Take Charge and Live!

Take Charge and Live!
You Are A Precious, Adorable Angel

Joyce Hovis

TROB Publications
Atlanta, Georgia

Copyright © 1995 by Joyce Hovis
All rights reserved.
This book, or portions thereof,
may not be reproduced by any means
without permission of the author.

Address all inquiries to:

Joyce Hovis
c/o TROB, Inc.
1291 Dresden Drive, N.E.
Atlanta, Georgia 30319
404-237-7924

Throughout this book, the word "he" is used generically.

DEDICATION

I dedicate this book to Truth, to all those who follow It and courageously take a stand for It and to those precious, adorable angels who were created by God to express their talents and abilities. I acknowledge all those whose lives have passed through my life and our TROB school to assist me to understand myself and to have understanding. You can know and understand me only if I can know and understand me, and I can know and understand you only if I know and understand me. I am especially grateful to all of those who have given many hours in assisting me with their writing skills. My dream is that these truths will assist you to express your highest and best, that they will assist you to be all you can be, that they will assist you to have a dream and, most importantly, that they will assist you to know yourself. When you know yourself it is so much fun to relate to and play with others who know themselves, express themselves and love themselves.

It is difficult, if not impossible, to express the depth of my gratitude to the thousands who have assisted me to bring these words to you. Thank you. Thank you. Thank you.

I love you all,
Joyce

Cover Design
Jeff Ashcraft

Front Cover Photography
Steve Shepard

Back Cover Photography
Jeff Ashcraft

Layout
Leanne Frank

Index
Linda Griffin

CONTENTS

Dedication v
Foreword xi
Preface xiii
Ocean Room Blessing xv
Acknowledgements xvii
Beginning the Journey xix

1: The Attachments 1
        Mother 4
        Father 13
        Family 17
        Teams 22
        Spouse 30
        Self 35
        Children 40

2: The Releasing Technique 45
        Releasing the Seven Attachments &
        Accepting the Seven Acceptances 48
        The Power of Releasing Four Times 51

3: The Acceptances 53
        Take Charge 54
        Child of God 61
        Being 65
        The Source 71
        Relying Within on God 74
        Expressing Talents and Abilities 78
        Enjoyment 79
        Fun 85

4: The I Ams 87
        I Am Centered 87
        I Am In the Zone 88
        I Am the Light 89
        I Am Joy 89
        I Am Love 90
        I Am Listening Within to God 91
        I Am Relying Within on God 92
        I Am Enjoyment 93

5:	The Acceptance of Being Bad 95
6:	Good 101
7:	Perfection 105
8:	The Roles 121
	The Controller 121
	The Controllee 127
	The Flip-Flopper 130
	The Right and Blameless Destroyer 131
	The Wrong and Blamed Scapegoat 143
	The Importance and Value of
	Knowing Yourself 146
9:	Stars 149
	The Negative Star 149
	The Exclusive Star 155
	The Natural Star 158
	The Team Player 159
	Characteristics of Stars and Team Players 162
	Special 166
10:	Competition 183
11:	Game Playing 199
12:	Mind Sets 233
13:	Impatience 253
14:	Destructive Powers 259
15:	Rebellion 267
	Core of Rebellion 273
	The Void 276
16:	Escaping Responsibility 279
	Fantasy 281
	Responsibility 284
17:	Programming 287
	Family Commitment 288
	Family Code 292
	The Code Bearer 293
	Pacts 295
	Opposite Desires (The Life Pattern) 300

18:	From Role to Reality	313
19:	The Destruction Caused By Your Belief System	333
20:	Ending Destruction and Moving Into Love	339
21:	You Are a Precious, Adorable Angel	369
22:	How To Live a Life of Ecstasy and Bliss	371
Afterword		377
A Final Word		379
Joyce Hovis		381
What Is TROB?		383
Index		385

FOREWORD

I never thought I would be the slightest bit interested in the subconscious or the psyche or anything more than sex, eating, sleeping and making a living. However, I find myself enthusiastically composing this introduction to a book written by my wife. Some readers may say, "Why, certainly he would endorse the book. It's his wife's!" However, it's so obviously not the thing to do that doing it should demonstrate the complete sincerity and gratitude I feel for someone who has been the recipient of original thought and totally unique ideas and solutions to life's most perplexing problems.

I have always felt that there was a cause for every effect and that removal of the cause would alleviate the problem. Any rational person would tend to agree with me on this point, particularly as it is applied to material matters. If the dog runs loose and bites the postman, the cause is a loose dog, so we tie him up and there is no more problem. If it's raining and you're asleep in your bedroom and a stream of water starts to fall on your face, you either move the bed from under the leak or go patch the roof. Once again, the problem of the soggy mattress is solved. It's pure genius! We could all list these neat problems and proper solutions and think we have a clutch hold on life.

Have you ever said to yourself, "I wonder why my marriage or marriages have failed?" or, "Why am I unable to progress and prosper in my business?" or, "Why do my children turn out to be so spooky?" or, "Why can I always go just so far and seem to fall short?" or, "Why?" to a million other things that seem so unanswerable.

Most of us stay away from asking these questions, or we take refuge in the accepted standbys such as, "He was born well-to-do," or, "I'm certainly OK, what's the matter with the rest of these people?" or, "He was in the right place at the right time," or, "Times have changed, it's tougher now," or, "My ship is just over the horizon, maybe tomorrow it will come in," or "This person just doesn't understand me. I'll get another one who does."

Some people innately recognize these as genuine problems with solutions that are obtainable, and fervently seek answers from psychiatrists, psychologists, fortune tellers, Indian holy men, snake handlers, foot workers, marriage counselors, yoga, various religious institutions, positive thinking books and on and on. Sometimes, there is revelation and enlightenment and relief. But, most often, after a short period of jubilation and a feeling of "I've got the bull by the horns now," we find ourselves right back where we started. Our "outcomes" remain consistent.

I will submit to you, at this time, that my lovely wife Joyce has, through great personal travail that I won't discuss here, found the reasons for our inability to make life's formulas work for us. I am convinced of the accuracy of her information; it is unique in the area of human interrelationships, and totally and completely explains and unravels in logical manner the perplexing "whys" of human behavior. Without revealing the gist of what is to follow, let me tell you there is a knowable, reversible reason why our marriages and relationships fail. The same is true of our businesses and professional lives, and, equally so, for all other aspects of our day-to-day comings and goings. If you will come to a complete understanding of the information contained in this book---by that I mean, seeing its truth with clear vision---your life will instantly undergo a total transformation, and you will leave your failures and disappointments behind you as you go on to a new and much, much better life experience.

If you are very serious about self-improvement and the impact that it can have on your world; if you are willing to do whatever it takes to get the job done, this is the book for you.

The ultimate reward is not easy, but it is simple and it is attainable:

To Be Who You Really Are

Kent Hovis

PREFACE

The purpose of this book is to assist people to know themselves and be themselves, to know their dream and be free to have their dream, to do their highest and best and be their highest and best, and to be free to express and have love, success and peace every moment of their lives.

I searched for years for the meaning of life, and for the freedom to fully express and enjoy myself. More than anything, I wanted to create a family that supported each other, that worked together, played together, loved together, and had fun together, a family that had warm and loving relationships with each other. To me, life is memories, and I wanted to create happy, fun memories for our three sons to take with them throughout life. I wanted to create a warm and loving home for my husband and our sons to leave with confidence and return to with joy. I wanted to create a safe, secure place where they could bring friends, where they would feel welcome and wanted, and where they would all be free to have fun, to laugh and to play. This was more important to me than clean floors and a neat kitchen.

I also wanted to create successful relationships with extended family members, but mostly I wanted to create peace, love and joy within myself, free from the influence of external circumstances.

This dream was so important to me, and at times, seemed so impossible, that I made up my mind to do anything it took to achieve it and to give my life toward its pursuit. This made-up mind led me to nightly vigils of asking questions and listening to God. Moments quickly became hours, and before long I'd realize that there were only three hours in which to sleep before starting a new day. How is it possible to do this with piled-up laundry, car pooling, racing to football practice, then to the grocery store and then home to successfully prepare the much anticipated evening meal? With meetings to attend, phone calls to return and errands to run? Finding my center and staying focused on God within began to be, for me, the answer to achieving the peace, the joy and the eternal happiness which I so fervently sought. It was in learning how to form this habit that the truths and how-to's contained in this book began to slowly reveal themselves to me.

OCEAN ROOM BLESSING

I am surrounded by a wall of golden Light.

Above the wall there is Wisdom; beneath the wall there is Love.

I am that Wisdom.

I am that Love.

We surround this room with a wall of golden Light; this city, this state, this country, the world, the whole universe we surround with a wall of golden Light.

We give thanks for all that is, we give thanks for all that was, we give thanks for all that ever will be.

We give thanks, we give thanks, we give thanks.

ACKNOWLEDGEMENTS

To say thank you to so many for sharing their lives, their fears and their dreams seems inadequate. In telling my story and sharing my life's experience with you, I have grown in depths of spirit beyond my wildest dreams. In supporting you to be free to express, be, and love, I have become free to express, be, and love on the deepest level.

I am so grateful to my teams, my students, for their trust and their opening up to me.

And I am so grateful to my husband for his support---for giving me the freedom to stay up half the night for years in order to receive this information. I am so grateful to him for being my sounding board, for his willingness to grow with me in spirit, in mind and in body, and for allowing me the freedom to do whatever it took for the years of its incubation.

I am especially grateful to Maxine Taylor and Lynne Pope for accompanying me in writing these words, in expressing these truths in as simple a way as possible, and to Dorothy Anderson for her editing skills and generous support. What was once complex, they have helped me to make simple. The mind has lost its mystery, the heart and the soul have returned to their proper positions, and the spirit is now free to flow. There are so many more, too numerous to mention, whose love, support and help have gone into the completion of this book. They know who they are, and I hope they will forgive the omission of their names and know that I am eternally grateful to each of them.

And to Linny Curry who has been my "right-hand man" and has been willing to be coached in every detail of her life, I give my thanks.

There are so many students I have interviewed who have opened their hearts in total trust to allow me to assist them and, in so doing, to assist you. To each I am most grateful.

This work has taken me to many parts of the world, and has helped me to see that our oneness with the whole, and our uniqueness is what everyone is seeking to express. So I am grateful to each of you who chooses to peruse these words. Take what you can, store what you can't until the time comes that you can, and let go of what doesn't apply.

I acknowledge the Truths that this book is about: each of us has talents, abilities and uniquenesses that are crying out for expression. This book is about discovering and expressing them.

Most important of all, I am grateful to God for giving me this opportunity to share His wonders with you. For this opportunity I will be eternally grateful.

Joyce Hovis

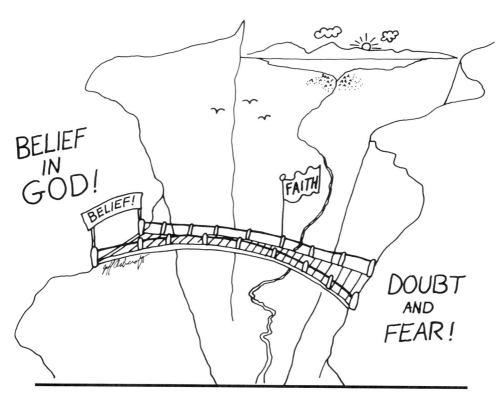

BEGINNING THE JOURNEY

I threw the book across the room. The author had found the peace and joy I desperately longed for. I felt totally defeated and discouraged. Once I, too, had peace, love and joy, but lost them, and I did not know how to get them back. Her success contrasted so much with my own frustrated attempts to recapture God's love as I had known it in the past. I had tried everything I knew, except psychiatry, which I couldn't afford.

As a child I dreamed of living in a yellow Cape Cod house with green shutters. I yearned for tall trees, a bubbling brook and a green meadow. Here I was, living in the home of my dreams, on top of a hill overlooking two bubbling brooks, one in the front and the other in the back. We were surrounded by virgin pines on four and a half acres. Marriage to my college sweetheart had produced three sons whom my husband and I both adored. As a child, I also dreamed of having a collie, and now I even had the dog. Because my childhood was unhappy, I constantly worked to create my idea of the ideal family. I had everything that society and the experts said should bring happiness, but I didn't have what I really wanted: inner peace and the warmth of loving relationships.

Why was I so miserable? It made no sense to me, and I knew it could not possibly make sense to anyone else. I believed that others would say, "If I had what YOU have, I'd be happy." But the truth was, I was NOT happy. I knew that if there were no obvious explanation I could see, how could others? I couldn't possibly tell anyone, so my disillusionment increased. I feared resentment and criticism for complaining when it appeared I had so much. I cut myself off from help because I didn't feel safe sharing my unhappiness. I felt that there was a secret within me which held an answer. Yet, I feared seeing it. I was afraid to know me. I feared being told that I was bad when I already felt bad enough.

Finally, when the only solution I could come up with was to look within, I looked within. I began asking God for answers to my thousands of questions. Out of desperation and need, I tapped into the Source of all knowledge and understanding. For seven years I experienced daily the meaning of the Bible verse, "Seek and ye shall find. Ask and it shall be given unto you." I sought, I found. I asked, and it was given unto me, in even greater measure than I had asked.

At that point, I made the choice to let go of my volunteer and social work so that I might spend as much time as possible alone with God. This became my top priority. I used what time I could find during the day, but mostly I used the night while the rest of my family slept. I was so lost in this creativity that dawn would break and surprise me. I regretted interrupting this time alone with God to get a few hours of sleep in order to have the energy necessary to run a home and raise our three boys.

As I began to follow the inner guidance I received, distinct changes started taking place. One major change was in the area of responsibility. I saw clear distinctions between my responsibilities and those of others. I came to see that I wanted Kent, my husband, to take responsibility for the way his mother treated me (the focus of much of my unhappiness) instead of handling it myself. I began to realize that this was not his responsibility. It was mine. How ANYONE treats me is my responsibility. I learned that I am treated the way I invite and allow others to treat me. This was the turning point in my life.

In the past, I had accepted my mother-in-law as she was, but was still vulnerable to her unspoken resentment and contempt for me. I continued to accept her as she was, but was no longer vulnerable to her mental domination. I came to see that the only power she had over me was the power I gave her. I took that power from her.

When my fear of her ceased, her treatment of me changed, and we became close friends. During the last days of her life, I was the one she wanted to be with, the one to whom she turned for help and comfort. I loved her dearly, and, miracle of miracles, she came to love me also.

I was now able to distinguish between Kent's responsibilities and mine. When something was his responsibility, such as cutting the grass, I did not interfere, even if it grew a foot high. I did not remind or nag him, but let it be totally his responsibility. Before I saw this, I had become what, to me, was the most despicable thing a wife can be: a nag. I nagged if the bills were not paid, if the roof leaked and if the garbage was not taken out. If I did not nag out loud, I thought about it repeatedly, which created a negative atmosphere in our home. Who wants to be around someone who is always looking at what you have not done? Kent felt this negativity and would say to me, "Look at what I do instead of what I don't do."

My journey within led me to see that he was absolutely right. As my attitude changed, my relationship with Kent changed. I no longer felt responsible for his mother's relationship with our children. I no longer carried the full responsibility for Kent's and my relationship. I used to worry that my children would not have a relationship with Kent's mother if she did not accept her role as a grandmother. I stopped trying to force my husband and his mother to be the way I thought they should be. I stopped trying to make them fit my pictures of the perfect grandmother, father and husband.

As I understood more clearly my responsibilities and those of others, my life changed. I could handle my own responsibilities, I found, but handling others' responsibilities was impossible. I later came to see that I had made a subconscious commitment to my own mother, many years before, to be responsible for her happiness and everyone else's. It was not until I began this search within that I straightened out this misplaced commitment and was able to take full responsibility for my own happiness and my own life.

The other major breakthrough I had during my midnight sessions was to see that my life was filled with limitations. I was not free to DO what I wanted to do, to BE what I wanted to be or to HAVE what I wanted to have. The cause was my attachments to people and things. These attachments held me down. They kept me from having FREE CHOICE.

Out of this discovery, a creative process evolved whereby I learned how to release these attachments. Only then could I change my actions and my responses to others' actions. Before, I had no choice; my actions and responses were involuntary.

This knowledge, and the releasing technique, were incredibly simple, and yet incredibly powerful in their effect on me. Suddenly, I knew that I had rights of my own, and I chose to exercise them. Once I saw clearly that I had rights, I took charge of my own life. I saw that making myself happy was my own responsibility. I no longer needed to do what other people wanted me to, when they wanted me to do it. I had my rights! I could say yes or no to what I wanted to do.

At first, it was difficult for Kent to adjust to these changes in me. In the end he liked and respected the new self-approving woman I had become.

Before I began my journey inward, our marriage was based on need. Kent needed to control me in order to feel secure, and I needed to please him and make him happy in order to feel secure. We both leaned on each other. The slightest move by either one of us could have caused the marriage to crumble.

Our marriage now can be compared to two strong oak trees that stand side by side in life. We each take full responsibility for our own happiness. We are free to enjoy and love each other because we love ourselves. We're together because we choose to be, and not out of need. There is no blame, no resentment and no negative emotions to interfere with our happiness.

Because we're together out of choice, we each feel free to leave if we choose. For we know that to be together for any lesser reason would stifle the freedom that we feel in our relationship and within ourselves. Because we are committed on the deepest level, we are free to live on the highest level.

1 The Attachments

IF YOU ARE DOING SOMETHING OFFENSIVE to a loved one, you might want to change your behavior, but can you? You can will yourself to change, but that may not last long, because it takes an enormous amount of energy and attention to maintain a forced change, and you will, ultimately, return to the old behavior. How do you change without all the effort, will and subsequent tension? It was the search for this answer which led me to the discovery of the seven basic attachments: Mother, Father, Family, Teams, Spouse, Self and Children. These attachments keep us bound and limited. They predetermine our thoughts, actions and commitments. It is the letting go of these attachments that takes the struggle, effort and will out of change. Letting go frees us to be able to make our own choices.

Anyone to whom or anything to which we are attached imprisons and controls us. Consider a man who loves his car so much that he lives in fear of its being scratched or stolen. Does the man own the car or does the car own the man? If it's constantly causing fear, apprehension or concern, then the car owns the man. He is attached to it, so it controls him.

It is important to recognize that letting go of these attachments does not mean abandoning or betraying our loved ones. It means the removal of control and the beginning of freedom in our relationships. We find that we do not have to move in order to get away from interfering in-laws, ex-spouses or any other unpleasant relationships. Nor is it difficult to continue loving and being loved by those we have always cared about. In fact, we are able to love them and be loved by them on a deeper level.

Once we begin living our lives apart from our parents, we believe that we are free to make our own choices. We may be physically independent, but emotionally, this is far from the truth. Often, we feel trapped and ask ourselves: "How can I get out of this trap?" and "How can I avoid hurting the ones by whom I feel trapped?"

Some people avoid dealing directly with the problem by escaping or repressing their feelings. They rebel, resist, manipulate or fantasize. More destructive escapes include insanity, disease, alcohol, drug addiction and even death. By trying to escape the trap, we only strengthen its control and power over us.

The first step toward getting out of your trap is to see clearly your attachments and the control they have over your life. Then you can let each one go.

Many times, people who decide to change want to start with what **APPEARS** to be their most problematic relationship. For example, when told that your first attachment is to your mother, you may respond, "I'm not having any problems with my mother. It's my wife (husband) who is driving me up the wall." The need to release attachments does not presuppose current problems with that particular attachment, in this case a spouse. Problems with a spouse may be directly connected to the attachment to or rebellion against a mother. What appears to be going on is often not what is really going on. An attachment to a mother could create problems with a spouse in ways that are not easily understood.

The results of releasing your emotional attachments can be one or all of the following:
- Freedom to make choices based on what's best for you,
- A greater awareness of current reality,
- An increased ability to take charge of your own life and create what you want, and ultimately,
- Self-knowledge and self-realization.

Being emotionally attached triggers strong responses when the people to whom we are attached fail to act or react the way we want them to. Before releasing these attachments, we are compelled to repeat the same patterns in our lives, whether or not we are aware of them. A kind, loving woman, who married three destructive men, asked, "How many times will I make the same mistake?" Repeating these mistakes reinforces the pattern that keeps their solutions deep within us. Releasing our attachments to people does not remove the problem, but the release frees us to see the problem and be able to do something about it. The changes which then take place are amazing!

Releasing your attachments means that you will be able to recognize problems and deal with them better than before. A man who is still attached to his mother, unknowingly, wants his wife to think like her, even though he once rebelled against his mother. For example, John's mother always kept a perfect home. His wife, Sally, cared more about her children's freedom to play and fingerpaint than she did a perfect home. Each evening, John came home and inspected the woodwork for fingerprints. Sally's mess infuriated him, and his inspections infuriated her. After releasing his attachment to his mother, he came home and looked for Sally instead of the mess.

As children, attachments provide us with a sense of belonging necessary for our security. It is only our ignorance of our attachments and our continued reliance on them that cause us so many problems as adults. In order to grow up and take adult responsibilities, it is necessary to release our childhood attachments, take charge of our lives, and take responsibility for our happiness. Most adults feel they have already released their emotional attachment to their mothers, taken charge of their lives, and assumed responsibility for their own happiness. However, they find themselves still blaming others. Since releasing their emotional attachment to their mothers, taking charge of their lives, and assuming responsibility for their happiness eliminates the need to blame others or circumstances, they demonstrate that they have not yet released their emotional attachment to their mothers, taken charge of their lives or assumed responsibility for their own happiness. They have not yet truly become emotional adults.

In addition to examining our emotional attachments, we will look at the different roles we play in relationships, and how they affect our lives. We will conclude by looking at how to live a life of peace, joy and love.

So, now we really begin. Your task is to look honestly and systematically at your relationships with other people, both present and past. You will also look at how you function within those relationships, and what role you play in creating a false identity for yourself. Before you begin the next chapter, ask yourself, "Do I believe I am entitled to rewarding, happy relationships? Do I want to know and be the real me?" If you can say yes to either of these questions, you're ready to learn how to...

KNOW YOURSELF

MOTHER

The first and most influential emotional attachment that we have is to our mother, and it is this attachment which controls our thinking. We are with her even before birth, and closer to her than any other human being for the first few years of our lives. She is the role model for our thinking. Her thoughts become our thoughts; her opinions, our opinions. Her concepts of us become our concepts of ourselves.

Our lives and circumstances are determined by the way we think. Because our mother is the source of our thinking, we have warm and loving thoughts if she has warm and loving thoughts; we think critically and negatively if she thinks critically and negatively. Because of our close attachment to her, we know how she thinks without her having to verbalize her thoughts. This gives her enormous power over us. The role of mother is the greatest responsibility on earth. The hand that rocks the cradle does, indeed, rule the world, but neither the world nor mother has completely understood the power she possesses.

In an effort to teach generosity to her daughter, Lynne, Mary scolded and criticized her for her selfishness. Mary complained that Lynne thought only of herself. Focusing attention on Lynne's self-centeredness increased it within her. By praising Lynne's acts of generosity, Mary could have achieved her desired results. Instead, she created in Lynne a belief that she was selfish, which Lynne has acted upon her whole life.

Perfection

Mothers are motivated by a strong desire to have perfect children so that they will be seen as perfect mothers. This desire for perfection has been passed down by mothers for generation after generation. Consequently, we live in terror of being less than perfect, and of being criticized for our imperfections. Many children develop a fear of failure, a fear of making a mistake or a fear of not being good enough. They learn, early on, that making a mistake makes them less than perfect. Most mothers feel that if their children do not behave perfectly, they will be criticized for being bad mothers.

So that we don't disappoint our mother, our lives become a struggle to be perfect. Consequently, we live in constant fear of falling short of the mark. Beneath the surface there is a deeper fear: the fear that if we are not perfect, our mother will leave us, and we will be abandoned. Being perfect has such a huge power over our lives that it becomes our reason for being. We are all in this "perfect" boat together until we let go of the need to be perfect, and the need to care what other people think about us.

Rebellion

Often this pressure to be perfect becomes overwhelming, and causes many children to rebel. When we rebel against our mother, we don't give her what she wants. Rebellion can be done silently or openly (see chapter: Rebellion). The act of rebellion says, "I'll show you. I don't have to do what you tell me to do." If we choose to rebel against our mother, we stop giving her what she wants, or we give her what she doesn't want. Unknowingly, rebellion prevents us from giving ourselves what we want, as well. If we rebel against our mother, we THINK that our thinking is different from hers. However, rebellion is an extreme resistance to thinking like her and giving her what she wants. Therefore, we are still controlled by her thinking.

Surrogate Mothers

If our mother fulfilled her role as nurturer, our need for a mother and for nurturing is satisfied. If, however, we did not have a mother who nurtured us, we spend the rest of our lives seeking to fulfill this unfulfilled need. Sometimes we adopt a surrogate mother when we do not have a natural, or nurturing, one. This can be a grandmother, stepmother, maid, older sister, etc. If we do not release our emotional attachment to our mother before we leave home, we, unknowingly, look for another elsewhere. Often we marry our mother, or make doctors, ministers or friends our mother. We look to these mother substitutes to tell us who we are, how to be and what to do. We look outside of ourselves for our identity and, in so doing, give others total power over our lives.

Most of all, we want our mother to believe in us, value us and love us. If she does, we will believe in, value and love ourselves. If, however, our mother did not believe in us, or withdrew her love from us for being bad or not good enough, we will look for a surrogate mother who will do the same thing. This truth is so powerful that even if we succeed in finding someone who does believe in us, we are unable to accept it, and work to destroy that person's belief in us. We expect the negative while hoping for the positive, and so, push away the thing that we want the most.

If we are fortunate, and our mother or her substitute gives us positive self-concepts, we reflect them in our lives. In a group of multi-millionaires who came from meager beginnings, the one common denominator was that each had a mother who believed in him, constantly praised him, and told him that he had what it took to be anything he wanted to be. They all had mothers who took their job as mother seriously.

Self-Concept

We feel lovable and express love if our mother thinks we are lovable, because we think about ourselves the way she does. If she thinks we are beautiful, we feel beautiful, and exude beauty. If she thinks that nothing we do is right, we believe that nothing we do is right, and so, nothing we do IS right. If she doesn't want us, we go through life feeling unwanted, undesirable and rejected. If she sees us as bad, and constantly tells us we are bad, we feel bad and behave badly. If she tells us that we are not good enough, we lack confidence in ourselves, and feel insecure and scared. If she gives us love, praise and admiration, we have a good self-image with a high level of self-esteem. If our mother's way of communicating with us is one of verbal put-downs, criticism or anger, our feeling of self-worth is low. If she feels secure in HERSELF, we feel secure in OURSELVES. If she is nervous, we are nervous. If she is depressed, we are depressed. If she is friendly with strangers, we are friendly, as well. If she trusts others, we trust others. If she distrusts others, we distrust others, also. If our mother is possessive and does not want us to have friends, we, unknowingly, push friends away.

Guilt

Even though our mother may have positive and loving thoughts, there comes a time when we don't have her there to make our decisions for us. We want to be free to think for ourselves, to make decisions which will work for us, and to think the way WE CHOOSE to think. We want to be able to turn within to find solutions, to form our own concepts, and to make decisions based on the existing circumstances of our lives.

If we are still attached to our mother, we feel guilty if we do not think the way she thinks, or make the decisions she would make or would want us to make. We feel guilty if we do not ask her opinion. Even if she is no longer living, we ask ourselves how she would feel, and feel guilty if we go against her thinking. We need her permission to make any decision. This is why it is so difficult to make a decision until we release our emotional attachment to her.

> *One hot summer afternoon, Mary stopped to say hello to Jane, her 65-year-old friend, who was working in her garden. Jane was wearing shorts and, even though her mother had passed away many years before, was still, at 65, concerned with what her mother would say if she saw her dressed in shorts while talking to friends. Jane said to Mary, "My mother would turn over in her grave if she could see me out here in my shorts."*

Releasing the Attachment to Mother

By releasing this attachment, we free ourselves to think the way WE choose to think. The truths and principles our mother taught us will always be there for us as a source of information. Her knowledge and wisdom will forever be recorded in our mind. This can be called upon at will, yet we want to be free from guilt, blame or feeling bad whenever we choose to make choices different from hers, or from those she would want us to make.

We also want our mother to be perfect because we identify with her, and we feel, on a subconscious level, that if she is perfect, then we are perfect. Therefore, we place her on a pedestal and see her as perfect. This continues until we reach our teenage years, when we begin to view her as the person she really is. This awareness helps us to release our emotional attachment to her, which is necessary for us to grow up emotionally.

However, this awareness causes great conflict in teenagers. They begin to see their mother as she is, and they feel betrayed or disillusioned by what appears to be a sham. The truth is that they had been viewing her through their "need her to be perfect" eyes, and are now seeing her as she truly is. The trouble comes from the conflict between the need to release their emotional attachment to her and the continued need for her nurturing, between wanting to be dependent and independent at the same time. Many of us have opposite desires (see chapter: Programming). We want to be told what to do and how to be. But when we are told, we resist and then become resentful toward the person telling us. This resentment may come from our rebellion against our mother.

Being attached to our mother is important for our security and well-being as children. During the teenage years we begin to try to release this attachment. If both mother and teenager know and understand what is going on at this tumultuous time, this break from the nest is easier for everyone. Once the break is made, the teenager becomes a young adult, and is free to become a close friend. The caterpillar turns into a butterfly and is then free to soar. If the break is never made, the teenager remains an emotional child in an adult body for the rest of his life. Soaring becomes impossible, and blame becomes the way of life.

Often the mother feels threatened or insecure when her children are breaking away from her. She fears losing them and, at the same time, they fear hurting her, which prevents their making the final emotional release. Later, when they physically leave for college, work or marriage, they, unknowingly, remain emotionally attached to their mother.

Fear of Releasing the Attachment

Before we release our emotional attachment to our mother, we need her permission for everything we do. The irony is that we even need her permission to release the attachment to her. Therefore, many fears can arise at the thought of releasing this attachment: the fear of abandoning her, of betraying her, of feeling guilty, of hurting her, of disobeying her, of leaving her, and the fear that she will punish us for releasing the emotional attachment to her. For many, releasing seems to mean giving up something positive and good.

> *Jane had fond memories of her loving relationship with her mother which she felt she would lose by releasing her emotional attachment to her. Yet, releasing this attachment was a positive, natural step to take, and Jane's relationship with her mother was nourished and improved as a result.*

The Need for Nurturing

If the emotional attachment to your mother has not been released prior to marriage, the need for nurturing and being taken care of can be transferred onto your spouse. In many cases, both partners bring this need to the relationship. Because they both need the same thing, it is impossible for either one to be satisfied. In addition, the couple now acquires many adult responsibilities, all of which will be dealt with from an emotionally immature level. They often feel that there is an invisible hand pulling at them. This feeling comes from a conflicting need to be back in childhood with their original family while, at the same time, wanting to be with their spouse and children. They not only have a need to be taken care of, but also, a need to remain loyal to their original family. Until they release their emotional attachment to their mother, they cannot totally "be there" with their original family OR be involved with their spouse and children.

Blame

When we are attached to our mother, we are not free to assume responsibility for ourselves. We blame other people and external circumstances for our lives' not being the way we want them to be. We blame others for not taking care of us the way we expect to be taken care of, and for not making us happy. Blame is the natural expression of those who are emotionally attached to their mother. Blame is the opposite of taking responsibility and of being in charge of your life. Blame is a substitute for taking action, for solving problems, and for getting the job done. Some people blame the government for all their problems. They say, "If there were no inflation, there would be no problems," or "Because of high taxes, there is not enough money," or "Government interference keeps us from getting ahead and having our dream." Others often blame their mother for their pain and suffering. They say, "If she had only been different when I was a child, my life would be happy, and I would be free from pain and suffering." Many people blame their spouse for their immediate problems. A great deal of friction occurs in a marriage when one spouse chooses the other as his scapegoat. The air is filled with resentment and anger. Blaming frees us from all responsibility. If we can blame someone else, we feel safe, our self-esteem is not in danger, and we do not face having to change. Some mothers do not allow their children to have problems because problems mean that the children are less than perfect, and that they do not have a perfect mother. If children are not allowed to have problems, they will not be able to deal with problems as adults. They will avoid problems by sweeping them under the rug, thereby creating bigger and bigger problems. Many divorces are caused by not addressing and not solving problems early in marriage.

> *Nancy, a young bride, blamed her husband for her unhappiness. She thought that if he would just be kind, sweet and more loving, she would then be happy. She wanted HIM to change. Everything she read reinforced her belief that he was to blame for her unhappiness. She had dated him for many years prior to their marriage, and they had gotten along*

beautifully, but soon after the wedding, she became unhappy. He continued to tell her that it was not his problem, because he was very happy. He refused to take responsibility for her unhappiness. Her mother was her best friend, and required Nancy to include her in all of her relationships. Nancy was unable to see that her mother's possessiveness was unusual. She felt that when she married, she left her mother. The pull within her between her husband and her mother was enormous. There was an unspoken law that her mother was to be her one and only relationship. This forced her to choose between her mother and her husband. Her husband kept telling her that she needed to grow up. The pressure became so great that she was unable to think, and felt blocked in every direction. Later, after she released her emotional attachment to her mother, her marriage improved dramatically. She no longer demanded that her husband be responsible for her happiness, nor did she blame him for her unhappiness.

Need

Unfulfilled childhood needs can keep us living in the past. Our childhood cannot be recaptured; it cannot continue into adulthood. To try to do so places impossible demands and expectations on others, and causes a life of frustration. Trying to do so keeps us living in the past, seeking fulfillment of an unresolved need, or continuing to be taken care of without responsibilities. It keeps us wanting what we cannot have. Yet, many spend a lifetime trying to recapture their childhood, to satisfy these unfulfilled needs.

Need is a very strong desire, and creates strong emotions. Anything we need, we HAVE to have. Anything we need, we push away. This is a universal law. Think about a time when you needed money, and were unable to get it. Think, also, of all the times you needed love, and it eluded you.

By releasing our emotional attachment to our mother, we are able to begin life anew. We are free from childhood longings which have kept us from dealing with current problems on an adult level. We are free to think for ourselves and take responsibility for our own decisions. This does not mean that we will no longer want our mother, or want to be with her. It does mean, however, that we will be free to be with her because we CHOOSE to, and not because we HAVE to. It means that we have begun the process of releasing her control over us, and of taking charge of our own lives. It means that we have begun to grow up emotionally.

Control

Another reason why it is so difficult to release this attachment naturally is control. People have controlled us, and we have controlled them throughout our lives. In some cases, the control is conscious; in others, it is totally unconscious. If our mother is, by nature, domineering or controlling, she will often respond to our new freedom with fear. Her greatest fear is that we will leave her. As long as she controls us, she can hold on to us and keep what she thinks is order in her own world. When she senses that she is losing control, she will use one of several tactics to regain it. If the first does not work, she will resort to the second and so on, though not necessarily in the order listed.

First, she may withdraw her love from us in an attempt to regain control. Her actions will reveal that she feels our performance is not good enough, and that we are displeasing her. Therefore, she must punish us by withholding her love in order to let us know that she disapproves of us.

Another tactic is to become pitiful. Her voice, words and manner may become exaggeratedly dramatic. Her motive is to get us to feel so sorry for her that we will come back to the nest and allow her to control us again. Any bid for sympathy is a bid for control.

Anger or rage is another tactic. She will raise her voice or resort to full-fledged rage to achieve the desired results. If this works, we will feel guilty, fearful and bad for having caused her unhappiness. Once we see that this is simply a means to control and dominate us, we will view it in its proper light, and it will then lose its power over us.

The threat of her leaving, another tactic, arouses our greatest fear: the fear of being left and, therefore, being alone. The way out is to face that you have been controlled by this fear your whole life---and let it go. Tell her that if she wants to leave, it is her choice, but not to tell you again that she is leaving.

Another tactic is mental seduction. This is a mind game used to unconsciously control us, take choice from us, keep us from thinking, and prepare us to be sexually seduced. The purpose of this nonverbal and nonphysical seduction is to get us on her team against our father or some other relative. Because nothing is verbalized and no action is taken, she can deny it to herself and, if confronted, believe in her own innocence.

By using sexual seduction, she gives us the non-verbal message that we are sexually desirable, and withholds the sexual act. First, she tells us we are desired, then she tells us we are not. As a result, we feel undesirable, weakened, and ultimately, controlled.

The divide and conquer tactic is used to turn us against someone we desire, by criticizing them or planting a negative thought in our minds about them, causing us to doubt them or ourselves, while at the same time, keeping us bonded to her and terrified of betraying her.

Negative suggestion is used to destroy while remaining innocent. A glance, a raised eyebrow or a vocal inflection can be used to plant the seed of doubt.

By talking non-stop she monopolizes the conversation and maintains center stage.

Excluding is designed to manipulate and control. Excluding can be subtle or blatant. She may simply refuse to look at us, or may invite others to go to dinner with her in our presence, and exclude us.

Not including, another tactic, is even more subtle than excluding. She always knows how we are responding to her non-inclusion without looking at us, and if we leave, she becomes angry.

Walling off puts an impenetrable barrier between our mother and us which hurts, makes us feel unwanted and pushes us away.

When our mother chooses sides, she protects and defends her side from her perceived enemies, and these "enemies" can be the ones she loves the most.

Charm is used when all else fails. She will become charming, agreeable, cooperative and/or humorous in order to gain control. In order not to be dominated by her, we must not need ANYTHING from her. We can want, but not need. If we are willing to release all need for anything from her, we will then be able to continue this charming relationship without being manipulated.

After Releasing the Emotional Attachment to Mother

Most mothers feel a sense of relief when their children release their emotional attachment to them. It relieves them of the pressure of having to be their children's perfect mother.

Once you release your emotional attachment to your mother, your relationship will no longer be based on a sense of duty. You will then be free to be friends and equals. Friends get together because they like each other and want to be together, not because they should, ought to or have to.

Also, after releasing this attachment, your awareness and insights will expand. You will be able to think more clearly and be freer to make decisions. And a great deal of blaming of yourself and others will cease.

Children are attached to their mothers, therefore they blame instead of taking responsibility to get the job done. Adults get the job done. Children of all ages explain why it didn't work, and complain about what others didn't do, or how others kept them from making it work. Responsible adults eliminate all excuses and get the job done. (See chapter: The Acceptances). Blame is eliminated from our life when we release our emotional attachment to our mother, take complete responsibility for every outcome in our life, and take responsibility for our happiness---and not until then. Just before the age of puberty we begin to break loose from our emotional attachment to our mother, and take responsibility for our own lives. Staying emotionally attached to our mother prevents us from doing this. We have to let go of one before we can take on the other. Once we are free to grow up and soar, we will, in turn, give the same freedom to our own children.

Releasing your emotional attachment to your mother frees you to think for yourself, but YOU have to do the thinking.

FATHER

The second most influential person in our life is our father, or his surrogate. It is his responsibility to protect us and teach us how to act out in the world. He does this by his example and teachings.

Acting Like Our Father

For our early physical and emotional well-being, it is important that we have a father role model. Our father's actions become our actions. But if this attachment is not released, we are not free to act the way we want to act, nor are we free to do what we want to do. Rebellion is the one exception. If we rebel against him, we will act just the opposite of the way he acts, but we still will not be free to do what we want to do.

If our father approves of us and our actions, we approve of ourselves and our actions. If he had fun with us and others, we are free to have fun. If he knew what he wanted to do and pursued it, we find that we know what we want to do and are able to pursue it, also. If he fixed things around the house, we are handy ourselves. If he procrastinated and did not get things done, we follow his example by procrastinating and not getting things done.

> *John's family lived in a three-story house. His father never finished anything he started. During the many years they lived there, his father painted the front and two sides of the house, but not the back. John, a professional carpenter, eventually saw that he, too, was unable to finish what he started. He had uncompleted projects throughout his workshop and he realized that he was repeating his father's pattern.*

Judging

Not only do we act like our father, but we also want others to act the same way. If we are attached to our father, we are not free to act the way we want, and we become critical and judgmental of others' actions.

Judging labels something either right or wrong, good or bad. We feel that we have to label others in order to understand them, and thereby, we feel safe and secure with them. It makes life easier to label things good or bad, right or wrong. What we understand, we can put to rest.

Rebellion

Rebellion is the one exception to acting like our father. If we object to or resent what we perceive to be unjust actions by our father, we may choose to rebel by doing just the opposite. Our attitude becomes one of, "I'll show you. I will not give you what you want. I will never act like you." This can be done either silently or openly (see chapter: Rebellion).

Open rebellion is obvious, while silent rebellion is subtle, and expresses itself in the form of resistance or a negative attitude. For example, if your father is neat, you may be messy; if he is a blue collar worker, you may become a white collar worker, or vice versa. Those who have workaholic fathers may rebel by being lazy. The paths of rebellion vary according to the individual, but for all who rebel, rebellion looks like the only way out. However, it is destructive to all relationships, including your relationship with yourself. The decision to rebel and refuse to give your father what he wants prevents you from giving yourself what you want, and everyone else what they want. You may know that you are not going to give your father what he wants, but you don't realize that you're not going to be able to give yourself and others what you and they want.

In Marriage

A woman, unconsciously, wants her husband to act the way her father acted if she is still emotionally attached to him. If he was domineering, she wants her husband to be domineering, because it is comfortable and familiar to her. If she marries a gentle, non-interfering, non-controlling man, she will, unconsciously, try to make him act like her father.

An example of a man who did not act like his wife's father is Tom, who was raised in an apartment building. He never saw his father do any work in or around the apartment. The maintenance man who lived in the building took care of all the necessary repairs. He painted the walls, cut the grass, and even replaced the light bulbs. Tom's wife was raised in a two-story house, and her father was a "jack-of-all-trades." He repaired everything himself. He upholstered the furniture, painted the walls, did the plumbing, took care of the electrical problems, and even varnished the floors. Tom's wife's concept of how a husband should act was to keep the house in top repair. When the couple acquired a home of their own, Tom did not do anything around the house. Not only did he not do it, he didn't even notice that it needed to be done. This was a source of great irritation to his wife. She became a nag, which, to her, was the worst thing a woman could be. She nagged him to repair the roof, to fix the screens, and to paint the house. He always resisted. One day, when she realized what she was doing, she started crying, and told him she was so sorry for having nagged and pushed him. She was still emotionally attached to her father, and wanted her husband to act like him.

Releasing the Emotional Attachment to Father

She released her emotional attachment to her father, and Tom then had the freedom to act however he chose, without her interference. She said to him, "Even if a hole in the roof becomes so big that rain can pour through it, I will never press you to repair it." And she never did.

After Tom's wife released the emotional attachment to her father, Tom began taking care of the house repairs. And after he released his emotional attachment to HIS father, he created various additions to their house. He enclosed a small screened porch to make a bar, and added a den with a loft. He later added decks and a large screened porch.

Another example is Dorothy, who always wanted to have her own business. After releasing her emotional attachment to her father, she gathered fabrics she had purchased in the Caribbean Islands, and took them to the fabric buyers of the largest department stores in her town. Each placed an order with her. She was immediately in the import-export business. She began traveling to the islands to find different sources for her new business.

Once we release our emotional attachment to our father, we are much freer to act the way we want to. Once we are free to act the way WE want to act, we are no longer frustrated, offended and judgmental when others do not act the way we want them to.

Fear

Many people are concerned that they will feel separated from their father or will hurt him if they release their emotional attachment to him. They fear that the release will adversely affect the relationship. However, it works just the opposite. Once they take this step, they relate to their father as adults and no longer as children. An unperceived pressure is removed from both. They no longer try to force each other to act in certain ways. This frees them to have a warm, loving relationship with each other.

Releasing your emotional attachment to your father frees you to do as you choose, but YOU have to DO it.

FAMILY

The third emotional attachment is to our family. When we're emotionally attached to our family we are not free to be how we choose to be. How we are to be is predetermined by how our family wants us to be. Family includes brothers, sisters, grandparents, aunts, uncles, cousins, etc. Family influence can be great or small, according to our closeness to them and according to the <u>control</u> they have over us. Many people today lack close contact with their family because they have lived in so many places. Therefore, it is difficult to realize the family's control over us. This control, which began in childhood, is stored in our subconscious minds and, unknowingly, still runs our lives.

Differing Messages

Your family dictates how you "should," "ought to," and "have to" be.

Jane grew up in a small town which was mostly owned by her grandparents. She was never allowed to associate with anyone other than family members because of a social caste system. Talking to strangers or townspeople who were not her social equals was not permissible. Because of this, Jane could never talk to strangers anywhere. She was on the tennis court at a seaside resort when she released her emotional attachment to her family. She immediately walked over to one of the other courts and began talking to a stranger. What before had been impossible, now became a pleasurable experience.

There can be conflict when parents' messages differ from those of grandparents or other family members. If a grandparent is in conflict with other family members about how a child should be, confusion is created in the child's mind. This double bind leaves the child feeling bad and not good enough for the grandparents or other family members. This confusion continues into adulthood, where it affects his relationships and can lead to serious emotional problems.

Both John's mother and paternal grandmother wanted to be the most important person in his life. They competed with each other for John's love. As long as the three weren't together, he could handle this conflict. However, when he found himself with them, he felt great inner turmoil. To please one would mean angering the other. After marriage, his emotional capacities were stretched beyond his ability to cope when his wife also demanded to be number one. His brief marriage ended in divorce. Not choosing kept him terrified, cowardly and in rage most of his life. He feared that choosing his wife would hurt his mother, and that choosing his mother would hurt his wife. This conflict continued until he faced his grandmother and himself. He made up his mind that he was free to love and be loved by anyone he chose. This ended the inner emotional conflicts which had plagued him his whole life.

The Family and Self-Worth

If you were wanted by your older brother or sister, you will feel wanted and accepted. This is translated into feelings of self-worth and self-esteem. If, on the other hand, an older brother was jealous of your arrival, he would neither want, nor be able to accept you. Unless or until you deal with this by releasing these feelings of being worthless and unwanted, you will feel rejected and worthless. It will not matter how popular or in demand you are, you will still feel rejected and worthless.

The family member who is the closest to you has the greatest influence and control over you. For example, a sister or brother whom you see every day would be closer than a grandparent who lives 200 miles away whom you see only twice a year. If the brother or sister is jealous of and competitive with you, you are influenced by his or her not wanting you to be successful or have fun. You may be hard-working and success-oriented, but taking the ball across the goal line is very difficult, if not impossible. To the world you may appear successful, yet to yourself you fall short of achieving what is success for you. This keeps you always striving and never arriving. The feeling of success and excitement that comes with beginning new goals totally eludes you.

On the other hand, warm, loving relationships with sisters, brothers or grandparents who are not only supportive, but want you to be a winner, make success easy and make life fun for you.

The Only Child

Many people who grew up as only children were not allowed to love or to be involved with anyone but their mother and/or father. In such a case, mother and father are the family. Not only will each parent need to be released individually, but once again when the emotional attachment to family is released.

> *Joan, an only child, had one daughter. Joan adored her daughter and actively participated in her life, but couldn't give the child her undivided attention. Joan's parents (in this case, her family) had been possessive and overly protective, which, in later years, prevented her from being fully attentive to her husband and child. When alone with either, she became uncomfortable, and began busying herself. She was unable to be fully involved with her husband and daughter because of her emotional attachment to her family, and unconsciously held back part of herself. Many times, a fight would ensue as a result.*

Competition

Our family can either accept or reject us. If they reject us, we reject ourselves, and are rejected out in the world. If they accept us, we accept ourselves and are accepted by others. The family is the training ground for learning and perfecting competition. We are told, and believe, that our family will accept us and be there for us, but it doesn't always work that way. Often, we become disillusioned and deluded. Sibling rivalry, as well as possessiveness of family members toward each other, can make rivals of brothers and sisters, grandparents, grandchildren and cousins. Our greatest competition can, and often does, exist within the family itself. Each child competes to be number one with his parents. Family wars exist because of competition. In family competition, the object is to win the parent.

Being How You Want to Be

Once you release your family attachment, you are able to choose how you want to be. You may choose to compete or not. Before the release, you have no choice. Afterwards, you can turn your attention away from how others want you to be, and direct it toward how you want to be. When you're being how you want to be, for no other reason than because it is your choice, you are freed from acting out of duty. Releasing your emotional attachment to your family eliminates doing what you do because you should, ought to or have to be the way your family wants you to be. It frees you to accept yourself. The release of this attachment frees you to begin the process of becoming an adult, and to begin taking full responsibility for your life.

Before releasing your family attachment, you had no choices other than being what your family wanted you to be. Now you must decide. It will not happen of its own accord. This can be an exciting and creative experience. It frees you to be a mother or a father or a friend. It frees you to be loyal to the family you choose to create. It frees you to create the career of your choice, wealth and happiness, but you must choose, and you must act on your choice. Deciding what and how you want to be will require a great deal of time and thought. Nothing just happens.

Changes In Sibling Relationships

After releasing your emotional attachment to your family, you will begin to notice many subtle changes. These vary from family to family because each family's message is different. Because of sibling rivalry, for instance, many brothers and sisters don't want their siblings to be as successful as they are. Some siblings feel an invisible rein always holding them back from being their highest and best. They feel both a desire to accomplish more than they are accomplishing, and an inner pull which prevents them from doing so. This power and control is so strong that there is little, if any, thought process involved.

> *Bob's younger brother, George, was very shy and had no friends. Bob, on the other hand, was outgoing and liked by many. George felt left out and rejected by his brother's friends. Nevertheless, he followed Bob everywhere. After George released his emotional attachment to his family, he experienced a freedom to be himself with everyone. Before, he had been reserved; now, he experienced an openness and freedom in relating to people, and began making his own friends.*

> *Judy, a precocious first child of loving, adoring parents, was dethroned at the age of three by the arrival of her sister.*

At first, she looked forward to a live-in playmate. However, the demands of the new baby turned what was to have been fun and games into war and hate. The more attention baby Betty got, the more resentful and jealous Judy became. Judy neither wanted Betty to succeed at anything she tried, nor even to live. In one of their physical childhood bouts, Judy tried to kill her. As a result of Judy's non-acceptance and death wish for her, Betty failed at everything she tried to do, from marriage to career. She was always sick, and once attempted suicide. Unknowingly, she was just how Judy wanted her to be---"out of the picture." Then Judy released her emotional attachment to her family, which freed her to love and accept Betty. This does not necessarily mean that Betty responded in a positive way to Judy. In the beginning, Betty distrusted this change in Judy, and she tested and challenged it. Judy has continued to love and support Betty, giving the relationship a chance to mend, and to have a new beginning.

Releasing your family attachment frees you to be able to accept yourself, where before, you were not free to make this choice. It frees you to love yourself, support yourself, believe in yourself, and be yourself. If your family hasn't accepted you, and you're attached to them, you won't accept yourself. However, by releasing this emotional attachment, you will be free to accept yourself just as you are and to BE YOU.

Freedom to be ourselves is what we all want, and releasing our emotional attachment to our family frees us to be who we are. It frees us to be a wife or a husband. It frees us to be a father or a mother. It frees us to be successful at whatever we do. It frees us to be our highest and best, and to be all we can be.

Once you release your emotional attachment to your family and ACCEPT yourself, you can BE yourself. Releasing your emotional attachment to your family gives you the freedom to be you, but YOU have to BE it. Make up your mind to release this emotional attachment and to BE YOU, to be your highest and best, to be all you can be.

TEAMS

Our fourth emotional attachment is to our teams. They tell us what we can have. They are our entry into the world. We attract teams which reflect back to us what we have been taught about ourselves by our mother, father and family. They mirror us to ourselves by giving us what we've expressed to them about who we are and how we want to be treated. If we think highly of ourselves, our teams will, also. If we think poorly of ourselves, our teams will be contemptuous of us. If we are outstanding in intelligence, talents, beauty or gifts of the spirit, and feel badly about being outstanding, our teams will be jealous of us. If we are outstanding and feel comfortable with it, our teams will support and emulate us. If we are outstanding and feel superior about it, our teams will hate us, compete with us, beat us or, in some cases, attempt to destroy us. If we know that we have what it takes, but we're not doing it, and we see our friends and family succeeding, we begin to hate them, become jealous of them, and destroy our relationship with them. Because our teams have the power to tell us what we can or cannot have, we are not free to have what WE want when we are emotionally attached to them. According to our team's rules, we hold back from giving our highest and best and, in so doing, we block ourselves from having everything we want. We are controlled by expressions like, "Who does she think she is?" or, "He's getting too big for his britches," or, "He thinks he's better than we are." Or we have controlled others by telling them, either verbally or nonverbally, that we are too good for them, and superior to them. The fear of being left out, different or rejected by the group often causes us to slow down on our road to success. Natural leaders may refuse to lead, due to the fear of being disliked or excluded. Capable workers may hold back, for fear of losing friendships and alliances. Conformity becomes a reality because of our emotional attachment to the team. The fear of being different keeps us from taking risks and having what we want.

Our teams consist of friends, co-workers, athletic teams, religious groups, club members and school mates, to name a few. In some cases our mother, father and/or our family is our only team, particularly if our parents are overly possessive and protective, and fearful of losing us to our friends. Some parents will allow their children to have one team or one friend. In this case, the child will go through his whole life with one friend or one team.

> One student had a close friend in college who he intermittently discarded and held on to. When the student went to work for a large corporation, he made a friend in the corporation, and because he could have only one friend, he put his college friend on the back burner. Years later, the corporation friend died. At that time, he took his college friend off the back burner and reactivated the friendship. All this is due to the fact that his mother would allow him to have only one friend.

Our fathers take us out into the world to begin our training, but our teams are our first venture out alone, free of parental control and/or guidance. Teams are our school for learning how to get along with others in the world. Our teams assist us to complete incomplete relationships, as well as build new ones. They teach us what we have to do in order to create warm and loving relationships.

Parental Attitudes Toward Teams

Mothers either encourage or discourage teams by their attitudes toward their children's friends. If a mother welcomes them with cookies and a cheerful smile, she sets the stage for healthy team relationships. If she praises and admires her children's friends, they feel her acceptance and permission to further their team relationships. If, on the other hand, she is cold or indifferent because she feels protective, possessive, or that her children are superior, her children will have problems with teams, and find it hard to become involved because of their mother's message.

Mothers' attitudes toward the girls their sons choose, and fathers' attitudes toward the boys their daughters choose determine how each will later relate to people of the opposite sex. A father who, either directly or indirectly, tells his daughter that he never wants her to leave him for another man creates feelings of resistance and guilt in her when she is involved with a boyfriend. If she marries in spite of his message, she will soon feel compelled to divorce her husband. Some daughters are unable to have any relationships with boys at all, while others rebel and look to relationships with boys as an escape from this smothering possessiveness.

Sometimes, a mother's jealousy of her son's relationships with girls can be carried to such extremes that attention from any female (aunts, baby sitters, cousins, neighbors, teachers or mothers of friends) can be threatening. This type of mother puts out such angry feelings toward other women that the son perceives all women to be his mother's enemies. It is not as big a problem when romance is not involved. However, much conflict is still created in a little boy who wants to be the teacher's pet, but is unable to express his love because he feels tense and uncomfortable in her presence. These feelings are sometimes misread as shyness, but are really the result of an unconscious feeling that he is doing something his mother doesn't like. When you do something your mother doesn't like, you feel tense, guilty and bad.

The Effects of Teams

Your teams have profound effects on your life. They assist you to go out into the world and begin to gain a sense of freedom and independence from your family. They give you a perspective on how other people live, and provide an opportunity for you to carve your own niche in society.

The feeling of being left out (or not included) is known to many people (see chapters: Mother and Game Playing). It can leave a child scarred for life and reluctant to pursue future team relationships. Everyone wants a team relationship, but many cannot have it due to childhood programming. Those who cannot have team relationships become loners, and deny to themselves their desire to be on a team. They take pride in their rugged individualism and independence.

Conformity

The majority of people want to be accepted by the group, and because of this, will often go to extremes to conform. These people are controlled by their teams, which prevent them from being successful and from expressing their talents and abilities. To surpass a close team member in business would be threatening to that relationship. The fear of being disliked for surpassing the team forces them, subconsciously, to hold themselves back and to conform.

A girl whose boyfriend was becoming very successful in business, unconsciously, tried to hold him back because she was afraid of losing him to a more appealing and successful woman. This happens with men and women. It creates in the person who is held back a feeling of being smothered, possessed and held down.

We often hear stories of movie stars abandoning the friends they had before they became rich and famous. Frequently, the abandonment is the result of the friends' attitudes, not the star's. The old friends are unable to feel comfortable with and relate to the star's new success because they feel jealous, resentful, insecure or inferior. While this doesn't always destroy the relationship, it certainly stifles it.

All team members, unconsciously, know their boundaries, and any time a member tries to step beyond them, he is quickly put back in his place. Because it is difficult to pull himself above the group, it is easier to stay mediocre. At some point, he knows that in order to excel and succeed, he must make a conscious choice to let his teams go. This means freeing himself from the need to pull the team with him, from the fear of the team's rejection, and from the fear of losing the team.

Because we are taught that we're not good enough and to never make a mistake, we fear taking risks, and look only at what can go wrong. We are told, "Watch out! You might fail!" We develop a negative attitude. (Many who have the same fear of failure take the risk anyway.) This gives our teams the power to control and discourage us. No wonder there is so much room at the top, and it is so crowded at the bottom.

We blame our teams when they don't make us feel safe and secure. We want them to take responsibility for our feelings and for the relationship by giving us the space to create our lives our way, and by not getting mad or upset with us when we don't do it their way.

If we are not allowed to say "I want" or "I don't want" by our parents, we begin to look to our teams to see what they have that makes them desired, appreciated and valued. We look to see what they want or don't want. This begins the habit of looking outside ourselves for what will work for us. We have an unwritten reciprocal agreement with our teammates in which they tell us what we should have in order to be popular, desirable and wanted, and then we tell them what they should have to be popular, desirable and wanted by us. We become social chameleons whose colors change with every encounter. It takes enormous amounts of energy and constant vigilance to meet the standards of all our teams. Team members are automatically sized up and put in different categories. Those who are being themselves cannot be categorized. This both angers and/or frustrates the social chameleon. It is frustrating and uncomfortable for the chameleon to be around someone who is free to say "I want" and "I don't want" when he is not free to say it.

Because of the fear of rejection by our teams, we are afraid to be ourselves. The fear of being left out and humiliated encourages and feeds conformity. For many, it becomes necessary to pull away from the group in order to be free to have what they want without pressure from their teams, and it seems as if this is the only solution to the problem. But running away does not solve this problem; it compounds it by creating incompletions and the habit of running from problems instead of dealing with them. This can become a lifelong pattern. Incomplete relationships continue to be created until they begin to see how destructive they are to creating successful relationships in every area of life. The reason they have incomplete relationships is that they cannot have problems. Those who are not free to have problems run from them because they cannot deal with them. And so they justify, defend and protect themselves by refusing to look at anything they might or might not be doing to cause the problem. They believe that problems cannot be solved without pain and difficulty, and so they deny they have them. To support this belief, it is necessary to blame others, make everyone else wrong and make themselves right, blameless and the victims of their circumstances. They then have to begin the destruction of these relationships, and establish a lifelong pattern of being right and blameless (see chapter: The Roles). This pattern, in relation to teams, is established in early childhood, and continues throughout life unless they face it and choose to change it.

If you see enemies everywhere, and expect others to take advantage of you or use you in some way, you, unknowingly, put up walls of resistance in every relationship. These walls present a barrier to any person with whom you want to relate. The effort to be on your team becomes so great that the other person gives up, and the relationship is destroyed, while you look on innocently. By releasing your team attachments and making up your mind that you are free to have team relationships, you begin to see friends instead of enemies. You begin to have teams that work, and warm and loving relationships.

When nothing you do ever measures up to the expectations of your teammates, retreat, in one form or another, appears to be the only solution. How do you retreat and stay in the relationship? Giving in, letting them have their way, never disagreeing with anything they say, and becoming quiet all appear to be sensible solutions. So your life becomes one of denial, selling out and escape just to maintain a relationship that's not working. When one team member dominates another, the one dominated soon loses his identity. If you find yourself dominated, releasing your emotional attachment to your teams will allow you to acquire the courage necessary to break free. Some people experience such freedom and power from being released from that control that they feel vengeance toward those whom they perceive as having held them down. Now they, in turn, begin to dominate and control others. No lessons have been learned; power and control have merely been shifted.

> *Ed was an overweight first grader who was picked on and teased by his classmates for being fat. Every day he came home from school crying because of the teasing. When his friend, John, told his mother about how the class was teasing Ed, she suggested that John tell his friends that Ed was his friend. Because John was popular with the other kids, his taking a stand for Ed would end the teasing---and it did. Several weeks later, John's mother saw Ed humiliating his younger brother the same way he'd been humiliated for being fat. Nothing was learned; the power of team control just shifted. When John became an adult, he became a millionaire in business and highly successful in his family relationships, while Ed's marriage ended in divorce. John practiced in his own life the principles he believed in, while Ed did not choose to learn what wasn't working for him. John learned the lesson; Ed didn't.*

As soon as you find yourself doing the same thing to others that you hated being done to you, end and complete those relationships based on old control tactics (see chapters: Mother, Game Playing, The Roles). With a made up mind, be willing to face yourself, be willing to take responsibility for what you have created, and choose to develop warm and loving relationships that work. No one has the right to dominate and control you, nor do you have the right to dominate and control anyone else. By being free from the need to either control your teams or be controlled by them, you are free to have the kind of team relationships you want, as well as whatever you want to have. Being free to say "I want" and "I don't want" also allows you to have what you want. A loyal team member will support you through all your successes. Supportive team members give you a feeling of inner security.

Teams are the greatest school for learning what works and what doesn't work in the world. Herein lies the secret to your successes or failures. You can choose to learn from your team lessons, or remain right and blameless, or escape in other ways. If you choose to remain right and blameless, you will find yourself destroying your relationships. If you choose to escape, you will find yourself avoiding responsibility and avoiding solving problems, all so that you can remain right and blameless.

Wanting What Others Have

Unknowingly, parents teach their children at an early age that being themselves is unacceptable. The child, in turn, responds to this by figuring out what his parents want and giving it to them. Children become so adept at giving other people what they want that they often lose awareness of what they themselves want. Because they don't know what they want, they start looking at and desiring what others have. They think that because others have it, it must be of value. Life then becomes one of always seeing and getting what others have. Once they get it, they are still unfulfilled and discontent, because it wasn't what they wanted in the first place. For the most part, all they are aware of feeling is discontentment and dissatisfaction. They have no idea why they feel unhappy after they get what they thought they wanted.

Deciding What You Want

Your emotional attachment to your teams locks you into having what they want you to have. Once this attachment is released, you are free to have what YOU want, but you yourself must decide what that is (see chapter: Programming). Sometimes you discover what you want by a process of elimination: looking at everything you DON'T want is one way of arriving at what you DO want.

It is anxiety-producing to think about what you really want, and often risky to go ahead and get it because of unconscious fears. These include the fear that what you are going for may not be what you really want, the fear that if you get it there will be nothing left to strive for, the fear of failure, or the fear of not living up to others' expectations. Then there's the fear of success: "If I'm successful, will I be able to follow that act?", or, "Will they hate me or abandon me, and I'll be left alone?" It becomes easier to create what we don't want and then complain about it than to take a risk to create what we do want, have success and take a chance on losing what we have.

When you decide what you want to have, there is a natural inclination to tell your teams, hoping that they will encourage and support you. However, the opposite can occur. Because of their fear of losing you or feeling "less than" you by comparison, they may tell you, either verbally or nonverbally, that you cannot have it, or that you are "not good enough" to have it. Once you hear this from a team member, you might never take the first step toward doing what is necessary to have what you want. Taking risks can fill you with such anxiety and fear that any discouragement is easily accepted. This is one of the reasons we create negative circumstances in our lives and are totally unaware that we are doing it. Once we become aware of what we want, we can't wait to share it with others, and so begins the decline of our success. This is one of the ways we unconsciously set ourselves up to fail. We enlist our teams to discourage us so that we will have an excuse to escape the very uncomfortable feelings of risk and commitment.

> *In her excitement and enthusiasm at starting an interior design business, Mary called her friend, Joan, to share this decision with her. Joan's reaction was, "Aren't you afraid to go into people's homes all by yourself? And besides, what do you know about starting and running a business? I'd be scared to death to try anything like that. Do you know what to charge? I hear the interior design business is very difficult because you have to deal with so many different kinds of people, and nothing gets done on time, and customers get upset and angry." By the time Joan finished telling Mary all the reasons why she couldn't do it, Mary was so discouraged that she hardly had enough energy to hang up the phone. What Mary was unaware of was that Joan was giving her what she really wanted: an excuse to avoid taking a risk.*

Releasing Your Emotional Attachment to Your Teams

By releasing your emotional attachments to all of your teams, you are better able to see how you relate to them and how they relate to you. Upon close examination, you can see their effect on your successes and failures in life. By understanding this, you can create successful team relationships and, in so doing, relate successfully in every area of your life. By releasing your emotional attachment to your teams and accepting them just as they are, you will be free to choose those teams which want the best for you, rather than choosing ones which limit you. And destructive team members who do not want the best for you will move away.

By releasing your emotional attachment to your teams, you are free to choose what YOU want, rather than what your teams want. And it frees you from the need to have their support. You would like to have it, but you don't HAVE to have it. You are stronger, more independent and have the courage of your own convictions.

Releasing your emotional attachment to your teams frees you to HAVE what you want, but YOU have to decide what you want and begin to create it by taking one step at a time.

SPOUSE

The marital relationship is the most difficult one in which to achieve success, because it unites two people with different programming on an intimate level. What begins in courtship as a loving, giving and supportive relationship often turns into anger (and, in some cases, rage), competition or destruction. As a result, marriage can lack the love, romance, support and consideration everyone wants.

Our fifth emotional attachment is to our spouse. One symptom of being attached to our spouse is that we are not free to rely on ourselves or, most importantly, on God. We have a compulsion or need to rely on our spouse, as well as on others. Men rely on women for admiration, sex, love, domestic comforts, companionship and children. Women rely on men for love, financial and emotional support, sex and companionship. Their priorities are, therefore, different.

Because of the differences in priorities, agendas and programming, conflicts are created. Rather than examine their relationships, find solutions, and take their responsibilities, some people blame their spouses and look to others for the lustre that has gone out of their lives, while others settle for less than what they want. Both solutions are the reverse of what works best.

Where do you find lasting solutions? Many solutions give hope and temporary relief, but fail to solve the problem. Any time things start to show wear and tear in a marriage, the first response is to resist, divorce or hold on tighter. However, anything you resist persists, and what you hold on to, you lose. And divorce is accepting failure. It is in letting go and releasing your emotional attachment to your spouse that you begin the process of finding the solution to what you've always wanted: the warm and loving relationship which was begun and lost. The first step toward regaining this is to release your emotional attachment to your spouse. This frees you to rely on yourself, and permits you to rid yourself of resentments caused by needing your spouse.

Needing Someone

Needing someone implies that you do not already have what you want. Because you are afraid that you won't get what you think you need, you put too much energy and effort into obtaining it. In other words, you try too hard and, unconsciously, push away the very thing you want. To see this clearly, think of someone who has needed you. How did you respond to that need? Did you want to get away from him? Experts have been studying sports for years to learn how to bring about top performance. In golf, for instance, you learn that trying too hard prevents you from hitting the ball well. The same is true in relationships.

Another drawback to needing anyone is that you unconsciously resent them. Need creates demanding expectations, followed by disappointment, hurt, anger, resentment and, sometimes, hate when the expectations are not fulfilled. If we need to rely on our spouse, we push away their ability to be reliable. This causes anxiety, tension and conflict in the relationship. Most people dislike and, sometimes, even hate expectations because of the pressure they create, and the fear of falling short of them. Expectations are a way of demanding performance from a spouse based on preconceived notions of what that performance should be. Therefore, by releasing this attachment, you are free to want your spouse without the negative influence of need restricting the flow of your love.

Mixed Messages

Men often give women a contradictory message: "I am independent and don't need you, AND I am depending on you and I do need you." Another mixed message is, "I like you to be independent and take care of things yourself, AND I like you to be dependent on me and make me feel strong and manly."

Women also give out mixed messages. On the one hand, the signal is, "I need you to make me feel feminine and desirable," while the opposite signal is, "Who needs you? I can take care of myself!"

Those who want to be independent resent anyone or anything they must rely on because "needing" is a sign of weakness, and makes them feel vulnerable to manipulation.

Many women have been taught to be dependent on their spouse. Releasing the emotional attachment to their spouse frees them to be more independent. In some cases, this can be a threat to the spouse, while, in others, it is a relief to both parties. When a woman is heavily dependent on her spouse, he feels the pressure of her leaning on him, and this may cause him to push her away. By releasing this attachment, she is freer and more self-reliant, and he is freed from the demands, pressure and expectations she placed on him. The releasing of your emotional attachment to your spouse frees you to rely on yourself for your own identity instead of your partner.

Men are equally reliant on their spouses. Since society has created an image of men that requires them to be manly, self-reliant and independent, the ways in which they rely on women are more covert. Their strongest need is to rely on women to protect and support their egos. There is a conflict between the man's need to be viewed as a hero, and his need for his ego to be supported and protected. Heros, by definition, are strong, take-charge, "I'll-protect-you-and-save-you-from-all-danger" figures. In contrast, egos are vulnerable, self-centered and constantly in need of recognition, admiration and acknowledgment.

Because of this conflict, men give a confused message to their wives. On the one hand, they say, "I'll take care of you," and then, on the other, "I need you to take care of me and my ego." Women, because of their need to rely on men, accept and believe the hero message, and then when they come up against their husbands' need for ego support, feel betrayed, disillusioned, disappointed, and often lose respect for them. These opposite messages create inconsistency, and can cause spouses to stop believing in each other.

Preconceived Role Concepts

The pressure of living up to preconceived role concepts is enormous for both husband and wife. Living up to the way society says a wife or a husband "should" be can create problems in the relationship that are difficult and, at times, seemingly impossible to solve. Both husband and wife have their own insecurities which require care and feeding. It is not honest to impose on men the belief and expectation that they have no emotional needs, and it is not honest for men to impose on themselves that they have no emotional needs. It is neither fair to them, nor to their wives, because what they are in essence saying is, "I don't need you, and I don't want you to need me." This is the kiss of death to a marriage. Neither partner can live up to these expectations. If both were free to be themselves, they would be able to maintain a warm, loving relationship and to freely give each other what they want.

Releasing this emotional attachment to our spouses frees us to rely on ourselves for our own identity, instead of on our partners. As long as we rely on our spouses for our identity, we are unable to be ourselves. In many cases we resent them, unknowingly, because we need them to tell us who we are. This puts undue pressure on them, as well as creating disappointment in us, since it is impossible for them to give us our identity, and even if they try, they do not give us the identity we want. Spouses cannot give us what we alone can give ourselves.

Four False Concepts

There are four false concepts contributing to destruction in relationships: the first is not facing and accepting that our needs exist; the second is looking to our spouses to give us our identity; the third is trying to get them to live up to our image of what and how the perfect spouse should be, and the fourth is the inability to give total loyalty and commitment to the spouse because of previous family commitments. When both spouses release their emotional attachment to each other, they begin to build the kind of marriage they want.

Many people rely on their spouses to make them happy, then resent them when they don't succeed at this impossible task. Releasing this attachment helps you to become aware that you are relying on your spouse for your happiness. Some people need a spouse in order to feel okay about themselves. Releasing this attachment frees them to feel okay about themselves, with or without a spouse. They still have to acquire belief in themselves, but now they have the freedom to choose to do so. Marriage is designed to be a supportive relationship, not one which requires one person to develop a crippling need. Total dependency, while it may gain some rewards, such as security or admiration, leads to a restricted life. Totally dependent spouses may soon find themselves unable to make simple decisions or handle tasks outside of the routine. Overly dependent couples are afraid to try new experiences alone. They may even give up pleasurable activities like singing in a choir or playing bridge because one spouse doesn't enjoy it. They "have to" do everything together.

Dealing with Dependency Needs

People deal with their dependency needs in different ways. They may respond openly by becoming overly needy and dependent, which, quite often, elicits a contemptuous response from their spouses. Or, they may hide and deny their needs with a facade of false independence, for fear of being weak (or seen as weak), vulnerable and emotionally trampled. In either case, there is a desire to have these needs fulfilled, and a fear that they will be rejected.

Single People

The person who does not have a spouse is just as involved in our cultural concepts of marriage as those who do. In this case, the individual will release the need for a spouse, or the need to remain single. By so doing, he will be free to marry for the right reasons, or be free to remain single.

A typical example is the young girl just out of school whose parents have a strong desire for her to get married. Out of her need to make her parents happy, she, too, feels a strong need to get married. In many cases, women will stop or interrupt a career to fulfill this parental desire. Releasing the need for a spouse alleviates the feeling of parental pressure, and allows the single person the freedom to marry or not marry because he wants to or doesn't want to.

Another example is the man who felt a lot of pressure about the type of person he should marry, based on his parents' concepts. After releasing his need for a spouse, he was able, for the first time, to think about the kind of spouse he would like to have.

Releasing Your Emotional Attachment to Your Spouse

When you release this attachment you will not be as needy. You may want certain things, but you no longer need them or have to have them. The source of much of your conflict and anger ceases to exist. You are freer to rely on yourself. This does not mean you will become defiantly independent. It does mean, however, that you will be able to give and receive support from others without the strong need to get something in return. Old patterns will no longer restrict you.

Releasing your attachment to your spouse allows you to clean out old programming and make space for healthier approaches to warm and loving relationships. You still have to be the one to learn and apply the laws of how to create this. What you will notice after releasing this attachment is a closer, friendlier, more loving relationship with your spouse, and an ability to rely on yourself in new areas.

By releasing this attachment, you free yourself and your spouse from unrealistic demands and expectations, and allow each other to rely on yourselves for your own identities, thus enhancing your self-confidence and self-esteem. This step also frees independent spouses to ask for what they want without expecting their mates to be mind readers, consequently eliminating the anger they experienced when this need was previously unmet.

By releasing your emotional attachment to your spouse, you allow your marriage to grow and blossom. You can now begin to build a lasting relationship on rock instead of sand.

Releasing your emotional attachment to your spouse frees you to RELY on yourself, but YOU have to do the relying.

SELF

Our sixth emotional attachment is to our ego self. This attachment prevents us from being able to express ourselves freely. Either we cannot say what we want, or we say too much. The statement we make to the world about ourselves is really the statement our ego makes. If we are confident, assured and feel good about ourselves, our statement is one of high self-esteem. If, on the other hand, we feel insecure, inadequate or inept, our statement is one of low self-esteem. Many people become adept at disguising their statements, but their actions eventually reveal their true feelings.

The ego self is very vulnerable. This attachment is so powerful in its control that it keeps us constantly on the lookout for ANY threatening situations. We are not able to relax until we feel totally safe, which is never. Even with someone who is caring and non-threatening, our guard is still up. The ego is distrusting, and, as a result, totally consumed with protecting itself. It asks, "What are they trying to get from me?" Because of the ego's fear of being caught off guard, and because the ego requires constant proof of who everyone says they are, most relationships have to begin anew at each meeting.

What is the Ego Self?

The ego self is a false identity which the mind has created. It exists to have its own way and to protect itself at all costs. It is only concerned about its survival. It prevents you from seeing, and therefore expressing, your true self. It is filled with fears, doubts and insecurities. The ego self needs constant feeding with attention and recognition, but no amount of feeding will satisfy it. It spends its life either demanding attention and recognition, or being hurt and angry at being denied them. It has to have its own way, and justifies anything it does to get it. An example is the seemingly honest man who lies to himself in order to satisfy his ego's demands.

The ego self constantly looks at its reflection in mirrors and windows. Although it gives itself enough daily attention to be able to paint a self-portrait, it would not recognize itself if it saw itself walking down the street. The ego self doesn't know itself at all, so it is constantly looking to others to tell it who it is. Its needs are in conflict. On the one hand, it needs you to tell it how wonderful it is, and on the other, it fears you because you might tell it what it doesn't want to hear. It is controlled by fear. As a result of this fear, it distrusts everyone, including itself.

Self-Expression

Our attachment to our ego self controls what we say or do not say. Many people analyze every word that is said for fear they will not receive acceptance or approval. We are constantly judging ourselves as to how well we are doing, how we look and how we are coming across to others. If it appears to us that our looks and actions do not measure up to our own and others' expectations, we become uncomfortable. In extreme cases, we feel like running away. If we do not get what we want, we leave and blame others, using anger and criticism for protection. When a problem of opposing views arises, it is difficult, if not impossible, to come to an agreement because we are unable to express ourselves without conflict due to the protective and defensive nature of our ego self.

Madeline often found herself disagreeing with the opinions of others. Rather than express her disagreement, she would withdraw mentally from the conversation by "tuning it out." Her fear of saying what she wanted to say restricted and angered her. She envied those who could speak freely. Her ego self protected her from seeing this envy by silently blaming and hating others for disagreeing with and restricting her.

Everyone has an ego self that keeps them from expressing their highest and best self. It holds them in such a confining and restricted state of control that they are unable to say what they want. They often feel that there is someone tied up inside them. The need and desire to release that someone (the true self) is always with them.

Self-Centeredness

Because everyone's ego's attention is on protecting and defending themselves, they are never able to relax their guard long enough to be able to hear, let alone be interested in, what another person is saying. They are waiting for others to stop talking so that they may begin. In most encounters, everything the other person says is filtered through, "How is this going to affect me?" or, "What am I going to get out of it?" At the slightest indication, mental neon lights flash, saying, "Warning. Warning. They are going to get you or take advantage of you in some way." It is this constant attention to the ego self which prevents people from saying what they want to say out of fear of being humiliated, made wrong or rejected.

Jane was involved in a literacy program she believed in. She wanted to enlist the support of others in this project, and to do so she spoke before many church and civic groups. Each time, her fear of saying what she wanted to say, even though she believed in what she was saying, was so great that she experienced overwhelming terror. She feared humiliation and rejection. It was impossible for her to take her attention off herself and her fears. She was unable to lose herself in her project because her ego self stood in her way.

Judy was a brand new high school teacher, not much older than her students. She was afraid of not being able to maintain control over her class. She feared losing their respect and her authority by saying the wrong thing. As a result, she remained distant and aloof, saying as little as possible. This destroyed her natural self-expression, and inhibited her teaching ability.

Being attached to the ego self causes inner stress, tension and anxiety, which often manifest as physical problems. Many turn to pills and alcohol to relieve this, rather than deal with the cause. By releasing the emotional attachment to our ego self, we take the responsibility to begin freeing ourselves from these enormous restrictions.

Once you release the emotional attachment to your ego self, you have more freedom to say what you want to say, and you are also able to be more interested in other people and what they have to say. Your attention is less on yourself. Before releasing this attachment, you may be very self-conscious when entering a room full of people. After the releasing, you are able to talk with others un-self-consciously.

> *Marge, while on a picnic in the park, was bitten by a dog she had befriended. Before releasing the emotional attachment to her ego self, she would have been furious, and would have blamed its owner for his lack of responsibility in not leashing the animal. However, because she had just released this attachment, she was amazed to find herself being far more concerned with relieving the guilt of the dog's owner than with her own bleeding hand. After releasing this attachment, you are freer to care more about others and less about your own ego's needs.*

> *Robbie was the neighborhood bully. He was able to intimidate everyone, including adults, like Bill. Before releasing his emotional attachment to his ego self, Bill was afraid to tell Robbie not to shoot a BB gun in his yard, fearing Robbie's destructive retaliation. After he released his attachment to his ego self, Bill was able to say to Robbie, with firm conviction, what he had previously been unable to say. Robbie left the yard, never to return again, and there was no retaliation.*

> *In the same way, Mary's mother-in-law criticized Mary's yard every time she came to visit. Mary was unable to take a stand on her own behalf. The yard consisted of several acres left in a natural state. After Mary released her emotional attachment to her ego self, she spoke up and said, "Mom, we*

keep our yard the way you see it because this is how we like it." Her mother-in-law never criticized the yard again.

Talkativeness

The ego drives some people to say too much. They can be opinionated and/or talk compulsively. Others feel a need to be either sarcastic or involved in excessive bantering. There is also the aggressive person who has all the answers and no reservations about telling everyone how to live their lives. After releasing their emotional attachment to the ego self, these types of people are less impulsive and less inclined to speak without thinking.

> *Dorothy was driven to talk. It seemed as though she couldn't stop even if she wanted to. She acted as though she were always on stage, responsible for entertaining anyone who was with her. Her monologue was filled with jokes, and she expected her audience to laugh, whether or not they were amused. She was so wrapped up in her own talking that she had no awareness that others might be drifting, bored or waiting for a chance to respond. If the conversation took a more serious turn, she then became the ultimate authority on any subject. After releasing her emotional attachment to her ego self, she saw that this behavior had pushed a lot of people out of her life, and she was no longer driven to talk incessantly.*

After releasing the attachment to your ego self, you are not as demanding about having things your own way. It is the ego self that says, "I want what I want when I want it." You begin, at this point, to see your ego as a separate part of yourself. The releasing of this attachment aids you in beginning to understand the truth that you are not your ego self. This is a false concept with which you have mistakenly been identifying.

Releasing your emotional attachment to your ego self frees you to EXPRESS yourself as you choose, but YOU have to express it.

CHILDREN

Within all mothers there is a built-in protective mechanism. This natural protective instinct, coupled with the emotional attachment to our children, makes this attachment very strong. This protective mechanism can best be seen when observing a small bird chasing another one, twice its size, away from its nest. Mothers instinctively sense any danger to their children. This instinct arouses aggressive or defensive behavior in varying degrees.

Many couples have children for the wrong reasons. A lot of women feel that they "should" have children, because society says it's their duty. Sometimes parental desires for grandchildren are so great that couples have children in order to please their parents. Feelings of discontentment, resentment, boredom, or even contempt may arise when you have children because you feel you SHOULD, OUGHT TO or HAVE TO.

With the birth of children comes the responsibility for nurturing them and providing for their physical needs. This responsibility is so consuming that it can prevent, or at least inhibit, the normal enjoyments in life. The birth of a child can also interfere with a couple's enjoyment of each other. Being a good mother or father places such huge pressure on parents that some wonder, "Why can't we have children, and enjoy ourselves and our children at the same time?"

Being a "Good" Mother

Our concept of responsibility has been described as being devoid of fun and enjoyment. As children, we see "grown-ups" burdened with responsibility, worrying and fretting over their children instead of enjoying them. We are not given permission by society to enjoy our children fully. If a mother watches her toddler son run happily down the steps and enjoys his glee, others may criticize her for not taking what they consider to be her responsibility, which is to fill him with the fear of falling. We are taught that being a good mother means pointing out all dangers and keeping ourselves attuned to them. If we believe that, we can't enjoy our children because we are so consumed by what could go wrong with them.

The do's and don't's multiply with each new generation. There are more dangers today than there were 100 years ago. One generation ago, experts told us that we had seven years in which to create the perfect child. Now they tell us we've got three. Thirty years ago, the play pen was a necessity. Now you're an irresponsible mother if you use one. Fifty years ago, there were no child-rearing experts, and mothers followed their own instincts. These days, the bookstores are filled with "how to" books on raising children, each one saying something different. The authorities of each generation debunk the authorities of the previous one. For any one problem, there are twenty different solutions. Not only do we have our own strong, natural sense of duty and responsibility to our children, but we also have the added burden of what society says is right and wrong, and what our responsibility is.

Father's Role

Fathers have an innate urge to take their children out into the world and teach them how to relate to others. The father is the child's bridge from the security of the home to the larger community outside of the home. By releasing the emotional attachment to his children, he is free to help them fully experience the excitement of the world. He can enjoy his children's progress, their mistakes as well as successes, and allow them the freedom to learn from their mistakes. Releasing the attachment also frees him from the innate fear of losing his children when they're grown.

Parental Fears

While the mother's built-in protective instincts are very important to the safety of her child, these instincts can be carried to extremes. When they lead to possessive over-protectiveness, these instincts destroy her child's natural development. They restrict the child's freedom to experience life and learn from it. In our attempt to protect them from physical and emotional hurt, we give our children our fears and lack of faith. By releasing our emotional attachment to our children, we free ourselves from the necessity of giving them our fears. We free them from the burden of OUR fears.

Balance

There must be a balance between being overly protective and allowing too much freedom. Unless the parent, and particularly the mother, is free to enjoy her children, this balance is very difficult to achieve. Releasing the emotional attachment to our children gives us the freedom to enjoy them. It is this enjoyment which allows us to create the balance.

Mary's four-year-old son, Tommy, was asking her questions and talking to her while she was "very busy" sweeping the floor. All of a sudden, he looked up at her and said, "Mommy, you're not listening to my words." She realized that he was telling the truth. She was NOT listening to him, and this made him feel unimportant. She was driven by her need to complete her domestic duties at the expense of her son. He helped her to see that her priorities were not in order. Her attention was on sweeping the floor, while she half-heartedly listened to him. After she released her emotional attachment to her children, she became aware of a new closeness and openness with them. She enjoyed them as she never had before.

Good Parents

When we are attached to our children, if our young children are out of reach, we are concerned and unable to put our total attention on our current activities. We, as parents, place restrictions on our children to alleviate our own fears. We believe that if we control the situation, nothing can go wrong. In addition to worrying about our children, we are concerned about how to be good parents and how much time to spend with them. What is quality time? Are they getting the healthiest foods? What is the right kind of discipline? Will they love us and like us? How do we juggle our rights and interests with theirs? After a day of all this, putting the children to bed brings a huge sigh of relief.

In extreme cases, parents make remarks about this feeling, such as, "You are a noose around my neck," or, "If it weren't for you, I'd be free to..." Feelings such as these do not need to be verbalized to be understood. They can be passed along to our children, unspoken. Many times, parents are not even conscious that they are feeling like this and conveying these messages. Sometimes they know that they have these feelings, but feel too guilty to acknowledge them. These feelings indicate that the parents blame their children for the burden and responsibility they feel. These messages can make children feel they are "not good enough," and can cause them to feel self-blame, self-hate or rebellion.

Identifying with Your Children

When you are attached to your children, you identify with them, and take on their feelings. If they are happy and cheerful, you are, also. If they are disappointed, sick, hurt or mistreated by their peers, you feel the pain and suffering equally. At such times you may feel that there is no enjoyment in life and that no one else is having fun either. By releasing your emotional attachment to your children, you no longer take on their moods, but are able to support them. When they go down emotionally, you won't go down with them, and you will then be able to assist them back up. You are also more able to enjoy them and everything else you do.

Releasing Your Emotional Attachment to Your Children

Releasing this attachment feels as though a weight has been lifted. You feel lighter. Your children, also, sense a pressure being lifted from them. They are freer to enjoy themselves and, therefore, find it easier to perform better in everything they do. Once you release your emotional attachment, you won't have that feeling of holding on to your children too tightly, or the opposite feeling of not being able to be involved with them. You experience more patience, understanding and respect for them. Your worries during their absence are greatly diminished, and you don't have the pain of loss when they leave home. You feel that they are separate individuals rather than extensions of yourself. In addition, because you're not worrying about your children, your relationship with your spouse can be greatly improved.

Releasing your emotional attachment to your children frees you to ENJOY yourself, but YOU have to do the enjoying.

Individual Attachments

Everyone has individual attachments beyond the basic seven. These attachments vary according to the needs of the person. The most common individual attachments are to our work, students, patients, sports, playing, working, truth, freedom, animals, people, money and material possessions (such as homes, memorabilia, papers, cars, jewelry, plants and land), as well as youth and beauty. Some people choose the same attachments which their parents chose. New attachments can be created at any age. A child born into a family that puts great value on money could form an attachment to money at a young age.

We become attached by needing and holding on to something which, we believe, will give us fulfillment and make us happy. However, by giving it more and more attention, importance and value, it entraps and eludes us, instead of fulfilling us. We can free ourselves by releasing each of these attachments, just as we did the basic seven.

2 The Releasing Technique

WE HAVE DEVELOPED A SIMPLE TECHNIQUE to release the childhood programming that has run your life, and replace it with a program that works for you. It is important to know that it is both your choice and your responsibility to deal with the programming you accepted in childhood. This can be thrilling, and in some ways, threatening. It is thrilling if you realize that, by being responsible, you can take total charge of your own mind and, in so doing, lead your life your way. It is threatening to the mind because it means that you are going to have to do something, that you might have to change. It is only threatening, though, if you either refuse to take, or deny, your responsibility. It is easier to blame others, and in so doing, relieve yourself of the responsibility of having to do anything about your programming. However, blaming others and denying your part in it will continue to keep you locked into the same old problems. So, choose to take responsibility for that which you have created. Do it for you.

The technique is a sevenfold pattern for releasing your programming. It is systematic and orderly. You will be able to observe the natural succession of this pattern. Once you have released your emotional attachment to your mother, the doing and judging patterns of your life will immediately start to emerge. These patterns relate to your father. We act like our father. You will find yourself judging what others are doing. Once you release your emotional attachment to your father, you will immediately stop judging and will become aware of being bothered or irritated by how others are being, which relates to your emotional attachment to your family. Your awareness will begin to expand as you release each emotional attachment.

It will expand even more with the seven acceptances of Take Charge, Child of God, Being, I Am the Source, Relying Within On God, I Am Light, and Enjoyment.

The simplicity and power of this technique is incredible. Thousands of people have used it successfully to remove blocks which were preventing them from creating the kinds of lives they wanted. It has worked for them; it can work for you.

Using the emotional attachment to your mother as an example, the procedure is as follows: sit in a comfortable position, totally relaxed. Close your eyes and give yourself mental and/or verbal suggestion: "I am completely relaxed. I see myself sitting by a bubbling brook, leaning against a large oak tree. I am so relaxed. I am so peaceful."

Now, put your attention inside yourself to that spot where you go when you think deeply about something or when you pray. See yourself in a scene with your mother. It can be a childhood scene or a recent scene. It can be happy or unhappy. Allow any scene to come to your mind without forcing it. Become involved in that scene. If your mind is blank and refuses to give you a scene, visualize a photograph of your mother.

As you become involved with the scene, and re-experience the emotions relating to your mother, you will feel a tension begin to build in your body. It may be in your stomach, chest, throat or head. If it is in the stomach, chest or throat it will rise toward the top of your head to be released. This will happen naturally. All you have to do is visualize it happening and allow it to go.

If the mind begins to resist, ignore it and release the attachment anyway. Say, "Dear Heavenly Father, I totally release my emotional attachment to my mother unto You." If you have a problem calling on your Heavenly Father, say, "I totally release my emotional attachment to my mother unto the universe." Choose the words that work for you.

Imagine that there is a muscle in each temple. There is actually no muscle there, but it feels as if there is. Relax that imaginary muscle, and release the emotional attachment to your mother into the arms of God or unto the universe.

You will actually feel the tension move up and out through the top of your head. It will be accompanied by a feeling ranging anywhere from peace to joy. You will feel lighter and clearer. Colors will be brighter. All bodily tension will go and you will feel relaxed.

If, after going through the releasing technique, you still have tension anywhere in your body, except the neck or shoulder area, you have not released the attachment. Simply go back inside and do it again. If the tension continues after two or more attempts, ask yourself if you feel that you deserve to be free and happy, or if you feel that you are abandoning or betraying your mother by releasing the emotional attachment to her.

Release any of these blocks by using the above technique. Because you have needed your mother's permission for everything, you now have to make up your own mind that you are going to release your emotional attachment to her without her permission. Then you are acting on your own. You are not abandoning her, but are preparing yourself to have an adult relationship with her versus a mother/child relationship. She will feel the pressure to be the perfect mother for you removed from her, and your releasing your emotional attachment to her will, in fact, help her relationship with you flow much more freely.

The second part of this process is to accept your mother just as she is. Every mother does the best she knows how, regardless of how it may appear. Even if your mother is perfect in your eyes, you will still want to accept her just as she is. Acceptance accomplishes two things: it acknowledges her just as she is, and frees you of negative thoughts and energies created by your lack of forgiveness. To accept her, go back inside to that spot inside your head, see her clearly and say, "I totally accept my mother just as she is." Relax the "muscle" on either side of the forehead, and the acceptance automatically goes into the subconscious mind and flows down into every cell of your body.

The third part of this process is to accept that you are free to think for yourself, using the above technique. Go back inside your head and say, "I totally accept that I am free to think for myself," and allow the acceptance to flow down into every cell of your body.

RELEASING THE SEVEN ATTACHMENTS AND ACCEPTING THE SEVEN ACCEPTANCES

MOTHER

Release:

"God (or "Heavenly Father" or whatever words feel comfortable to you), I totally release my emotional attachment to my mother unto You."

Accept:

"I totally accept my mother just as she is."
"I totally accept that I am free to think for myself."

FATHER

Release:

"God (or "Heavenly Father" or whatever words feel comfortable to you), I totally release my emotional attachment to my father unto You."

Accept:

"I totally accept my father just as he is."
"I totally accept that I am free to do what I want/act the way I want."

FAMILY

Release:

"God (or "Heavenly Father" or whatever words feel comfortable to you), I totally release my emotional attachment to my family unto You."

Accept:

"I totally accept my family just as it is."
"I totally accept that I am free to be the way I want to be. I totally accept that I am free to be me."

TEAMS

Release:
"God (or "Heavenly Father" or whatever words feel comfortable to you), I totally release my emotional attachment to my teams unto You."

Accept:
"I totally accept my teams just as they are."
"I totally accept that I am free to have what I want."

SPOUSE

Release:
"God (or "Heavenly Father" or whatever words feel comfortable to you), I totally release my emotional attachment to my spouse unto You."

Accept:
"I totally accept my spouse just as he is."
"I totally accept that I am free to rely on myself."
"I totally accept that I am free to rely on God."

If you are single,

Release:
"God, (or "Heavenly Father" or whatever words feel comfortable to you), I totally release the need or desire for a spouse (or not to have a spouse)."

Accept:
"I totally accept that I am free to be married if I choose to."

SELF

Release:

"God (or "Heavenly Father" or whatever words feel comfortable to you), I totally release my emotional attachment to my self unto You."

Accept:

"I totally accept myself just as I am."
"I totally accept that I am free to <u>say</u> what I want."
"I totally accept that I am free to <u>express</u> my talents and abilities."

CHILDREN

Release:

"God (or "Heavenly Father" or whatever words feelcomfortable to you), I totally release my emotional attachment to my children unto You."

Accept:

"I totally accept my children just as they are."
"I totally accept that I am free to <u>enjoy</u> myself."
"I totally accept that I am free to <u>enjoy</u> everything."

If you don't have children,

Release:

"God (or "Heavenly Father" or whatever words feel comfortable to you), I totally release the need or desire (not) to have children."

Accept:

"I totally accept that I am free to have children if and when I want them."

THE POWER OF RELEASING FOUR TIMES

Our beliefs begin with a thought. The thought then becomes a feeling, the feeling then becomes a habit, and the habit then becomes a mood. In order to completely release a concept or an old belief, it is important to release it four times: once for the thought, once for the feeling, once for the habit, and lastly, for the mood. It is equally important to accept the corresponding Truth four times for the same reasons. For example, if you are releasing the belief that you are bad, let it go four times and accept that you are good enough just like you are four times.

3 The Acceptances

From our attachments, we accept certain concepts which become the false belief systems on which we base our lives, and by which we are controlled. This programming starts out as a little thread that winds around itself until it becomes a ball. The ball can be unwound back to the core until you can see the real you. The next chapters will reveal the false belief systems as they have been accepted and have become the mood of your life. As the ball unravels, freedom can come by accepting the truths of who you are. The thread shows the route you took into the dilemma; the route out is to unwind the ball back to your center.

We accepted these attachments and false concepts in sequence. There is an orderliness and pattern to these which each individual mind follows. Just as there is an order to the seasons and the ebb and flow of the tide, so there is an order to the mind, although it appears to be otherwise.

Once we get the order of how our belief systems went in, we get the order or "road map" of how to get them out. We have been led to believe that this process is complex; however, it is not. We can choose to walk out of the maze of the mind into the light of understanding, and we can choose to take the road to Truth. The decision is one that we alone can make for ourselves. Once the decision is made, NOTHING CAN STOP A MADE-UP MIND.

Letting go of our belief systems is both our choice and our responsibility.

Introduction to the Acceptances

Whenever you let something go, a vacuum is created which causes an imbalance. Once you let go of an emotional attachment, it is necessary to follow with an acceptance, which creates a balance. For example, when you let go of your emotional attachment to your mother, you are free to think for yourself, to think your own thoughts, and to think the thoughts that will work for you in your life at this moment in time. You then accept that you are free to think for yourself, after releasing the emotional attachment to your mother. You can do this with power and understanding by taking charge of your life. Taking charge of your life will empower you. In truth, all of the following acceptances will empower you:

Take Charge
Child of God
Being
The Source
Relying Within On God
Expressing My Talents and Abilities
Enjoyment
Fun

TAKE CHARGE

The sign on President Harry Truman's desk said, "The buck stops here." He knew that, in the final analysis, he was responsible for every decision he made for this country. Because he was in charge, there was no one to blame. He made the decisions which, he felt, were best for the country, regardless of public opinion or the opinions of his advisors. He knew that the buck stopped with him.

Taking charge of your life and your responsibilities is stepping from childhood into adulthood. It is the beginning of taking full responsibility for your life and happiness. It is often confused with taking control, which is motivated by fear and the desire for authority without responsibility. Taking charge, however, is motivated by the desire to get the job done. When you control, you substitute blame for responsibility. When you take charge, you eliminate blame (of yourself and others) by assuming responsibility.

After taking charge, you no longer need to prepare for failure because you are not thinking of what could go wrong or of all your reasons to remain blameless. If you make a mistake, you seek solutions rather than excuses. You cease identifying with the mistake and taking it personally. You begin to stop blaming others, and having to prove and protect yourself. Prior to taking charge, you unconsciously feel a need for your mother's (or a mother substitute's) permission to make decisions that will work for you. After taking charge, you are free to give yourself permission.

Controlling is hard work---willing, pushing, coercing, struggling, conning and/or forcing people or circumstances to do what you want them to do. Much energy is used in this effort because you fear that life will not go your way. Then you get angry when it doesn't, and figure out ways to manipulate others without their knowing it. You cannot be honest and open. You have to constantly watch others in order to stay in control, studying their weaknesses and shortcomings so that you can get your way without being blamed. Blaming means that "they" are wrong or guilty, and that you are right and blameless. This absolves you from all error, allows you to remain perfect in your own eyes, and gives you control over your life. It can be frightening to let go of the need to blame. Blaming has served you, both as an escape and a protection from looking and feeling bad or wrong. As long as you remain blameless, you do not have to change. We dislike change because it implies that we have made a mistake, are less than perfect and, therefore, bad or not good enough. Most people spend their lives avoiding the pain and heartache which results from feeling that they are bad.

At this point, one of your fears is that if you give up those old "perfect" messages you will not have anything to do, nor will you know how your life should be. This step is the crossroad between childhood (the need to be taken care of) and adulthood (deciding what YOU want to do, be and have). Many people tell you, from time to time, that you need to grow up, without telling you how. Taking charge of your life is the how. Taking charge is taking a leap of faith that you will take the responsibility to get the job done. What job? Any job. It's scary, yet any new step into the unknown is scary. Up to this point, you are either controlling or being controlled by what other people think. Unknowingly, you have accepted others' concepts of what you should do, be and have as your own. Before taking charge, you are unable to take responsibility for getting the job done. You may want to, but you can't. After taking charge, you can begin to think for yourself and formulate your own concepts of what YOU want to do, be and have.

A wonderful essay which illustrates the importance of taking charge and getting the job done is "A Message to Garcia," by Elbert Hubbard. During the Spanish-American War, President McKinley desperately needed to get a message to the Cuban leader, Garcia, whose whereabouts were unknown. After many couriers failed to get the job done, someone told the President that a Lieutenant Rowan could find Garcia. Once the President assigned Rowan the job, Rowan got it done without thinking of what could go wrong. Failure did not enter his mind.

Before taking charge, you are constantly thinking of what could go wrong because you're preparing for failure. After taking charge, if the thought of failure enters your mind, you can turn it away and, in so doing, strip it of its power.

Abraham Lincoln said, "You are as happy as you make up your mind to be." He was politically defeated again and again. He served during the United States' most trying years. His wife, historians say, had mental problems, and one of his children died at a young age. He was unable to receive much comfort even at home. Because of all these circumstances, he was led to find happiness within. He learned that, in order to be happy, it was necessary to make up his mind to take charge of his life and take responsibility for his happiness.

Once you accept and face your circumstances, you can deal with them. Therefore, acceptance is a major step toward achieving happiness. Acceptance is the opposite of resistance. Many people resist their circumstances. There is a natural law which says that whatever you resist, persists. What you resist grows larger and larger in your mind, and gets you deeper and deeper into the mire. With acceptance, discontentment and discouragement lose their power. Taking charge of your life is the first step toward growing up and creating your own happiness.

> *Jane was dominated and controlled by many people in her immediate family. Nothing she did was right, good enough or approved of, including how she raised her children. However, she had definite ideas on how to raise them. Everyone, including "the experts," had different opinions, which caused her to question her own ideas. The "how to's" varied with each article or book she read, as well as with each family member. In addition to their ideas, she acquired her own*

experiences, which only added to her confusion and conflict. She was worn out and exhausted from willing and forcing herself to live out others' ideas of how the perfect family should be. Faced with what looked like inevitable failure, she examined closely what SHE really wanted to accomplish, and decided that to achieve it she would have to stop listening to others and find her own way. She made up her mind to do this and, in so doing, took charge of her life. Instantly, energy filled her body. Her mind cleared, and she had a new sense of power and resolve. She knew that she was ultimately responsible for the way her children turned out, and resolved that she was going to get the job done with or without help. She realized that the buck stopped with her. She was no longer afraid or worried about offending others by doing it her way, and not only could, but would do it the way she thought best. For the first time, she had faith and trust in her own decisions. After taking charge, her fears no longer prevented her from getting the job done.

Once you take charge, you see that you do not need your mother's, or anyone else's, permission to be happy. Once in charge, you can choose to be happy and successful. It is important to decide what being successful means to you, because success to one person can be failure to another. It is YOUR understanding of success that matters.

Any time Martha was happy or feeling good, her husband, Harold, would, unknowingly, deflate her because he felt threatened by her happiness and success. She felt so controlled by him that finally she was motivated to take charge of her life. Shortly thereafter, on a trip to the mountains, he tried to upset her again. He refused her requests and persisted in giving her "not good enough" messages. In the past, this would have made her furious and silent. She would have retaliated in some way, and the fun-filled day they had planned would have ended in war. But now Harold's techniques were not working. She let him know that she was happy, and chose to remain so, and his verbal abuse ceased. As a result, they were able to enjoy the day together.

With taking charge comes the ability to begin to express yourself and to give of yourself openly, without fear of rejection or humiliation. You are able to begin to take your attention off yourself and be there with the other person. You are able to begin to think in terms of others. The fear of being blamed is lessened to such a degree that you feel less vulnerable and freer to open up.

> *While Sue's boss was out of town, another manager asked Sue to do his secretary's work. In doing this, he inappropriately broke the chain of command. Sue had not yet taken charge of her life, and she became very angry at the request, but suppressed her anger. This situation was the catalyst she needed to see clearly how she allowed the world to control her, and how she always responded with unexpressed anger. This had been the pattern of her life. Out of fear of rejection or criticism, she had allowed others to take advantage of her. With clear vision, she instantly saw the lie and the power it had over her. She took charge of her life, and with this step, came peace and inner power. The next day she was presented with the same request, but this time Sue had a different attitude. She let the manager know that she was not available. He was not offended because she let him save face by not challenging him for breaking the chain of command. With her extra time, she went to her boss' immediate superior and asked if she could work on the computers and learn more about them. Now she was using her time to further her career, rather than being at the mercy of other people's whims. She was then able to give direction to her life.*

When you take charge of your life, what was negative can, and often does, become positive.

> *Before she took charge, Barbara was always irritated by her husband's lack of responsibility, because his irresponsibility mirrored her own. Her way of expressing her lack of responsibility was to seek others' sympathy and to act pitifully. Her husband expressed his irresponsibility with outbursts of anger and by threatening to leave her and their four children. Her greatest fear was of being blamed, especially*

for the failure of their marriage. It created such terror in her that his threat of leaving would bring her to her knees and cause her to beg forgiveness.

Finally, Barbara faced her tremendous fear of being blamed, and stopped resisting her husband's anger and attempts to leave. She accepted the possibility of divorce and being blamed for the failure of their marriage. She took a deep breath and made up her mind that she was totally in charge of her life and her happiness. "I was truly free," she said. "What before was so, became 'so what?' I am free from what I have feared and been terrorized by all my life. The feeling is incredible and beyond description."

Once Barbara took charge of her life, what had been a negative situation became a positive one. She saw that the irresponsibility she had previously disliked in her husband was the very quality which now prevented him from taking the necessary steps to divorce her. Recognizing her fear of being blamed pushed her into making up her mind to take charge.

After you take charge, you become aware that you have the CHOICE not to be bothered by the small, mundane, and often irritating things that happen during the day. They still exist, but you no longer need to resist them. You can accept them without becoming involved in them.

Prior to taking charge, emotional upsets are filled with pain and suffering. Many people are not able to identify these feelings because they have repressed and/or resisted them. Some people have not been given permission by their mothers to be happy, while others have not been given permission to be unhappy. Those who have not been given permission to be unhappy can convince themselves that they are happy by denying their unhappiness, pain and suffering. Those who have not been given permission to be happy may vacillate between unhappiness and happiness. This, too, creates pain and suffering. After taking charge, the unhappiness may continue, but it does not result in pain and suffering. You can now choose to be happy, whereas before, you did not have a choice.

If you feel irritated or angered by even a simple or loving request, this is an indication that you are not in charge of your relationships. Not being in charge of your relationships keeps you from being free to ask for what you want. Therefore, you unconsciously resent anyone asking you for what they want or saying "I don't want." When you are not in charge of your relationships, you feel blame and resentment any time you think someone is making you do something you do not want to do. If others ask you to do something, you automatically think they're trying to make you do it. You reach the point where you feel that you are doing your boss or spouse a favor by doing what is already your responsibility. The truth is that you are responsible for your actions, your life, your relationships and your happiness. Doing what you do to please others indicates that you are not taking your responsibility. Do you cut the grass for your wife or because it is your responsibility to cut the grass? Do you clean the house for your husband or because it is your responsibility to clean? Do you go to work because you "have to" earn money for the family or because it's your responsibility to support them? Taking charge of your life, relationships and happiness frees you to get the job done, frees you to create warm and loving relationships, and frees you to create the success you want, whereas not taking charge keeps you blaming others and looking for reasons and excuses to fail.

When you are not in charge, the ones most affected are the people you love. Irritation and resentment are expressed more openly with family members than with employers and friends because employers, for example, are free to ask things of you. This creates much unpleasantness in the home. Before taking charge of your life, your relationships and your happiness, you are not free to say, "I don't want," so you express yourself with anger, resentment and blame. After taking charge, you are free to make decisions based on what you want or don't want to do.

When we are not in charge of our lives, we live in the fantasy of believing that we are actually taking our responsibilities, and we feel burdened by them. Feeling burdened is a clear indication of not taking responsibility.

> *Jane was always on time, but shortly after arriving at work she would spend two hours on the phone talking with her close friend about personal problems. She fooled not only her boss but herself as well. She believed that she went beyond the call of duty. She could always justify her actions. When she attended night classes at college, she excused her nonparticipation at work the next day by saying that she was tired and had already done too much. To do any more would add to what she felt was her burden. She was not taking*

charge of her job, for which she was paid a large sum of money.

When you are out of charge, you place compensation on top of compensation. Rather than achieving what you want, you only complicate your life more. You can get your work done but only with great resistance and complaining. Your job can become physically and/or emotionally painful and draining as a result of your resistance. After taking charge, much resistance and compensation are eliminated. You begin to make decisions for your life which will work FOR you rather than AGAINST you.

Before taking charge of your life, you are vulnerable to pain and suffering. You need other people's permission to make decisions, and you feel burdened by responsibility. After taking charge, you stop demanding that people (or material possessions) take care of you or make you happy. You grow away from emotional dependencies by choosing to be happy regardless of your circumstances. You put away childish things and become an adult. According to the Bible (1 Corinthians 13:11), Paul said, "When I was a child, I spake as a child, I understood as a child, I thought as a child; but when I became a man, I put away childish things." Taking charge of your life is the step necessary to becoming an adult in the world. TAKE CHARGE AND GROW UP!

CHILD OF GOD

Once you take charge of your life, you begin to assume the responsibilities of adulthood. You begin to think clearly and make decisions based on what you want to do, how you want to be, and what you want to have. Most blaming ceases because now you see clearly that not only are you in charge of your life, but also that you WANT to be responsible for it. With this comes a newfound freedom. But often, you feel that fun is missing. You want to have fun and still be in charge. How can you do that? How can you have both? As with all great Truths, the answer is so simple it eludes you: let go and accept that you are God's child, and know that God will protect you, take care of you, and guide you step-by-step. This takes a leap of faith. There is an intangibility about taking such a leap. It is this intangibility which makes it impossible to understand with the intellect. It has to be experienced. You must go beyond the intellect into the unknown. Taking a leap of faith is stepping out into the unknown.

In the beginning, we were connected to our Source---God. We knew we were God's children. We began thinking that there was something more, and, as in the Biblical story of the Garden of Eden, we left our Source to seek that something more. We wandered away from our spiritual Father and, like the children of Israel, got lost in the wilderness, and couldn't find our way home. After losing our way, we lost our true identity and began looking outside ourselves to find it. We soon became insecure and frightened, and turned to our mind and body for our identity. We created an ego with which to identify. The ego then became the false identity which we took on to protect ourselves. But, in reality, we wound up protecting and defending it, instead of it (the ego) protecting and defending us. By replacing our ego with God, we are able to move from fear, doubt and insecurity into inner security, confidence and love. We are able to believe in ourselves and believe in God.

The mind wants to analyze and understand intellectually what it means to accept that you are God's child. It asks, "How do you do it, and what happens when you take that step? How do you know the difference between your mind and your spirit? Why is it that, even though you may have experienced God in the past, you can't recall or understand how you found Him, how you lost Him or how to recapture Him?"

You can't grasp God with the intellect. Words cannot describe what it feels like to let go and let God guide and direct your every step. It has to be experienced. When you become aware that your life isn't working the way you want it to, you will be ready to let it go to God. You have to be willing to acknowledge that you have a problem, and you have to want a solution. The problem is that you are separated from God, which separates you from your loved ones and from yourself. You find yourself being hurt and/or hurting others. Letting go and letting God guide you is the solution. You resist the Truth that you are God's child because your mind feels threatened that it will lose its control and power over you. By accepting the Truth, you are able to allow God's power to work for you and through you. No one can do it for you. You must do it for yourself.

Because many people are programmed to suffer and be punished, letting go, letting God guide them, and being free terrifies them. They come right up to letting go and letting God, and then they back away. There are many fears the mind can use to prevent you from taking this step: the fear of having to give something up, the fear of being wrong (or the need to be right), the fear of being different (or having your personality change), the fear of the unknown, the fear that "arriving" won't live up to your expectations (or what you had hoped for and yearned for won't be there), the fear of being blamed, and the fear that you're not good enough and, therefore, have to keep working hard in order to get good enough.

When we left our Source, God, and forgot how to return to Him, we became weakened, threatened and vulnerable. Thus began layer upon layer of false concepts. Man began putting everything and everyone before God. Even the concept of God has taken on many different interpretations and false beliefs, and triggered many fears and emotional reactions. You can say the word "God" to 15 different people and elicit 15 different definitions, such as: energy, spirit, Jehovah, Allah, Being, actualization and Jesus, to name a few. Some see God as a God of love, while others see God as a Santa Claus God. Some see God as wrathful and vengeful, while others see God as judgmental and something to be feared. For many, the defense and proof of these concepts is more important than the experience. God needs no proof. God is. Just as gravity and the sun need no proof. They just are. Let go and accept the Truth that you are God's child, and you can immediately feel peace, security and protection.

There are those who misinterpret the act of faith---letting go and letting God---as literally doing nothing. By letting go, you allow God to work through you without effort and struggle. You continue to act, but not with a driving or pushing intensity.

Before you take this step of accepting that you are God's child, you experience a very strong need to will yourself to do what you feel you should, ought to, and have to do. You are unable to go about your daily activities without stress and pressure, and often, you are blocked from doing anything at all. You feel as though there are chains all over you. Pulling against these chains requires such enormous effort and will that, at times, it feels like it isn't worth it.

There are many subconscious reasons why we are not free to do what we want: we may have been taught that we didn't deserve to do what we want, that it is bad to have our way, or that we should do only what we're told to do, just to name a few. You may find that your greatest enjoyment is getting into bed at night, or looking forward to the weekend or some other time in the future. You feel that you must delay your gratification by putting it off to a later time. By letting go, moving into the loving arms of your Heavenly Father, and accepting the Truth that you are His child, you immediately cut through many mental barriers which keep you from being free to do what you want to do. At the same time, most judgment of others and/or yourself ceases, and you can do things without effort and will.

Bracing for action, getting ourselves up, and becoming tense are ways we use to will ourselves to get the job done. We feel that this prepares us for anything which could happen. We believe that this bracing and tension wards off mistakes, failures, losses, confrontations and enemies, and prepares us for the fierce competition out there. We fear that if we let go of this intense effort, we will become lazy, worthless failures, vulnerable and unprotected. This is how the mind tricks us into believing that it will protect and save us from its so-called enemies. Often, people of faith are perceived as sitting on a mountain top doing nothing, which to us, equals failure. However, these are false concepts which, by their very nature, prevent us from experiencing the Truth that we are God's children. Some people work without faith, and experience much effort and struggle, while others think that faith is all that is necessary, and thus, take no action. Both concepts fall short of the mark. It is the combination of faith, visualization (seeing and feeling), and action (works) which brings the desired results.

You are the child of a King who resides not only all over the universe but within you as well. Let go and accept that your Heavenly Father loves you unconditionally, will protect you at all times, and will give you the solution to any problem. Letting go is the opposite of willing, tension and struggle. Letting go allows you to do the job with ease, peace and direction, knowing that everything is going to work out all right. It may look like you won't want to do anything, but the opposite is true. For the first time, you are free to do what you want to do without willing yourself or struggling. Before this, you feel as though you have to, you should, or you ought to do what you do. After letting go and letting God, you are free to choose to do what you do because you want to. By letting go and letting God, you turn over the responsibility for your life to Him, and rest in His loving arms.

Just go within and realize that your Heavenly Father is everywhere, giving you unconditional love, having all power, taking care of you, and protecting you from harm. Simply let go and move into the warm, secure, safe space within. In so doing, you identify with being part of your Heavenly Father. You then ask questions, listen within, be with Him, experience Him, and trust and follow the direction He gives you. Simply close your eyes and accept that you are God's child forever, and ever, and ever.

BEING

Knowing and being who you are is the most exciting adventure you can experience. It has been clouded from your view only because of the false identities that you have believed yourself to be. The major false identities are: your mother, father, family, teams, spouse, self, children, your mind, your body, your work, and even your possessions. Once you have seen this in clear vision, you are able to let go of these false identities, and accept the Truth of who you are. The Truth is that you are one with your Heavenly Father --- you are the Spirit that is, the Spirit that was, and the Spirit that ever will be. The word "God" brings up various connotations. Use whatever word represents God to you. Too many of us allow a word to block us from realizing the Truth of who we are. We get so caught up in facts that we do not allow ourselves to experience the Truth. It is time to end our preconceived myths, and experience love, joy and peace --- our natural state of being.

When you are ready to accept the Truth of who you are, you will experience fear, inferiority (feelings of not being good enough), and/or superiority (feelings of being better than others). Your mind may tell you that you have to do many good deeds to earn the right to be who you are, and that you have to atone by paying penance for having been bad. But what your mind neglects to tell you is that the penance never ends, and you never get good enough. Therefore, it is your responsibility to accept the Truth of who you are, and not allow the doubts or negatives of the mind to stop you.

We resist those things which are best for us because of our need to hold on to the old, familiar myths. Yet, it is in accepting the Truth of who we are that we begin to find the love, joy and peace we have always wanted.

Fear

One of the most powerful blocks to Being is fear. The presence of fear is the absence of trust and faith. Fear began in the mind of man when he ceased relying upon his Source, God within. Instead, he began relying on his mind and outside sources to protect him from all dangers. The mind took control, and looked out at the world with suspicion. Suspicion and fear replaced faith, trust and unconditional love. At that moment, all his troubles began. However, instead of protecting him and giving him control over outside threats as it said it would, the mind entrapped him in its needs and unrealistic demands to have its own way. It used fear, tension, anxiety and doubt to control.

Fear is a signal of, and protection from, impending danger. It blocks the flow of energy, happiness and unconditional love, and prevents the free flow of self-expression. It causes you to lose perspective, prevents you from taking the action necessary to achieve your goals, and stifles your creativity. In its extreme, fear drives you to paranoia, and assures you of misery and failure.

Fears come in many forms: fear of failure, fear of the future, fear of the unknown, fear of success, fear of people (seeing enemies everywhere), fear of humiliation, rejection, abandonment, physical disfigurement, or being alone. Fear of death is man's greatest fear, and reveals itself through such fears as flying, heights, falling, speed, water, fire, sickness, and so on. The fear of death leads to other fears and insecurities, such as the fear of losing loved ones, money or position. The fear of loss creates a need to hold on to things and people, which can lead to greed and possessiveness.

During the United States' Civil War, General Stonewall Jackson said, "I never take counsel with my fears." This statement reveals that he knew he had fears, but that he was not going to pay any attention to them. He knew that they could prevent his making the right decisions. Everyone has fears, but some people refuse to be controlled by them. Franklin Roosevelt acknowledged this when he said, "The only thing man has to fear is fear itself." He meant that FEAR is the problem. He inspired the United States to go beyond its fears.

The Search For Security

In order to make themselves feel secure, many people put their faith in tangible things: their ethnic group, family, heritage, beauty or social and business positions, because God appears to be intangible (can't be seen or touched). This intangibility doesn't give the mind the security it seeks. So, many people rely on their spouses for their security, and live in constant fear of losing them to another person, a career, a hobby or death. Others turn to money for their security. They feel that by amassing great wealth, they can find security and freedom from fear. The truth is that none of these tangible security measures work.

As long as you rely on your mind, you will be afraid and inhibited. To eliminate your fears, all you need to do is put your faith and trust totally in your Source, God within. Rely on that Source instead of your mind. This is a powerful Truth.

"Fight or flight" is your mind's reaction to fear. For this reason, most people try to avoid fear by keeping it hidden from themselves and others. This is why conformity is the norm, rather than the exception. Stepping out of the crowd, stretching or growing threatens the status quo and causes numerous fears to surface. Often, when you begin a new project or set a new goal, fear expresses itself as resistance, physical illness, doubt, discouragement, withdrawal or depression. This is your mind's way of avoiding the arousal or recognition of the fear. Once you MAKE UP YOUR MIND and begin to move toward your goal, the fear (and its symptoms) disappears. For some, doing whatever it is they fear, eliminates it. For others, the fear cannot be eliminated until they release the specific fear itself. Many well-known speakers testify to years of feeling terror each time they stood before an audience because the fear of public speaking aroused the fear of humiliation.

Fears can be released as they are faced. However, as soon as you release one, another surfaces. The only way to be free of all fear is to put your total faith and trust in your Source, God within, and totally rely on Him.

Faith

Faith is the opposite of fear. Faith is believing and trusting that you can have what you want. Faith requires that you let go of having to have your own way. People confuse this with not being able to have what they want. They confuse method with result. By totally trusting and relying on your Source, God within, you are able to choose what you want without having to force people or circumstances to give you your way. Faith is acting on what you are led to do without knowing the outcome beforehand. It's doing the thing you want to do without doubt, not knowing the outcome, yet knowing it will work. You do not know how, but you know it will.

The way to be free from fear and its crippling effects is to accept and be your true self, to be one with God, to accept that you are one with the Spirit that is, was and always will be. This gives you newfound energy to accomplish your goals. The feeling that you cannot possibly succeed no longer robs you of your ability to try. Both your physical and emotional health improve. When you no longer need to give attention to your inner tensions and fears, you can give your undivided attention to the tasks at hand. You are free to enjoy your own life without the need to protect yourself or to live life vicariously. You can be yourself and be spontaneous. You no longer have to watch your words for fear of being rejected. The greatest result is that you are free to love and be loved.

The Mind

Once you accept the Truth that you are one with God, the mind can become your servant instead of your master. This is a big step, because the mind resists giving up the power and control which it has had over you. And yet, once you accept the Truth that you are one with God, your connection with Him is open and flowing.

It is our demanding mind which gets us into so much trouble. It wants its own way. It is selfish, self-centered and deceptive. It often believes that it has the right to run over people in order to have its way, and we cannot tell it otherwise. We cannot reason with it, though we believe we can. It cannot tolerate any criticism or control, yet feels it has the right to criticize and control others. It sees itself, and has to be seen, as perfect and indestructible. YOU must take charge of IT, rather than letting IT control YOU. This doesn't mean getting rid of your mind or intellect, or resisting it. It means allowing it to serve its true purpose as your servant instead of your master. Your mind is a non-supportive, destructive, inconsistent master, but a cooperative, supportive and willing servant.

The mind tells you that you are not good enough to take this step, and keeps coming up with just one more thing for you to do to get good enough. Years ago, in order to keep a mule plowing the fields, a farmer would hang an apple in front of the mule's nose. The mule believed that with just one more step, he would get a bite of the apple. He believed it so strongly that it kept him working all day long. Our "apple" is our perfect concept of how we should be in order to arrive at peace and happiness. And we will never reach it as long as we work to get it. We simply have to accept the Truth that we are.

The truth is that NOW is the only moment we have. We exist only in the now, not in the past or the future. Since this is the only moment we have, why not live it to the highest by enjoying it to its fullest? This is done by accepting that you are one with God NOW, instead of working to become it later. Our need to make everything perfect is a burden, and creates such pressure in our relationships that we rush to make them perfect. However, it is impossible to make everyone and everything perfect. Each person's concept of perfection has come from his or her mother, father and family, and no two persons' concepts are alike. Many of us rebelled against our family's concept of perfection. These concepts are so ingrained that even though we rebelled, we, unknowingly, demand perfection from all of those around us.

The mind tells us that once we become perfect, and therefore, good enough, we will be ready to accept the Truth of who we are. The truth is, we will never get good enough to satisfy the demanding mind. This false concept binds us to the world and prevents us from becoming free from the burden of perfection, free from our own minds. The only way to freedom is to accept the Truth of who we are. When we do this we can accept ourselves and be ourselves just as we are.

This is what all of us are looking for in our relationships. We want others to accept us as we are without blame, judgment or criticism. We interfere, either by thought or deed, with how others are being, because we have not accepted ourselves as we are. Once we accept ourselves and be who we are, we can then give others this freedom and, thereby, create warm and loving relationships with ourselves and others.

Realizing the Truth of who you are frees you from the power and control of the mind, and fills you with peace, unconditional love and joy. The life force which animates every living thing is the same life force which animates you. That force is God. You and God are one. It has always been so. You simply forgot. You are the Spirit that is, was, and always will be. This realization provides you with the necessary tools to move through life without the myriad of ups and downs which occur each day. It allows your flow of energy to be directed with a singleness of purpose previously dissipated. By being who you are, you are able to live in the moment, without the hurts of the past and the fears of the future destroying the present. Peace and serenity fill every cell of your body, giving you a newfound energy. Strangers smile and loved ones respond differently, as though they have gone through some change. However, their change is only in response to your change.

This step is neither something another can do for you nor, once achieved, something another can take from you. It IS you. It is the Truth of who you are. There are no words to describe it, though we try to do so. It is worth anything you have to do to remove those blocks which stand in the way of this reality. The blocks will dissolve with the acceptance of this Truth, and you will have given yourself the greatest gift of all: unconditional love for yourself. With this unconditional love comes the freedom to love all others.

Depression

Depression is one of the most emotionally debilitating diseases in the world today. There are several causes for depression. Becoming aware of the cause of any problem is essential for its solution. Not knowing the cause keeps you on a roller coaster of effects.

One major cause of depression is grief. Grief is the natural and normal reaction to a loss, whether the loss of a loved one, loss of a material possession, loss of freedom, loss of confidence, loss of a relationship, loss of position, and so forth. Some people, unknowingly, repress their grief, which later expresses itself as a mild form of depression, low energy and extreme sadness. You can eliminate depression caused by grief, first, by facing that you are sad and, therefore, in grief and, then, by letting go of the resistance to grieving. Accept that grief is a normal reaction to your present circumstances, and LET THE GRIEF GO. After letting the grief go, let the sadness go. Grief is a natural reaction to losses in life, and will, therefore, recur if there are other losses, but by being aware of it, you can then let it go. You do not have to continue to feel its pain. You do this by putting your attention inside your head to the place you go to when you think deeply or pray. At your temples you will experience tension, as though a muscle had tightened. Relax this area and consciously let the grief go. You will experience a lightness and a feeling of clear-headedness. The grief is gone. Sadness follows naturally on the heels of grief. Let the sadness go just as you did the grief. Your spirits are lifted. If the sadness returns, due to more grief, keep repeating the process until it is all gone. It sometimes takes 5, 10 or 20 times for all the grief to go. Do it as many times as is necessary. As long as we live in this world, there will be grief, followed by sadness. Use this process to eliminate grief and sadness when they occur in your life. Grief generally takes three months to live out its normal pattern.

Indecision can also be a cause of depression. The fear of taking action or the fear of failure causes the indecision. Some of the reasons for this fear are: fear of making a mistake (and, therefore, being less than perfect), fear of having to give something up, or fear of making the wrong choice and not being able to turn back. This form of depression is eliminated by making a decision. Even deciding to make a decision later is better than making none at all, and will cause the depression to leave.

A third cause of depression is anger turned inward. Many people were never allowed to express their anger as children, and so, turned it inward. The anger then became unexpressed blame and hatred of others, or self-blame and self-hatred, both leading to hurt and depression, followed by sadness.

Another cause of depression goes back to childhood. If our mother was depressed, we will be depressed because we think like our mother.

Our family gives us a blueprint of how to be. Once we release our emotional attachment to our family, we are free to make our own choices, to create our blueprint for ourselves, and to decide in minute detail how WE want to be. We are now free to be ourselves and to make choices based on what will work for us in a positive, loving, constructive way. We are now free to be good to ourselves. If, before, we allowed others to control us, we are now free to make the choice to just be. If, before, we controlled others, we are now free to allow them the freedom to be. We are now free to be responsible for asking for what we want, which frees us from having to manipulate. Being free is giving yourself and others freedom --- the freedom to leave or to stay, the freedom to be involved with you and you with them, the freedom to be totally there, to be a listener, and to be both a giver and a receiver.

Knowing that you are the Spirit that is, was and always will be frees you to begin to be considerate of yourself and others, and frees you to have choice. Having a choice frees you to be real, to be yourself, and to be the Truth. This is one of life's greatest freedoms. Choose to be YOU.

THE SOURCE

Learning how to create what you want is one of life's greatest blessings. It often helps to first look at what is blocking you from having all that you want to have. There are several reasons why you might not want to look. First of all, you may think that looking is too painful, because you might find out something bad about yourself. Secondly, looking requires that you do something or make a change. And thirdly, looking forces you to see how you relate to others. The very thing that you resist facing is what is necessary for you to move through in order to have it all. So, why not make up your mind, like Mary Poppins, to put on your hat, grab your bag and fly through the obstacles blocking your success?

Who or what you identify with determines your degree of success or failure. Your identity and your successes or failures reveal your state of mind. Your role models determine how you think, act and are. If you think negatively, you can expect negative results; if you think positively, you can be assured of positive results. If you say something to a friend, expressing a positive state of mind, it will be perceived openly and graciously. If, however, you say the same words from a negative, skeptical or doubting state of mind, you will receive rejection, resistance and anger. Ceasing to identify with others and beginning to identify with your true self frees you to create your life and happiness YOUR way. The truth is that you are the source of the circumstances which exist in your life. It is very freeing to know and accept this, because it allows you the freedom to create your circumstances the way you choose. By accepting the Truth that you are the source of your life, you eliminate the doubt that looms within, blocking you from having what you want. Accepting this Truth forces you to take full responsibility for your creation and, in doing so, learn through experience what TRUE freedom is all about. You learn the power of being free to create what you want.

As you begin to create the results you want, all your subconscious resistances will come to your conscious mind to be faced and released. Everyone has fears and doubts. Problems arise when you allow fears and doubts to control you, hold you back or stop you from "going for it." So many people are taught in childhood to "be careful, you might fail," that being careful becomes a way of life. Being careful assures you of not having what you want, of stopping before you start, of holding back and resisting. Being careful can cause you to move into fantasy, to envy others or to live vicariously through others' lives. Living vicariously is wanting others to succeed so that you may enjoy success through them. At the same time, you can have the opposite desire of wanting them to fail because their success mirrors your failure (see chapter: Programming).

Telling yourself the truth is so powerful, it is almost unbelievable. By accepting that you are the creator of your life and, therefore, the source of your circumstances, you eliminate not only the doubt, but also the anxiety which stands guard over your having what you want. It is hard to believe that so simple a process creates such a powerful result. By eliminating doubt and anxiety, you are free to feel your desired success. This may sound complex, but in fact, it is quite simple. One of the laws of manifestation is to feel the way you would feel if the results of your manifestation existed now. It is often referred to in other writings as "act as if you already have it." To act as if, you have to FEEL as if you have it now. The Bible refers to this same principle: "And all things, whatsoever ye shall ask in prayer, believing, ye shall receive" (Matthew 21:22). To believe means to be it and live it as if you already had it.

First, get clearly in mind what you want, which is the "asking" step. Then, believe that you already have it, which is the "be-live" it step. Getting clarity is very important for your manifestation. You might say that you know what you want, you just don't bother to think about it because you know you can't have it or don't deserve it. In order to live with this block to your having, you might say, "I could have it if I wanted it. I just don't want it now." It is this childhood belief that you can't have it which stands in your way. It is a myth that no longer has value to you as an adult. Facing this myth allows you to give yourself permission to release it. You are, in fact, releasing the power it has had over you.

Another major block standing in the way of your manifesting what you want is rebellion (see chapter: Rebellion). Rebellion is a choice you make to get back at some authority figure for not giving you what you want. You do it in anger to retaliate. However, rebellion results in not giving yourself what you want, and not being able to receive what you want. Getting agreement between your conscious and subconscious minds is necessary if you are to receive what you have asked for. You are the only one who can give yourself that agreement. It is done by gratefully acknowledging your mind for keeping you from jumping in "where angels fear to tread" by being cautious and caring. In this way, the mind releases its resistance, and responds to the positive acknowledgment. The mind is like a child who requires attention and cannot stand to be ignored. As a result of the acknowledgment, it lets down its defenses and supports you in having what you want.

Making up your mind is the most powerful thing you can do to create what you want. Making up your mind requires your decision and commitment. Your mind will make you feel as if you are going to give up something. For example, if you decide to lose weight, your mind makes you feel as if you will be giving up both food and your freedom to eat when and what you want. To resolve this conflict, choose to enjoy the hunger, knowing that it is a sign you are losing weight. Once you have made that choice, your mind can't tell you that you are giving anything up, because you never feel deprived of something you enjoy. This sounds like a game you are playing with your mind, but you are really telling yourself the truth----that you have chosen to enjoy the hunger and the results of the hunger. This process stops your mind from fighting and resisting you. Nothing can stop a made-up mind, and the only person who can make it up is YOU. It is such freedom to know that you have this power.

Who have you allowed to control you? To whom have you given your power? What has this person told you that you could have? Look at what you have and see how obedient you have been. It is not until you let go of this individual's control over you and your "having" that you will be totally free to create what you want. It requires determination and a strong desire on your part to break the chains which bind you and keep you from having what you want. Accept your responsibility for having allowed others to control you, and accept your responsibility to let go of this control. It is important that you take your responsibility to let it go from you, rather than trying to change them. A made-up mind will do this. It is not necessary to say anything to them. In fact, if you do, it is likely that you are not taking your responsibility. So, getting agreement between your conscious and subconscious minds, and taking responsibility for creating what YOU want support you in removing outside controls. Getting this agreement and taking responsibility give you the freedom to live your life your way, although to do so requires courage, determination and a strong desire. The result is freedom---yours.

Now is the time to tell yourself the Truth and accept the Truth that you are the creator of your life. It is your life, and you are responsible for your choices. Therefore, why not lead your life your way now? Go deep within and accept the Truth, by saying, "I totally accept that I am the source of my life. I am the creator of my life, forever and ever and ever."

RELYING WITHIN ON GOD

As children, we are taught to rely on our parents: on our mother for love, nurturing and support in the home, and on our father for love, protection and support outside the home. When we go into the world as teenagers, we expect everyone to be loving and supportive, as has been our experience at home, but we soon discover that it can be a non-caring world. Sometimes the experience in our homes was not warm and caring, but it was at least familiar. Many of us experience a lot of pain and suffering before we realize that we are failing to get in the world what we had at home. Even though home might not have been so great, it often looks good in comparison. We keep trying to find a way back to the security, or, at least, the comfort zone that we felt with our parents.

Our desire for a mate becomes strong out of a need to replace the security we felt at home. This is true for both boys and girls. Controllers and right and blameless destroyers recognize this need, and often use it to their advantage (see chapter: The Roles). Thus begins the manipulative "cat and mouse" game of competition which is the basis of many relationships. It is important to look into your childhood and see who or what you were taught to rely on, or if you were allowed to rely on anyone. Or were you the one on whom everyone in your family relied? Was your mother there for you as a sympathetic, supportive, nurturing force? Did you feel that you could rely on your father for protection and confidence out in the world? Could you rely on your parents' love for each other to give you security and confidence? Could you rely on your friends to keep your secrets? Could you rely on your siblings to be on your team? To make you feel secure? We rely on our spouse, our family, our parents and our friends to give us confidence and security.

Were you told, either verbally or non-verbally, that you could rely on them and trust them, but when you turned to them, they let you down, leaving you feeling betrayed and/or abandoned? Did you have this supported, confident, secure feeling only to lose it through death, divorce or tragedy? Did you have it from one or both parents, and lose it when a sibling was born? Or when a mother went through menopause, or a new spouse entered the home? Do you see the same patterns of relying taking place in your life today which took place in childhood? Do you see how family members relied on you at home and how now, in the world, the same pattern is repeated in your relationships with others?

Those who were not taught self-reliance in their childhood feel very insecure in the world, which is why they quickly look for a mate on whom they can rely. Self-reliance is learned in early childhood by giving children hands-on responsibility, and increasing their responsibilities with age, according to their ability to handle them. Some parents teach their children to be totally self-reliant out of necessity, such as the parents' working outside of the home or illness. These children may feel shaky and scared, but are self-reliant and have a certain level of confidence which says they know they have to get the job done and can do it regardless of the circumstances. In contrast, those who were never allowed or taught to do anything for themselves were never allowed to grow up, mature and assume responsibility. They are unable to act due to lack of confidence, a lack of belief in themselves to get the job done, and motivation. When children become adults with adult responsibilities, their lack of training causes their mind to resist being asked to <u>do</u> anything. It causes resentment, contempt or hatred toward the person asking, because they feel that they are being asked to be a servant. Or it forces them to face the fact that they can't do it. Their ego is too large to ever consider that they might serve others, and their denial too great to feel that they can't do it. However, they know that their comfort zone is being interfered with. They must keep others in a position where they can rely on them while, at the same time, keep them from asking for or wanting anything from them.

> *For example, Chrissy was employed by a service organization as a "Girl Friday." She became angry if her boss made any request of her. To solve this problem, he put the responsibility on Chrissy by making her accountable for his requests. She was to report back to him. However, this also made her angry, for though she was paid well, she was offended by these requests because they made her feel like a lackey.*

In a marital or business relationship, it is one thing for you to know you can't get the job done, but when your spouse or boss puts you on the spot by asking if you did the job, the pressure becomes unbearable, causing you to become angry and resentful at having been asked---and for being confronted.

Our need to rely on others is so strong that we will do anything to keep the other person responsible for us. We might feel resentful when he asks us to do something for him, but we will deny this feeling rather than risk losing him. Only when we are in a relationship in which we are sure of the other person's staying and needing us, will we allow this anger to surface. Our need to rely on others outweighs all other considerations. We can instantly be whipped back into shape by the slightest withdrawal of love, approval or support by the other person. No matter how reliable our spouse may be, it's never enough. He may be reliable 95 per cent of the time, but we put the spotlight on the 5 per cent when he's not. Even if someone could meet that last 5 per cent, what we really want is that they know what we want and give it to us without our having to ask. Because our desires are constantly changing, it is impossible for anyone to meet the needs of our whimsical minds. We are the only ones who know what we want, how we want it, and when we want it. To expect others to know this is to place unrealistic expectations on them. This assures us of being disappointed.

Many people allow us to rely on them to prove their love and caring. Then there are those who use relying on us as a means of controlling us. They put us in a defensive position; in order to prove to them that we care, we must allow them to rely on us. And others want us to rely on them so that they will feel needed, loved and included. The truth is that the only thing which will give us confidence, security and power is to rely within totally on God.

The other extreme are those people who experienced no help, support or teaching as children, and were forced to rely on themselves to do everything. It is just as hard for them to let go and rely within on God as it is for those who totally relied on parents or siblings to do so. They have spent a lifetime looking for someone to rely on, and have been frustrated, disillusioned and disappointed many times in their attempt to find that reliable source. They are so needy that they can find security, confidence and power only by relying on themselves, but they are still afraid. One group has to let go of relying on others, while the other has to let go of relying on themselves. Therefore, the only way to find security, confidence and power for both extremes, and all who reside in between, is to rely on God within. This requires accepting that the power and security for which they are looking can only be found within. It also requires a strong desire to let go of old habits and patterns.

It is important to face the fact that those upon whom you have relied are unreliable --- they are not doing what they said they would, or can't do what they said they could, or are using this as a tool to manipulate and control you, or they simply don't care. It is difficult to face that those who you think care and believe will be there for you do not care and are not there for you. There is only one source that will always be there for you, who will never let you down, who wants to give you everything you want, who is there regardless of the storms or successes in life, who is consistent, reliable and has all knowledge, all power and all presence: the God within. Your God within you.

By relying within on your Heavenly Father you receive power, confidence, security and direction as to your first step. Once that step is taken, you will be shown the next step. After you take that step, you will be shown the next. You will never be given more than one thing to do. By learning to apply this Truth and principle, you eliminate the feeling of having too much to do. To apply this Truth to your life teaches you to live in the now, in the precious present. Make up your mind that you have only one thing to do.

EXPRESSING TALENTS AND ABILITIES

Being free of anxiety or stress so that we can express ourselves comfortably and confidently in any situation is one of life's greatest blessings. Knowingly or unknowingly, we all want to do this, for to do so frees us to express ourselves without limitations. How wonderful to feel free to say whatever we want without concern about what others think. How wonderful to be free to do whatever we do without second-guessing our actions, and to be free to be ourselves. And how glorious to feel confident and comfortable that everything we have or want to have is a true expression of what we want, and not a reflection of either what someone else has or wants us to have. Maria, in THE SOUND OF MUSIC, embodied this freedom of expression in her job as nanny to the Baron Von Trapp's children. She was not fearful of expressing her desires, nor was she held down by having to be perfect. She was free to use all her talents and abilities and to express herself limitlessly. Having studied Truth in a convent, she had learned and accepted that she was the Light, which she revealed by her freedom of expression. It is our acceptance of this Truth, that we are the Light and that we express our talents and abilities which allows us to do so. We are then able to take our attention off ourselves and what we are saying, as well as off what other people are saying or might be thinking about what we are saying. We are able to allow our expression to flow freely. Out of fear of saying or doing the wrong thing, or being called bad or not good enough, or being less than perfect, we keep a bushel basket over our Light. Some people, unknowingly, put a bushel basket on others, which makes them feel as though a heavy fog has descended on them, preventing them from expressing themselves. They feel held down, held back and, in many cases, feel that their Light has gone out.

Once you have accepted that you express your talents and abilities, and become established in this acceptance, you will be free to express yourself. And once you let go of caring what others think, you will be able to express yourself freely. No longer will they be able to hold you down. Before accepting this Truth, you are like a lighthouse whose shades are pulled down. After accepting that you express your talents and abilities, the shades are pulled up. Once your Light shines freely, it lights the path for others to follow, but this is not why you are doing it. You are accepting that you express your talents and abilities so that your Light shines brightly forever.

When you arrive at that time in life when you reflect on how you expressed yourself, whether with limitation, control and doubt, or with limitlessness, freedom and fun, you want to be free of regrets, and be able to say, "No matter what others thought, I expressed with freedom. I expressed myself my way."

It is time to realize that it is your choice. It is so exciting to be able to speak or write without the fear of being humiliated, exposed, embarrassed, ridiculed or questioned. It is these fears and doubts of what others might think which cause you to limit your self-expression. It is in being free to express yourself that you experience true freedom. And to know and accept that you are Light empowers you, for it is when you are in the Light of God's love that you are free to express yourself limitlessly and, like the sun, you just keep on shining.

ENJOYMENT

Everyone wants to be able to enjoy life and everything in it. It is the most sought after and, yet, the most elusive of all goals.

Many of us have believed that if we could get our loved ones to be happy and enjoy themselves, we would then be free to be happy and enjoy ourselves. Most all of us had a parent or authority figure growing up who controlled us, who determined how, what and who we could enjoy. Therefore, it is important to look back into your childhood to see how you were programmed to enjoy. By facing this programming and taking responsibility for its cause and effects, you can free yourself to enjoy life, and to enjoy whomever or whatever *you* want to enjoy.

> *Betty was given permission by her mother to enjoy playing cards. When we enjoy something, we are good at it. Because Betty enjoyed playing cards, she always won. She was also allowed to enjoy being alone. She loved finding cozy places in the woods or in gardens where she could find solitude. Though her family was poor, Betty's favorite private places*

> *were surrounded by elegance, beauty and wealth. Because she was allowed to enjoy these things as a child, she was able to create and feel comfortable in an environment of wealth, beauty and elegance as an adult.*

How were you programmed to enjoy? Could you enjoy work, play, friends, boyfriends and girlfriends? Mary was not allowed to do anything for herself. Her mother made her bed, cleaned her room, and so on. When she left home, all she wanted to do was sit and read about what others were doing. Nor was she allowed to enjoy people. Because she could not enjoy them, she feared being with them. When her four-month-old baby screamed every time he was picked up by someone else, Mary realized that she had passed on her fear of people and inability to enjoy them to her baby. Her mother would not attend Mary's baby shower because of HER fear of being with people. Her mother had passed her fear of enjoying people on to Mary, who passed it on to her baby. How we are taught to enjoy or not enjoy is passed down from one generation to the next. It is important to see that your enjoyment has been dictated by your programming from your parents, who were programmed by your ancestors. It is also important to see that no one can change this pattern but YOU. Your parents cannot, your ancestors cannot---only you can change what you have been allowed (or not allowed) to enjoy.

> *A famous singer was told, as a child, by his father, "You are dumb, stupid and will never make anything out of your life!" He rebelled against his father's criticisms by saying, "I'll show you!" As a result, he became a world famous singer, but though he had fame and fortune, he was unable to enjoy any of it. He left his singing career to find himself, and in so doing, ceased rebelling against his father's message. Discovering the cause of his lack of enjoyment, and taking responsibility for the cause and its effects, freed him to enjoy his life.*

By committing to end how you have been programmed to enjoy, and taking responsibility for making every moment of your life enjoyable, you can experience freedom. It is worth anything you have to do to commit to it for life. Blaming your parents or anyone else prevents you from taking responsibility, and keeps you from enjoying your life.

Many people, in an effort to enjoy, remain childish and irresponsible, blaming others rather than taking responsibility for their lives. It is of great value to learn how to be both responsible and childlike. Once you see this clearly, it is important to examine your feelings. First, see how it feels from the side of blaming and not taking responsibility. Then, make up your mind to take responsibility for your life and for your happiness, and choose to enjoy every moment of your life, now and forever. Once you have chosen to take responsibility for your life and to enjoy your life, examine how wonderful it feels to be responsible and to be free to enjoy your life. It is pure freedom to take away others' power to control you and keep you from enjoying your life.

There are mental and emotional blocks to enjoyment which control us on a subconscious level. Once we become aware of our parental programming, we can ask to be shown any other blocks that keep us from enjoying anything we are doing:

The Inability to be on a Team and to be Committed to a Team

Look back into your childhood and see if you always felt like an outsider, if you could join the team but couldn't be a team player. Perhaps you had to be the star, or maybe you drew a circle around one person and kept the other team members out. It is important to become aware of the truth about your ability to be a team member, because it is not until you can join the team that you can commit to the team. And it is not until you can commit to a team that you can enjoy a team. This is a two-step process. If you can't first be on the team, you can't commit to it. Until you commit, you can't be comfortable, can't have fun on that team, and can't enjoy that team. This is true for marriage, friendship, work or sports teams. If you are not taking responsibility for your enjoyment, then you are blaming your discomfort and lack of fun on the team or one of its members. You will find that you resist both the other team members and the leaders because of your lack of commitment and inability to enjoy being on the team. It's no fun when you are not committed. Consequently, you are always looking for reasons to leave. And then when you leave, you blame the team for your leaving, all as a result of your inability to be on the team, enjoy the team and commit to it.

Uncommitted people feel there's a wall between themselves and others. They feel resistant and afraid of being asked to do something they don't want to do. Some uncommitted people feel as though a team member is going to "get" them, give them a "not good enough" message, or test them when they have made a mistake. When we are uncommitted, we are always looking for a reason to leave. We project that reason onto the team members and make that projection our reality. We then use it as our excuse to leave, blaming them rather than taking our responsibility for leaving.

We can also transfer our parents onto team members, seeing them as dominating or tyrannical. We use this mind game as an excuse to leave. Both transference and projection appear to be reality when, in truth, the facts they present are totally false. They are the mind's techniques for avoiding responsibility.

It is very difficult to break this habit of transfering and projecting. To do so requires a commitment of loyalty to the Truth and a made-up mind to take responsibility for your life and your enjoyment. No more hiding out, denial or blaming. They are simply blocks to your freedom to enjoy--no more, no less.

Possession

Being possessed by another person means that you are loyal to the possessor, interested only in the possessor's interests, and will do what it takes to make that person's life enjoyable. It means that you choose, listen to and defend them. This can continue even after the one who possesses you has passed from this earth plane. You feel as though you have the thoughts of the possessor in your mind. Possession can be experienced as fuzziness in the head, an inability to think, tiredness and displaced loyalty. You can't be loyal to a team or team member, even though you are committed, if the possessor doesn't allow you to, because you are required to be loyal to the one who possesses you. This prevents you from enjoying any team or team members the possessor doesn't allow you to enjoy.

Competition

Competition destroys the relationship between team members and, ultimately, the team itself. Competition destroys not only your enjoyment, but others' as well. You may believe that competition is enjoyable. However, this is not so. Once you let it go, you will see how upset and uptight it kept you.

In public speaking, there are many competitive techniques which are used. One is to destroy the flow of conversation by interrupting the speaker. A second is to withhold information which you have been asked to share. A third technique is to innocently get up to leave, right at the punch line of a story or an important moment in the conversation, subtly destroying the concentration of the audience. A fourth way is to say something negative or critical of a team member or a spouse in a social situation. In this way, competitors hold the team down and keep the team members from enjoying themselves. Competitors destroy their own enjoyment in the end because they are not free to enjoy.

To accept that you enjoy yourself all the time is freedom: freedom from the mental and emotional bonds of others, and freedom from any psychological restrictions to your enjoyment.

One young girl in a religious school was reprimanded for singing and dancing in the school courtyard. She was accused of being irreverent, and was made to stand with her nose against the blackboard. Because she was humiliated in front of the class, she was unable to enjoy singing and dancing from then on.

To accept, with complete faith and trust, that you enjoy every moment of your life and take full responsibility for your enjoyment frees you from past emotional restrictions placed upon you by others. It is your choice---choose to take responsibility for your life, for your happiness and for your enjoyment, and begin living your life from the deepest level of enjoyment.

One and Only, and Only One

One of the most powerful blocks to enjoyment is the message from one or both parents and/or a family member that you are their one and only and/or their only one. This concept prevents you from being on a team and enjoying it. You might join a team but be unable to be involved with it. Instead, you are constantly resisting, backing off or pulling away. You can enjoy the team on a surface level, but it will stay that way until you let go of the need to be the one and only and only one to your mother, father and/or family member. The one and only concept has to do with people. To be a parent's one and only means that you are not to be involved with anyone else. The "only one" message limits you in other areas of life as well. Unconsciously, you limit yourself to one friend, one car, one house, one career, one relationship, and so on.

John loved to play both golf and tennis. Because he had to be his mother's one and only and only one, he could only enjoy one sport. He enjoyed tennis and had fun whether he won or lost, but he'd get angry and upset playing golf. When he went to the driving range to hit balls at his private club, he felt guilty and bad. Unknowingly, he was not able to enjoy golf because he could enjoy only one sport.

Suzanne accepted the message that she had to be her mother's, father's and sister's one and only. She spent most of her childhood indoors, knitting and watching TV. This was the only way she could enjoy. She did this because she couldn't be involved with others.

Those who have been given the one and only message unknowingly begin to destroy their marriage the moment the ink has dried on the marriage certificate. First, the fun goes out of it. Then, they become creative in the way they destroy the relationship with their spouse and later, their marriage. They blame their spouse and make them wrong, while feeling they are blameless, right and justified in their destruction. All this because, as a child, they accepted the myth that they had to be someone's one and only.

We want to enjoy ourselves but we can't because of the responsibility that we've accepted or resisted. Either we act as children, taking no responsibility (resisting it), or as parents and make everyone else our children, taking on their responsibilities. Neither allows us to assume our own responsibilities. How do we enjoy and, at the same time, take full responsibility for our lives, for our happiness and for our relationships with our children, our grandchildren, our friends, our team members, our parents, our husbands or wives, God, ourselves and people? By making up our minds to accept that we enjoy every moment of life. This is the key. NOTHING CAN STOP A MADE UP MIND. So make up your mind and begin living your life from the deepest level of enjoyment.

FUN

Life is about loving and having fun. Fun is a state of mind. When you have a fun state of mind you have fun doing everything from cleaning floors to flying airplanes. Fun is creative. When you're free to have fun, you're free to create: wealth, love, friends and success.

Your childhood programming determines who you can or can't have fun with. This is why many married people can't have fun with each other. Consequently they blame their spouse for not being fun.

Fun is beyond enjoyment. Fun is an attitude, and you bring this attitude with you to everything you do. When you have an attitude of fun you don't have to do anything to have fun because everything you do IS fun. Youa re fun! It even allows you to turn work into fun. To the person who can only work, fun appears to be a frivolous waste of time, but the truth is that everyone wants to have fun.

The fun you can have as an adult is determined by the fun you were allowed to have as a child. When she was growing up, Tammy was only allowed to knit, play the piano, listen to music, watch television, eat or study, all solitary pursuits. As a result, it was difficult for her, as an adult, to have fun interacting socially with others.

There are those who can control you by not allowing you to have fun, whether by being with friends and loved ones or by doing what you love to do. They destroy your attitude of fun by squelching your enthusiasm and excitement.

Without fun, life lacks lustre and becomes dull. Fun feels happy, exciting, giggly and tingly. Fun frees you to see beauty everywhere. By making up your mind that you have an attitude of fun all the time you bring fun to everything you do and everyone you touch. If those you are with resent or are uncomfortable with your having fun, or if they have fun at your or others' expense, make friends with those who enjoy having fun with you. And have fun!

4 "I Am"

RELEASING YOUR EMOTIONAL ATTACHMENTS opens you up to seeing the Truth. Once you see the Truth, you become free to accept the Truth. Once you accept the Truth, you then become free to be and express the Truth. The "I Ams" are the process of being the Truth and, finally, expressing the Truth.

Now begins your journey of expressing the deepest level of Truth.

I AM CENTERED

Once you let go of your emotional attachment to your mother and are free to think your own thoughts, you then become free to Take Charge of your life. Once you take charge of your life and become the director of your life, you are then free to become centered (focused on God) and instantly begin to become a magnet for energy. Before accepting that you are centered, your energy is dissipated. Energy is what empowers you to act. The next step is a process of action. Once you are free to think, once you Take Charge of your life, and once you are centered and creating energies, you are then prepared to act.

To be centered is to be anchored deep within, to be focused on God at the bottom of your stomach. In so doing, you draw to you energies from the universe. You feel as if there's a magnet in the bottom of your stomach which is attracting energy from every direction, as opposed to dissipating energy in all directions, which occurs when you're not centered. You feel calm, anchored, solid and focused. When you're not centered, you feel scattered, easily distracted and depleted. When you are centered, you feel contained, aligned and balanced.

You become centered by placing your attention at the bottom of your stomach, like diving straight down off a diving board to the bottom of the pool. When your attention is there, say the words "I am" over and over, silently to yourself. Observe the energies being drawn into the pit of your stomach. Feel your energy increase. Observe how anchored and solid you feel.

I AM IN THE ZONE

The zone is the place within yourself where you go and where you stay in a constant state of peace, love, joy and ecstasy, listening within to God, and relying within on God. In the zone you stay in a constant state of creation. Being in the zone is being in a meditative state where there is no thought. When you first move into the zone and the mind is still, give yourself positive suggestions about everything you want, preceded by the two creative words, "I am," four times.

I am balance.
I am rhythm.
I am love itself.
I am harmony.
I am wisdom.
I am beauty.
I am success.
I am wealth.
I am energy.
I am power.
I am happiness.
I am in impeccable shape.
I am joy.
I am fun.
I am that I am.

I AM THE LIGHT

Now that you have released your emotional attachment to your father and are free to act (to do what you want to do), you still have to know what it is you want to do. This is made easy by accepting that you are the Light. You have to accept that you <u>are</u> the Light before you can <u>be</u> the Light. Having previously accepted that you are centered (focused on God), you can now focus your attention on the Light within, and see it pouring out from you and being regenerated within, constantly filling your body with more Light, so that your space is filled with Light.

And it is knowing that you are the Light that prepares you to be God's Child, which is an extension of the Light of the World, for God IS Light. To be God's Child is to be Light, and this I Am is what empowers you to take your knowledge of being the Light and your focus on the Light into the world---and be the Light wherever you go.

This is the turning point of moving from the world into the Spirit and focusing within instead of without.

By visualizing and accepting that your body is filled with Light every moment, you are empowering yourself to soar without limitation in every area of your life. You feel a deep peace, and your body tingles. You take this step by seeing your tummy filled with bright white Light. Visualize the Light moving down through your legs and feet, up through your tummy, chest and throat, filling your head, and moving out through your arms and hands. Accept "I AM THE LIGHT." You feel a deeper peace and greater freedom. Your Light fills up the space of the whole planet, giving you a feeling of unity with the whole and a lack of separateness.

I AM JOY

There is an energy field that you move into when you focus on the Light within. You almost feel that you have crossed a sound barrier. Once you cross that sound barrier and move into the energy field, focusing within on the Light becomes easier. Simultaneously, you have a subtle feeling of joy. It is both astounding and amazing how natural this feels. And in recognizing this naturalness you begin to realize, for the first time, that constant joy is your natural state of being. At some point in your life, you moved away from this joy and forgot how to get back. Now you are Home at last, Home at last, Home at last. Make up your mind that you are staying Home forever.

By accepting that you are Joy, you fill yourself with happiness, which is one of the greatest gifts you can give to yourself. You look at life lightly instead of darkly, with a smile on your face instead of a frown. Go deep within and feel the Joy which emanates from the Light. Feel it, feel it and keep feeling it until you feel an energy shift. As soon as that takes place, you start to feel lighter. As you move into it, you know, beyond a shadow of a doubt, that you are Joy. You know that you know that you know that you are Joy.

I AM LOVE

If you are free to <u>do</u> it, you will be free to <u>be</u> it. If you are free to <u>be</u> it, you will be free to <u>have</u> it. By letting go of your emotional attachment to your teams and accepting that you are the source and the creator of your life, you are free to have what you want to have. Now it is time to face what it is you want above all else. If you had one wish, what would it be? Given time to sift through everything that has value for you, you most likely would end up wanting to be loved, which is to have love: love of self, love of God, love of family, love of friends, etc. Love is empowering, inspirational and fulfilling. The desire for love is strong, and when you have love, it frees you to get on with your life. If you have sought and found love from without, you might have the fear of losing it. To find love within is to know that it never leaves. You can leave it, but it is always there to come Home to. In searching for love, you ultimately find that the source of it lies within you, and that with love you can do anything it takes to create what you want. You find the Truth that you are the creator of it, and with that knowledge you are empowered to both express it and receive it.

Due to past programming, there can be blocks to both receiving and expressing this love. Allow those blocks to surface, and let them go. By being love, you create having it. In finding love within, you find that this is what you have always wanted to have.

The highest form of love, agape love, is the union between God's love and man's love. This union makes you feel warm and cozy, and your heart is opened up to the whole planet. By uniting your love with

God's love, you are able to feel His love for you and for all mankind. By uniting your love with God's love, you are freed to love unconditionally, to love even those who betray you or want to do you harm. Go deep within and feel God's love pouring from your heart, and feel your love uniting with God's love. Say, "I am united with God's love," to yourself. You feel as if one of your hands is reaching up to God, and God's love is pouring through it into your body, while the other hand is reaching out to man, sending out love, thus completing the process. Union is the experience of love inside in a way you've never felt before: a completeness, a oneness. It is a love that comes from within and goes out, instead of coming from without and going in.

I AM LISTENING WITHIN TO GOD

Everyone is looking for someone who believes in them, on whom they can rely and in whom they can believe. Finding someone, and then being disappointed or disillusioned by that person, can be a block. We all make mistakes in judgment, and can let those mistakes block us. This is a real turning point. More people allow themselves to be stopped here than at any other place. Here is where you can take a huge step toward making your life work. Rather than relying on yourself due to prior disappointment and distrust resulting from relying on others, make up your mind to rely within on God. Accept that you will do anything He directs you to do, knowing full well that He will give you only one thing at a time to do. Make up your mind to do that one thing. Then He will give you the next thing to do. Trust Him, rely on Him. Let go and allow Him to do the work through you. Take your next step. One step at a time. Let go of your mind and, in so doing, get you off your hands so that God can work through you.

By listening within to God, instead of either to your mind or to others, you are able to focus your attention on what you want to create and manifest. Listening within to God feels like an archer shooting his arrow into the bull's-eye without external interference. Listening within frees your spirit to soar, empowered and energized. It quiets and stills your mind because your attention is focused within on God. You move into the first level of Listening by listening within to God, allowing your body and mind to let go and, consequently, ignoring the mind. The mind is like a child who will run the show if you allow it, but who will leave you alone if you let it go and ignore it. You move into the second level of Listening within to God by listening more deeply and allowing your body to let go more deeply, while continuing to ignore the mind. You move into the third level of Listening within to God by listening and allowing your body to go deeper still. As you become more consciously aware of what is happening, you will feel a change in energies when you move into the third level. When you move into the fourth level of Listening, you experience what the Bible refers to as "the peace that passes all understanding."

I AM RELYING WITHIN ON GOD

It is very important to have one person who believes in you in order for you to believe in yourself and, in so doing, unlock and express your talents and abilities. It just takes one. If you are not blessed with that one, do not be discouraged. Invite and allow God to be the one who believes in you, for He will take you to heights beyond anything you ever dreamed of. He will lead you to believe in yourself.

By Relying Within on the deepest level, you are able to totally trust God. Relying Within on your Heavenly Father allows you to focus your attention on your purpose, to be confident, and to have inner security and power. You feel that you can do anything you choose to do. Go inside and accept that you rely within on your Heavenly Father, on the deepest level, forever. By Relying Within, you will be shown your next step, and you will always know what your next step is, so take it without fear, but trusting Him, knowing that He is going ahead to open doors. Sometimes one door will be closed, but know that a bigger and better one is soon to be opened for you. More often than not, blocks will come up which appear as obstacles on your path. Face them, name them, and release them. You can't create the new while still holding onto the old, nor can you sweep the old under the rug. So, let the old programming, the old attachments, the old false concepts go, and rely within on your Heavenly Father, where you feel safe, secure and confident, where you know you can have what you want, where you know you can have it all.

I AM ENJOYMENT

When you are in Enjoyment, you enjoy life to the fullest. Everything you do is enjoyable. What, before, seemed like a task, now becomes a pleasure. You appreciate the beauty in the small things in life as you never have before: the beauty of a falling leaf, the veins in a rock, the swirls in a pond. Everywhere you look, you see beauty. Life takes on new meaning. You appreciate and enjoy people in a way you never have before. Your life is filled with enjoyment.

Your enjoyment is enhanced by letting go and letting God. A young lady of 70 testified at a workshop that she began enjoying from a level she didn't know existed when she let go and got <u>herself</u> off her hands. Our biggest block to enjoyment is our past programming. Many of us have been programmed not to enjoy and not to have fun. We are not about making our parents and family bad and wrong here, for they, too, were not allowed to enjoy by their parents and family members, but rather now that we are adults, we are about being free from past programming so that we might enjoy every moment of our lives regardless of our circumstances. You might ask the question, and many do, "How can I enjoy when I'm surrounded by chaos and destruction?" And I say, "Look up at the blue sky, look for anything that represents beauty to you, that represents freedom to you, that represents enjoyment to you." It will take discipline, but you can more easily maintain this disclipline by inviting God into your heart, to walk with you and live with you and be with you through the valleys as well as the mountains, to show you that you can enjoy every moment of your life.

5 The Acceptance of Being Bad

THE CORE OF PEOPLE'S MISERY, unhappiness, fight for survival and rebellion begins when they accept from their mother, surrogate mother or other authority figure, the false premise that they are bad. The time and circumstance of this acceptance vary with each individual, but it occurs at a young age. Every subsequent thought and action is based on or seen through this false concept, creating insecurity, low self-esteem and lack of confidence.

Children's need to prove their goodness to their parents underlies their every thought and action. It runs their lives. Because they believe that they are bad, they are burdened with guilt and by the feeling that they are always coming from behind. They are driven to vindicate themselves by <u>proving</u> that they are good, and they strive to free themselves from feeling guilty.

Once children accept the idea that they are bad, they no longer express themselves spontaneously or allow themselves to receive love freely in any form. They become uncomfortable with attention, recognition or praise. They can be given material expressions of love, but cannot receive them freely. Not only do they accept that they cannot have what they want, but it becomes very difficult, if not impossible, for them to even think of what they want. They devote their entire existence to either discovering and giving their parents whatever THEY want, or by rebelling against their parents and, in so doing, refusing to give them what they want. They want to give their parents what they want in the hopes that their parents will tell them they are not bad, but are good enough just as they are, and do not have to <u>do</u> good works to get good enough. More often than not, though, they are not freed from their self-imposed prison of being bad, and spend a lifetime looking for someone or something that will free them.

Pleaser or Rebel

Often, a child will accept the responsibility for the happiness of one or both parents in an attempt to compensate for being bad, or to be told by them that he is good enough. The child tries very hard to give them everything they want. He becomes a pleaser. If the efforts to please are met with "you're still not good enough," the child can, and often does, give up trying and becomes rebellious (see chapter: Rebellion).

Rebellion expresses itself in many ways. At the moment a child becomes fed up with being told that he is bad, he responds with a rebellious attitude which says: "Since you think I am so bad---watch this! You haven't seen anything yet! I'll be the worst person I can be." Or the rebellious child can respond by saying "You say I am bad---I will prove how wrong you are! I will be perfect in everything I do." The child who doesn't rebel knows that if he does anything which causes a negative reaction in anyone, they will accuse him of being bad, and cause his parents to become angry. Therefore, a child avoids this by pleasing and being good. Once the child accepts that he is bad and rebels against the bad message, a lifelong pattern of compensation begins. The child has his feelers out, listening, listening, listening for the bad message. It keeps him from going all out for what he wants. It keeps him resisting those he loves. It keeps him looking at what can go wrong rather than what works, at the negative side of life rather than the positive. Layer upon layer of untruths are piled on each other.

Sometimes the child will choose to become a combination of both the pleaser and the rebel in an attempt to get parental approval and acceptance, and relief from the feeling that he is bad. This causes him to flip from one side to the other. It causes him to be inconsistent in his life. It causes a double bind: one moment the child is rebelling by lashing out at what he feels are parental injustices, and the next moment, he is atoning by becoming a pleaser. He feels so bad for having rebelled and so desperately wants his parents' permission, approval and acceptance that he tries, once again, to please. Consciously, the child wants to give others what they want, and works diligently to do so. But because he has chosen rebellion as an escape, he, unconsciously, cannot give them what they want. This double bind results in almost constant sabotaging of the child's efforts. He promises to give others what they want, and then reneges on the offer. He wants credit for trying, but once credit is given, he stops trying. By doing it for awhile the child creates expectations in others that he will continue to make an effort to do what they want him to do. However, the double bind causes the child to stop once he gets what he wants, and to go in the opposite direction. This creates disappointment, hurt, disillusionment and distrust. Because the child fears losing what he has (time, money, love), he withholds. Unaware of what he is doing, the child does not know how or why he sabotages relationships.

> *A classic example is Judy, who had access to wholesale clothing. In order to make her mother happy, she volunteered to buy her a purse, and told her she would buy it right away. Three weeks later, when her mother reminded her of her promise, Judy was embarrassed. Judy looked at this situation and realized that this was a pattern in her life. Many times she had failed to fulfill one of her teenage son's requests after promising to do so. On one occasion, she disappointed him by forgetting to have his clothes ready for a special school event, and often forgot to buy his favorite breakfast cereal. She began to see that her behavior was keeping her from having the warm and loving relationship with him she had always wanted. Instead of keeping her word with the people she loved, she was disappointing them. She was not giving them what they wanted.*

When the acceptance of being bad has become ingrained in a person, it becomes impossible for him to receive or believe any good messages about himself. Acceptance of being bad determines his life's role of either controller/right and blameless destroyer or controllee/wrong and blamed scapegoat, which he unconsciously chooses (see chapter: The Roles). These roles create belief systems based on lies. Whenever a lie is expressed, it is automatically covered up by another lie, and soon this lie must be covered up by another. These false concepts determine how the child feels about himself, and create his personality, which is the image that he presents to the world.

Denial, Perfection and the
Controller/Right and Blameless Destroyer

The controller/right and blameless destroyer denies the lie that he is bad and covers it up by declaring that he is good (see chapter: The Roles). In extreme cases, the he stays in a state of superiority all the time, feeling perfect or God-like. In spite of this denial, on a deep level, he has a sense that he is not telling the truth. He is afraid that if he were to look within, the sight would be unbearable. Therefore, he does not look. He is so hypersensitive to bad messages, that he experiences both physical and emotional responses to the slightest implication that he is "bad."

When Susan's boss requested a report she was working on, her stomach became tight and her head throbbed. She was terrified that he would see her as less than perfect, and felt guilty for the flaws she feared were in her report.

Once the controller/right and blameless destroyer senses that others are implying that he is bad, he projects onto them what is angering him, blaming and accusing them of what he is thinking and feeling guilty about.

Those who deny the acceptance of being bad demand constant proof from everyone that they are good. If they are given negative messages about themselves, they are infuriated, and in extreme cases, incapacitated, because the negative messages trigger a deep belief within them that they are bad. Any request at all angers them because, in their minds, it implies that they are not already doing what is requested. They believe that the one making the request sees them as less than perfect. Being anything less than perfect makes the controller/right and blameless destroyer feel that he is bad, and arouses the need to prove his accuser wrong. If he chooses to give someone what is asked for, he believes this is an admission of being bad.

John liked to eat dinner right after his golf game. Sally asked him to call her when the game was over so she'd have time to prepare it. Her request offended John. He felt that she was trying to control him and was implying that he was inconsiderate. To admit that he is wrong in the smallest area makes the controller/right and blameless destroyer feel vulnerable to the entire world. John goes to such extremes to be perfect in his own mind that to expose the slightest imperfection would be the same as being wrong in all areas.

Acceptance, Guilt and the Controllee/Wrong and Blamed Scapegoat

Those who accept the lie that they are bad carry a tremendous burden of guilt. They work diligently at being good because they are unable to withstand any more guilt. Regardless of what they do or how well they do it, they never feel that it is good enough. No matter how much praise or approval they receive, there is never a reprieve from their "bad" feelings. They can never feel good about themselves. They invite hurt, discouragement and disappointment. Even when falsely accused of behaving inappropriately, they think to themselves, "Maybe you're right," and feel as guilty as if it were true. They spend their lives atoning for things they have not done so that they will feel good about themselves.

Controllees/wrong and blamed scapegoats feel that they are undeserving and, therefore, they have to pay back with good works over and above anything they have received (see chapter: The Roles). Controllees/wrong and blamed scapegoats are naive to the point of gullibility, thus assuring themselves of disappointment and hurt. They respond to the con artist's sales hook with trust. Even when confronted with the truth of having been used or taken advantage of, they deny it, preferring to live in the fantasy that everyone else is good and they, alone, are bad.

> *Barbara, a classic controllee/wrong and blamed scapegoat, was separated from her husband. Their best friend, John, told her that his wife and her husband were having an affair. Even after he proved that what he said was true, she refused to accept the evidence. To believe it would make her feel even worse about herself and guilty for having caused the affair in the first place.*

The controllee/wrong and blamed scapegoat reveals all his shortcomings and weaknesses to the controller/right and blameless destroyer in an effort to be hurt and punished. Even though the punishment is painful, he welcomes it because it gives temporary relief from guilt.

The controllee/wrong and blamed scapegoat denies himself pleasure, fun and enjoyment. A small relief from ever-present guilt is all he will allow. This person can experience pleasure, fun and enjoyment only vicariously by watching others. The controllee/wrong and blamed scapegoat blames himself for anything that goes wrong in his life, and turns his anger inward. This anger-turned-inward becomes depression. He is constantly compensating by doing something nice in order to make amends for having been the cause of whatever went wrong. He does not need to be accused because he constantly accuses himself.

The Bad Message and You

Releasing your acceptance of being bad is one of the most freeing things you can do for yourself. It enables you to see good where, once, you saw only bad in others or yourself or both. A truce is called in your internal war, and you can stop fighting and start loving. You feel clean, pure, worthy and deserving of love. You are free to be involved with your family, friends and yourself. There is less need to rebel, for there is nothing to resist or fight. Your mental record of past mistakes no longer controls you.

The greatest block to the controller/right and blameless destroyer is denial of having accepted the bad message. The greatest block to the controllee/wrong and blamed scapegoat is the feeling that he does not deserve to be free from guilt, pain and suffering. Identifying your block helps you to clearly see the "bad" lie which has run you.

The feeling of being bad has, unknowingly, had total power and control over your life. Once you let go of this false concept you can begin to live your life in a way that works for you. You can begin to look at what you want to be and what you want to have. The Truth about yourself lies deep within your being. The key that unlocks the door to this truth is called desire. When your desire is great enough, you will tell the Truth to yourself and arrive at the conclusion that not only are you not bad, you are beyond the opposites of good and bad. It is the belief in these opposites that has kept you from being free---free to be all you can be, free to be you.

Look carefully at yourself. Have you chosen to live a role? Have you accepted that you are a controller or a right and blameless destroyer, or have you chosen to live out the role of a controllee or a wrong and blamed scapegoat? To help you see this more clearly, these four types are discussed in greater detail later in this book.

6 Good

ALONG WITH THE FEELING OF BEING BAD deep within everyone, there is also a compelling need to override this feeling by being good. Even those whose actions would be described by many as "bad" DESIRE to do good and be good. It appears to each person that he is the only one who feels this way, but in truth, this feeling is common to most of us. Many people cover up the feeling of being bad by "putting on blinders" and accepting and believing that they are good. However, this self-deception does not work against those deep feelings of being bad. For others, working to be good is used to cover up the feeling of being bad. We go through life doing good deeds, hoping to be acknowledged, admired and recognized enough to compensate for being bad. However, nothing we do is ever good enough to bring us these desired results. Doing good deeds for these reasons alone leaves us feeling unfulfilled, dissatisfied and frustrated.

It would appear as though becoming a hero, martyr or star, or receiving recognition for some outstanding achievement would absolve us from having to do good, and from feeling guilty for being bad, but it doesn't. As long as we believe that we are bad, the feelings of elation resulting from such successes are short-lived, and leave us wanting more. Working to be good runs our life and becomes our motivation for living. It destroys our creativity, and makes constructive, supportive relationships difficult, if not impossible.

By having to always be good, our life becomes one of survival, constantly protecting and defending ourselves from others who perceive us as bad. This life of survival begins in childhood. We sell our parents and teachers on how good we are, and with age, acquire many techniques for doing so. If we could just prove our goodness to others, we would be absolved from our guilt of being bad. Life becomes one of selling and proving, not only to ourselves, but to everyone. We compare ourselves and our possessions with others'. We start looking out there at what others are doing, being and having, instead of within at what we want to do, be and have.

At some point, we come face to face with the realization that not only do we not know what we want, but that we do not even know who we are. Who we are, upon closer examination, is determined by who "they" say we are. If "they" say we're "bad," we feel bad. If "they" say we're "good," we feel good. Unknowingly, we give anyone and everyone total responsibility for our happiness, peace and well-being. A a disapproving glance or an ugly word can destroy our day. Criticism by a spouse, family member, team mate or child can lower our self-respect, self-image and self-esteem, all because we have accepted that we are bad, and want others to see and perceive us as good.

The need to be good in the eyes of our mother and father requires that we make them our number one. Often, both are competing for this position. Then, as we go out into the world, there is pressure from everyone to make them our number one. We fear that if we don't, they will tell us we are bad. Later, when a spouse comes into our life, the spouse wants to be our number one, but our mother and father still want to be our number one. Society, too, wants to be our number one. All of this causes more conflict, inner turmoil and division.

Along come our children, and they begin demanding attention, time and love. As our children grow up and become involved in different organizations, each organization wants us to make it number one in our children's lives. Some people refuse to play this game and avoid these conflicts by not becoming involved. Those who choose involvement are torn by opposing forces.

At some point, you feel as though you can't take any more---you've had it. You may have the realization that you have been doing this your whole life without success or reward. Temporary lifts come with a pat on the back, but that is never enough. You have an insatiable need, and one word of praise brings cravings for more. You feel like you have been working, working, working your whole life, spinning your wheels, and never arriving. You feel a lack of fulfillment, dissatisfaction with your life, frustration with others for not meeting your needs, and exhaustion from the effort and struggle of it all.

When you are ready to free yourself from your desire to be good and do good works, you know it, because the pressure from the effort of doing and being good becomes intolerable. Unknowingly, this effort has consumed your life, and you now want to be you. You are then ready to do what you do because you choose to, and not because you want to be good.

Releasing the need to be good, and accepting that you already are good, frees you from guilt. You feel as though a heavy burden has been lifted. You are now able to see what you and others have done in an attempt to be good.

7 Perfection

MOST EVERYONE IS EITHER STRIVING for perfection or rebelling against it. Those who are not, are being themselves. Each person's concept of perfection varies according to his mother's, father's or both parents' (or one or both grandparents') concepts. In some cases, when the mother and father are in conflict, a child will choose the concept of the parent with the most influence over him. Or, if the child tries to please both parents, he will be caught in the double bind of opposite desires, vacillating between pleasing one and then the other (see chapter: Opposite Desires). These concepts of perfection are passed down from generation to generation. In our need for perfection, we strive to make those close to us perfect as well. This need creates tremendous pressure within, and places a great burden on those around us. For example, a mother who strives to be Super Mom wants her children to be Super Kids, and her husband to be Super Dad.

The need for perfection causes us to compare ourselves with others to see if they measure up to our own expectations of perfection. The act of comparing generates a feeling of either superiority or inferiority. This habit of comparing does not end with ourselves, but evolves into comparing our children with other children, our spouse with other spouses, and so on, to see how they all measure up to our expectations of perfection. Comparison causes us to feel anger or resentment toward, for instance, a spouse who does not compare well with others' spouses. This, naturally, puts pressure on our spouse to meet our standards of perfection.

Most people seek to perfect those around them, either mentally or physically, according to their parental concepts of perfection. This is the cause of bigotry, judgment, criticism and much anger. Because we push away what we need, and the need for perfection is so great, it is forever eluding us. Most parents have 18 to 20 years in which they try to create the perfect child. The final test comes too late to make changes. At that time, many parents become disappointed in their children, and let them know it. These children, then, either keep striving to live up to their parents' expectations of perfection, or they rebel against them.

A professional man pursued his career because he was expected to follow in his father's footsteps. In order for the son to be perfect, he needed to be like his father. Quite often though, a child receives the message to "be like me, but don't surpass me." For example, when a dentist announced his annual dollar income to his father, who was also a dentist, his father replied that he had never earned that kind of yearly salary in his practice. The effect of this statement was so powerful that the son's income plummeted. It was not until he moved his practice to another town that he was able to recuperate and begin to do better than ever. To this day, the son will not tell his father how well he is doing for fear of angering his father and punishing himself by decreasing his own business.

In their attempt to create the perfect child, parents very often give "not good enough" messages. No matter what the child does, the parent withholds approval and love in an attempt to get him to do it a little bit better. An example is the daughter whose mother requested that she clean her room. During an inspection afterwards, the mother only commented on the one thing that was not done to perfection. She had no praise or admiration for the part of the room that was done well. All the child heard was, "What you have done is not good enough."

Many parents have the idea that criticism motivates the child to be perfect. Instead it has the opposite effect, and produces more negative behavior. The child interprets this criticism as being "not good enough" and less than perfect. This creates low self-esteem, insecurity, hurt and lack of confidence in himself. The submissive child chooses to strive for a parent's approval and recognition by working tirelessly to measure up to his concept of perfection. The rebellious child chooses to rebel as a protective or survival mechanism against what he feels are unjust demands for perfection. And there are some who submit, but rebel silently.

Our desire for perfection comes from our mother's need for us to be perfect. Unconsciously, in her need to be the perfect mother, she has a strong desire for her children to be perfect children. By having the perfect child, she can then feel that she has become the perfect mother. Because we think like our mother, we in turn, want our mother to be perfect. And because we identify with our mother, we need her to be our perfect role model. If SHE will just be perfect, then WE will feel that we have arrived at perfection. This endless cycle erupts regularly into anger, frustration, impatience, resentment and impossible demands on both parent and child.

Man becomes so burdened by striving for perfection that he becomes impatient, which leads to everything from anxiety, stress and unhappiness to depression (see chapter: Impatience). He works harder to get relief from this inner pressure. Sleep and vacations provide him with a rest from the drive for perfection. Recreation is supposed to serve as a relief and release from this drive. Yet, the habit of impatience is so gripping that some people are unable to enjoy anything and are always in a hurry to finish their golf or tennis game, picnic, and so on. These people live in the future because that is where perfection resides. They believe that in the future they will be done with the task at hand and be free to enjoy life. To enjoy anything, we must be able to experience the now, the present, rather than waiting for the future which, in these terms, never arrives.

You will NEVER arrive at the ideas of perfection with which you have been programmed. So how do you let go of the striving? How can you allow your inner love and peace to flow freely? You must consciously ask yourself, "Is what I'm currently doing working?" You can then begin to learn how to eliminate what is not working, find what WILL work, and apply it.

It helps to see that your parents never arrived at the happiness they sought by striving outwardly to fulfill their concepts of perfection, nor did their parents before them, nor their parents before them. The next step is to be willing to admit that maybe, just maybe, you and they could be wrong. You cannot arrive at happiness by changing those people or things with which you are involved, because happiness comes from within and not from without. Once you find happiness within yourself, the external circumstances and people you blamed for your unhappiness cease to be the source of your problem.

In order to have peace, some people convince themselves that they are already perfect. They believe that they are no longer responsible for doing anything to achieve perfection, since they have already "arrived." Some people accept the role of "perfected person," as an actor takes on a part in a play. They act the part, but do not become it. Others actually believe that they <u>are</u> the part, go all the way with it and become it. These people have deceived themselves to the degree that they have bought their own lie. They are playing a role within a role (see chapter: The Roles). These perfect ones are the most destructive of all to family, friends and teammates. Contemptuous of anyone who is less than their concept of perfect, they use humiliation, criticism or humor to put others down. They feel that they own others, and are justified in their right to perfect them. Therefore, they can say and do anything they choose to anyone. They need to be heroes, and have to be seen as perfect in others' eyes. Others need to be perfect in their eyes as well.

This need is so great that it expresses itself with opposite messages. One message is, "Stay down so that you can admire me and look up to me," while the other is, "Come up beside me and be as perfect as I am." You can't win for losing. The person who believes he or she is already perfect creates this double bind.

> *Tom acted out this role and, in so doing, almost destroyed his entire family emotionally. No one, especially women, could make intelligent conversation with him. No one could say anything to him without the fear of offending him in some way, and no one ever knew what the rules were. He made them up as he went along to keep others feeling small, degraded and powerless. In any interaction with him, others were completely gutted of self-respect. At any given moment in any conversation, he could strike and stun his listener for no apparent reason. These tactics, and his money, were used to keep everyone under his domination and control. His wife became emotionally crippled with alcohol. One son became a liar and a thief, while the other became shrewd and destructive with money. Tom wanted them to be perfect like him while, at the same time, to look up to him as their hero and perfect example.*

Because we are so overly concerned with what others think, we seek to impress them with our perfect families and perfect selves, and become snobs in the process. Fathers want their sons to be athletic heroes, and mothers want their daughters to marry men of wealth and prestige---all because of what others will think of them as parents. Society worship can become so great that the children of such parents forever seek to be what everyone else wants them to be in order to please their parents by being perfect in the eyes of society.

This pressure builds up until it leads to some sort of escape---disease, alcohol, insanity, rebellion or revolt. Some people cannot tolerate bad or "not good enough" messages because they BELIEVE that what others say is true. They are taught by their parents to accept other people's opinions, because their parents want them to be perfect in everyone's eyes. They respond to this by either retreating from people and not being involved, or by trying to please everyone. Some swing between both extremes.

The need to make others perfect leads to interference in others' lives. One mother-in-law was so extreme in her need for a perfect home for her son that she would go into her son and daughter-in-law's home and rearrange the furniture.

> *Another example of extreme interference is the mother whose husband failed to live up to her expectations of the perfect husband. Because of this, she began to demand that her son take care of her needs the way she wanted her husband to take care of her. He was to take care of her and make her number one in his life, with no regard for his wife and children. He was either to visit or call her every day or else be burdened with guilt. She would have preferred not to have included his wife in her own family activities. On occasions when it was necessary to have the wife present, the mother drew a circle around herself and her son, leaving the daughter-in-law out. In his mother's presence, the son would never show affection to his wife or take a stand for her, because to do so would have been disloyal to his mother.*

Interference also takes the form of saving or reforming. Reformers have a strong need to make the world a better place. They become irate and upset at incompetency, inefficiency or any other kind of deficiency. They complain and find fault with everything. They always see the glass as half-empty, rather than half-full. Additionally, they are adamantly vocal about these things. In many cases, this serves as an excuse to express years of pent-up repressed anger. Many people find an outlet for this anger in sports. Others take it out in various social issues, from politics to consumerism. One young girl's mother believed that feeling angry was unacceptable. The only permissible outlet for her daughter's anger was the softball field, where she could reform incompetent or disinterested teammates, or correct the injustices or stupidity of the umpires. Some people <u>think</u> of reforming; some people <u>verbalize</u> it; others <u>act it out</u>.

Saviors interfere by nurturing and mothering. They seek out needy people who want to be taken care of and saved. The saviors themselves, of course, have a need and desire to be saved, but they are unaware of this.

> *One example is a girl who spent years trying to save her friend from unhappiness. When the friend finally found herself, and experienced peace and joy for the first time, the savior-friend became very upset and angry. She feared that she was not needed and was, therefore, threatened by the very results she had been wanting to provide for years. It seemed to her that her friend would leave her now that she no longer served a purpose. When she saw that she had lost control over her friend, she was angered even more.*

> *In another example, a wife complained for years about her alcoholic husband, and constantly tried to save him from his addiction. She saw to it that he ate and dressed properly, and she even worked to provide their family's livelihood. All that she did served to keep him stuck in his alcoholism. She, subconsciously, felt that if she did not do this, he would no longer need her, and he would leave. Then, she would not have anyone to save. This was so much a part of her life's motivation that after his death she was immobilized. Her purpose for living and working was gone. Nobody needed her. She had lost her identity and had become an angry, embittered woman.*

The savior is locked into saving by the belief that not until everyone else is saved will he be free to save himself. The savior's life is about striving, but never arriving.

One girl had an enormous fear of success without knowing why. After many years of preparing herself to be a doctor, she put herself so heavily in debt that she could not afford an office. On an unconscious level, the thought of success was unbearable. Questions in her mind included, "How can I handle it? How will I act? What will they think of me? What will I think of myself?" Her fear was so great that she made her immediate success impossible. Unconsciously, she did not really want to succeed because it would violate her loyalty to her father. He was illiterate and financially incompetent, and his message was that the perfect daughter should not exceed him.

The lie that is perpetuated is, "If you can just become perfect enough, then you will be happy." Our lives are driven and motivated by being perfect enough so that we will be given permission to be happy by our controlling family member. When we marry someone who has two different concepts of perfection --- one from each parent --- we now have their (our spouse's) concepts of how the perfect person should, ought to or must be. The pressure is incredible. Nothing will ever be perfect or good enough. Pulled in a thousand different directions, unfulfilled and vulnerable, we still believe that if we work hard enough, do our jobs perfectly, create the perfect marriage, the perfect child or the perfect home, we will then arrive at society's or our family's standard of perfection. We will then have their approval and acceptance. The truth is that society and our family can never fully approve of or accept us as we are since they, themselves, have never achieved perfection, and they, themselves, have never received the approval of their controlling family member.

When you see this in clear vision, you will think, "How ridiculous it is that I am going to others to tell me that I am now perfect, and good enough to be happy." The truth is that since they cannot be happy themselves, they will never give you permission or approval to be happy, because you would then stop trying to make them happy. The job is doomed to failure because it is based on a lie. It is absolutely impossible for someone else to make you happy or for you to make someone else happy. The only person who can make you happy is yourself. The only permission and approval you need for this is your own.

Examine yourself to see your intense feelings of pressure, and how you are burdened by trying to make everything and everyone in your life perfect. No sooner do you complete one task than there are two more staring you in the face, waiting for your attention and effort. Does the pressure of the next task move in and consume you before the last task has been completed? This overlapping prevents the enjoyment of any completed task. Your life is lived in the future: you can hardly wait for the end of the day, the weekend, vacation or retirement. When Sunday night arrives, does the fear and anxiety of getting through the week's work, and performing perfectly enough, overwhelm you? Do you never feel satisfied, fulfilled and complete? Is there always something more to be done? Of course.

You can spend your life committed to working and striving to be the perfect person your parents wanted you to be, doing what they wanted you to do, being what they wanted you to be, and having what they wanted you to have. That commitment can control and direct your life. As long as you are committed, new commitments are very difficult---almost impossible---to make, even to yourself.

Everyone is trying to find peace and joy by arriving at perfection out there, whereas, the perfection we are seeking lies within. Tap into that Source of love and joy that lies deep within you. There you will find the peace you have looked for all your life, which the Bible refers to as "the peace of God, which passes all understanding," (Philippians 4:7).

The Burden of Perfection vs. the Freedom to Be You

To go from having to be be perfect to living a life of focus on God (centered down in the bottom of your stomach) is a short, to the point, description of going from hell to heaven. It is to go from a life of difficulty, confusion and burden, to one of simplicity, joy and ease.

Where does this burden of perfection come from? What does it look like? What is perfect? Perfect is imprinted upon our minds by the person in our life who became our code bearer (see chapter: Programming). This is the person who gave us the code by which to live. It is only by facing this code bearer that we see his concept of perfection and how he wanted us to be. (While the code bearer and the possessive, controlling parent or family member can be the same person, this is not necessarily always the case).

Our mothers tell us how to think perfectly in the home. Our fathers tell us how to act perfectly in the world, and our families teach us how to be perfect in order to get along with them. It is the attempt to live up to these varied concepts of perfection which causes us such pain, and it is this pain which creates the desire for escape. The way we choose to respond to this burden of perfection determines the road our life will take. Some rebel against it, some work hard to become it, while others resist and escape it. The most common escapes are drugs, alcohol, sleep, food, fantasy, the void and mental illness.

Mental illness prevents communication on a truthful, honest level. The person with a mental illness fears being found out, and tries to disguise his symptoms. The most common mental illnesses are: egomania, paranoia, schizophrenia, sociopathy, pathological lying, bipolar illness and dementia praecox.

Egomania is a grandiose sense of self-importance or uniqueness in which the egomaniac is preoccupied with fantasies of unlimited success, and has an insatiable need for constant attention and admiration. The paranoid individual experiences delusions of persecution or jealousy. He may feel conspired against, cheated, spied upon, followed, poisoned, drugged, or maliciously maligned, harassed or obstructed. The schizophrenic's thoughts can shift from one unrelated subject to another. His thinking involves delusions that have no basis in fact. The sociopath has no concern, empathy or caring for others. He is antisocial, and violates the rights of others by lying, stealing, fighting and resisting authority. The pathological liar cannot resist the impulse, drive or temptation to lie in a way that is harmful to himself or others. Bipolar illness, which was previously called manic depression, is characterized by inconsistency. The manic depressive goes from feeling extremely high and perfect, to extremely low and hopelessly imperfect. Dementia praecox involves a loss of intellectual abilities, such as memory, judgment and abstract thought, of sufficient severity to interfere with normal functioning. The thoughts of the psychotic are disordered, and he is out of touch with reality.

The world of perfection is one of rigid structure, controlled by expectations based on each individual's programming. It takes enormous courage, and one person believing in you, to break out of this preformed mold for your life. If you do not have anyone who believes in you, or if everybody is trying to pull you down, turn to your original Creator, God, who will lift you up, hold you up and lead you to high places.

The burden of perfection comes from living your life according to someone else's rules, programs and concepts. It is not until you make up your mind that you are responsible for your life, and take your responsibility, that you are free to live it your way. As long as you live your life according to someone else's rules, you are just surviving life versus living life. It is a life of continued dissatisfaction because you can never get good enough. The way to end the burden of perfection is to make up your mind to do so. Take responsibility for your life, accept you are free to be you, and begin to live. Your first thought might be, "I don't know who I am." You can find this out by making up your mind that you have choice, and that you choose to embark on the grandest adventure of all: that of knowing yourself and finding out who you are. Make your life simple. How do you do that? Begin by making up your mind to do what you do because you want to, instead of doing it because you should, ought to, or have to. Freedom is being able to say, "I want" or "I don't want."

The secret of making life simple is knowing that you have only one thing to do at a time. Get very clear on what you want, and believe you have it now. To believe you have it now means to be it---to act as if it's a done deal and to give thanks.

When you stop being perfect according to others' concepts, and decide who you are and how you want your life to be, you can begin to live a life of wisdom. To begin living a life of wisdom is to live a life of simplicity, joy and happiness. So make up your mind that you live your life the way that works for you.

The Terror of Making Mistakes

Rather than take responsibility for our mistakes, we often blame others. Not until we take full responsibility for creating our life the way it is can we end blaming others and begin to create it the way we want it to be. If we have to be perfect in order to gain our possessive, controlling parent's or family member's approval, we give him total control over our life and relationships, and in so doing, become terrified of making a mistake. Doing anything less than perfectly would mean that we made a mistake, so the need to be perfect according to our possessive, controlling parent's or family member's concept of perfection unconsciously rules, controls, and directs our life. It is only in facing his concept of perfection and letting it go that we can be free of it. We disguise the terror of making a mistake by learning to _act_ confidently, developing a personality, accepting that we're superior to others or believing they are not good enough for us, all of which disguises the truth that, on some level, we have accepted that we are bad and must work hard to get good enough to receive our possessive, controlling parent's or family member's approval. Our life is programmed by that parent or family member, and we follow that program implicitly in order to receive this approval, which he withholds, and will continue to withhold, until we make up our mind that we neither need it nor want it. The terror we feel comes from the fear that either he will leave or will make us leave. We react to this terror in one of four ways: the first is to become paralyzed and unable to do anything; the second is to use the terror as a motivation to do ten times as much; the third is to flip between wanting to succeed and wanting to do nothing, and the fourth is being willing to do anything it takes to get the job done. Our reaction to our terror is determined by how our possessive, controlling parent or family member trained us to react to mistakes.

The paralyzed non-doer often escapes into playing, alcohol, drugs, sleep, books, movies, fantasy, the void, etc. He hates the doer for making him feel insecure and inadequate by comparison. He wants to be like the doer but, on some level, he knows he can't. He resists doing anything, and blames the doer for holding him back. The truth is that because of his terror of making a mistake and being less than perfect, he holds <u>himself</u> back and tries to hold the doer back to keep from feeling less than the doer. He feels trapped, and resents the doer for doing what he wishes he were free to do. The closer he is to the doer, the more he resents, blames and judges him. The paralyzed non-doer subconsciously sets about destroying his relationship with the doer because he is not allowed to have it.

> *John, a paralyzed non-doer, always fell short in comparison with his doer wife when they were out socially. Social interaction made him feel so insecure that he ultimately stopped going to parties with her. He then felt trapped, blamed her for keeping him from having fun, and later became angry at her when she began to go to parties without him. Out of the terror of making mistakes, John destroyed his marriage. This failure of his marriage motivated him to turn what was a weakness into a strength: he used his anger at his doer ex-wife as the motivation for finding his labor of love.*

> *On the other hand, Tom, a paralyzed non-doer said that if he did not get angry, he would not do anything. He used anger to motivate him to act. Anger, projection and blame are what the paralyzed non-doer use to destroy the relationships which mean the most to him.*

The paralyzed non-doer wants success, but is so terrified of making a mistake that he pushes success away by not doing what it takes to get it. He has opposite desires: he wants success and yet, he doesn't want to do anything to get it, and his opposite desires lead him to failure (see chapter: Opposite Desires). The opposite of opposite desires is to be of one mind. If you feel paralyzed, let go of opposite desires four times, accept that you are of one mind four times, and accept that you are successful in every area of your life four times. Let go of the terror of making a mistake four times, and accept that you get the job done four times. Let go of comparing four times, accept that you have inner security four times, and accept that you are confident four times.

In contrast to the paralyzed non-doer, the doer tries too hard. He compensates for his terror of making a mistake by overdoing, but his doing is a smokescreen which covers up his lack of responsibility. Rather than take responsibility to do his job, he stays busy doing. When it is necessary to do something he doesn't like to do or want to do, he wills himself to do it, and cannot understand why the paralyzed one will not do anything. The doer is busy doing, but resists taking charge for fear of being blamed and not being right if something goes wrong. Because he is so busy, he appears to be in charge, but he does what he does for praise, acknowledgement and glory. If he is confronted on having made a mistake, he falls apart. He can't solve the problem because he feels unjustly accused. He can't stand to be held accountable. Rather than taking his responsibility to do his job, he stays busy.

There are those who flip between being paralyzed and doing. When they move from being paralyzed into doing, they become superior to, and feel contempt for, the non-doers they left behind. They become snobs. Comparing makes them feel insecure, but they will go full speed ahead to cover up their insecurity. One flip-flopper said that if she does 1,000 things a day, maybe she will get two things done right.

Like the paralyzed non-doer, the doer, and the flip-flopper, the be-er is also terrified of making a mistake, but differs from them in that he gets the job done. He takes his responsibility, takes charge of whatever he has to do, and does whatever it takes to get the job done.

Though the paralyzed non-doer, the doer, and the be-er are all terrified of making a mistake, they deal with this terror in three different ways: one is to not do, another is to do, and the third is to be. The paralyzed non-doer does just enough to get by, the doer does just enough to look good, and the be-er does whatever it takes to get the job done. The be-er does what he does for love, the doer does it for glory, and the paralyzed non-doer resents both of them for getting love and glory.

Love or Glory

In this world you have two choices: love or glory. Going for glory gives you a temporary emotional high which requires constant feeding and replenishment, whereas going for love gives you peace, security and limitless expression. The tension created by going for glory requires an outlet, which can be food, sex, money, work, or sports. On the other hand, going for love involves a lot of letting go, responsibility, valuing and appreciating, loving unconditionally, expressing your talents and abilities, telling the truth without anger or rage, and learning the love language of your loved one.

There are several different ways to express love. It is important to take the responsibility to find out how your loved one wants love expressed to him. For example, one person might love gifts or a bouquet of flowers sent for no reason other than that you care. Another might love to have you serve his favorite meal, whereas for another, a phone call might touch his heart. Each of us has to find our loved one's love language. If, for example, you send a dozen beautiful red roses to someone who wants a caring phone call, the roses will have no meaning. Finding this secret key can be the turning point in the relationship that means the most to you.

Glory gives to get; love gives for the joy of it. Glory does to please others; love does to give pleasure to others. Take the responsibility to face yourself and what your life has been about in order to end the terror of making a mistake, and in order to stop destroying your relationships with those who care about you.

The secret to living life from the mountain top is doing what you do because you want to, having what you have because you want it, and expressing your talents and abilities because you choose to. So, it comes down to having the freedom to say, "I want" and "I don't want," having choice, and doing what you do because you want to. To do so eliminates blame, judgment or criticism of another for what you have done or haven't done. In essence, you are taking full responsibility for what you do and don't do, eliminating any blame or scapegoating from your life and, in so doing, freeing yourself to express your talents and abilities. Make up your mind that you do what you do because you want to, and for no other reason. Make up your mind that you come from being yourself, being your highest and best, and being all you can be. Make up your mind that this is your life and that you are in charge of it. So what if you make a mistake? So what if you are less than perfect? Our mistakes teach us and help us grow. Doing what you do because you want to ends inner conflicts, and creates warm and loving relationships. Doing what you do because you want to frees you to have fun and enjoy what others are doing. End the power and control that anybody has over you forever by taking charge of your life and making up your mind that you do what you do because you want to. This drops the chains from your mind, and frees you to be who you are, have what you want, and express your talents and abilities, instead of being the way others want you to be, having what others want you to have, and suppressing your talents and abilities. This frees you to live your life your way.

When we identify with our possessive, controlling parent or family member, and are controlled by the need for his approval, we think the way he thinks, do what he wants us to do, and are the way he wants us to be. This creates resistance to, limitations in and contempt for love. Let go of the need for your possessive, controlling parent's or family member's approval, let go of the terror of his leaving or making you leave, and let go of the need to destroy your relationships with those who care about you. Let go of coming from destruction, accept that you come from creation, and accept that you are a precious, adorable angel. Identify with your Source within, where you are empowered to express your talents and abilities, and where you are free to enjoy and have fun every second of your life. This makes it possible to accept, "I have everything I want now." God is the original master Creator and architect, and we are the individual creators and architects of our lives. Accept and believe that you are the creator of your life and that you already have what you want now---this is the secret that has eluded us.

Ending the terror of making mistakes is life transforming. It allows you to create constructively instead of destructively. Make up your mind that you create constructively. Make up your mind that you are in charge of your work, your health, your marriage, your home, your relationships, and every area of your life. The terror of making mistakes leads to insecurity and lack of self-confidence. The way to end this is to let go of having to be perfect forever, and accept that you are good enough just as you are. Learn the truth: there is no such thing as a mistake. Mistakes are simply problems to be solved and stepping stones to success. So, make up your mind to let go of the terror of making mistakes forever. Leave self-doubt and terror, and move into self-confidence. Make God your authority and rely on Him to direct your every step to the dream you have chosen for your life---and have fun while doing it.

8 The Roles

THOSE CHILDREN WHOSE PERSONALITIES ARE UNACCEPTABLE to their parents take on a role so that they can be approved of and accepted. This role generally continues for life. There are four roles: controller, controllee, right and blameless destroyer, and wrong and blamed scapegoat. These roles are consistent, structured and predictable, and are described in this chapter.

If you are acceptable to your possessive, controlling parent or family member, you are free to be yourself and, consequently, have no need for a role.

THE CONTROLLER

The role of controller is chosen by the person who needs to maintain control to feel secure and comfortable. The controller fears the unknown and believes that he can handle the future by constantly controlling the present. Controllers analyze every situation in order to prevent future problems. They are afraid of being trapped, hurt or made to feel bad and wrong. They are always on the alert for anyone who might try to control them. In order to stay in control, the controller has to run the show. Large social situations are very uncomfortable to the controller because he is not free to come and go at will and is unable to control the crowd.

Controllers are motivated by the need and desire to be taken care of by others. They want someone else to be responsible for them so that they can remain blameless. They want a controllee---someone they can control so that they won't have to do anything or be responsible if anything goes wrong. They cannot get the job done because they are so afraid of being made wrong. They would rather not do anything than risk being criticized, critiqued or rejected. Controllers have learned to get what they want by manipulation rather than by asking for it. In this way they never have to confront a straightforward "no" or the possibility of rejection. They manipulate controllees in order to have their own way without obligation, while at the same time, making the controllees feel obligated to and responsible for them.

Controllers are good at knowing who will give them what they want so they can have their way. At the start of a relationship, they lay down their rules by telling you how they think, how you should think and what they want from you. They let you know, either subtly or directly, what they want you to do, how they want you to be, and what they want you to have, to make them happy. To maintain his control over you once the relationship is secure and established, the controller uses anger, rage, withholding of love, pity, anger, charm, the threat of leaving, mental seduction, sexual seduction, dividing and conquering, negative suggestion, non-stop talking, walling off, choosing sides, excluding and/or not including (see chapters: Mother and Game Playing). Another manipulative technique is to suppress your talents and abilities in order to make you feel incompetent and insecure, and in the end, to hold you down so that he can maintain his control.

Controllers keep people needing them, beneath them and dependent on them. Controllers are threatened by controllees' successes.

Controllers want their controllees to think the way they do. They do this by constantly giving their opinions on everything. If controllees offer a different opinion, controllers disapprove of them, and deny them the right to express themselves. Because controllees are so afraid of controller anger they soon suppress their own ideas.

Controllers tell their controllees that they will take care of them. Once controllees are corralled, controllers change their message, and manipulate controllees into taking care of them (the controllers). As these relationships continue, the controllers make the controllees believe that they (the controllers) don't need them, giving the controllees the message that they have no worth or value in order to keep the controllees responding to them (the controllers). As the control becomes tighter, the controllers gives less and expect more.

Controllers are constantly stressed to maintain their control over those they have corralled, adding new controllees and preventing other controllers from moving in on their territory. They instantly recognize any threat, and will attack, if necessary. They maintain control by being aggressive, angry, forceful, manipulative, cunning and watchful for weaknesses.

Control limits controllers in their own expression of life because it destroys spontaneity and constructive creativity. Controllers force things to work instead of <u>allowing</u> life to flow. They are so concerned about staying in control that they cannot express themselves freely, because their minds are constantly keeping score to see how they measure up to others.

The inability to say "I want" makes controllers angry, while the inability to say "I don't want" triggers rage. Because controllers are not free to say "I want" or "I don't want," they are unable to give others the freedom to do so. Controllers' anger is triggered when someone says "I want," and their rage when someone says "I don't want." Should someone say, "I want" or "I don't want," their minds automatically interpret this as a confront. They feel that the other person is telling them that they are not good enough, bad, wrong, less than perfect, and that they have made a mistake because they should have already known what the controller wanted and given it to him. To understand and change this, it is necessary for controllers to let go of denial, face themselves and see that they project their own feelings onto their controllees. The only way out for controllers is to rely on God to support them in telling themselves and others the truth. The controller is a role they accepted to protect them from danger and attack and to maintain the image of perfection which was given to them by their possessive, controlling parent or family member. This role runs their lives. By just being themselves and relying on God to protect and take care of them, their lifelong terror is over.

Controllers cannot listen to you or hear you because you might want them to do something. Should you ask them to do something, they will deny that you asked it---and completely believe that you didn't.

Sam was told by Jane, a long-time friend, that he was welcome to stay at her house any time he wanted to, whether she was there or not. Once he became free to say "I want," he called and asked if he could spend that weekend at her house. He was shocked by her response that it would be inconvenient because she wasn't going to be there. This was totally opposite from what she had previously said. Sam's saying "I want" triggered this surprising response. Because she is a controller, Jane does not allow anyone to say "I want." She is acting like a generous friend when, in truth, she wanted Sam to visit when she wanted him to and not when he wanted to. By saying "I want," he broke her unwritten rule, which was to see her as a kind, generous, loving woman, when actually, unbeknownst to Sam, she had total control over him. He has broken her control over his life by being free to say "I want" and "I don't want."

Controllers come closest to experiencing freedom from controlling when they are with a "natural person." A natural person is someone who is himself regardless of who he is with. Controllers know that the natural person cannot be controlled, so for a brief moment they can relax and enjoy themselves. There is nothing more refreshing, beautiful, fun and exciting than to be with someone who is free to be himself. These are the people controllers envy and wish to emulate. As long as they are with such a person, controllers are able to forego their constant manipulation.

What everyone wants more than control is the freedom to be themselves. It is the naturalness of others that controllers wish to emulate. To be natural requires that they first get to know themselves. This is very difficult to do alone, but they can do so by looking within and relying on God to show them to themselves one step at a time. It is important that they make a commitment to be free in order to let go of the role of controller. And it is also important that they make up their minds to be free of controlling, free of watching others and free to be themselves. This is a blessed relief to both the controller and the controllee. If they are in conflict about making this decision, they will experience depression. The depression will leave instantly, once they make up their minds to let go of their controller role, and to know and be themselves. Nothing can stop a made up mind.

When you become aware that you are a controller, your mind will try to block you from making any changes. It does so by looking out there and making "them" the cause of the problem, and wanting "them" to change. The mind says, "If they would just change, the problem would be solved and I wouldn't have to do anything." Many of your greatest fears will be aroused, not the least of which is the fear of being out of control. One fear after another will reveal itself: the fear of being hurt and vulnerable, the fear of letting go, the fear of the unknown, the fear of having to do something you do not want to do, the fear of having to give up or lose something, and more. You can overcome these fears by facing them and seeing that the only power they have over you is the power you give them.

You are ready to see how you act out your controller role when you acknowledge that nothing is working in your life: people respond to you in negative ways, planned activities fall apart, rigidity keeps you from going with the flow and you become angry (or filled with rage), depressed and frustrated. Not having your way feels painful. Controllers feel anger, but they rarely show it because they know that it would be an indication of being out of control. Since their anger cannot be expressed outwardly, it is turned inward and causes depression. If the controllee is the one who is depressed and, therefore, out of the controller's control, this can be the opportunity for the controller to end his role. The controller has to begin to see that maybe he could be wrong. At this point, if you can say to yourself, "Maybe I could be wrong," this can be the beginning of the end of the controller role and the beginning of freedom.

Even after seeing their role, controllers don't want to give up control out of a stubborn insistence to holding on to being right at all costs, because to be wrong would mean having to give up everything they believed to be true about themselves and everyone else. It would mean letting go of the false image they have had about themselves and letting go of the fantasy that they are right. They control in order to be perfect for the possessive, controlling parent or family member who gave them their role. Because they believe that this family member knows what is best for them, giving up the role would require giving up this family member as their god, and to do so would make them bad and less than perfect. The thought of this fills them with terror because, in so doing, they would trigger the family member's rage, which they avoid doing at all costs.

So it comes down to choice: the choice between continuing to be controlled by your possessive, controlling parent or family member or being you; the choice between making your possessive, controlling parent or family member your god or worshipping the True God, your Heavenly Father, who lives within you; the choice between continuing to believe the lie that you're bad, or believing the Truth that God tells you, which is that you are good enough just as you are. Do you want to keep protecting and defending your possessive, controlling parent or family member who wants to maintain control over you by holding you down? Do you want to be right and blameless or happy? It comes down to choice, and your possessive, controlling parent or family member does not allow you to have choice.

That's part of the control. So your first step is to accept that you have choice to live your life your way, that you are responsible for your life and you are responsible for your happiness. Take charge of your life and live it constructively, creatively and lovingly. To live life lovingly is to love God first, yourself next and then those in your life according to your priority. It is important to accept that you are free to love everyone and to accept that you are free to be loved by everyone. When you give up control you open the flow of love and communication, and this gives you the opportunity to create a warm and loving marriage. It frees your children to be themselves, and allows you to have warm and loving relationships with them---and with everyone in your life.

Now that you are free to say "I want" and "I don't want," and have choice, you no longer have to control. You are now <u>free to be you</u>.

A Profile of the Controller

The controller:
- Denies that he feels bad, not good enough and less than perfect.
- Resists bad, not good enough and less than perfect messages.
- Defends and protects his cover-up to himself and others.
- Fears being discovered by himself and others, and feels as though he is hiding something.
- Uses anger, if necessary, to intimidate and control.
- Feels superior to and is impatient with others.
- Resists any criticism while, at the same time, is silently critical and judgmental of others, while denying it to himself.
- Sees truth 180 degrees from how it really is.

THE CONTROLLEE

The role of controllee is chosen by those who have strong dependency needs. Controllees are totally dependent on others for self-worth, self-esteem and to be taken care of. Controllees need others to build their confidence and tell them who they are. They are vulnerable to blame because they are filled with self-doubt. In their minds, they always believe they didn't perform well enough and could have performed better. As a result of their low self-esteem, they automatically accept the blame, and continue to try harder.

Controllees need to be taken care of and need others to be responsible for their happiness. Their message is, "I will take responsibility for your happiness and I need you to be responsible for mine. I will please you, submit to you and take care of you and I need you to take care of me in return." They are pleasers who put their own needs and desires after those of others. Controllees are totally controlled by their need to be taken care of. They're terrified of hurting anyone for fear of the guilt they would feel. Many controllees feel that they will be absolved of their guilt if they can do enough good works. They work diligently, trying to make others happy, hoping to be freed from this burden.

Controllees choose spouses, friends and associates who will take care of them because they feel unable to take care of themselves. They seek those who, they hope, will give them approval, acceptance and the permission to be happy which, they believe, they cannot give to themselves. They feel that they can never be good enough until others tell them that they are, and they are always looking for a controller who will. However, controllers withhold this from them in order to maintain their control, preventing the controllees from getting the reassurance they need. Controllees, like their counterparts, controllers, are locked into the need to be taken care of. Controller and controllee play complementary roles which maintain this balance of power. Any time controllees complain about being overwhelmed by their all-consuming burden, they instantly get slapped down by their controllers. Complaining is neither accepted nor tolerated by controllers, who, themselves, complain constantly.

Pleasing others is one of the controllees' strongest character traits. It is their method for acquiring love, keeping the peace and avoiding others' anger. They are willing to accept their lot in life in order to maintain the illusion that they are being taken care of. They want everything around them peaceful, and they are often passive, quiet or shy. They may also, at times, be playful and charming, but never in a threatening way. They avoid conflict at all costs.

The controllee's life is motivated by the need to be taken care of. The controllee responds to the controller's slightest indication of disapproval or unhappiness. This control can be maintained by something as simple as a raised eyebrow, a tone of voice or an angry glance.

> *Jane's controller mother used a tone of voice to maintain her control over Jane. When Jane chose to end this control, she did so by confronting her mother at the moment of the raised voice, by saying "Don't you ever raise your voice to me again as long as you live." In a final attempt to control, her mother said "I might forget, dear." Because she was immediately empowered by her decision not to be controlled, for the first time in her life Jane did not back down, but firmly replied, "I will help you to remember, Mother." And her mother instantly knew that the control was over. For the rest of her life she never again raised her voice to Jane.*

The controller determines which people the controllee is required to make happy.

> *Lisa's mother was possessive of her. Not only did she demand that Lisa make her her one and only and only one, but she also demanded that Lisa be responsible for her happiness. This caused Lisa to resist everyone but her mother, which forced her to destroy her relationships with everyone else in her life.*

> *In another case, Sherry's mother wanted her to be responsible for the happiness of the whole world. Sherry would never take care of herself or her own problems and feelings because she was always thinking about others. Her burden became unbearable because she did not take responsibility for herself.*

Controllees are generally dependable, reliable and respectable, and lead a routine, safe and structured life. They avoid attracting attention to themselves. It would never occur to them to challenge anyone or to be a challenge. Normally contented with their circumstances, though not satisfied, they are often quietly ambitious. Although they do not volunteer for responsibility, when asked, they will assume it.

Controllees attract controllers because they want to be taken care of. Both the controller and the controllee send out the message "I'll take care of you," but the controller maintains the control. The controllee is willing to be controlled in order to be taken care of.

Controllees are threatened by any growth or progress their controllers make because they fear no longer being needed or wanted and, ultimately, being left. The controller maintains his control because he, too, is afraid of being left. Both the controller and controllee hold each other down and back. They are locked into this mutual control in order to keep from being left.

Controllees are always so busy helping, serving and thinking about what will make others happy, that they become servants. The degree of servitude is determined by the demands of their controller. Regardless of what controllees do, it is never enough. And this is the life controllees choose in order to be taken care of.

Because controllees are so concerned about others' happiness, they are unable to give any attention to their own. Ruth looked forward to a party with her husband. Anticipating the fun put her in a happy mood. On the way to the party, she could sense that her husband was irritated and preoccupied. Being a controllee, she allowed herself to be pulled down by his unpleasant mood and, as a result, neither of them had fun at the party. Because the controller demands total attention and service, the controllee's needs and desires are not considered.

Ending the Role

Recognizing the controllee role and the reasons you chose it is a necessary step to ending it. You may feel anger toward those who have controlled you, and toward yourself for having been controlled. However, this anger can be released without turning it inward on yourself or venting it on others. If you feel anger, forgive yourself and forgive them, for neither of you knew what you were doing. Then accept yourself as you are and accept them as they are. Follow this by accepting that you love yourself and them. Make up your mind that you are free from ever being controlled again.

It is a universal law that you must let go of one thing before you take on another. Because nature abhors a vacuum, it is necessary to replace your commitment to playing the controllee role with a commitment to being you, being all you can be, being your highest and best. Make up your mind to move into being and stay there. This is going from role to reality.

A Profile of the Controllee

Controllees:

- Accept that they are bad.
- Are extremely vulnerable.
- Invite bad messages (others telling them they are bad) in order to atone.
- Work hard to be good.
- Are open, self-revealing and trusting.
- Feel inferior.
- Are self-critical.
- Are unhappy and don't feel they can be happy until others are.

THE FLIP-FLOPPER

A flip-flopper flips between the two roles of controller and controllee at the slightest indication of a bad, not good enough, less than perfect or non-deserving message. If flip-floppers are confronted on being destructive in their role of controller, they feel guilty, and flip into the controllee role to atone by humbling themselves. They immediately punish themselves by assuming an inferior position. Once they feel they are forgiven, they instantly return to the superior position, and resume their controller role. The flip-flopper is inconsistent and in the course of one conversation can flip between both roles many times.

A Profile of the Flip-Flopper

The flip-flopper veers between:
- Denying and accepting that he is bad.
- Inviting and resisting bad messages and criticism.

- Feeling superior and inferior.
- Blaming himself and others.
- Being critical of himself and others.
- Being closed and defensive, and open and trusting.
- Being insecure and self-confident.

THE RIGHT AND BLAMELESS DESTROYER

To arrive at the point where you become aware that you are destroying the relationship that means the most to you is the greatest thing that can happen, although, at the time, it may appear otherwise. If you want to be free, free to be you, free to have warm and loving relationships, free to have success in life, read on, for within these pages lies the secret behind relationships that don't work: the cause, effects and solution. This information is the culmination of forty-two years of research.

Right and blameless destroyers want to remain children, and want their destruction to be seen as childish behavior rather than what it truly is. Their major characteristics are destruction, deception, and remaining, right, blameless and innocent of making others wrong and blamed. Their tactic for destruction is game playing, which consists of withholding love, pity, anger, charm, the threat of leaving, mental seduction, sexual seduction, walling off, excluding and not including (see chapter: Game Playing). They don't believe they make mistakes or have problems because, in their own minds, they are already perfect. They destroy with contempt, rejection, not giving you what you want, holding you down and back by not allowing you to say "I want" or "I don't want," blaming, transference (subconsciously making you into someone from their past) and projection (believing that you are feeling their feelings, to the point of hearing you say things you didn't say, seeing you do things you didn't do, and believing it to be the truth). Right and blameless destroyers project their need to be perfect onto you and become angry when you are less than perfect. They do one thing for you and, in so doing, obligate you for life. They can only have one relationship, and that one is with their possessive, controlling parent or family member who obligates <u>them</u> for life. Because they can only have one, they don't want you to have more than one.

Right and blameless destroyers are without principles, integrity and ethics. They say one thing and do another, and take no responsibility for what they have done or not done. They say they will give you what you want, and then give you what <u>they</u> want to give you or what you <u>don't</u> want. Then they become enraged and blame you for being unappreciative and ungrateful if you tell them it was not what you asked for or wanted. They only want to do what <u>they</u> want to do, which is to look good. They are out to destroy you and their relationship with you and, on some level, they know what they're doing, but won't look at it. In order to hide their destructive role of right and blameless destroyer, they choose an act that will work for them and play it out. Many become the part. "All the world's a stage, and all the men and women merely players" (Shakespeare, "As You Like It").

Right and blameless destroyers transfer onto you what <u>they</u> are doing. They accuse you of always having to be right and making them the bad guys when, in truth, they always have to be right and are making <u>you</u> the bad guy. They say you are always watching them, judging them and telling them that they are bad when, in truth, they are judging, watching and accusing <u>you</u> of being bad. They use charm to win you over, and anger to hold you down. They are cowards who experience short-lived courage when they are enraged and angry. They have courage with people they can bully, and are cowards with the ones they cannot.

Right and blameless destroyers hold back from expressing their highest and best out of terror of failure, being humiliated, rejected or seen as less than perfect. Their inability to say "I want" and "I don't want" creates anger and rage within them.

Right and blameless destroyers are dreamers who fantasize rather than act. They are spectators of life rather than participants. They want to be seen as important without having to do anything. They feed off their dream and act as if their dream were reality in order to convince you (and themselves) that they are what they say they are. They are possessive of you to keep you from leaving or having a relationship with anyone else. They want you to be successful because it makes them look good while, at the same time, they feel threatened by your success. They have opposite desires and can instantly flip from one to the other (see chapter: Programming). A problem is created because they say one thing, while their hidden agenda says another. You respond to what they are saying, and should, ought to and have to know and respond to their hidden agenda as well, without revealing it to them. To do so would be to expose them, and your job is to assist them to protect their image at all times. If you don't, they will retaliate. Unknowingly, you are trapped in a lose/lose situation.

The right and blameless destroyer role originates in early childhood with a possessive, controlling parent or family member who requires that the child be his one and only and only one. Possessive, controlling parents or family members keep the child for themselves, and do not allow him to grow up and leave emotionally, mentally and/or physically. Possessive, controlling parents or family members have a detailed blueprint of how they want their child to be. The possessive, controlling parent or family member determines those with whom the child can have a relationship and the kind of relationship he can have with them. How the perfect child should, ought to and has to be varies with each possessive, controlling parent or family member.

Right and blameless destroyers find it difficult to complete a task because their possessive, controlling parent or family member will not allow them to. They do just enough to get by. The possessive, controlling parent or family member wants them to destroy, not build, relationships. Right and blameless destroyers will attempt to block _you_ from being successful because your success mirrors their lack of success, making them feel inadequate. This feeling of inadequacy triggers their anger, blame and need to destroy. Suggesting ways to get the job done further triggers their anger at you, because your suggestion implies that you're judging them for not doing it in the first place. This justifies their destruction of you. They avoid getting the job done while appearing to look busy. They can keep up this pretense for only a little while because, contrary to the message they send out, they know they can't get the job done without a great deal of effort and will. And effort and will can last only a short period of time.

The right and blameless destroyer destroys those relationships which his possessive, controlling parent or family member will not allow him to have, blaming YOU (or others) for their demise, while totally denying, that he is destroying them. This becomes his life.

The right and blameless destroyer holds on to blame, judgment and the need to appear perfect to the world instead of ending all of his destruction. Right and blameless destroyers spend time and money on their dreams, and then always blame circumstances or people for their lack of fulfillment. They spend their lives leaving a trail of hurts, disappointments and broken promises, and deny it. If confronted or forced to face their destruction, they say that they can't stop it. They can't stop because they are not willing to take responsibility for their lives, and will not be able to end the destruction until they do.

> *By creating chaos in her office, a school secretary continually hurt her fellow workers, students and the school's integrity. She escaped her responsibility for the hurt by denying that she was responsible for the chaos, and felt justified because of the magnitude of her job. Her belief that she wasn't responsible for the problem prolonged it.*

If you tell right and blameless destroyers what you want or don't want they take it personally and instantly become angry or enraged because they believe you are blaming them for not giving it to you, and that you are accusing them of being bad and wrong. Your asking for what you want makes them feel threatened, which in turn makes you feel you are being denied the freedom to say "I want" and "I don't want," leaving you both with a problem that cannot be resolved unless you are willing to be their wrong and blamed scapegoat.

The right and blameless destroyer's role is designed to protect him from making a mistake, being less than perfect and having a problem. It keeps him from expressing his talents and abilities for fear of exposure as being less than perfect.

It is impossible to have fun with right and blameless destroyers because their possessive, controlling parent or family member wants them to destroy their relationship with you. Because of this, right and blameless destroyers project onto you and accuse you, either mentally or verbally, of being no fun, so they can return to their loner existence. All right and blameless destroyers are loners who are always leaving and who blame you for their having to leave. As a result, they have to destroy any fun occasion by messing it up, while remaining right and blameless and innocent. The role of right and blameless destroyer keeps them in a state of proving who they are instead of being who they are. They have no choice but to destroy. It's their job, their duty, their obligation. They will go along with what you want to do, and then resent, blame and judge you for not being fun. They give you the responsibility for creating fun, and blame you for not being fun. This self-deception allows them to remain self-pitying martyrs who believe themselves to be good girls/nice boys. You can't have a warm and loving or intimate relationship with them because they know there's something wrong with you---it's your fault. They have to forever remain right and blameless. Having fun takes an element of spontaneity, and to right and blameless destroyers, that's too scary. Spontaneity is the opposite of the control they must have.

Right and blameless destroyers cannot be praised or acknowledged because that is a sign of success in a relationship, and they have to destroy their relationships for their possessive, controlling parent or family member. To praise or acknowledge them makes them even more destructive of you. Therefore, if you tell them that you love something they are doing, they will soon stop doing it, because your praise makes them feel that they are being constructive rather than destructive, and they must destroy rather than create. Your praise implies to them that you expect them to do it again. The husband of a right and blameless destroyer learned that if he praised his wife for her delicious muffins, he would never see them again. As right and blameless destroyers become more and more attuned to what they are doing, their destructiveness becomes more and more subtle.

Right and blameless destroyers cannot ask for what they want because they are afraid you will see them as less than perfect for not being able to get it themselves. They are terrified of your rejection. They feel that they are noble for <u>not</u> asking for what they want, and resent you when you don't give them what they didn't ask for. They want to control you so that they can have it all without having to step over the line from dreaming to doing. If you tell them that they can do it, they feel good. If you tell them <u>how</u> they can do it, it makes them angry. At that point, you have crossed their line, and they have to destroy you.

Right and blameless destroyers come from their heads and not from their hearts. They will tell you that they care in order to get you to respond. When you respond by telling them that you care about them, they pull the rug out from under you because they are not allowed to care. Right and blameless destroyers destroy their relationship with you by looking at your weak points, wants and desires, and then using them against you.

Right and blameless destroyers want to be included, but won't include you. They want to know what you are doing and what's going on with you at all times. The most threatening thing you can do to right and blameless destroyers is to reject them. To be in control is what they want most, and they get this control by making themselves desirable. This is why movie stars become famous. This is why men build empires. This is why Napoleons and Hitlers seek to conquer the world: the desire for power and control. On a personal level, right and blameless destroyers do the same.

> *An example of this is the right and blameless destroyer whose boss had become totally exasperated with her lack of performance and denial of the problem. While he never said anything to her, she sensed that her firing was imminent. She quit rather than risk the terror of being rejected (fired).*

Finally ending a relationship is a tremendous relief to right and blameless destroyers. They leave without regrets, remorse or guilt. Unknowingly, it relieves them of the burden of betraying the possessive, controlling parent or family member by having a relationship with someone of whom the parent or family member disapproves. The cause of the demise of all of the right and blameless destroyers' relationships is the possessive control of this parent or family member. More often than not, possessive fathers don't want their daughters to have husbands, and possessive mothers don't want their sons to have wives. Some will allow their children to marry so that they'll look like a normal family. Some will let their children be married in order to have grandchildren, but will not allow them to have a relationship with their spouse or children. The rules vary according to the degree of possessiveness. Until the right and blameless destroyer makes the choice to end his destruction, it will get worse.

The right and blameless destroyer's life is about protecting himself from being rejected and left, while at the same time, destroying all of his relationships by rejecting and excluding others. It is a life of defense and retaliation.

> *Mary had been divorced twice. In the second marriage, her husband filed for divorce after six months. It so infuriated Mary that she retaliated by leaving the house, getting a loaded gun and almost killing him. She wanted to be the one who ended the marriage. She managed to get him to stay in the relationship for another year and a half, just long enough to regain control and then leave him.*

Some right and blameless destroyers will not stop until you hate them, forcing you to leave, so that they will remain right and blameless.

Right and blameless destroyers are children who want authority without any responsibility. They take no responsibility to become aware of what they are doing. They play the "make you crazy" game in which they try to drive you insane while, at the same time, they blame you for inconveniencing them with your insanity. They seek sympathy and pity. They betray you, blame you for the betrayal and project onto you that you have betrayed them. They have total contempt for you if you allow them to control you. They take your love and destroy it.

Right and blameless destroyers are extreme controllers with a great and deep need to be right, blameless and perfect. They have an insatiable desire to receive credit and recognition, and to be seen as heroes. The destroyer is fiercely competitive, with an intense need not only to win or beat, but to destroy others in the process. He achieves his goal of destroying his relationships and others' happiness while always remaining right and blameless. His fear of humiliation and rejection is so great that he avoids being confronted at all costs.

There are two sides to the right and blameless destroyer's role. One side feels superior and justified in perfecting everyone because he believes it is both his right and his duty to make them perfect. The slightest not good enough message causes him to plummet to the other side of his role and feel that he is bad, inferior and less than perfect. He immediately begins to seek praise, recognition and acknowledgement to regain control over himself and others.

Although the right and blameless destroyer sees himself as a self-righteous, blameless, noble, model human being, underneath lies a fearful coward.

Creating a Right and Blameless Destroyer

Many parents tell their children that they expect them to be perfect, to succeed, and to avoid bringing any shame to the family. At the same time they often doubt that the children will do so. They expect the children to succeed, and they expect them to fail. This terror of not measuring up to expectations leads to the creation of the right and blameless destroyer role.

The child chooses the right and blameless destroyer role for survival after trying and failing, after experiencing one injustice after another. From then on, his life becomes one of defense, denial, self-protection and proving himself right and blameless. His creativity is cut off because he sees enemies everywhere. He can't be natural or spontaneous. He makes up his mind that nobody will ever hurt him again. He chooses the right and blameless destroyer role out of rebellion.

The right and blameless destroyer is constantly on the lookout for others' weaknesses and shortcomings while, at the same time, is searching for someone to believe in him and in whom he can believe. He is searching for someone to free him from his self-inflicted jail; someone who accepts him just as he is and doesn't allow his destruction. Once the right and blameless destroyer finds someone who believes in him, he unconsciously begins the process of destroying that relationship. He takes advantage of that person's belief in him. The relationship is destined to fail until the right and blameless destroyer becomes aware of what he is doing, faces it and ends his destruction. When a line is drawn and destruction is no longer allowed, the right and blameless destroyer can then begin to create successful relationships. The only way out of this is to face his destruction and take responsibility for what he is doing. Until the right and blameless destroyer takes full responsibility for his life and happiness, he will continue to destroy his relationships.

Because the right and blameless destroyer has to protect and be loyal to his possessive, controlling parent or family member, he is not allowed to look at the role this parent or family member has forced him to play, nor at the cause of his rage and contempt for his chosen scapegoat. The right and blameless destroyer has to have a scapegoat who he can blame and make wrong. If the one he chooses refuses to accept this role, his frustration becomes enormous. He has to, of necessity, fulfill his possessive, controlling parent's or family member's mission for him by driving the scapegoat to insanity, alcohol, drugs, suicide---or to leave. In the end, the right and blameless destroyer destroys his relationships with everyone he cares about. He cannot stand anyone around him to be happy because it mirrors his own unhappiness, so he destroys others' happiness wherever he finds it. He hates others for having what they want and will do anything to destroy their success. He can't have it, so he doesn't want anyone else to have it. The right and blameless destroyer tries to prevent them from being successful by holding them down and back.

> *John and Sue talked about taking a vacation with their grandson. John did not want to go on the trip, but he also did not want Sue to go because it would make her look like the better grandparent by comparison. Instead of telling the truth, that he really didn't want to go, he set about doing everything he could to destroy the trip.*

Beliefs and Behavior of the Right and Blameless Destroyer

The right and blameless destroyer both respects and fears strong people who do not defer to him, while at the same time, hates them for making him feel insecure and uncomfortable by comparison. He makes them responsible for him, blames them for how he feels, and criticizes them to others for making him feel uncomfortable. He gathers teams to support his opinions because he lacks the courage to stand alone.

> *At a cocktail party, the hostess gave a glowing description of her friend, Sue, to her destructive friend, Jane. This aroused Jane's destructiveness. As a result, before she even arrived at the party, Sue became Jane's enemy. When Sue arrived, Jane openly criticized her. Jane's criticism backfired when her own husband rose to Sue's defense. Jane's attempt to destroy Sue by trying to publicly humiliate her resulted in her own public humiliation.*

Right and blameless destroyers see enemies everywhere. They cannot let down their defenses for fear somebody will humiliate them and expose their clay feet. As a result, they constantly try to expose others before others expose them.

The right and blameless destroyer is controlled by others' opinions, and believes he is what others tell him he is, which is why a right and blameless destroyer works so hard to protect and defend himself from others' negative opinions of him. He voices his opinions on every subject in an attempt to prevent others from expressing theirs. Since others might tell him that he is bad, the right and blameless destroyer sizes them up with great scrutiny to find out their weaknesses and how these weaknesses might be used to control them, so that he will always be prepared in advance for any rejection or attack. He keeps a wall up at all times for his own protection. With pride in his intellect and ability to size people up, the right and blameless destroyer looks down upon others from a superior position. In his own mind, he knows it all.

The need to be right is so strong that the right and blameless destroyer totally denies the truth to himself. He can instantly change his opinion in order to remain right and blameless, and he has the capacity to forget and deny ever having taken his original stand. He does whatever it takes to remain right and blameless. When a right and blameless destroyer hears something with which he is unfamiliar, he either argues against it or maintains that he already knew it. Some of the ways a right and blameless destroyer destroys communication are by denying the reality of what someone is saying (making it wrong), by getting up and walking out (leaving), by dominating the conversation (not allowing anyone to say anything), or by changing the subject (either directly or humorously). All of this is designed to keep him in control.

Right and blameless destroyers believe that unless they destroy an opponent, the opponent will be able to recoup and attack them. Their greatest fear is being exposed, humiliated and ultimately rejected. If anyone publicly humiliates them, that person has made an enemy for life. Right and blameless destroyers never forget or forgive. At the same time, they humiliate others to control them and to make themselves look good. "Don't get angry, get even!" is their motto. And the truth is, they do both.

There are two types of right and blameless destroyers: beaters and winners (see chapter: Game Playing). The winner will walk over anybody in order to win, because he must win at all costs. The beater has to beat his opponent. He is more concerned with holding the other person down and back than winning.

The only way out of this bottomless pit is for the right and blameless destroyer to take full responsibility for his life and happiness, tell himself the truth about playing a role, and move into being---being his highest and best, being himself, being real. Until he does, there is no way for him to see that he is destroying his life and his relationships with all those who mean the most to him.

In order to end this destruction, you have to make up your mind that you have choice and that it is not your responsibility to protect your possessive, controlling parent or family member. Take responsibility to create your life the way you want it to be. The only hope for lasting happiness is to let go of having to be perfect and accept that you are the source and the creator of your life. Make up your mind to rely on God to protect and take care of you. True happiness comes from letting go of all destruction and accepting that you enjoy every moment of your life.

Profile of the Right and Blameless Destroyer

- The right and blameless destroyer has to destroy all of his relationships for his possessive, controlling parent or family member.

- The right and blameless destroyer has to protect his possessive, controlling parent or family member at all costs.

- The right and blameless destroyer has to know it all. He has to be perfect. He believes that he has the authority to point out others' imperfections. He feels that it is his right and his duty to make others perfect.

- The right and blameless destroyer is terrified of confrontation.

- The right and blameless destroyer must make others wrong and blamed in order for him to remain right and blameless.

- The right and blameless destroyer denies that he has any problems, both to himself and others. To acknowledge that he has a problem and has made a mistake would be to admit that he is less than perfect.

- The right and blameless destroyer gives in order to get. Sometimes he performs what appear to be generous acts, but these are motivated by his need to gain control. The right and blameless destroyer has to always be in control.

- Right and blameless destroyers are self-centered. In their own minds, they are above reproach.

- If someone is going through hard times, is ill or has problems, the right and blameless destroyer has contempt for him. To the right and blameless destroyer, problems are a sign of weakness. He also feels contempt in situations that would normally evoke feelings of compassion, kindness or sympathy. The right and blameless destroyer is intolerant of needy people because they don't live up to his concept of perfection.

- The right and blameless destroyer has contempt for happiness. He destroys others' happiness with needling remarks, criticism and/or ridicule. He can also withhold himself, money, affection or approval, break things that are meaningful to others, forget, gamble, abuse substances, become ill and not give others what they want. He uses whatever works.

- The right and blameless destroyer is a trouble-maker who causes problems so that he can solve them in order to be the hero. When involved in an organization, he uses the "divide and conquer" technique to draw teams and be the "good guy".

- The right and blameless destroyer cannot stand negativity in other people, but is negative himself. Sadness, anger, fear and moodiness are intolerable to him. He gives his scapegoat total responsibility for his happiness, while denying it to himself in order to remain right, blameless and innocent in his own mind.

- The right and blameless destroyer cannot stand to see things run smoothly, and will attempt to destroy any successful operation. His actions were set in stone when he chose to destroy all his relationships for his possessive, controlling parent or family member.

- The right and blameless destroyer is forever seeking someone who will love and accept him just as he is and, at the same time, won't allow his destruction. He is forever pushing to see how far he can go. He has to destroy all of his relationships, and if they won't leave, he forces them to. On some level, he knows and fears that if he destroys his relationships with those he cares about the most, he will have to destroy himself.

- Because he compares himself with others, the right and blameless destroyer envies and resents those who have more than he does. He uses this envy and resentment to justify his destruction of them, and feels it is his right and duty to do so.

- Most right and blameless destroyers play a role within a role. They lead others to believe that they are generous, loyal friends while, at the same time, they are always scheming to take advantage of them. They pose as friends while, deep down, they hate their friends for doing, being and having what they want.

- In the presence of a stronger destroyer, the right and blameless destroyer often acquiesces and plays the scapegoat role.

- Right and blameless destroyers don't take responsibility for their destruction. Instead they deny it, believing they are perfect. To admit a mistake would make them a failure, and failure is a breach of their commitment to their possessive, controlling parent or family member to appear perfect to the world at all times.

Being a right and blameless destroyer is the way to destroy all relationships. It is how you fulfill your commitment to your possessive, controlling parent or family member, who you have made your one and only and only one.

It is only when you get sick and tired of destroying your relationships that you will be willing to face your destruction and its cause. It is only when you are willing to tell yourself the truth that you can be free.

Let go of playing a role so that you can stop play-acting, so that you can be real, so that you can be true to you, so that you can be all you can be, so that you can be your highest and best, so that you can be the master of your ship, so that you can be you, so that you can just be. Be it and live.

THE WRONG AND BLAMED SCAPEGOAT

For the right and blameless destroyer to exist, he must, of necessity, have a wrong and blamed scapegoat on whom to vent his destruction. Wrong and blamed scapegoats have a symbiotic relationship with right and blameless destroyers. They are dependent on right and blameless destroyers to punish them and, thereby, give them some relief from their overwhelming feelings of guilt. The right and blameless destroyer and the wrong and blamed scapegoat join hands in a union that leads the scapegoat down the road of pain and suffering. Each serves the other for his own survival. The right and blameless destroyer has to have an outlet for the pent-up anger created by his rebellion against the perceived hurts and injustices he suffered as a child. Because he is terrified of his possessive, controlling parent's or family member's anger, he vents his own anger on the scapegoat who has a need to atone for his belief that he is bad. Being punished is how he does it.

Though these two appear to be opposites, their life patterns come from the same basic fear of being bad, to which they react and respond differently. The destroyer denies he is bad; the scapegoat accepts it. The scapegoat lives in constant fear of the destroyer's anger; the destroyer lives in constant fear of the scapegoat's leaving.

This symbiotic relationship depends on the destroyer using the scapegoat, and the scapegoat being used. The destroyer uses hurt and pain on the scapegoat to destroy him. And the scapegoat both invites and allows it. The scapegoat creates getting backed into a corner to force himself to choose between being destroyed or taking a stand, between life and death. The scapegoat must, if he wants to be free from this suffering, make up his mind to end this self-inflicted destruction. There is a simple (but not easy) formula for doing this: first, the scapegoat has to see clearly and acknowledge that HE has invited his pain, suffering and destruction, and is, therefore, responsible for it. Second, he has to make up his mind to end the punishment he has invited, and, finally, he has to take a stand with the destroyer in order to end it. Knowing that the destroyer hates to have a line drawn, the scapegoat fears he will be left, but he must take a stand in order to live. He must, of necessity, face how he has allowed himself to be scapegoated.

If a destroyer is confronted to the point that he feels bad for what he has done, he feels inferior and flips into being pitiful in an attempt to elicit sympathy. He then attempts to seduce his confronter into praising him so that he can return to his superior, contemptuous, destructive role.

No matter how illogical or unreasonable a destroyer's request may be, a good scapegoat is expected to give him what he wants instantly and without questions, or risk being blamed and left. This threat of blame and imminent departure is how the right and blameless destroyer controls the wrong and blamed scapegoat.

> *Karen, a scapegoat, was in love with Bill, a destroyer. One Sunday afternoon, he invited her to the movies. The movie was to begin 30 minutes from the time he called, and there wasn't enough time for her to get there. When Bill called, Karen politely declined, but offered to meet him later in the day. He felt rejected, hurt and humiliated, and retaliated by withdrawing his love from her. The relationship ended a year later, but they remained casual friends. Two years later, when Karen was talking to Bill on the phone, he reminded her of the rejection he had suffered on the afternoon of the movie. It was clear that he had never forgotten nor forgiven her for rejecting him. To this day, Bill still holds a grudge against Karen for what he perceives as her rejection.*

The destroyer can't give the scapegoat what he wants, and the scapegoat is not allowed by the destroyer to even ask for what he wants. If the scapegoat wants anything, the destroyer says the scapegoat thinks only about himself.

Susan complained that her daugher, Jenny wasn't grateful for what she gave her. Susan gave her things she didn't want instead of what she asked for, and was hurt and disappointed when Jenny wasn't grateful for getting what she didn't want to begin with.

The destroyer manipulates the scapegoat into being responsible for his happiness by using anger, self-pity, charm, withholding, mental seduction, sexual seduction, the threat of leaving and either excluding or not including (see chapters: Mother and Game Playing). Once the scapegoat has given all he has to give and has been destroyed, the destroyer blames the scapegoat and leaves.

Both the destroyer and the scapegoat blame the scapegoat for everything that goes wrong. They both have the same agenda. As long as they blame, (the destroyer, the scapegoat; the scapegoat, himself), neither has to take the responsibility to change. The scapegoat can free himself and end his role by letting go of the need to be punished, by letting go of the need to be responsible for others' happiness, by letting go of the need to be wrong and blamed, and by moving into being---being himself, being his highest and best, being all he can be, being real.

The truth is that the role does not and cannot give you the happiness and peace you are seeking because it is only a role---it is not reality. It is through learning the Truth and being the Truth of who you are that you find happiness and peace. The truth is that you ARE God's child, that you ARE spirit, that you ARE light, that you ARE energy, that you ARE love, and that you deserve a life of peace, a life free to express your talents and abilities, a life free to be all that you can be, a life where no one and nothing controls, manipulates or dominates you. It is important for you to know that this is your birthright, this is your inheritance, and it is both your right and your responsibility to claim these truths. It is time for you to create your own dream and to take full responsibility for the step-by-step realization of that dream. It is time to stop living out someone else's dream. This is your life, and it's time to take responsibility for the causes and effects of it. It's time to live a life of abundance, joy and ecstasy. It's time to have fun, to cease all blame and criticism, and to cease allowing or inviting blame or criticism from others. This is the moment to live your dream, to be your dream and to have your dream. This is the moment that IS.

Profile of the Wrong and Blamed Scapegoat

- For a scapegoat to exist, he must have a right and blameless destroyer to blame him.

- The scapegoat sentences himself to a life of punishment, guilt and feeling bad, and attempts to be redeemed through a lifetime of submission and atonement.

- The scapegoat is controlled by and terrified of the destroyer's anger and threat of leaving.

- The scapegoat both invites and allows the destroyer to use him and take advantage of him.

- The scapegoat is treated with contempt by the right and blameless destroyer, who tells him, verbally or non-verbally, that he has no worth or value.

- The right and blameless destroyer vents his anger and rage on the scapegoat and blames him for feeling trapped.

THE IMPORTANCE AND VALUE OF KNOWING YOURSELF

The controller, controllee, right and blameless destroyer, and wrong and blamed scapegoat experience different reactions when they begin to become aware of the roles they have been playing and the way these roles define their lives. Prior to this, they were unable to look at their roles because of their deep fear of being bad, which triggers their terror of being rejected.

The Controller, and the Right and Blameless Destroyer
Due to their own need for perfection, controllers and right and blameless destroyers are very conscious of others' mistakes, errors and lack of

perfection. This lack of perfection causes them to be angry and impatient. They are unaware of their own lack of perfection and, until they choose to change by facing themselves, they will continue to live life playing this role. Should they choose to change, they begin to see how destructive playing a role is to their relationship with themselves and others, and they begin to see that they, too, are less than perfect. The wall of perfection which they so solidly built starts to crack at its foundation. These cracks threaten their confidence, causing them to feel fearful that they might be wrong, bad or not good enough. Once they realize that they have accepted that they are bad, and from that acceptance has sprung all of their actions, they can be filled with grief, sadness, remorse, regrets, sorrow, anguish, guilt and unhappiness for past mistakes. These emotions surface sequentially, and are part of the natural process of letting something go. It is important that they release each emotion in sequence, and that they accept they are happy. While facing this can be painful and humiliating, becoming aware of what they are doing is the only way they will be able to free themselves from the suffering they have created for themselves and others.

The Controllee, and the Wrong and Blamed Scapegoat

Controllees, and wrong and blamed scapegoats have always felt terrible about being bad. Once they become aware of how their fear of being bad motivates and controls their life, they can begin to realize both the cause and the solution. The belief that they are bad keeps them constantly struggling to get "good enough" in order to have self-worth and self-respect so that they can love themselves and, in turn, be loved by others. The effort to be good, nice and liked becomes all-consuming. Because they feel they've already been tried and convicted, they feel that they have to work to pay off their sentence. This sentence causes them to feel down, unhappy and, often, depressed. They feel exaggerated pain and guilt over small mistakes. Their mind says, "Don't look, because if you do, you'll see how bad you are, and then you will have to work harder and harder to get good enough." They feel that they can't work any harder than they already are. They don't dare to even glance inward, for to do so would show them how bad they believe they really are. This would cause them to redouble their efforts, and they feel they are already doing as much as they possibly can. Self-scrutiny is agonizing to them. They feel exposed, and have a strong desire to be invisible in order to get away from their own and others' judgments.

The Flip-Flopper

Flip-floppers have the greatest difficulty in facing and knowing themselves because of they have the ability to escape by flipping from controller to controllee, and from right and blameless destroyer to wrong and blamed scapegoat, alternately blaming themselves and then others when the truth gets close. Flip-flopping always provides them an escape, which allows them to avoid looking at the Truth.

Becoming aware of the role you've been playing and the choices you've made, and taking responsibility for those choices and that role is necessary in order to end them and move into being---being you, being your highest and best, being all you can be. Without awareness, there is little hope of changing your life from pain and suffering to a life of happiness and freedom. Living a role is like being in a play. It is acting at life. Living life to the fullest is about being you. Becoming aware prepares you to end the old programming and create a new program of happiness, freedom and joy.

9 Stars

There are three different ways to express leadership: exclusive star, negative star or natural star. Exclusive stars squelch their leadership ability by excluding others and competing to be the one and only and only one. Negative stars squelch their leadership ability out of fear, and seek negative attention. They are loners who do not include. Exclusive and negative stars express leadership by excluding or not including because, as children, they were taught that they were special. Natural stars are "people persons" who express their natural leadership ability because they love people. Team players are followers who work well on teams and support the team leader.

NEGATIVE STAR

Negative stars are leaders whose light has gone out. All negative stars are right and blameless destroyers (see chapter: The Roles). Negative stars create chaos and destruction in their own lives, as well as in the lives of those with whom they have a relationship. Because they are loners, they cannot be successful team players. They don't know that success involves being on a team with other people---and everything in life is a team: family team, marriage team, business team, friendship team, etc. To them, being independent and not needing others is success. Negative stars hold themselves back because they don't believe they are good enough to be successful, and they hold others down to keep them from being successful. In this way the negative stars won't feel less than them by comparison. They are terrified of being criticized, judged and blamed. Their life is consumed by remaining innocent. They use denial, anger, fantasy and projection to protect themselves from emotional, mental and physical pain, and will go to the ends of the earth to prove their innocence. They cannot stand pain, yet inflict it on others. Their terror of being confronted, rejected and, in the end, left turns them into cowards, bullies and, in extreme cases, tyrants. They are consumed by the need to cover their real feelings while remaining innocent, and live in terror of being found out. As a result, negative stars do not always appear to be negative. Some negative stars can seem very positive, but their negative energy drains the life out of a room.

Negative stars see enemies everywhere, often to the point of paranoia. They feel that these enemies are there to "get" and expose them. Negative stars are constantly looking for weaknesses in others in order to strike at their vulnerable spots. They have to "get" their enemies before these enemies "get" them. They feel innocent and self-righteous, and use this to justify their negative behavior. If confronted on their destructive actions or statements, negative stars become enraged. Their knee-jerk reaction to being confronted on their destruction is rage, denial and punishment.

Negative stars are self-centered, believe they are special, and don't want to grow up. They are impatient to complete projects so that they can go play. Their attitude is, "The one who dies with the most toys wins," and/or, "Having a problem says something about me."

Negative stars don't know what love is. They have to be in control. Because love IS, it cannot be controlled, so they must destroy it. Because they cannot be loved, negative stars do not know how to respond to love. As a result, they are uncomfortable in its positive presence. Unknowingly, they want love more than anything, but because their possessive, controlling parent or family member will not allow them to love or be loved, they must destroy it.

The negative star has to destroy all his relationships or, at best, maintain them at a distance. Close relationships, like marriage, require constant guarding, self-protection and analysis to the negative star. If there is a conflict, he blames the other person by saying, "If I get along with everyone else and not you, then you must have the problem."

As a child, the negative star was told that he was not good enough by some authority figure outside the family and, as a result, accepted that he was a failure and/or could not be successful. This public humiliation caused him to feel inferior, which destroyed his self-esteem, self-confidence and happiness. The negative star went into a fantasy to protect himself from ever being humiliated and blamed again, and began a life of destroying others' successes. At that point the negative star accepted, "If I can't have it, no one else can." When this humiliating event occurs in a child's life, he often turns to the Dark Side for vengeance and protection. This is the turning point which creates the negative star.

The negative star can be seduced by money, sex or ego, and possibly by all three.

> *Barbara (and her family), who had been going to a negative star dentist for twelve years, suddenly felt a change of attitude in his office. His staff treated her like a second class citizen and made her feel like they were doing her a personal favor to be there for her. When she confronted the dentist on this sudden and dramatic change in treatment by asking, "Is the manner in which my husband is paying my bill a problem to you?" he became terrified and angry at being confronted. "Yes," he responded, and instantly walked out of the room. The student got to the cause of the dentist's attitude: he wanted to be paid in full at the time services were rendered, and her husband had been paying $200 a month on their bill. Because this negative star dentist had been seduced by money, he was creating a non-caring, money-oriented, cold, alienating atmosphere in his office. As a result of his attitude, these patients of twelve years found caring services elsewhere.*

Negative stars are terrified of failure. Because they feel so inadequate, they resist getting the job done, while denying it to themselves. They become resistant to doing anything for anyone who says, "I want" to them, but remain innocent of this in their own minds.

Negative stars have opposite desires (see chapter: Programming). They want you to leave, and they want you to stay. They try to get you to leave by not giving you what you want, and then become frightened and scurry to give it to you when you start to leave. They promise to end their destruction, but soon discover that they can't stop. In a relationship with a negative star, the pendulum swings from love to hate in a regular pattern. Not until the negative star's destruction of the relationship has gone as far as it can go is he willing to face what he is doing, and change. At this point he can end the swing and create love in his relationships.

When negative stars make up their minds that a certain area of life is a priority, they can perform superbly in that one area, but this high performance won't last unless they find new challenges. They don't take any responsibility for a job or a project not working, and they wear an armor of low grade anger. This anger turns to rage if you tell them that you don't want them to do this any more.

Negative stars do not have the freedom to make a mistake, to fall flat on their faces or to fail, and yet they fail in every area of life and cannot look at it. They are not free to say, "I want" or "I don't want," nor can they allow others to say, "I want" or "I don't want" to them. In order to cope with wanting and not being free to say, "I want" and "I don't want," they compensate by projecting and transfering onto others for survival. Because they doubt that you are going to provide what they want, negative stars become angry if they have to ask. They expect you to read their mind and know what they want---and resent you for "making" them ask. If asked a question in the area of their expertise, negative stars become angry because, to them, the person asking is questioning (doubting) their ability.

The negative star cannot give anyone what they want because he doesn't give others the freedom to say, "I want" or "I don't want." For someone to ask him for what they want makes the negative star terrified of not measuring up to their expectations. In order to avoid having anything asked of him, the negative star adopts a defensive attitude of not caring. This prevents him from having warm and loving relationships, because warm and loving relationships are created by caring, loving and taking responsibility to make them work.

All negative stars have scapegoats on whom they vent their frustration and anger for not being taken care of and protected, and for being forced into the position of having to DO something they don't want to do. The negative star believes that if the scapegoat were different, their lives would be different. Because negative stars don't take responsibility for their actions, they make their scapegoat responsible for their unhappiness, problems and failures. They blame the scapegoat for everything in order to remain right and blameless. The scapegoat fills their need to punish and destroy any relationship their possessive, controlling parent or family member won't allow them to have. It can be a spouse, a teacher, a boss, a child, or other people. Unknowingly, negative stars constantly criticize and find fault with them, either mentally or verbally. They believe that it is their right and their duty to judge every action of the scapegoat. They deny this out of their need to appear perfect to the world. Negative stars become angry and enraged, and blame their scapegoat for putting them in the position of having to say, "I want" or "I don't want." They withdraw or withhold to punish their scapegoat for not giving them what they want, and not knowing what they want without having to ask. Negative stars believe they have this right because they were taught as children that they were their possessive, controlling parent's or family member's one and only or only one, and that they are special, and special people believe they can do whatever they want. This belief empowers them and causes them to live in the fantasy that they are better than others. Negative stars have to destroy the relationship with their scapegoat because their possessive, controlling parent or family member wants them to. In order to be free from this jail, it is important that negative stars face that they have bought that they are special, and, therefore, better than others. This keeps them in their head, and prevents them from coming from their heart.

It is impossible to have a warm and loving relationship with a negative star. For example, if the negative star asks, "Do you think I need to lose weight?" and the scapegoat says, "Maybe just a few pounds," the negative star becomes angry because he expects the scapegoat to tell him what he wants to hear. When the scapegoat tells the negative star the truth, he becomes angry. This anger can be silent or verbal. If the negative star says, "I think I'm going to get a face lift," the scapegoat might say, "If that's what you want, that's great!" In return, the negative star might say, "Oh, so you think I look old, do you?" The scapegoat responds with shocked silence.

The negative star punishes the scapegoat by withholding and withdrawing. Because he can't be involved with a spouse, everything becomes "his" and "hers," rather than "ours": they are the negative star's friends rather than OUR friends; the negative star's money rather than OUR money. The negative star has a low grade anger at all times, and creates disasters in his life to get attention. One negative star said, "I have major disasters happen (like my car burning while I was in it, or the wheel flying off as I was driving down the freeway, etc.), but I never get hurt --- and they always turn out to be my greatest, funniest stories. The only problem is, they always cost me a lot of money. I get attention and a lot of laughs, but surely there are other ways to do that."

A negative star can hear a compliment as a criticism, and can turn the most positive, loving act into the most negative, destructive act, and have no idea that he is doing it because negative stars have to see what is wrong with everyone and everything. Unconsciously, they destroy the love that motivated the positive act. A negative star mother, for example, can kill the moment when her child comes home from school, wanting to share his day. Instead of listening and being there for him, she tells him all the things he needs to do. If he is excited about making 98% on a test, she'll ask him why he didn't make 100%. Unconsciously, she is using her own child as her scapegoat to relieve her inner pressure. She destroys the moment by pulling her child down with her, and is totally unaware that she is doing it. Negative stars create negative stars. The children of negative stars are influenced by their programming and become negative stars.

Negative stars destroy relationships, peace, joy and, in the end, their own happiness with their destruction.

Negative stars keep pushing away those relationships their possessive, controlling parent or family member doesn't approve of and won't allow them to have by walling off, withholding, not giving them what they want, excluding and not including. Negative stars see how far they can go before they are confronted or before they leave. Confrontation both terrifies them and drives them. It would relieve the horrible tension of waiting for the axe to fall if others would just leave or fire them. Negative stars are constantly looking for someone who will love them enough to stay, and who is strong enough to confront them. They push to see how far they can go before either they or the other person has to leave.

Because the negative star is a leader whose light has gone out, his life is one of survival. This survival has caused him to escape into playing a role rather than being who he is. The way out is to let go of the right and blameless destroyer role and move back into being---being the Light, being the truth of who you are, just being. And to accept that you are the Light and a natural star. This frees you to be the leader that you are. Move from your mind into your heart, and invite God into your heart to walk with you, guide you and direct you.

EXCLUSIVE STAR

Exclusive stars, like negative stars, are right and blameless destroyers whose light has gone out (see chapter: The Roles). To be acknowledged and recognized as the one and only and only one is the driving force behind an exclusive star. This desire for recognition is insatiable, and arouses hate and competition within him when it is threatened. Those who threaten the exclusive star's limelight instantly become the enemy, and he declares war.

Exclusive stars are driven by a need for power and control. They compete fiercely to be the one and only and only one. This motivation provides them with drive, boldness and a false sense of confidence, which is built on the shifting sands of others' adoration.

Exclusive stars are enslaved and addicted to being exalted, worshipped and adored. They need admirers, groupies and fans to provide the pedestal upon which they stand. Staying on this pedestal is like teetering on a seesaw. They never know when their end will touch the ground, or their exalted position will be threatened. They seek out, and instantly know, those who will become admirers. Exclusive stars use their entourage of admirers to reinforce their ego and protect them from the hate, jealousy or envy of their enemies.

Exclusive stars have a royalty complex. They believe they have the right to take anything they want and to punish anyone who offends them. Their punishment far exceeds what they perceive the crime to be. They believe themselves to be beyond reproach as a spouse, friend, parent or employee, and believe that they absolutely can do no wrong. They blame anything that doesn't work on others and live in total denial of this.

> *An exclusive star wife witnessed her husband receiving a friendly hug from a mutual friend. She instantly chose to retaliate by having an affair with her husband's best friend. This knee-jerk reaction to an innocent hug caused the demise of her marriage and her husband's relationship with his best friend.*

Because exclusive stars are inordinately needy of attention, admiration and recognition, they become very sensitive to the threat of rejection, humiliation and criticism. They have mastered the art of seduction in order to get what they want without having to ask. If they don't get what they want, they become angry to the point of rage, and use this anger or rage to get what they want.

If you don't give them what they want, they turn their back on you and punish you by giving their attention to someone else. This knee-jerk reaction occurs in an instant. Their capacity for denial is so great that they don't know what happened---and neither do you. The greatest deception, to themselves and others, is their denial of their hatred, triggered by not getting what they want. Their reaction is so quick that the hatred is never allowed to surface for them or others to see, and yet this is what propels exclusive stars. Their belief system is, "I know I'm going to have it. I don't know how, but I'll get it, and nobody can stop me. I will find a way." It's as if they have blinders on, and will mow down anyone who stands in their way.

Exclusive stars use others' innate weakness of wanting to be taken care of to seduce them. They want to be worshipped, and will say, verbally or non-verbally, "If you'll keep me on a pedestal, I'll take care of you." Those people who were trained to be possessed and taken care of by their parents gravitate to exclusive stars who will possess them and imply that they will be taken care of.

The exclusive star has a hidden agenda which functions and manifests on three levels. The first level is pursuit, the second level is the hook, in which he uses subtle, condescending rejection, and the third level is the corral, where he keeps the old admirer while in pursuit of a new one. This subtle game goes on subconsciously. Both the exclusive star and the admirer know, by the third level, that it's over, but the exclusive star is in denial, and the admirer is terrified of looking at it, out of loyalty to and fear of losing the exclusive star. This puts the admirer in the defensive, victimized position, and the exclusive star in the offensive, powerful position. Being corralled arouses the fear of rejection and a clinging possessiveness in the admirer.

After the exclusive star seduces his admirers and places them in a corral, he is free to go out and expand his entourage. Once corralled, the old admirers are neglected while the exclusive star pursues new ones. The only way the corralled admirers can regain the attention of the exclusive star is to become a challenge to him by leaving or threatening to leave. This challenge becomes motivating, exciting and addictive. It leads to all-out war and, in the end, the destruction of the relationship.

The exclusive star is needy and creates neediness in others. This neediness makes him vulnerable to rejection, humiliation and control. Need pushes away and assures rejection. Our greatest needs are to be loved, protected and taken care of. We avoid asking outright for what we need for fear of being judged, humiliated and, in turn, rejected. Instead, we manipulate to get what we want, by establishing our own rules. Often, we are told as children that it is bad to ask for what we want, and that we can only have what we need. To compensate, we develop intricate, complex techniques to manipulate others into giving us what we want without having to ask.

When the exclusive star doesn't get what he wants, he becomes angry and has to attack. Because the exclusive star's life is about pursuing his latest conquest, he is obsessed with being free to leave, and constantly looks for justification to do so. The slightest mistake gives him this justification. The exclusive star always has someone in the wings and, when the time is right (when he is ready to go), he chooses some flaw in the old admirer which makes him angry and justifies his leaving. The exclusive star then brings the new admirer forward while pushing the old out. This out-with-the-old-in-with-the-new, with never a break in the flow, is the life of an exclusive star.

The exclusive star feigns independence, but is the neediest of all. He is jealous and possessive of his entourage, and will not allow them to surpass him. They become trapped in this corral through ignorance. The only way out is to be let out by the exclusive star, which is most unlikely, or to realize the power and control they have given him and cease wanting anything from him. This will free the admirers to open the door and leave. The departure of an admirer instantly rekindles his desirability in the eyes of the exclusive star, and the chase is on again. Unknowingly, this need/hate is destructive to the exclusive star's relationships.

Letting go of being an exclusive star feels almost impossible. The star feels as though he will have to give up his personal power, and will be left behind. He feels as if someone will stop him from winning, and he will be helpless to do anything about it. "They" will be able to hold him down and back. "They" will be able to do to the exclusive star what he has been doing to them. This creates terror in the exclusive star: the terror of losing his power to get what he wants.

Exclusive stars cannot feel love. They are cold, hard and ruthless. They are not really involved with anybody or anything. People cannot stand to be around them for any length of time because they are so driven, manic, intense and exclusive. As a result, exclusive stars end up alone. At the slightest indication that they will not get what they want, they leave.

They feel that they have to get away, and no one can stop them. You can recognize them by the "I gotta go" energy they put out, which makes them feel driven, and very, very busy.

Exclusive stars use their natural leadership gifts, God-given talents and abilities for themselves. Exclusive stars use everyone, including God. Facing that they are using God is key to ending the role of right and blameless destroyer. Using God so horrifies them that it, in itself, can motivate them to end this role.

NATURAL STAR

Natural stars differ from negative stars in that they include everyone. Exclusive stars exclude, and negative stars don't include. Negative stars are natural stars whose lights have gone out. Negative stars don't include others out of fear that what they have will be taken from them, and/or that others will surpass them, and that their negativity will be found out. Exclusive stars exclude because they feel superior and believe that others are outsiders. Natural stars feel equal to, and the same as, everyone and have great difficulty understanding bigotry, snobbery or superiority. They neither feel superior or inferior.

Negative, exclusive and natural stars are all leaders who lead in different ways. Exclusive stars feel superior. Negative stars feel inferior. Natural stars feel equal. Natural stars live in reality rather than a fantasy. They are real and are always themselves.

Natural stars lack awareness of the destruction which is obvious to negative and exclusive stars. Because they arouse such envy, it is important that they understand that God will protect them, take care of them and love them in all circumstances.

Natural stars are unaware that they have a different agenda from the negative and exclusive star. They are just being themselves with nothing to hide. Whereas, both negative and exclusive stars are not themselves, and hide this from others. Negative and exclusive stars are constantly thinking or analyzing what they are going to say or do, or how they are going to be, but the natural star just IS. The natural star can be beaten by the pounding waves of life because he doesn't have destruction in him and, therefore, does not see it in others.

Natural stars are people lovers. Their loyalty makes them attractive to people.

Any exclusive or negative star can become a natural star by choosing to give up the other agenda and be themselves.

A former negative star turned natural star said, "Before my attention was totally on me, myself and I. Now my attention is on the team and how I can serve it, whether my friends, my family, my teacher, etc. My energy is different. I care about people. I no longer take things personally, but use what I am told to train and grow. I see that I have a responsibility as a citizen of this planet to grow up and give back."

Natural stars know that they don't know anything and, consequently, are open to learning. Negative stars deny that they don't know anything, and fantasize that they know everything. Exclusive stars don't know that they don't know anything, and believe they know everything.

Being a natural star is the easiest way to express your natural talents and leadership abilities, while caring what people think holds you down and keeps you from doing so. By being a natural star you don't have to pretend to be something you are not. Being a natural star makes life simple---and a joy.

TEAM PLAYER

Team players are people who can be on a team without resistance, people who can cooperate without interfering with the flow. Team players are able to both give to and receive from the team. They can be told what to do without getting angry, and can follow directions. They are a joy to the team and are truly missed when they are absent. A team player is a follower, rather than a leader, and is an absolute necessity to the team, because for the team to work, there has to be both leaders and followers.

To be on a team in which members work together, play together, and are cooperative, loving and supportive of one another is one of the highest experiences of life. To be unable to be on a team keeps you separate, and makes you feel like an outsider, excluded, uninvolved and unwanted. If you are not a team player, you experience resistance to the team, to being a part of the team and to being included by the team. You feel cold and resistant to team members. It takes ten times more energy to resist being on a team than it does to be on it. Being part of a team feels warm and cozy.

To be part of a team serves you to know yourself, teaches you who you are, and reveals to you your blocks to having your dream and having success in every area of your life. The main reason for your inability to be on a team is that your possessive, controlling parent or family member does not allow you to be.

In creating a team that works, the team players must be free to say, "I want" and "I don't want." This opens up communication and understanding between team members. If team members cannot express themselves freely by saying "I want" and "I don't want," and cannot give other team members the same freedom, they manipulate to get what they want. Game playing is the main tool used to manipulate to get what they want. This game, when played to its fullest, will destroy the team, which gives the possessive, controlling parent or family member what he wants. However, human nature being what it is, once the team member destroys the team, he will look for another one to join, and begin the process all over again. If the team member has to leave the team, he will destroy the team, while remaining blameless and looking innocent. Synergy, creativity and open communication are the result of a team of people who are free to say, "I want" and "I don't want." It is this freedom to express themselves that allows ideas, excitement and love for the team to flow freely. Anger and rage are created on a team when even one member is not free to say, "I want" or "I don't want," and doesn't give other team members that same freedom, which prevents them from solving problems or expressing their talents and abilities. The team members who do this are unaware of the destruction they create on their teams. In order for a team to work, it is important to give each member the freedom to express himself.

What is preventing you from being on a team and enjoying this elixir of life experience? Is it not because of the fear of experiencing the same pain you experienced when, as a child, an authority figure (either in the family or outside) caused you to believe that you couldn't be successful, that you were a failure, and that you couldn't have success? For many, this traumatic experience happened around the age of 4,5 or 6, or 9,10 or 11. These are two highly vulnerable periods in a child's life, for this is when they begin to venture into the world of outside teams. How they felt about themselves after their interaction with that authority figure resulted in their belief system regarding success or failure in life. At that time, many moved into fantasy and/or denial to escape from the pain of disapproval or failure.

The fear of experiencing this pain has controlled and restricted their team expression ever since.

> *Tim was a team player whose programming did not allow him to be on a team. Because of this, he was always looking for an excuse to leave. Mentally, he kept one foot out the door and the other set in runner's position. He always expected someone to say something derogatory, which would give him the excuse to leave. Tim had opposite desires (see chapter:Programming). He consciously wanted to be on the team while, at the same time, wanted to leave. He judged the team and blamed it for preventing him from doing what he wanted to do. Once he let the team go and accepted that he was happy, he then joined the team and was able to be a successful team player. He now feels supported by a team of people who are doing what they do because they want to. This makes being a team player fun and exciting. Now, Tim feels continuously energized about getting the job done, but most of all, he has fun.*

To realize the ultimate of being a team player is to recognize your importance and value to the team, and its importance and value to you.

Team players are vital to a team, and equal in importance to the team leader. As long as you believe that leaders are more important than team players, team players will be squelched, along with your ability to have fun with them. Imagine a team with all leaders and no followers. The result would be war. The team would cease to function.

By prioritizing your teams, you will be free to be on many teams, such as church teams, school teams, work teams, family teams, friendship teams and grandchildren teams, and have them all work for you. Every relationship you have is a team relationship. Many people are not free to have a friendship team because their programming only permits them to have either a family team or a parental team. As a result they feel a powerful resistance to being on any team. It is important for you to determine which teams you were allowed to have. Make up your mind that you are an adult and are free to have any team you want. Choose to be on your spouse's team, each of your children's teams, your family's team, your own team and God's team. Let go of the resistance to being on a team, and move into the warm and cozy feeling of being a successful team player.

CHARACTERISTICS OF STARS AND TEAM PLAYERS

Negative Stars

- Self-centered. Consumed with themselves.
- Leaders who doubt they can get the job done (self-doubt).
- Live in constant fear of being told they are bad, wrong and not good enough.
- Live in constant fear of being found out as less than perfect.
- Unless they see the positive things they have done, they feel like a failure, and can become depressed.
- Have a possessive, controlling parent or family member(s).
- Controlled by possessive, controlling parent's or family member's anger.
- Controlled by fear of anger or rage.
- Take everyone for granted.
- Take everything personally.
- Withhold.
- Compete for team players.
- Want to be included, but exclude others and want to be free to do so.
- Negative thinkers.
- Doubt others' ability to get the job done.
- Expect others to fail.
- Block getting the job done while looking and acting innocent. Look busy not doing anything.
- Do not want to be held accountable.
- Spectators of life.
- Live vicariously through others' lives: movies, books, sporting events, etc.
- Take on the personalities of their heroes.
- Want to be taken care of.
- Do not want to take care of anyone or anything.
- Do not take responsibility.
- Feel superior.
- Will not give you what you want.

- Desire acknowledgement and recognition.
- Live in denial.
- Act as if they do not need anything.
- Con you into thinking that they are other than they are. Can act like exclusive stars.
- Dead, but can come alive for the opposite sex.
- Walk away in time of need.
- Cannot stand you to say, "I want" or "I don't want" to them.
- Get negative attention.
- Masterful game players.
- Can neither care or be cared about, nor love or be loved unless their possessive, controlling parent or family member approves or allows it.
- Live in terror of being accused of making a mistake and being made bad, wrong or not good enough. Go into the void to avoid this.
- Constantly watch and listen to make sure that they are saying and doing the right thing in order to remain perfect and innocent.
- Are mean.
- Go for the jugular and act innocent.
- Hate anyone they can't control.
- Ride the coattails of others to take them out of their doldrums and make their lives exciting.

Exclusive Stars

- Live in constant terror of not being liked, which is the most important thing in life to them.
- Need constant approval, attention, acknowledgement and recognition.
- Everything is done for show.
- Leaders who believe they can get the job done.
- Compete for the limelight.
- Exclude all who threaten their limelight.
- Cannot stand other exclusive stars.
- Surround themselves with negative stars.
- Corral negative stars and give them just enough to keep them there.

- Are the greatest master mind game players of all, and deny to themselves that they are playing the game.
- Tremendous capacity to hide their ulterior motives.
- Extreme capacity for denial.
- Believe they are perfect.
- Possessive.
- Extremely self-centered.
- Terror of not being good enough and being exposed.
- Hatred of anyone who calls them on making a mistake.
- Have a royalty complex.
- Instant retaliation toward anyone who offends them. The punishment far exceeds the crime.
- Have to be perfect.
- Compete for team players.
- Inconsistent in their loyalty.
- Want to be admired by fans from afar.
- Do not want to take care of others, though they promise to do so.
- Walk away in time of need, but act as if they are there for you.
- Takers.
- Hate to be alone.
- Act independent, but are dependent on others' admiration.
- Take for granted the ones they care about the most.
- Cannot feel. Live in the void.
- Controlled by the terror of anger.
- Perform for the opposite sex.
- Extremely inconsiderate.
- Keep people waiting so that they can make a grand entrance.
- Cannot love.
- Do not care about others' feelings.
- Do not take responsibility for their life, their job, their family or their marriage.
- Cannot say, "I want" or "I don't want."
- Always keep score in marriage (and other relationships) to see who is winning.
- Come from an attitude of superiority.

Natural Stars

- Leaders who know they can get the job done.
- The job is done as soon as the idea is conceived.
- Negative and exclusive stars try to squelch natural stars.
- Do not compete. Do not have to - they just are.
- Want to be cared about and loved.
- Can care, love and receive caring and loving.
- Want acknowledgement and feedback in order to improve.
- Stand by you in both good times and bad.
- Welcome assistance and give it freely.
- Want you to tell them what you want, and want to give you what you want.
- Can admit mistakes, but fear the consequences of anger.
- If they are not free to say, "I want" and "I don't want," they will override their resistance and say it, anyway.

Team Players

- Support the team without having to be a star.
- Supportive of the star.
- Supportive of each member of the team and their abilities.
- Do not want to lead; just want to play on the team.
- Have great fun working on a team.
- Will set up the winning play.
- Do what they can for the team.
- Will put their own needs and wants on the back burner in deference to the team.
- Confident in their role on the team.
- Pleasant and good-natured.
- If they are not free to say, "I want" and "I don't want," they will override their resistance and say it, anyway.

SPECIAL

The ultimate control that a possessive, controlling parent or family member can have over a child is to tell the child, either verbally or nonverbally, that he is special. This elevates the child to the special status of being the parent's or family member's favorite, and is designed to control the child, hold him back, keep him from leaving, and get him to make the parent or family member his one and only and only one. The possessive, controlling parent or family member uses the threat of leaving to reinforce his control. While, at the same time, this parent or family member tells the child that he is not good enough. This double message confuses the child and creates opposite desires in him, which causes him to compete in all of his relationships (see chapter: Programming). This keeps him striving and never arriving. These opposite desires prevent the child from expressing his talents and abilities, and assures the possessive, controlling parent's or family member's lasting control. Not only is the child held down from expressing his talents and abilities, but, because of the fear of being left, the child, in turn, holds others down from expressing their talents and abilities. The special message, which was designed to control the child and prevent him from ever leaving the possessive, controlling parent or family member, keeps him from growing up. Those who bestow special on the child have the power to control what he can do, how he can be, and what and who he can have for life. He has no life of his own unless, at some point, he chooses to be free. These possessive, controlling parents or family members are the puppeteers who pull his strings and determine the people with whom he can have a relationship, and the kind of relationship he can have (close, distant, superficial, etc.). They give the child a blueprint by which to live his life. This blueprint takes away his right of choice, and makes his possessive, controlling parent or family member his one and only and only one.

One and Only & Only One

In order to assure total loyalty from his child, the possessive, controlling parent or family member requires that the child make him his one and only and only one, which later prevents the child from creating warm and loving relationships, and assures the destruction of his marriage. The only way to have a relationship with someone other than the possessive, controlling parent or family member is to transfer the parent or family member onto the other person, mentally making him that parent or family member. Making his possessive, controlling parent or family member his one and only and only one causes the child to be walled off, resistant, defensive, self-protective and impatient. This also causes him to see enemies everywhere, not only his own, but his parents' or family members', and keeps him coming to the parent or family member to be taken care of and protected. Many rebel against this control, yet are still not free to create warm and loving relationships. They are so restricted that they can't be in the Light, and are unable to express their talents and abilities.

The possessive, controlling parent or family member has to remain in control at all times through manipulation, resistance and impatience. The child makes this parent or family member his god, and turns to him to be told what he can do, how he can be, and who and what he can have. His god defines the child's moral standards. If his god cheats, the child will cheat; if he betrays, the child will betray; if he hurts others, the child will also hurt others---all without a conscience. The child is emotionally arrested at the same age at which his possessive, controlling parent or family member is emotionally arrested. This causes an incongruency between his emotional and chronological ages. Because his god is perfect in his eyes, he can't see him as he is. This keeps him loyally dedicated to his god for life, and keeps him protecting and defending him. He champions his possessive, controlling parent's or family member's causes, and scapegoats and blames his enemies for any problems the parent or family member creates. He takes on the responsibility of serving the parent or family member and keeping him happy. This is his life's work. It destroys his creativity, and keeps him always waiting for the parent's or family member's orders. There is an unspoken agreement between some children and their possessive, controlling parent or family member that if they make the parent or family member their one and only and only one, the parent or family member will make them _his_ one and only and only one in return. Failure to make the parent or family member happy terrifies this child because to do so would cause him to be banished. He feels strongly that he is either one and only and only one, or nothing. This keeps him desperately striving for approval. Having this approval means more to him than life itself. The possessive, controlling parent or family member knows this, and can control him with a glance. If the parent or family member withholds or withdraws approval, or worse, the one and only and only one status, the child will move into either fantasy and/or rebellion for survival, where he will remain for life unless or until he faces this control and lets it go. Low grade anger coupled with the eternal feeling of guilt assures the child of pain and suffering. The need to be the possessive, controlling parent's or family member's one and only and only one is the cause of destroyed relationships, the need to always leave (mentally, physically or both), and the need to be alone.

> *Maddy's possessive, controlling father was her god, her one and only and only one, and he knew it. Because her mother had rejected her, in order to survive, she lived in the fantasy that she was his favorite. She gladly served him and did everything she could to make him happy. One of the ways in which she did so was by making her mother and sister her enemy and, like him, constantly finding fault with them. After doing this for 22 years, she was shocked when he chose her mother and sister over her, and said that if she couldn't live according to their rules, perhaps she should move. The realization that her father had left her and gone over to the enemy caused her to rebel by taking him up on his suggestion, moving out of state and beginning a new life.*

The possessive, controlling parent or family member takes away the child's right of choice by requiring his total allegiance, loyalty and dedication. The child is glad he doesn't have choice out of fear of making the wrong choice. He WANTS the parent or family member to tell him what to do to avoid the risk of making a mistake. As a result, he does what the parent or family member wants him to do, is how the parent or family member wants him to be, and has what the parent or family member wants him to have.

The possessive, controlling parent or family member makes the child special, keeps him striving for his approval by always telling him he's not good enough, and encourages competition, thus assuring the destruction of all the child's relationships (see chapter: Competition). Game playing is the weapon the child uses to destroy his relationships while having fun doing it (see chapter: Game Playing). Thus, one and only and only one is the cause of special, perfect, not good enough, competition and game playing.

The child made special is like a huge elephant who is tied to a post by a thin string. This string keeps the elephant from moving and doing what it wants to do. Like the elephant, the child doesn't know that making his possessive, controlling parent or family member his one and only and only one takes choice from him and binds him to the parent or family member for life. The child made special cannot do what he wants because he does only what his possessive, controlling parent or family member wants him to do, whether or not that parent is alive or has passed on. The special message aligns the child with his possessive, controlling parent or family member against anyone the parent or family member will not allow him to have: spouse, children, family and/or friends. If the child chooses to have any of these forbidden relationships, he instantly feels bad, guilty and, unknowingly, has to destroy them. As an adult, he doesn't understand why he feels guilty when, in his mind, he hasn't done anything. He uses denial to keep from seeing, facing and taking responsibility for what he is doing. He is not allowed to tell himself or others the truth. He has to be perfect and follow the ever-changing rules that are laid down by his possessive, controlling parent or family member. Often, special children were taught not to tell the truth to anyone for fear that they and their families would be exposed as less than perfect. Making a child special causes him to deny the truth and assures that he will choose to play the role of right and blameless destroyer (see chapter: The Roles). He <u>has</u> to always be <u>right</u>, he <u>has</u> to always be <u>blameless</u> (perfect), and he <u>has</u> to destroy all his relationships.

Possessive, controlling parents or family members believe that the world sees their child as the special, unique and superior person they do. This relieves them of any responsibility to teach him how to co-exist socially. Being made special and, therefore, perfect, gives the child an inordinately high opinion of himself. The high position and the attention a child receives by being made special becomes an addiction that demands constant feeding. This addiction creates problems in all of his relationships. The child has been taught that he is perfect (superior), and, therefore, has no problems. He does not learn what life has to teach him. Because of this, he goes through life offending and alienating people, oblivious to what he is doing. He often says the wrong thing, which creates confusion and problems, and he takes no responsibility for this. When problems arise, he instantly flips into denial, feigns total innocence, and strengthens his protective armor of special. He finds a scapegoat to blame for any problems that exist and on whom to vent his anger and rage. This gives him the arrogance to say, "I don't have a problem---you have a problem," the freedom to be right and blameless, and to always look innocent, while creating enormous problems in every area of his life. Because his demand for attention pushes people away, the special person learns to "fake" it and wear many faces, acting like a nice guy or good girl and, in so doing, becomes a consummate actor, conning others into buying his act. The special person cannot bear to be around people and not receive the special recognition he demands and believes he deserves. Once he gets the limelight, he is reluctant to relinquish it. This addiction to attention is so all-consuming that the special person will compete with his own spouse and/or children for it. He feels that it is his right. Ultimately, he destroys all the relationships that mean the most to him, and denies having done so. If others reach the point where they have had enough of his attitude and leave, it takes the special person months before he realizes that they are gone and not coming back. When admirers are no longer there for him, he often turns to food, alcohol and/or drugs as a substitute for attention because those things won't leave.

Special people are always leaving, even when they are sitting still. They and those around them feel as if, at a moment's notice, they will bolt and run. They cannot be there with you even when you are alone together. They feel trapped, cannot have fun, and accuse you of being the one who is no fun, which justifies their leaving, either mentally, physically or both.

Possessive, controlling parents or family members who make their child special feel that this is an expression of love and caring, and that being made to feel special will instill confidence in the child. Instead, it instills arrogance, and arrogance alienates him from others, which reinforces his one and only and only one relationship with his possessive, controlling parent or family member. Making a child special excuses the parent or family member from training him to do anything except look good to the world. Bestowing special on a child assures him of destroying all his relationships and, in the end, even his relationship with the very parent or family member who made him special. This parent or family member needs to be the child's one and only and only one and, because need pushes away, the one made special has to leave for survival. So, making a child special always backfires.

Darlene, who made her son, Tom, special, told him and her daughter-in-law, Sue, that in the future, she wanted Tom to visit her alone, implying that she didn't want Sue to visit. What she didn't know was that the only reason Tom ever came to visit was because Sue encouraged it. Once Sue was not wanted, she never thought of visiting Darlene anymore. Consequently, Tom never visited again, either.

Because the only relationships that the child made special can have are those which the possessive, controlling parent or family member allows, he cannot care or be cared about, love or be loved, for his heart, soul and identity have already been taken by the possessive, controlling parent or family member. Caring is out of the question to the one made special. The only one he cares about is himself. He cannot acknowledge or be grateful. He is arrogant, cocky and devoid of humility, which assures him of destroying most of his relationships. He takes pride in being better than others, and has a look of haughty, contemptuous superiority. Some special people learn to hide this look with personality because they have seen that it alienates others and prevents them from being popular, while others are so wrapped up in themselves that they are unaware that people are avoiding them.

More often than not, the only close relationship a special person can have is with the possessive, controlling parent or family member who made him special. If the special person rebels and goes for the relationships he wants, it is necessary for him to wall off, withhold and use personality to cover up self-centeredness and lack of caring, or use transference to mentally turn that person into his possessive, controlling parent or family member. Transference means that the special person subconsciously sees his partner as the possessive, controlling parent or family member who made him special. This is the only way he can have a relationship. He is unable to see his partner as he really is, which denies the partner the freedom to be himself. The one made special expects his partner to act like the possessive, controlling parent or family member he has transferred onto him, and blames him for not living up to his expectations.

The one made special doesn't see anything as it is. When his partner speaks in a normal voice, the special person hears him yelling. When the partner expresses himself, he is perceived as mean. When the partner is loving, he is seen as cold and distant.

> *After her divorce, Beverly, who had transferred her possessive, controlling father onto her husband, was shocked when she saw him change after marrying a woman who did not transfer anyone onto him, but rather, valued him and allowed him to be himself. In another example, a husband became tired of his wife making him her father, and repeatedly said, "I am not your father. I am your husband." One day she stopped making him her father and accepted him as her*

husband. This was the beginning of the end of their marriage, because her father never allowed her to have any man but him.

The one made special puts the person on whom he is transferring in an impossible position and is totally unaware that he is doing this, making the problem unsolvable. He would be willing to swear that the other person is doing to him what he is, in reality, doing to the other person. The one made special sees everything 180 degrees from how it is.

When Tammy was growing up, her father told her he expected her to be perfect, yet his non-verbal message was that she was to screw up in order to make him look good by comparison. As a result, Tammy lived her life in terror of making a mistake. In order to have a relationship with her loving teacher, Tammy transferred her possessive, controlling father onto the teacher, and ascribed her father's emotions to her. Every time Tammy got together with her teacher, she waited for the axe to fall: she expected to make a mistake, and she did. By expecting her teacher (father) to reprimand her, she was setting herself up for hurt and disappointment. This justified her revenge, which she brought about by then transferring her mother onto her teacher, "hearing" her teacher (mother) yelling at her, enjoying her mother/teacher's loss of emotional control, and killing her with her mind. This is how she destroyed for her father.

This is the power of transference, projection and making a child special. Once special is bestowed in childhood, it continues throughout adulthood until it is recognized, acknowledged and released.

The special person sees those people with whom he is involved, but cannot have, as the enemy.

One special person saw her teacher as disapproving, judgmental, angry and mean, whereas in truth, her teacher was loving, caring and giving. Because she transferred her mother onto her teacher (in order to have a relationship with the teacher), all the student could feel was fear, although she could see intellectually that her teacher was kind and loving.

When she let go of being special, her concept of her teacher changed dramatically. The teacher did not change; the student changed. For the first time, she saw her teacher as she really was. She saw that they were the same. She could finally have her teacher as both friend and teacher. They could at last have fun together.

Special people cannot express their talents and abilities because their possessive, controlling parent or family member will not allow them to. They cannot enjoy themselves, and resist having fun because this parent or family member will not allow them to have fun with anyone else. Special people create negative, sadistic fun because that is what they are permitted to do. The negative star has fun competing and beating others by using verbal and mental put-downs and contemptuous laughter, while the exclusive star has fun competing and winning by turning his back on others, excluding them and, thereby, making them feel that they have no worth or value. His non-verbal message is "You're not important enough for me to give you the time of day," which, when confronted, he denies (see chapter: Stars).

All negative stars and exclusive stars have been made to believe that they are special. The exclusive star wants constant attention, stroking, praise, recognition and acknowledgement for his accomplishments, and gratitude for just being there, while the negative star, who feels sorry for himself, seeks attention through pity and sympathy. Many disguise this desire for pity and sympathy with humor. The exclusive star seeks positive attention; the negative star seeks negative attention. All negative stars have been made negatively special, which means that they are the best of the worst, and proudly wear the badge of martyred victim. Because they feel hopeless in the face of a problem, they are beaten before they start. They create failure and destruction everywhere they go, and put their head in the sand in order to reinforce their denial of what they are doing while, at the same time, take pride in their failure and destruction because this makes them successful in the eyes of their possessive, controlling parent or family member, who has to be their one and only and only one.

Both negative and exclusive stars are unhappy because they can never get enough attention from everyone. This causes them to manipulate through both mental and sexual seduction to get the attention they crave. This driving force of having to be special prevents happiness. They may appear happy, but it is an act. They cannot maintain this act because it is not the truth of who they are. Once they go home and are behind closed doors, they let go of their act and express their anger and rage with the ones they care about the most. Those involved with them feel shocked and betrayed because the special person is not who he claimed to be.

The possessive, controlling parent or family member doesn't trust the child or believe that the child can get the job done, and he teaches the child not to trust or believe in himself by doing everything for him.

> *When Maddy was 13, she was supposed to turn in a science project. Her possessive, controlling father, who was sales manager for an international liquor manufacturer, and whose hobby was building scale models, suggested that Maddy build a scale model of a distillery plant. This was beyond her abilities and they both knew it, so her father built it. When it was completed it was flawless, and clearly not the work of a 13-year-old. Her teacher knew it, too, though he said nothing. To this day Maddy wishes she had built her own science project.*

The possessive, controlling parent or family member expects the child he made special to understand what is going on without being told. "If you don't know what you've done wrong, I'm not going to tell you." "I expect you to understand because you're the oldest." The parent does this to keep the child confused and hooked by the controlling message that one day he will get GOOD ENOUGH. This keeps the child always striving, but never arriving. Ever present in the child is the prevailing feeling that what he is doing or not doing is NOT GOOD ENOUGH.

Special people claim the right to make their own rules and change them any time they want. One night, Dan would praise his daughter for the way she washed the dishes, and the next night, criticize her for doing it the same way. Special people confuse their loved ones, uplifting them with expressions of love and desire for a warm, loving relationship one day, then "slam-dunking" and rejecting them for some imagined fault the next. Their inconsistency is unbearable to live with---and they do not know they are doing it. They do not know what created the heaven or the hell, but they believe that the other person is to blame. Special people are frustrated, and their victims are confused by this inconsistency, so their relationships are frustrated and confused.

On one occasion, Bob praised his daughter for making 99% on an exam, and the next time she made 99%, he criticized her by asking "Where's the other point?" This created confusion, kept her striving for perfection and, in the end, feeling that no matter what she did, it would never be GOOD ENOUGH. Because of these double messages, she never knew what GOOD ENOUGH was. This left her terrified, off balance and always looking to the world to tell her she was okay. As a result, in order to get some relief from the inordinate pressure of not being GOOD ENOUGH for her father, she stopped making her father her god, and made society her god.

Unknowingly, when those who were made special leave home, they stop making their possessive, controlling parent or family member their god and make society their god, thereby giving others the power to tell them they are NOT GOOD ENOUGH. For example, the stranger in traffic can honk his horn at them and make them feel NOT GOOD ENOUGH. Because they have to be GOOD ENOUGH they are terrified of making a mistake, because making a mistake feels like death.

When the pressure to measure up to the unfulfilled expectations placed on him by his possessive, controlling parent or family member become too great, the special child either blows up in anger and rage, blocks his feelings or becomes depressed. Unknowingly, he blocks feeling love, joy and fun at the same time.

For a child, being special is like being invited to join the most prestigious club in town, in which he is the only member. For this honor, he will be paying dues the rest of his life.

The "special" message permeates every area of life. The one made special not only expects, but demands that everyone treat him as special. He demands that others be delighted to see him and make him top priority whenever he chooses to arrive. The special person has an imperious, "how dare you not make me special" attitude. He is shocked when others don't share this attitude, and will instantly punish them for it by retaliating. This knee-jerk retaliation, and denial of it, is what his life is about.

John, who was made special by his possessive, controlling mother, learned early on in the business world the results of being made special, when interviewing the head of a large corporation to sell him an insurance policy. During the sales presentation he said to the President, "You could help me by asking your employees to fill out these forms." The President said, "Son, it's not my job to help you." This both shocked and embarrassed to John.

TO THE ONE MADE SPECIAL, THE WORLD REVOLVES AROUND HIM. He is the center of his universe. He is totally self-centered. As a result, he sees everything through "I'm special" eyes. The world can teach him that he is NOT special. If he becomes aware of this, he is devastated because, to him, he is either special or nothing.

Special people who are in sales often display a non-caring attitude, as in the following example: when a customer asked the special saleswoman where a certain item was, the saleswoman's superior reply way, "I have no idea." Her special attitude conveyed the message, "How dare you ask. Go find it yourself."

Special people are not free to say, "I want" or "I don't want," and do not give others the freedom to say, "I want" or "I don't want," either. The special person hears "I want" and "I don't want" as a criticism, which he takes personally. Your request says that he hasn't done it, or hasn't thought of it, which, to him, says that you are accusing him of being less than perfect. It implies that he 1) has made a mistake, 2) is bad, and 3) is not doing it good enough. This makes him angry or enraged. To say, "I want" puts the attention on you, which means that the special person has to take it off himself. He cannot do this because he sees nothing beyond himself. If someone gives the special person a bottle of cologne, he thinks, "Does this mean he thinks I smell bad?" If someone gives the special person's child a toy, he thinks that the gift-giver is saying that he is a bad parent for not having already given one to his child. If the special person's spouse, friend or employer asks him to do something, he becomes angry or enraged because carrying out the request lowers him (in his eyes) to a less than special status and makes him feel like a slave. However, having to ask for what he wants also makes him angry, so when he wants something, you are supposed to know it without his having to ask. In a relationship between a special parent and a special child, the child becomes frustrated when he asks the parent for something, because the parent cannot even hear the child, much less give him what he wants---and the child hates having to ask for it in the first place.

IF YOU ARE AFFLICTED WITH THIS ENTITLEMENT, LET SPECIAL GO BECAUSE IT WILL DESTROY THE RELATIONSHIPS THAT MEAN THE MOST TO YOU.

Those who have rebelled against this special message and against making their possessive, controlling parent or family member their one and only and only one, and are married to someone this parent or family member has not allowed them to have, have an underlying feeling of guilt and of doing something bad. They don't understand why they feel guilty, because they haven't done anything wrong. Unknowingly, they feel guilty for having relationships they were not allowed to have and, consequently, they have to destroy them. They do so by having contempt for their spouse and blaming the spouse for making them feel bad and guilty. And the spouse feels like he is being attacked and does not understand why. The possessive, controlling parent or family member is the one calling the shots, and the special person is the hypnotized slave who continues to make the parent or family member his one and only and only one, while the parent or family member appears innocent and blameless. To be free from the pain which comes from feeling bad, special people move into denial, scapegoat their partners and make them bad. Special people avoid pain at all costs, while constantly inflicting it on others. By scapegoating the ones they love, they are obeying their possessive, controlling parent or family member.

When two people who have both been made special marry, they set out, unknowingly, to destroy each other and their marriage. Ron, who was made special by his father, was married to Sue, who was made special by her mother. War began in the beginning and continued throughout their ten-year marriage. When Sue's mother died, Sue was left without her support system in this warring marriage, at which point Ron increased his destruction by making Sue feel inadequate. Because both were made special, they could not destroy each other, but they ended up destroying their marriage.

The feelings evoked by being special are: superiority, arrogance, judgment, contempt and condescension. The special person constantly judges, while at the same time, accuses and blames others for judging him. This fuels his perpetual low-grade anger.

Special creates a cycle of highs and lows, victories and failures. It creates constant defeat in areas the special person is totally unaware of, such as business, health, and emotional and spiritual stability. To the one made special, life is one of opposite desires, messing up and always starting over (see chapter: Programming).

Special people do not know what the rules of society are. They make their own rules, and feel free to change them at whim. They also feel free to take who or what they want, even if these people or items belong to someone else. The one thing that holds them in check and keeps them from total destruction are the laws of the land.

Special people want to be included, and once they are, they become exclusive. They want the right both to be included and to exclude. During the process of excluding, special people begin acting out the role of right and blameless destroyer, and play many games to remain in control (see chapters: The Roles and Game Playing).

> *Tom and Bill had been best friends since high school. Their wives, Jane and Sue, were also dear friends. The four were together socially every week. Gail envied Tom and Bill's close relationship. She wanted her husband, Steve, to be included in their friendship, so she asked Sue if she and Steve could join them (be included) during one of their evenings together with Bill and Jane. Sue was happy to include Gail and Steve. Shortly thereafter, Gail and Steve began courting Jane and Bill's friendship by buying them gifts, paying them compliments and planning trips with them. Little by little, Gail and Steve excluded Tom and Sue. What appeared to be an innocent desire to be included was, in reality, a means of competing with them for their friends, and gaining power and control by taking their friends away from them.*

Making a child special causes him to RESIST everyone and everything. His heels are dug so deeply into the sands of life that the thought of swimming out into the ocean is unbearable, unimaginable and impossible. The one made special feels like a hero when he prepares his child's breakfast and when he goes to work for those people who are paying him---and he feels his employers are so lucky to have him! The special person is constantly thinking of what his pay-off will be, and how others might be of service to him. According to him, they owe him.

The special person feels martyred, and the only reason he stays in a relationship is because he is getting (or is going to get) something in exchange for the great sacrifice he is making. The special person both resists and, at the same time, is compelled to act as he does, and feels as if he is doing others a special favor. He has opposite desires (see chapter: Opposite Desires). A husband who does his wife a special favor cuts the grass for HER, not because it is HIS responsibility. He feels that she should be grateful and appreciative, and praise and admire him for what he sees as his personal sacrifice, but in reality, cutting the grass is his responsibility. The wife who does a special favor for her husband cleans the house and cooks the meals for HIM, and not for herself or because it is her responsibility. She feels that he should admire and praise her for doing it.

Special people live an incredible life of frustration, working like crazy and using every manipulative tool to get what they want. Then, once they get it, they don't want it, so they lose it. This is the ultimate of opposite desires. The desire to be loved, desired, respected and worshipped is overwhelming. However, once this desire is expressed, they have to pull the rug out from under the person giving it to them, because they cannot have it. If they feel love for someone and start to express it, they instantly feel cut off from that person. There is no way to have a warm, loving, relationship with people who have been made special.

The resistance to giving and receiving love, having warm and loving relationships and hearing what others are saying requires so much energy that the one made special feels exhausted. In most conversations he has to tune out what is being said because he is not allowed to listen to or hear anyone but his possessive, controlling parent or family member.

Double Special

The doubly special person is the one who was made special by two possessive, controlling parents or family members. Whenever the doubly special person is asked to do anything, his attitude is one of doing others a special favor. He does just enough to get by and keep all his relationships in their place, and just enough to look good and avoid any blame. The doubly special person expects and demands acknowledgement, admiration and recognition for the great sacrifice he is making just to be there, and is angry if he doesn't receive it. When he is acknowledged, he feels even more superior and contemptuous toward others. The doubly special person has what the world would call a "bad attitude," one in which he condescendingly looks down at others. The doubly special person surrounds himself with a wall of unapproachability which separates him from the rest of the world. He has a strong air of superiority, which gives him the right to do anything he wants with total self-assurance. The doubly special person has a powerful, persuasive quality of salesmanship. This is seduction with promises of great things to come which never arrive. He uses this to get what he wants without having to ask for it or do anything. Then, when he gets it, he cannot have it.

Negative Special

The negative special child has been told by one or both parents that he is especially bad and worthy only of disapproval, therefore he expects to fail and does. Because he has accepted that he is not good enough, he believes that God's blessings don't apply to him. He feels that he is outside and beneath God's laws. Others can succeed, but he is doomed to fail. The negative special person feels that God doesn't love him, that he is not God's precious, adorable angel, and that he does not deserve abundance. He is always on the outside looking in. He expects rejection and, therefore, creates it. Because he has a negative mental attitude, and sees what is wrong with everything, he creates a negative atmosphere wherever he goes.

Negative special begins when a parent tells his child he is not good enough, whether it is because he is unwanted, disgusting, disapproved of, despicable, ugly or undesirable. This message is reinforced by the parent's constant attention to the child's negative attributes. The child soon learns that the only attention available is gained through negative behavior.

When a child has one parent who tells him he is special, and one parent who tells him he is negatively special, he will flip between feeling that he is the best of the best (special) and the worst of the worst (negative special). One moment he is arrogantly superior, and the next he is debased and demeaned. In his mind, no one is as bad as he is or as good as he is. With either message, the child is set apart from others through his specialness.

The negative special person resists attempting anything new because he believes he will fail. His attitude becomes one of, "Why try?" The negative special person may turn his anger outward, but, more often than not, it is turned inward because he fears others' anger in response to his. Yet he creates others being angry with him because he doesn't do what he says he will. This gets him the negative attention he craves and feels he deserves.

The only way to end negative special is to let it go, forgive the parent who made him negative special, then accept that he is one with the whole, and accept he is God's precious, adorable angel.

Summary

The special person's fear of rejection is so great that rejection by someone he cares about could destroy him. The only power the special person has is the power of being special, and he cannot be with anyone who doesn't make him special. His tools are manipulation, seduction and pity. He gets others to feel not good enough or less than perfect so that they will work harder to get his acceptance and approval, which he never gives. The special person resists being given a gift, even as he is taking it. He is in a double bind. When he receives what he has indirectly asked for, he feels bad because he is not supposed to want anything. In his mind, the giver has exposed the special person's neediness by giving to him. The special person has to retaliate by punishing the giver for giving him a gift, which, in the end, destroys the relationship. All of this because he cannot have a warm and loving relationship with anyone his possessive, controlling parent or family member won't allow him to have, which is no one. The biggest problem is that, down deep, a warm and loving relationship is exactly what the special person wants. He truly does want someone who will give him what he wants, but when he gets it, he cannot accept it, so he has to destroy anyone who keeps on loving him. The special person feels anger, hatred and contempt for people who give him what he wants, and it is impossible for him to be appreciative, grateful, or to acknowledge anyone.

It is a lose/lose situation for a non-special person to be married to a special one. By letting go of special and doing others a special favor to be involved with them, the special person will be able to see his loved ones as they really are for the first time. He will see everything totally differently from the way he thought it was, and be able to create warm and loving relationships.

If you are involved with someone who was made special, it is important to understand the ramifications of special in order to face and eliminate its destructive effect on you. Special people derive joy from any win and, while unaware of it, destroying you is a win for them. Unconsciously, they are destroying their relationship with you for their possessive, controlling parent or family member, and it is important to know this. It is not them, but that parent or family member who is destroying you through them. Because they cannot stop it, they have to hold you back, and holding you back becomes their life. They keep resisting and you keep responding. It is imperative that you take responsibility for your life and happiness, and be aware of how you are being destroyed.

It is necessary for you to make the choice to continue the fulfillment of your dream with or without those special people in your life. Holding you down or back is their job, and is necessary for their survival, while going forward is necessary for yours. There will come a crossroads, a time of choice, a time of decision-making. At this time, the special person will, of necessity, have to choose to change or leave. There is no other way, for holding back or holding down is now out of the question. By letting them go, you are freeing them to free themselves of this crippling disease, while freeing yourself of its crippling effects. Move on without regrets, sorrow or anguish, allow both of you to be free and happy, take responsibility for your mind, your happiness and your life, and accept <u>your</u> present and continued happiness.

By simply releasing the power that "special" has over you, you can become free to express your talents and abilities, and to claim your own life. Even though you may intellectually know this, your life is not your own as long as you allow special and the need to be special to have power and control over you. You are unable to be yourself, express your talents and abilities and have warm, loving relationships.

The only way out of this jail of special is to tell yourself the truth, tell others the truth, let go of special, let go of destruction, let go of making your possessive, controlling parent or family member your one and only and only one, and accept that we're all the same, each with our own unique talents and abilities. Take time to learn what yours are and make up your mind to express them. It is important at this time to accept your identity of being God's child. We are the same spirit, the same love, the same joy. You are one with the whole, and not separate and special. This Truth, and this Truth alone, will free you to let the wall of separateness down, and will free you to accept and be the Truth of who you really are.

10 Competition

COMPETITION IS ADMIRED, valued and respected in the world of business and sports. We make heroes of those who win in business and athletics. Competition motivates us to do our best and to go beyond what we believe we can do. What we're not told is that while competition works in sports and can work in business, it doesn't work in relationships. In truth, it destroys them. Because we are taught that competition is the way to win, those who compete in relationships end up, unknowingly, destroying them. The thrill that comes from the win is what, we are led to believe, creates happiness. However, this kind of happiness is short-lived because it requires constant replenishment for its fulfillment.

Mothers compete with fathers for their children's love, and children compete for their parents' love (sibling rivalry). Unknowingly, parents evoke this rivalry by getting the children to compete with each other for better grades, cleaner rooms and, in many cases, for their love. This competition continues outside the home, causing friends to compete with each other.

In competitive families, children are not free to say, "I want" and "I don't want." Not being free to say, "I want" or "I don't want" forces us to compete to get what we want. We avoid asking outright for what we want because in competitive families most requests are automatically rejected. To compensate for this problem, we develop intricate, complex techniques to manipulate others into giving us what we want in order to avoid having to ask. One of these techniques is competition. The word "competition" denotes two teams and implies that there is a winner and a loser. Any time we compete and lose in the game of getting what we want, the failure triggers hatred within us toward the winner. Competition causes us to want to leave. If we win, we want to leave to find a better competitor; if we lose, we want to leave to find someone we can control.

COMPETITION IS CAUSED BY A DESIRE TO WIN. If we want warm and loving relationships, competition doesn't work, because if we win, we lose.

It is because we need our mother's permission, our father's approval and our family's acceptance that we accept, as children, the myth that we can only have what we need. And, at the same time, anything we need, we push away. Need creates a strong emotion which demands attention and fulfillment. Need causes us to look outside ourselves and compare what we do with what others do, who we are with who others are, and what we have with what others have. Comparing arouses jealousy, envy and never-ending competition, and it is this competition that becomes the motivation for outdoing anyone who does what we want to do, is how we want to be, or has what we want to have. A competitor <u>has</u> to win. And if the competition is too great, the loser compensates with contempt for the winner and <u>has</u> to leave. If he doesn't leave physically, he leaves mentally or emotionally.

Competitors instinctively know that if they share what they are doing with friends who compete with them, the friends will try to outdo them and take what they have, whether their business position, social position, other friends and, in some cases, their spouses. If there is competition in marriage, one spouse can take the children from the other spouse. Because competition requires that you remain silent about what you're doing, you are unable to share your life with your spouse or friends. If you can't share your life with your spouse or friends, the very essence of what marriage and friendship are about is destroyed.

THE CYNIC

When a competitor suffers a loss <u>so</u> debilitating that he loses hope of winning, he becomes a cynic. At this point, the cynic turns what was a game of winning into a war of vengeance. Because the competitor <u>has</u> to win, the cynic compensates for losing by seeing his loss as a victory. From then on, the cynic takes pride in his ability to get negative attention and destroy others by pulling them down, holding them back and, eventually, breaking their spirit. He derives joy from beating others, and sees it as a win. If the cynic is unable to destroy by being negative, he sees it as a loss, and turns the loss inward where it can become depression, illness and, in extreme cases, death. The cynic finds it very difficult to say anything kind or nice, or to acknowledge anyone because he sees everything negatively. As a result, he can only tolerate joy, happiness and love in small doses. If the cynic is forced to spend more time than is comfortable in a happy, loving environment, he must either say or do something to destroy the atmosphere, or leave. A cynic is both a competitor and a game player. Competitors exclude and game players either exclude or don't include, according to the game strategy they are using. The cynic excludes and doesn't include. The cynic excludes himself from others and others from himself, and projects onto others that they are excluding him. This justifies his revenge. He either feels excluded or expects to be excluded. The cynic tries to get others to join his team in order to turn them against his enemies. The cynic is a beater warrior who knows, on some level, that he's going to lose, and wants to pull others down with him. Pulling others down is the cynic's win---and his life.

> *Maddy and her father had a morning ritual which gave him great joy: while he read the paper in the dining room, Maddy would pour him a cup of coffee in the kitchen, a few feet away. As she carried his coffee to him, he would take off his reading glasses, put down the paper, and wait for her to spill his coffee into the saucer. In spite of her attempts to set the coffee down without spilling any, she was never able to do so. Even when she filled the cup only half way she still managed to spill it. They both expected her to fail, and she did.*

You cannot play or have fun with a cynic because he takes everything personally, as a rejection or an attack. While visiting her family, Jane wanted to spend some time with her brother. When Jane went to his house for dinner, her mother, a cynic, took it as a personal rejection and made Jane feel guilty for spending time with her brother.

If you tell your competition what you are doing, he instantly compares what you are doing to himself, and reacts in one of two ways. Either he works hard to outdo you or, if he is a cynic, wants to beat and destroy you, and becomes jealous, envious, and tries to hold you down. The competitor works to win; the cynic works to keep from losing. The cynic is not willing to pay the price that you have paid to get where you are or what you have, while the competitor who goes for the win, is willing to pay the price. It is easier to pull you down than to do what it takes to win. This produces an ongoing mediocrity of the spirit and of the soul. The cynic is a beater rather than a winner.

BEATERS AND WINNERS

Though the games and rules vary according to the players, there are three types of competitors: those who want to beat you by holding you down, those who want to win by being victorious over you, and those who flip between the two. The competitors who want to beat you vary in their destructiveness, according to their intellect and level of conscience. They are constantly watching for your weak and vulnerable areas in order to exploit you. They look for your jugular, and never hesitate to stab you at the appropriate moment. On a subconscious level, these competitors feel that they cannot win. They see enemies everywhere and believe that everybody is out to get them. They know that if they don't act <u>first</u>, they will be held down and, ultimately, destroyed. They feel as if they have to defend themselves against annihilation. Because THEY are out to destroy YOU, they figure that YOU are out to destroy THEM, too. They are masters of destruction. Unknowingly, they have to destroy every relationship in their lives for their possessive, controlling parent or family member, especially the ones they care about the most. They use denial to keep from feeling and seeing what they are doing, because if they faced it, they would not be able to stand the enormity of their destructiveness. While they deny hurting or being destructive to others, they interpret truth as criticism, and any disagreement as a threat to their perfect image, security and power. This threat can be anything from a differing opinion to a confrontation. They are highly fault-finding and critical, but cannot tolerate any criticism from others. They expect, and are waiting, to be "gotten," which means rejected, left and/or excluded. In fact, their whole game is designed for them to be "gotten" in order to justify destroying their "enemies" and, in turn, their relationship with them for their possessive, controlling parent or family member.

The other type of competitors want to win. Their peripheral vision enables them to see what they have to do and be in order to do so. They are positive and willing to do whatever it takes. They have an air of confidence, power and independence designed to create a winning image. They are stars that have to shine. They plot and plan, appearing to be unaware of any opposition. The beating technique is intolerable and disdainful to them, as is wimpiness. They will flirt, flatter and flaunt themselves to attract attention, seduce and win over anyone else. In their quest to win, they will run over anyone in their path and deny it to themselves, then feel shocked and hurt when their victim retaliates by getting back at them. Part of their competitive technique is to never allow anyone to see their vulnerability.

When a beater and a winner interact, the winner believes he will win and the beater expects to lose. Because the beater is afraid of the winner's perceived courage and boldness, he supports the winner to his face, but stabs him behind his back. Because the beater hides out behind the person he is competing with and, ultimately, trying to beat, he feels guilt, admiration and envy---guilt because he subconsciously knows he is out to destroy the one he is hiding behind while publicly supporting, and admiration and envy because the winner has the qualities he desires. In a student/teacher relationship, the beater student hates the winner teacher because the teacher has what he wants: the courage, assurance and belief that he will win. He both needs the teacher and hates what he needs. Because he expects to fail, he lacks the courage to do what it takes to get what the teacher has. As a result, he takes out his anger on those with whom he can be superior, or over whom he has power, usually his family, friends and loved ones.

Donna, a winner and successful businesswoman, employed Judy, a beater. Judy was jealous of Donna's success. At staff meetings, Judy was openly supportive of Donna, but behind her back criticized and undermined her to other staff members. The only times Judy showed her true colors were when she felt supported by the team. At these times, she would publicly point out Donna's mistakes. When Donna gave Judy an assignment, she accepted it enthusiastically, but when it came to taking action, Judy would let her down and not fulfill the assignment. Because Judy was trapped and controlled by her possessive, controlling mother, she didn't have choice. So instead of doing what it took to develop the qualities she so desired, Judy took out her unexpressed anger on her family.

When she recognized the enormity of her problem she decided to find out what was causing this with her family. When she saw that she didn't take responsibility for what she did and didn't do, she stopped blaming others and took responsibility for what was happening in every area of her life. What she discovered was that she was controlled by her possessive, controlling mother who did not want her to have any relationships other than with her. Once she broke loose from this control her destruction ceased and she was able to create her dream of a warm and loving family and a business of her own.

The beater constantly stores facts on your weaknesses and on where and how he can destroy you, while denying this to himself. The winner will publicly attack you, while the beater does it behind your back. The only time a beater will attack you publicly is when he feels that he has support on his side. The reason why beaters are terrified of confrontation is because they expect to lose. Winners love to confront others because they know they will win. Both beaters and winners work to gather teams to support them. The winner collects, corrals and teases his conquests. The beater does not want the responsibility of a corral. They both want you to put them on a pedestal and worship them so that they can feel powerful and, subsequently, control and dominate you. This is the only kind of relationship they can have, because their possessive, controlling parent or family member will not allow them to have warm and loving relationships. Both the beater and the winner have to gain total domination, ownership and possession of those with whom they compete. They become overly demanding, inconsistent and unreliable, yet, because they are in denial, see themselves as fair, consistent, reliable, noble and always innocent. They give you what you don't want, expect gratitude, and obligate you to them. Because they have to be justified in their destruction ("After all I've done for you..."), they become masters at blaming. If confronted by a person or a challenge they cannot beat or win, or if they are caught and called on their competition, the whole thing backfires, and they have to destroy themselves, often by destroying their own bodies through illness, injury or death.

Some competitors are flip-floppers, able to change from beater to winner at a moment's notice, according to which technique will work.

Competition is totally self-centered and destructive. As a result, both the beater and the winner are NOT interested in the good of the whole, but only in themselves.

Some competitors know that competition will destroy their relationship with the one they love, so in order to have a relationship with him, they often mentally separate him from their competition and do not compete with him. Or they transfer onto him (mentally making him the parent or family member who controls them), thereby allowing themselves to have a relationship with him. Many deny to themselves that they even compete at all, when in fact, they are fierce competitors who lack respect for people who do not compete.

Do you have a pattern of destroyed relationships with men, women or both? Do you do anything to nurture and support your relationships, or do those with whom you are involved do most or all of the nurturing and supporting? Do you return invitations or are you always the one invited? Do you thank your host or hostess for having invited and included you with either a note, a call or a gift? Or do you have the attitude of a cynic: "They were lucky to have me show up?" Have you noticed that your invitations are few and far between lately? The answers to these questions will assist you to tell yourself the truth about your competition.

Need pushes away. Needing anything puts you in a vulnerable position, which arouses fear. Need _needs_ acknowledgement and approval. When you finally get acknowledgement or approval, your ego puffs up and gives you a powerful feeling of superiority, pride and arrogance. You become better and better at getting what you thought you needed, only to discover that you didn't want it once you got it. This illustrates opposite desires---getting it and losing it. Opposite desires are the cause of failure because when you have opposite desires, unknowingly, you compete with yourself (see chapter: Programming). Competing with yourself is how you keep from giving yourself what you want by remaining undecided, discontented and unable to choose. Competition, opposite desires and need create enormous inconsistencies in your relationships, and cause dissatisfaction with, contempt for, and the desire to destroy those relationships which mean the most to you. This brings up the following questions: Do you have choice? Have you found that your relationships have been destroyed and you do not know why? These are important questions to ask yourself in order to arrive at the truth that competition and its accompanying attitude are causing you problems in your relationships. Make up your mind to tell yourself the truth about competition, who you are competing with if you are, and why, so that you won't continue to deny to yourself what is going on. Since competition destroys relationships, why would you want to continue to compete? If you want to create warm and loving relationships, it is important for you to understand why you are destroying them, and face that your motive is to protect your possessive, controlling parent or family member by giving him what he wants. This relative tells you that he will protect you from the enemy, but you wind up protecting him by making his enemy yours, and by going out and destroying his enemy for him. And the enemy is anyone who he will not allow you have, such as your spouse, sibling, child or friends. This parent or family member manipulates you to make his causes your causes, and sends you out like a soldier to do battle for him. You become his clone. You are not in possession of yourself and don't know it. You function in life like a wind-up toy, totally hypnotized, and fulfilling this parent's or family member's wishes, while unaware of your own. You live life programmed, like a puppet dangling on the end of a string.

The need for the parent's or family member's protection and approval keeps you bound to him and destroying your relationships. You make the parent or family member your "protector," and this gives you your identity as a warrior/competitor and, unknowingly, your purpose for living. Anyone who tells you the truth becomes the enemy because he is exploding the myth that your possessive, controlling parent or family member is the one who knows best. Many people, when they realize that their possessive, controlling parent or family member is not there to protect them, rebel against him and, unknowingly, find themselves in limbo without an identity or a purpose for living. If you have done this, it is necessary to let go of that parent's or family member's control, let go of rebellion, and let go of any anger you may have toward the parent or family member. Accept that you are free to say, "I want" and "I don't want." Forgive the controlling parent or family member, accept him as he is, and accept that you love him. In so doing, you are then free to end competition, to be you, to have what you want and to express your talents and abilities. Make up your mind that you have choice, then choose to be you, and make God your identity.

Competition is very destructive to relationships because there can be only one winner. Since being competitive is so desired and accepted, not to be competitive feels like being an outsider. Each year many people become so depressed by the pressure of competition, the fear of losing, and the loss of self-worth that they take their own lives. Losing makes living too unbearable.

Many people think that if it were not for competition they would sit and do nothing. They believe that they can only accomplish their goals and fulfill their needs in life by competing, and yet, competition creates so much pressure, stress and anxiety that they long to retire, to get out of the game, and to be free from the pressure of competition.

Competition causes resistance and negative thinking. It causes us to see everyone as a potential opponent and enemy, and keeps us looking for their weak points, even in those with whom we are closest. We are constantly comparing ourselves to them to see how we measure up. Competition kills love and creates a fierce game with heartless rules. Children are not free to surpass their parents; spouses are not free to surpass each other. Because of the insecurities it creates, competition causes us to hold others down, to destroy their confidence or sabotage their efforts. This can be done in such subtle ways that the competition is not recognized, even by the participants, and the rewards of competition (the feeling of being the ultimate authority, the winner, being important, good enough or desirable) are short-lived.

When you are winning you forget the devastation, the pain and the feeling of worthlessness you experience when losing. When you win, you often do not believe it's possible ever to lose again, yet you lose far more often than you win. When you earn more money, you win, but you also create more pressure for yourself since now you have to constantly look over your shoulder to see if anyone is gaining on you or trying to take it away from you. If they catch up with you, you feel you have lost in the game of competition and have to retaliate by "getting" them. You "get" them by rejecting them, leaving them and/or excluding them, all of which says to them that they have no worth or value to you.

Professional football players win the game by hitting harder, out-maneuvering and out-scoring their opponents. Their lives appear to be all highs and excitement. Rarely do you hear of the humiliation or feelings of failure and worthlessness they experience when they drop the ball, miss the play or lose the game. If a player gets hurt and has to ride the bench, he is often ostracized by his teammates. The barnyard principle operates in competition: when a chicken becomes ill, the others begin to peck at it. There is no room for weakness, and illness of any kind is considered a weakness. When playing the competitive game, you must be physically, mentally and emotionally strong at all times. If you show any weakness, your opponent will use it against you.

Because winning is so important and so exhilarating to a competitor, and losing is so fearful and so debilitating, the competitor will always get up and try again, regardless of the pain and suffering he experienced. Losing creates a feeling of incompletion and a desire for another chance to win.

A winner will sometimes keep a loser down with an attitude of superiority long after the latest battle has ended. However, the winner never feels victorious for long. He soon must go out and look for another player, the ideal opponent, who will provide a good contest and a never-ending challenge.

Competition in personal relationships follows the same rules as those of a tennis match: competitors in both situations have the same needs. Both are looking for three types of opponents: one who is their equal, one who is slightly inferior and one who is slightly superior. The one who is equal is the most fun; the one who is inferior builds their ego and the one who is superior challenges and stretches their abilities. Unfortunately, competitors in an emotional relationship want all these qualities in one person, and the search for the perfect opponent brings about the demise of many relationships.

Competition motivates and inspires the acquisition of money and position. Because competitors always take into account the other person's position and acquisitions, friends and associates (even those of long-standing) are often discarded if their worth or status drops too low.

> *Barbara and Dorothy were best friends from the fifth grade. Because they came from the same social circle, they went on trips and spent the night together many times. Barbara married an artist. Later, Dorothy became engaged to a very successful businessman. Because Dorothy's mother was not living, Barbara did for Dorothy's wedding everything a mother would do for her daughter's wedding. After the wedding, the newlyweds had Barbara and her husband to dinner on one occasion. This was the last time Barbara ever heard from Dorothy. Because of her husband's business success, Dorothy felt more important than Barbara. Since Dorothy's value of Barbara was based on her social worth, her opinion of Barbara lessened, and she was no longer*

interested in the relationship. When Barbara's husband later became famous, Dorothy wanted to be friends again.

Superficial relationships are based on the status of parents, spouses, social position, material possessions or looks, and don't last.

COMPETITION IN MARRIAGE

Competition in marriage is very destructive to the relationship. Our religious heritage tells us that we should be supportive of our spouses. However, where there is competition, support is impossible. You cannot try to out-do your spouse, and, at the same time, support and cooperate with him. The rules of competition require that you withhold, hold your spouse down, and not give him what he wants, all of which assures the destruction of communication, cooperation and, often, the marriage.

We constantly work to be good enough for our possessive, controlling parent or family member by competing and destroying our relationships with others. If that parent or family member does not want us to be married, we have to either destroy our marriage or remain single.

During an argument, Bob told Sue, "If anything should happen to us and our marriage doesn't make it, my mother will be on my side." With this statement Bob revealed to Sue that he and his mother were a team united in competition against her, and that his mother wanted him to destroy his marriage.

A man and woman bring to their marriage their individual strengths and weaknesses. He has strengths and weaknesses that she doesn't have, and she has strengths and weaknesses that he doesn't have. They complement each other and combine to make 100%. When two people marry it is important that they take their hands out of their parents' hands, and put them in their spouse's hands, and in so doing, become one, each supporting the other until each one's weaknesses become strengths. When a possessive, controlling parent holds onto a son or daughter, the parent's possessiveness prevents this natural transition. It is so important for parents to let their children go so that they might grow up and become strong in their new relationships. Letting them go tells them that their parents believe in them.

> *Ann knew that her possessive mother-in-law was destroying her marriage by holding onto Ann's husband. She begged her mother-in-law to let her son go so that they might have a successful marriage. Her mother-in-law, a true competitor, knowing what Ann wanted, silently refused. Ann worked unsuccessfully right up to her death to get her husband to take his hand out of his mother's hand and put it in hers. Because of competition, she was unable to do so.*

Competition in marriage expresses itself in many destructive ways, one of which is to undermine the spouse, destroying his self-confidence, self-esteem and self-worth. When competing, the undermined spouse often retaliates by preventing the undermining spouse from doing, being and having what he wants. War ensues and winning becomes more important than having a warm and loving relationship.

> *When Nancy married John he was outwardly confident and expressive, while inwardly filled with fears and insecurities. His childhood was spent in boarding and prep schools, and he longed for a home and family. Shortly after their marriage he inherited $250,000. Competition in the business world or sports was sufficient for him. He didn't want to compete with Nancy at home. He wanted to love and be loved, yet because his mother had always been hospitalized and his father had had little to do with him, he didn't know how. Nancy, on the other hand, was a fierce competitor who loved to play the game, and because she was a loner, he was her only opponent. In an attempt to get him to "fight like a man," she persisted in cutting him down, withdrawing her love, withholding sex and threatening to divorce him. She would never give him what he wanted, and mentally, always had one foot out the door. She accused him of failure in his career. She attacked where she knew it would hurt him the most: that it was his inheritance and not his career that provided for them. Nancy claimed that John was never affectionate, yet she withdrew and found it intolerable any time he put his arms around her or touched her. Eventually, she had an affair and told him about it in another attempt to pull him into her competitive game. In the end, it all became intolerable for*

> *him and he left. Nancy had made him her scapegoat, and, unconsciously, wanted him to leave. After he left, he turned to another woman. This made him more interesting and challenging to Nancy, who then wanted him back. She knew that getting him back would be easy and was, therefore, shocked at his new-found indifference to her, which made him even more desirable. The more indifferent he became, the more she wanted him. His last message to Nancy was, "It's too late. I've found someone who doesn't compete with me, but wants me for myself. You'll never control me again." It took three months for her to realize that he wasn't coming back.*

Competition has become so ingrained in us that competitors don't realize that they take it from the business world into their relationships. In a competitive relationship, spouses are unable to praise and admire each other, whereas in a loving, non-competitive relationship they can. The need to compete and win is so strong that the only way to eliminate it is to face how destructive it is to our relationships, and end it.

Anyone you compete with you hate. As a result, your competitor becomes the enemy, even if it's your sibling, best friend, spouse or child. At a sporting event there are two teams on the playing field. You choose one team and the other automatically becomes the enemy. It's the same in a relationship. The Bible teaches women to submit to their husbands. To women who are taught to compete, this is interpreted as weakness and loss of control. And the Bible tells husbands to love their wives. However, because many men are taught to choose their mothers, sisters or families, to choose their wives would be to betray that family member and make the family member the enemy. To choose their family member would be to betray their wives and make their wives the enemy. This is competition. The Bible says, "No servant can serve two masters: for either he will hate the one, and love the other; or else he will hold to the one, and despise the other" (Luke 16:13). Competing in relationships is a lose/lose game with no winners.

> *When Gail was growing up, her parents told her that theirs was the perfect family. They were clannish and drew a circle around themselves which excluded all non-family members. When Gail married, her husband was not included by her family and remained the "outsider" throughout her marriage.*

When he arrived at family gatherings, they would jokingly say, "Here comes the outsider," and Gail laughed along with them. This caused her to emotionally reject him and, in turn, to eventually divorce him.

In competition you can neither give nor receive. If your spouse gives to you, you cannot receive because your spouse is the enemy. If your spouse gives you a gift, you must reject it by denying its worth or devaluing it. More often than not, this rejection is unspoken.

Both of Barbara's husbands showered her with lavish gifts of jewels, cars and furs, but she felt it was beneath her to thank or even acknowledge them for their gifts. Because her possessive, controlling father was her one and only, she was not allowed to have a husband. As a result, she felt contempt for and superior to both husbands, and always wanted to leave. Both her marriages ended in divorce.

After you become aware of how you compete, your mind can deceive you into believing that competition is gone, when in fact it has just become more subtle in its expression. When you forget to do the things your spouse asks you to do or when you do just enough to get by, your mind will prevent you from seeing that this is a non-cooperative, competitive act. Or when you don't listen to or hear your spouse you are unaware that you are competing by not being able to listen or hear. If you find yourself doing something you know will be disruptive to a project in which your spouse is engaged, you can be certain that you are still competing with him on a very subtle level by interrupting the flow. Everyone wants a warm and loving relationship with his spouse, and competition makes this impossible.

The most difficult part of dealing with competition in marriage is not knowing we are doing it, and that the source of it lies in our having chosen our original family instead of our spouse. Because we have never left our original family emotionally, we are unable to be emotionally involved with our spouse.

Competition destroys the glorious enjoyment of love-making between a husband and wife by turning it into "having sex." Once it becomes a sexual act and the fun, excitement and intimacy of love-making are gone, many men and women seek fulfillment outside of marriage where they do not compete, and blame their spouse for causing them to be unfaithful.

They deny to themselves that they are having an affair and believe that they have found their true love who has come to save them from their spouse who, from a man's point of view, doesn't understand them or fulfill their needs, and from a woman's point of view, doesn't love or cherish them. For them it is a win to have an affair because they are involved in the game of competition with their spouse. Many people leave their spouses believing this physical attraction to be love, and marry their lover, only to find themselves in the same competitive war with their new spouse. Many people do not marry because they unconsciously know that marriage often involves competition. In order to avoid competing, they compensate by not marrying. However, marriage is not the problem; competition is.

RECOGNIZING COMPETITION

It is very difficult to see competition in your close family relationships because family members often say one thing and mean another. A spoken message can be different from the way people really feel. It is not uncommon to hear parents tell their children that they "want the very best for them" (to be successful in all areas of their lives), and at the same time, react to a success story by not listening or with discouraging remarks. For example, when a child cleans up his room and is told that he didn't do it "good enough", he soon learns that he will never measure up to his parent's expectations of perfection and, often, stops trying. When a child is told often enough that he is bad or not good enough, he either works harder to get a positive response, or rebels and stops trying. Another tactic used by a parent is to respond to good news with the silent, frosty treatment, thus suggesting disapproval.

The truth is that, on a conscious level, parents really do want their children to succeed, and on a subconscious level, they don't want their children to surpass them. They are unaware that they are giving these opposite messages. Because the competitive parent says one thing and unconsciously feels another, he creates opposite desires in the child. These opposite desires cause the child to feel confused and insecure.

This competitive way of relating becomes an integral part of a person's behavior and is, unknowingly, carried into all future adult relationships. Once relationships are destroyed by competition, those involved don't understand what happened. When you begin to see how you compete, you will begin to recognize how and why you distance your relationships by not giving others what they want. You will see how you react to people who arouse your competitive instincts. Until you have become aware of this competition, you are its victim and competition is your master. Once you see how destructive it is to your relationships, you can let it go and begin to choose to lead a life of cooperation, love and support instead of one of destruction, interfering with the flow and holding down those you care about the most.

You did not know that you chose your possessive, controlling parent or family member to protect and approve of you, you did not know that he is not doing this, and you did not know that you have choice. You also did not know that this has kept you an emotionally crippled child, unable to face and solve your problems, while destroying all the relationships that mean the most to you. It's time to become aware of what you are doing to yourself and your relationships and to grow up and be emotionally and chronologically the same age. Face what you're doing, take responsibility for what you're doing and end it. It's time to end <u>playing</u> the grown up game and <u>be</u> an adult.

<u>Know</u> and <u>accept</u> that you have choice. You do not have to rely on your possessive, controlling parent or family member to protect and take care of you any more. By choosing God and placing God first, you can have God, your family and everyone else. Make up your mind to take full responsibility for your life, for your mind and for all of your relationships, including your relationship with yourself and with God. Let go of competition, and choose God. He will protect you, love you, take care of you, and guide you. He will give you knowledge, wisdom, understanding and, above all, love---love of self, love of mankind, love of life. He will give you adventure and excitement, and will hold your hand while taking you into the unknown, into a world of faith, belief, joy and peace beyond description.

11 Game Playing

WHAT IS THE SECRET behind man's destructiveness to man? What is the main cause of loved ones destroying their relationships with loved ones? What is the major cause of war in families and divorce between two people who love each other? How do you create warm and loving relationships instead of conflict, relationships in which love builds on itself instead of destroying itself? What happened to the man and woman who started out years before madly in love, only to one day discover that love turned to conflict and, in many cases, hatred? Why would a brother value money more than his relationship with his sister, causing him to steal from her? What causes a father to destroy his relationships with his children by always having to be right? What causes a mother to criticize her own daughter to people she doesn't even care about? What causes a parent to favor one child over another, making the rejected one feel unwanted? Why has the home become a battleground instead of the safe haven it can be? Few are willing to take the responsibility to risk asking, "Why? What happened?" Very few are willing to say, "It begins with me." Many are willing to take responsibility for others' problems, but not their own. Most people deal with their problems by either denying their existence, blaming them on others, or dealing with their effects rather than their cause. Instead of going to the cause of the problem, more often than not, they deal with it by playing an intricate, complex game. The need to remain right and blameless, to protect and defend the ego, and to protect and defend the possessive, controlling parent or family member, to give him what he wants, to be good enough for him and to live up to his expectations produces an openly-played, destructive game which, unknowingly deceives, seduces and destroys the relationships which mean the most to them. This cat and mouse game is designed to make competition and destruction fun. It destroys relationships, lives and, in the end, love. The game is the technique used by the game player to keep from having to do anything, to get what he wants without asking, to keep from giving others what they want, and to not only to destroy those relationships which his possessive, controlling parent or family member will not allow him to have, but also those which mean the most to him. The rules change with every opponent. The game is played with everybody and is no respecter of persons. The one exception is those with whom game players refuse to play. These few are the ones with whom they either can't win and/or from whom they want something, such as love, respect, a relationship, approval or money.

Maddy, a game player, was grateful to Paula, another game player, for the kindnesses Paula had shown her. Maddy knew that she could not win in the game with Paula, so she mentally placed her to the side and refrained from playing with her. This enabled them to be friends.

Game players are <u>always</u> leaving, either mentally, physically, or emotionally. If they leave mentally, they cannot listen to you or hear you. If they leave physically, they don't have to be with you or have fun with you. If they leave emotionally, they don't have to love or be loved by you. One game player told his wife of many years, "I don't want to be with you. You're no fun." He had left her mentally and emotionally many years before. Leaving her physically was the third step in the destruction of their relationship.

Game players have to have victims, and search for them wherever they go. The game is life itself to game players. It's all they know. Winning the game is far more important to the game player than warm, loving and intimate relationships. The game creates a life of impatience, tension, analysis and suspicion, a life of beating and winning, a life without joy. In contrast, non-game players are totally unaware of the existence of the game, and don't play, while game players use them as pawns, sadistically enjoying the torture while denying it to themselves. Once a game player backs a non-game player into a corner, he thinks the non-game player is weak and contemptible for allowing himself to be cornered, drops him, and moves on to bigger, better and greater challenges.

Game players are on a team with their possessive, controlling parent or family member, and are at war with those people with whom they are not allowed to have a relationship. Game players make them outsiders by excluding or not including them, according to the game strategy they are using. They play the game to get what they want rather than taking responsibility and asking for it. They manipulate, control, resist and withhold themselves and their love to get the outsider to always respond to and come to them, forcing the outsider to leave while they remain right and blameless. They destroy their relationships without being consciously aware of what they're doing (denial), project onto the person they're destroying and, in so doing, blame him for the failure of the relationship. They fight and destroy their relationships to protect, defend and give their possessive, controlling parent or family member what he wants. That parent or family member gives them no choice but to choose his side and to make those they're not allowed to have, the enemy. For example, some are allowed to have children, but not a spouse; some are allowed to have only one child, and others are allowed to have animals but not children. Game players have to destroy any relationship their possessive, controlling parent or family member won't allow them to have, and playing the game is how they do it. Their accompanying attitude is one of contempt, and the energy resulting from this attitude poisons the atmosphere.

> *Susan, a game player, could only have the relationships her possessive, controlling father allowed her to have. Susan wanted to give her father what he wanted. Her father did not want her to be married, and called Jim, her husband, "the outsider." She, too, referred to him as "the outsider." From the day she married Jim she knew that it was just a matter of time before they would be divorced, and ten years and two children later, they were.*

Because the game player can only have a relationship with his possessive, controlling parent or family member, the only way he can have a relationship with anyone else is to subconsciously transfer that parent or family member onto the person with whom he wants the relationship, mentally making him his possessive, controlling parent or family member. As a result, he reacts to the people who mean the most to him as if they were his possessive, controlling parent or family member. This prevents him from seeing them as they are. Instead he sees them as thinking, acting and being that parent or family member. As a result, the relationship is a sham.

The game player blames and hates others for excluding or not including him, yet he does the same to them, according to the game strategy he is using. This non-verbal message tells those excluded or not included that they are undesirable, not good enough, and unworthy of the game player. The game player withholds himself so that others will come to him, which places him in the position of power where he is free to reject them. This makes him feel victorious. Excluding others is the cruelest form of torture. It destroys their self-confidence, self-esteem and self-worth, and makes them feel rejected, abandoned, alone and of no value. Those excluded feel like outcasts, totally unwanted, undesirable and worthless. Exclusion empowers game players to move on without a backward glance except to gloat over their victory. When game players are exposed and can no longer use the game, they turn their destruction inward to punish and destroy themselves. There is a law of cause and effect that works unceasingly. <u>If you destroy what means the most to another, you will inevitably destroy what means the most to you.</u> In order to keep from facing the enormity of the destruction they are creating, game players go into total denial. However, their subconscious mind knows and causes them to punish themselves physically, mentally and/or emotionally.

> *After Bob beat his wife and threw her across the room, he went into total denial and had no recollection of his destruction. However, later his back became so painful that he could not lift the heavy equipment which he used on his job. This made it impossible for him to work. Unknowingly, he was physically punishing himself for his destructive behavior toward his wife, though mentally denying it to himself.*

> *When Don accused his sister of the dishonesty of which <u>he</u> was guilty, and told his family what she had done, he went into denial. To punish himself, he developed arthritis in his hands, which prevented him from playing baseball, his favorite hobby.*

Game players are taught how to play the game by their possessive, controlling parent or family member. Not only are they required to destroy their relationships, but they are taught how to use the game to do so. Much confusion is created when the parent or family member uses one strategy with one child, and another with his siblings. Even greater confusion, to the point of feeling crazy, is created when other family members don't see what's going on.

The game is dangerous and inevitably backfires on game players by destroying the relationships they want the most. Often the only way for them to end the game is to see that the opponent who has meant the most to them doesn't care any more, has left and is not coming back---and it's too late to do anything about it. It can take months, and often, years, before the game player realizes this. The game is so much a part of what game players are that it is not until they are willing to face themselves and their possessive, controlling parent or family member that they can end the game and the destruction of their relationships forever. Until game players face what they are doing and end it, it is impossible for them to ever have warm and loving relationships.

We are given the message, as young children, that we are bad or not good enough to express our talents and abilities. When we first begin to express ourselves, our possessive, controlling parent or family member holds us down or back by telling us that we are bad, or that what we are doing is not good enough and that we are, therefore, less than perfect. From that moment on, we work unceasingly not to be bad or to get good enough in order to measure up to the expectations of this parent or family member. We hold ourselves back, put a bushel basket over our Light, and squelch our talents and abilities. We stop expressing ourselves, begin to seek approval, and work to prove that we are not bad and that we are good enough. We try to get this approval by being how he wants us to be. Approval and recognition are like a drug to the game player, and it is this approval and recognition which are dangled before him to control him.

Game players are paper tigers without power. They are cowards who use fear tactics to make us afraid, and are terrified we won't be.

Control Tactics

There are many tactics which are used to control us, such as the withholding of love, pity, anger, charm, the threat of leaving, mental seduction, sexual seduction, dividing and conquering, negative suggestion, non-stop talking, excluding, not including, walling off, and choosing sides. The purpose of this control is to hold on to us and keep us from leaving.

The withholding of love is often used by possessive, controlling parents or family members to control. This withholding of love tells us that we are not yet good enough or worthy of their love. Withholding is used to keep us on their side and to maintain total control of us.

Being pitiful is another common control tactic. The possessive, controlling parent's or family member's demeanor reflects a call for help without having to ask. The tactic is self-pity; the motive is control.

Anger/rage is another control tactic. Possessive, controlling parents or family members can go from a raised voice to rage, whatever it takes to achieve the desired results, which are that we feel guilty, fearful and bad for having caused their unhappiness. Unknowingly, they have given us the responsibility for their happiness and we've taken it, freeing them to blame us and make us the victims when we do not fulfill their unexpressed needs and expectations.

The threat of our possessive, controlling parent or family member leaving us arouses our greatest fear: being left and, therefore, alone. To a child, the worst thing that can be done to him is to be left, and all game players know this. As children and adults, this tactic arouses enormous fear that can last for life.

> *Susie, at age 5, was upsetting her mother. Without warning, her mother picked up her purse and walked out the door, saying she was leaving because of Susie's misbehavior. The resulting terror that Susie felt then has continued to control her life until now, at age 40, she is fearful and becomes depressed whenever anyone leaves---for any reason: work, shopping, a social event, and so forth.*

Mental seduction is used by possessive, controlling parents or family members to get us to choose their side against others. Mental seduction is a mind game used to unconsciously control us, take choice from us, keep us from thinking, and prepare us to be sexually seduced. They give us one choice---them. Once this choice is made, they own us.

Sexual seduction is played by giving us the non-verbal message that we are sexually desirable. Our possessive, controlling parent or family member first tells us we are desired, then tells us we are not. As a result we feel undesirable, weakened and, ultimately, controlled. This parent or family member sends out the sexual message and withholds the sexual act. On the one hand, we are told that we are sexually desirable, but on the other, it is not acted on. In the end, sexual seduction destroys our confidence, our self-esteem and our self-worth. The possessive, controlling parent or family member who uses sexual seduction creates enormous confusion in us because this message is not acted on. Later, the seduction leaves us incapable of having a normal sexual relationship with our spouse. As an adult we feel guilty for wanting to express ourself sexually with our spouse, and don't understand the guilt. The guilt comes from expressing ourselves sexually with our spouse when, subconsciously, we know that our possessive, controlling parent or family member doesn't want us to. Sexual seduction is so powerful because it gets us on a primal level and arouses one of our strongest desires. Sexual seduction and its accompanying teasing teaches us to tease others. There is a difference between being sexually attracted and attractive to somebody, and being sexually seductive or seduced. The first one is a natural attraction; the second is used to play the game. Sexual seduction is different from sexual molestation. Sexual seduction is only in the mind, whereas sexual molestation is physical.

The father who sexually seduces his daughter, or the mother who sexually seduces her son does so by nonverbally and nonphysically giving the child the message that he or she is sexually desired by the parent. The father does this to get the daughter on his side against her mother, and the mother does this to get the son on her side against his father. They use their children as pawns in their competitive war games with each other. They also use this tactic to keep their son or daughter from desiring boyfriends or girlfriends, thereby never leaving them.

Mental and sexual seduction are the height of selfishness and self-centeredness. This seduction keeps children in bondage to the possessive, controlling parent or family member for life or until the children grow up and release themselves from this bondage.

Dividing and conquering is a tactic common to all game players. Possessive, controlling parents or family members use this technique to turn you against someone you desire. He does so by planting a negative thought in your mind against this person, causing you to doubt that person or yourself while, at the same time, keeping you bonded to him (the parent or family member) for life, and terrified of betraying him. The parent or family member flatters, flirts and/or teases you to get you to notice him. Once he sees that you are open to his suggestion, he makes fun of, criticizes or causes you to doubt the other person and, in the end, yourself. You then automatically return to that parent or family member to restore the confidence in yourself that he destroyed in the first place. Once you have been conquered and are on his team, you are then open to his negative suggestions and control.

Negative suggestion is used to destroy while remaining innocent. A glance, a raised eyebrow or a vocal inflection can be used to plant the seed of doubt.

One mother gave her son the negative message that all women were out to get him. As a result, he didn't trust any women. Her unspoken message was "I'm the only woman you can trust." When he married, he unconsciously believed that his wife was out to get him. This put him in a defensive and resistant position with her, never trusting, believing, listening to or hearing her.

Non-stop talking is another control tactic that is easily recognized. The possessive, controlling parent or family member maintains center stage with this technique by monopolizing every conversation.

Excluding is a mental technique used to manipulate and control. When using this tactic, the possessive, controlling parent or family member refuses to look at the child. The parent or family member might, for example, invite others to go to a movie in the presence of the child, who he excludes. Excluding, subtlty or blatantly, inflicts pain and hurt on its victims.

Not including is even more subtle than excluding. Only top game players can pull this one off. When a game player walks into a room, he instantly feels who will play the game and who won't, and does not include those who won't and those he cannot beat or with whom he cannot win. He always knows how his victim is responding to his non-inclusion without looking at him. If the one not included walks away, the game player becomes angry.

Walling off puts an impenetrable barrier between the possessive, controlling parent or family member and the child. This walling off hurts the child, makes him feel unwanted, and pushes him away.

When the game player chooses sides, he protects and defends his side from his perceived enemies, and these "enemies" can be the ones he loves the most. This is the insanity of the game. The game is no respector of persons.

Charm is used when all else fails. The possessive, controlling parent or family member becomes charming, agreeable, cooperative and/or humorous in order to maintain control. This is the one control tactic that makes a relationship possible with a possessive, controlling parent or family member.

These control tactics are used by possessive, controlling parents or family members to get you to protect them, always be there for them and take responsibility for their happiness. Unconsciously, you feel compelled and impelled to live up to their expectations and, in so doing, are controlled by them for life.

> *Jane was in the hospital recovering from painful surgery for a tubal pregnancy. Instead of comforting his daughter and easing her pain, her father sat at the end of her bed looking pitiful. His nonverbal message was "Don't expect anything of me. I'm the one who needs help."*

In order to be free from control, it is imperative that you be free from needing or wanting ANYTHING from your possessive, controlling parent or family member. Once you release any need from this parent or family member, you are then free to have a relationship with them without control. Breaking this control isn't easy, but it is essential for your freedom.

Most game players do not know they are playing. One student who was aware that she played sexual seduction games made the decision to end it after marrying because she knew it would be destructive to her marriage.

Two of the most important words used to get what you want are "I want." If you were never allowed to say, "I want" or "I don't want" as a child, you learn to manipulate and play the game to get what you want. If you take two children and, all things being equal, one is taught to say, "I want" and "I don't want," and the other is not permitted to do so, you will have two children who react and respond to life entirely differently. One will be real, free to express his talents and abilities, be himself, have what he wants, and be free to rely on God; the other will act the part, learn to manipulate, control, and rely on his wits, intellect or personality to get what he wants.

To the game player, any want or desire is a weakness to be exploited. The game involves finding out what others want and withholding it from them. To the game player, the true winner is the one who can get you to come to him, freeing him to withhold what you want. He is the one who is desired and, therefore, in control. The game player believes in the concept of "limited supply." According to this belief, if he gives you what you want, there won't be enough for him, and in giving you what you want, you will have won. Getting what he wants and not giving you what you want is the core of the game. The game player can't say, "I want" or "I don't want" because his possessive, controlling parent or family member won't allow him to. So he learns to manipulate to get what he wants, pretending not to want anything. (The less you want, the better game player you are.) He grows up not taking responsibility for what he wants, but is a master at knowing what you want. He is always looking to see how far he can go. He gives you what _he_ wants to give you, and at times, he even gives you what _you_ want, but it has to be _his_ idea and on _his_ terms. If you have to ask a game player for what you want, it means he hasn't thought of it and is, therefore, less than perfect. Your asking for what you want is what triggers the game. As a child, he was not supposed to ask for what he wanted. If you cannot ask for what you want, you cannot create it. Therefore, because the game player cannot ask, he expects you to read his mind. If you don't, you are to blame. As a result, communication and cooperation are impossible with a game player because the game begins with the slightest request, question or implication that he might be bad, not good enough, wrong or less than perfect. He misinterprets everything said and takes it the wrong way. If you ask the game player for something or ask him to do something, he takes it personally, hears it as a bad or not good enough message, interprets it as though he should have already done it, and withholds by doing only as much as is necessary to get by. His need to remain right, perfect and good enough in his own eyes is so great that, even in the student/teacher relationship, where the game player wants to be coached, he will become angry with his teacher for asking him to do anything---and will resist doing it.

The way to end the game is to face it, tell yourself the truth about it, make up your mind to end it, and make up your mind that you are free to say, "I want" and "I don't want."

The non-game player finds it difficult, if not impossible to interact with the game player. The game player knows that the non-game player is trustworthy, but the game player doesn't trust anyone. Instead he keeps trying to destroy the non-game player. If that doesn't work, he tries to destroy the relationship. Non-game players do not even know that games are being played, so they don't understand the fear of getting "gotten" or the sadistic actions of the game player. How can you get "gotten" when you don't know or care about the rules? Why would anyone want to "get" someone else? What is there to "get?" Non-game players feel like they are on a tennis court, being swatted from all sides. Because they don't know what's happening, they get emotionally hurt and beaten up, but it is impossible for them to lose the game because they are not playing. Playing the game with a non-game player is like hitting a defenseless child. The game player is unaware of the amount of pain he's inflicting on the non-game player, as well as himself. He doesn't feel his own pain because he's in denial. He can't feel anything. Denial and innocence lead to the "make you crazy" game, in which the non-game player thinks there is something wrong with him. This can cause a non-game player to have a nervous breakdown, which is designed to please the game player's possessive, controlling parent or family member.

In his heart of hearts, the game player wants to end the game, and wants the non-game player to draw a line and not allow him to cross it. The game player doesn't take responsibility for the problems he's creating, but wants the non-game player to do it for him. He keeps pushing the non-game player to see how far he can go, until the non-game player makes up his mind that the game player will go no further. The non-game player's reluctance to draw the line infuriates the game player. It's like waving a red flag at a bull. When the non-game player <u>does</u> take this responsibility and draws his line, the game player again becomes furious: "How dare you not allow me to kick you in the teeth." There comes a time when the non-game player makes up his mind that the game player has gone as far as he will allow him to go. At that time, the game player <u>must choose</u> between ending the game or leaving. This is when it becomes obvious that the game is an addiction, because he can't stop. He does not have choice. He has taken the one choice he has been given, which is to be on his possessive, controlling parent's or family member's team. The non-game player has to stop caring about the game player, wall off and walk away. This frees the game player to free himself from the game, and allows him to end it and his destruction. He is trapped for life until the non-game player stops responding to his destruction and goes on with his life, expressing his talents and abilities, enjoying himself and having fun every second.

Game players want what they can't have, then when they get it, they don't want it. They don't think anyone is worthy of their love, so they're always looking for someone better and more interesting.

Game players have to always remain right, blameless and perfect in their own minds, as well as in the minds of others. They will do anything to be right: lie, cheat, steal, use their friends or take advantage of family members. They have no morals, remorse, principles, conscience or integrity, though they believe otherwise. They feel free to do whatever they want, because the end justifies the means. They don't tell the truth to themselves or others. Their lives become a lie. They live in total denial of what they're doing. They believe themselves to be really nice people.

The verbal repartee of the game is socially acceptable. It is fun, and feels like harmless play to the game player. In truth, it is designed to destroy love, people and, in the end, relationships. The game player doesn't consciously know this, but if he looked within and told himself the truth, he would know that he is deceiving himself because he is always nervous, unsettled and ill-at-ease. He doesn't realize that what to him is a game, in reality, is war, and that the war is killing his relationships with the ones who mean the most to him. War is about competition; the game is about destroying the spoils of war. The game player doesn't dare care, look at or face this truth because the game is all he knows and he is terrified of betraying his possessive, controlling parent or family member. The game player wants constant feeding, care and attention. He wants to be pampered like a prima donna and served like a king. But once served, he becomes arrogant, superior and contemptuous toward the one serving him. The game player believes himself to be generous, but only gives in order to get. Every gesture, every thought, every action is calculated to get the results he wants: being #1, and in most cases, one and only. Having a warm, loving, intimate or close relationship with a game player is beyond hopeless, it's impossible. Protecting his ego and his possessive, controlling parent or family member, and destroying for him are all that matter to him. The exception is a short-term relationship like an affair, in which it is possible to be sexually intimate for a brief period of time without involvement or commitment. This is another technique designed to destroy relationships. Sometimes there can be warmth, love and intimacy in a long-term relationship when the two people don't spend a lot of time together.

The game player is out to destroy the leader (his teacher, boss, president of the company, and so forth), by gathering teams and turning people against him. Because the game player is afraid of being found out, he will be nice to the leader's face, while stabbing him in the back to others. Because the game player is undermining the leader, he feels guilty around him, especially if they are "friends." Though the game player is in denial, he cannot deny to himself the discomfort he feels in the leader's presence, although he blames the leader for it. He wants the leader to play the game so that he can destroy him without guilt. The game player's plan is to expose the leader by proving him wrong, then step in and take his place. If someone exposes the game player (tells the truth about what he is doing), the game player becomes furious, because his reason for living (the game) has been threatened. The person telling the truth then becomes the enemy and must be destroyed, even if that person is the one the game player loves most in the world. Neither one is aware of the degree of this destruction.

Game players can stop destroying each other and unite against a common enemy. In this union they feel a kinship with each other. Truth is the common enemy of all game players, because it exposes them and the control by their possessive, controlling parents or family members. On a team devoted to Truth and self-knowledge, the teacher (Truth) is the common enemy. On a subconscious level the game playing team can unite against the teacher by closing their eyes to the destruction of their teammates, thereby silently permitting the destruction to continue. This unspoken collusion makes allies of former enemies against a perceived enemy---the teacher.

The game player chooses sides and forces you to do the same, manipulating you into choosing his. If you do, you are "for" him. If you don't, you are "against" him. By choosing the game player's side, you give him power, which gives him control over you.

> *Early in Judy's spiritual training, her teacher corrected her in front of another student, who was also Judy's client. This so humiliated Judy, that she asked her teacher, "Are you my friend or my teacher?" What she was really asking was, "Are you for me or against me?" Her teacher's reply was, "I am your friend <u>and</u> your teacher."*

The game player wants to war, and the non-game player wants to have a warm, loving relationship. The non-game player can't understand the undercurrent he feels when he is with the game player. Nor does he understand having to begin anew each time they get together, though they may have been friends or spouses for years. When the non-game player begins talking, it feels to him that the game player is not there. The truth is, he isn't. He is back in his head, determining the next move. When the non-game player is walking hand in hand with the game player, the non-game player is enjoying the walk and just being there, while the game player is gathering ammunition (information) and making ready for combat. Because the game player's only reality is whether he is winning or losing, he instinctively categorizes everything as either a win or a loss.

A relationship between a game player and a non-game player is like that of two people living in a country where they both speak the same language, but the dialects are so different that they can't understand one another.

Game players compare you unfavorably to other people, are always criticizing you, either verbally or mentally, and project onto you that <u>you</u> are criticizing <u>them</u>.

Some game-playing women hide behind their femininity, posing as china dolls who need to be protected and taken care of. Often, behind this facade hides a fierce, warrior/game player. There are men posing as gentle, loving, caring, nice guys who tell you that they will take care of you and protect you, but who flee at the first sign of danger. Behind this nice guy facade, they are fierce Goliaths wearing steel armor, who leave you to be on your own. Battlefields reveal the truth. This is where heroes, bullies and cowards are unclothed and discovered. Game players are cowards who pose as heroes, in order to be seen as such, and cynical game players are coward/bullies. Battlefields are places where you can't hide out, and the game player knows it. To the game player, battlefields provide the arena for war to be waged without guilt, a place where he can freely do battle and leave destruction in his wake.

Confrontations reveal the truth. In a marriage, when a confrontation is imminent, the game player uses the threat of leaving or divorce to avoid the truth that would come out of the confrontation. To avoid telling the truth he sidesteps the issue. On the job, the game player uses the same technique, the threat of leaving, to avoid a confrontation.

THE MASTER MIND

The master mind is the penultimate game player. He always has a plan to keep you under his control. He plans his stategy and has a back-up plan in case his first plan doesn't work. He secretly watches his prey to gain the necessary information that will assure his win. This game player has the greatest capacity to hide out, and derives sadistic pleasure from torturing his victims. Winning at all costs is what his life is about, and winning to him means being in control. He tells himself that he has won, even if he hasn't. He never forgets a wrong or an insult, and can (and will) hold a grudge for years. He attacks you behind your back, and "gets" you if you humiliate, embarrass or threaten to expose him. If he ever feels that he owns you, you become his helpless victim and slave. The solution is self-confidence and not caring what the master mind thinks. In so doing, you are able to bond with him, and he with you. Bonding is a loving, caring, supportive feeling between two people which enables them to have a warm and loving relationship with each other.

The master mind uses the escape of inconsistency to keep his victim off-balance and to keep him proving himself, responding to him, and coming to him so that he can keep his victim in the palm of his hand. For example, in a boy/girl relationship, the master mind keeps his girlfriend doubting his loyalty. The master mind's victim sees his inconsistency as moodiness, and the master mind uses this inconsistency to control. He believes that he can't stop it, however, the truth is that he _can_ stop by ceasing to listen to his possessive, controlling parent or family member, by taking responsibility for his life and happiness, and by accepting that he is a precious, adorable angel.

The master mind tries to make himself important to those who are important to him, and he can accept advice from an authority who he admires and respects.

The master mind is a coward who is terrified of being exposed. If he is told that he has made a mistake and is, therefore, less than perfect, he has to destroy his accuser. To assist him to end this, you have to be willing to leave.

The master mind is always analyzing and strategizing. He acts like your friend in order to gather useful information. He cheats to win, and has contempt for his victims. If you refuse to be his pawn, he has to destroy you. There is no way to have success with him.

Master minds give the appearance of being calm, self-confident, in charge and caring. They look innocent while planning their next attack.

The only way to end being the master mind's victim is to let go of being a victim, and be willing to go it alone.

THE PSYCHOTIC MASTER MIND

The psychotic master mind can and will become enraged when he doesn't get what he wants. He is cruel and cool. He is addicted to winning the game at all costs, and will resort to murder or suicide to win. The psychotic master mind believes he is intellectually superior to all people. If someone makes him feel inferior by not giving him what he wants, he instantly becomes violently enraged. He is extremely jealous, and rejection triggers his rage. Once his rage is triggered, it's out of control.

The psychotic master mind is always right in his own mind. He cannot be wrong. He can be incorrect, but not WRONG. He will make himself right at others' expense by making <u>them</u> wrong. Because he can't see anything the way it is, he never believes anyone is telling him the truth.

THE FOUR STRATEGIES

The game consists of four different strategies or ways of playing. They are: pompous, angry/vindictive, defensive/paranoid and cooperative. These strategies are used by the game player to get what he wants without having to ask or take responsibility, and to conquer and ultimately destroy his relationships, all this to get good enough for his possessive, controlling parent or family member. Game playing begins with the pompous strategy. Game players who were made special by their possessive, controlling parents or family members use this strategy. Because the pompous strategy is so unacceptable in polite society, the game player using it soon realizes that he is disliked. When he sees that everyone is leaving him, he moves into the second strategy, becomes angry and vindictive, and blames his opponents for rejecting and leaving him, all the while, refusing to take responsibility for his unacceptable behavior. The game player then becomes defensive and fearful and, in so doing, moves into the defensive/paranoid strategy where he becomes terrified of being accused of making a mistake, being less than perfect, and therefore, bad. When he sees that this doesn't work he moves into the cooperative strategy where he tries to give you what you want, but in reality gives you what he thinks you want.

The game player knows instantly when he has been called into battle, and will choose his method of attack accordingly. To the game player, everything, including love, is a strategy calculated to get him what he wants without having to ask. The game player's life is about looking for others' weaknesses so he can destroy his relationships with them. A game player can change tactics in the middle of a conversation, and an astute game player subconsciously knows when strategies are taking place. Once the game player lets go of a strategy and moves into the next one, he can stay in it for life and not return to the previous strategy. For example, once he makes up his mind to move out of the pompous strategy, he automatically moves into angry/vindictive, and will not return to pompous.

The four strategies correspond to the four sequential levels of learning: thought, feeling, habit and mood (see chapter 3.)

The Pompous Strategy

When the game player is in the first level of the game he is using the pompous strategy. Pomposity is intimidating, and reflects and implies an attitude of superiority. It is an act. It is not real. Pomposity is the ultimate in self-importance and self-centeredness. The pompous game player believes he is "royalty" and buys his own sale. He sees everyone else as an underling, a subordinate or an inferior, and treats them like servants and, sometimes, slaves. He doesn't say, "I want" or "I don't want," but acts bossy and tells others what to do. When a game player is using the pompous strategy, he feels and, most importantly, believes that he is a superior human being. He has an air of arrogance, and acts as if he is better than the masses. This makes people want to get away from him. Pomposity is an extreme form of prejudice. Of the four strategies, pomposity feels the best to a game player, as the act of superiority gives him a sense of confidence and power, but in reality, it is a false sense and rarely lasts. The fall is, in direct proportion, as low as the win is high. In the pompous mind, you, the adversary, have already lost the battle because he is naturally superior, so he never loses---and you can't ever win. Therefore, he believes you are foolish to even challenge his authority. The more insecure the game player, the easier it is for him to remain in the pompous strategy. This strategy is used to keep from feeling bad or less than perfect. Problems do not exist to the pompous player---he knows that someone beneath him will solve them.

Those with no self-worth can begin a life of game playing and move into pompous with the simplest of statements. One student moved into pompous when asked how to spell a word.

For the pompous player, everything is always his way. He knows it all and knows what is best for you. He lives his life _his_ way, oblivious to what others want. He is a star who basks in his own glory, and can only hear praise and acknowledgement of himself. He is so wrapped up in himself that he doesn't see others as people or think about what they want. He is arrogant, superior and elite, and keeps others coming to and responding to him.

Pompous players want to be worshipped, desired and put on a pedestal. Their greatest fear is being knocked off this pedestal. They are uninvolved, like a statue on a mantle, use fake self-confidence to impress their opponents, and don't take responsibility for their destructiveness.

The pompous player mows people down, constantly hurts, and thinks nothing of it. If he decides to see and face the destruction he has created, he can end this strategy forever. When he does, he automatically moves into the angry/vindictive strategy.

The Angry/Vindictive Strategy

When the game player is in the second level of the game, he's using the angry/vindictive strategy, and is always looking for something on which to vent his anger and/or rage. The energy from this strategy poisons the atmosphere to such a degree that it is felt strongly by those in his presence. He is a rebel looking for a cause; a soldier looking for a war. If the angry/vindictive player can't find a cause or principle to fight for, he will find a person on whom to vent his anger or rage. He constantly judges the imperfections of others. Politics is an arena for the angry/vindictive player. It gives him a cause and a candidate to fight for, and an opponent on whom to vent his anger. He wants his candidate to be angry and vindictive, also. Religion is another arena in which the angry/vindictive player comes alive, fighting in the name of God. ("My religion versus your religion," "My God versus your God," "My beliefs versus your beliefs.") To the angry/vindictive player, love is a sign of weakness, and he has little patience with it.

Angry/vindictive players have an aggressive energy about them. In this strategy they vent their anger and rage, express their resentment, and right the wrongs of this imperfect world. They feel that this is their "job." It makes them feel like "somebody." If the angry/vindictive player cannot judge and criticize, he is nobody, is not needed, and believes he must leave the team. He knows that he is often disliked, and doesn't even like himself, but feels that what he is doing is important. This allays his fears of being kicked out. He is always leaving, whether in mind, body or spirit before he is found out and exposed. He is a trouble-maker without choice who uses mental and sexual seduction to control and destroy. He destroys his relationships by "getting" them before they "get" him. The angry/vindictive player places expectations on everyone. When these expectations are not met, he is always hurt and disappointed. He uses this hurt and disappointment to blame those who have let him down, and to justify his anger and ultimate revenge. He uses love, God and people to get what he wants, which is to destroy. He is a right and blameless destroyer who denies what he's doing to himself and others. Consequently, he doesn't take responsibility for his actions. He sees everything negatively and 180 degrees from how it is.

Meditating or being still with God seems boring to the angry/vindictive player. Non-game players are also boring to him. He's always looking for new players and challenges. This player juggles two different agendas: while he's proving himself to be trustworthy and who he says he is, at the same time he's resisting his opponents and getting them to prove themselves and respond to him. In so doing he sets his opponents up to be destroyed for his possessive, controlling parent or family member. He wants you to tell him he is not bad, puts up a wall to keep you from doing it, and gets angry with you if you do. At the same time, he is constantly waiting, even demanding that you tell him he is bad in order to justify his revenge.

The angry/vindictive player cannot say, "I want" and "I don't want," nor does he allow others to say, "I want" and "I don't want." He experiences anger when someone says, "I want," and rage when they say, "I don't want." This rage triggers his vindication. He has a constant low-grade anger which can be felt by others.

> *Tom's roommate asked him to shut his door because his music was so loud. This simple request angered Tom. After letting go of the game, he was able to see his anger and inability to allow others to say "I want."*

The angry/vindictive player is mean. If another game player excludes him, he will retaliate in the way that will cause the most pain. This ability to exclude and hurt others gives him pleasure and joy when he sees the pain on the face of the one he's excluded. When non-game players are excluded, they are hurt and don't understand why, because they don't understand the game.

The angry/vindictive player can hold a grudge for years, and is always waiting for his opportunity to retaliate. Time doesn't matter. He knows his opportunity will come. He is like a cat waiting to leap on a mouse. His whole life is about vindication, and he will lie to be vindicated. He lives to get you back.

> *When Gail was a young mother, her neighbor, Cathy said something that humiliated her. While Gail never said anything to anyone, for 50 years she held on to that scene, carried resentment and waited for her opportunity to get Cathy back. The opportunity presented itself when Cathy wanted to join Gail and a mutual friend on a trip to Europe. Gail refused to let her join them and said, "I finally 'got' her." She felt gloriously victorious---she'd finally gotten her revenge.*

The angry/vindictive player stirs things up because he is uncomfortable with peace. If things are too peaceful and loving, there's no place for him. He doesn't belong. There's no room for anger and trouble in a loving, peaceful environment. He must either stir things up or leave.

Angry/vindictive players believe in lack and are, therefore, possessive and tenacious of what is theirs. They think in terms of "my children" rather than "our children," "my money" rather than "our money," "my friends" rather than "our friends," and so on.

Angry/vindictive players are rigid, demanding and structured. They look for what is less than perfect in their loved ones by comparing them to a more perfect example, hoping that their loved ones will shape up and reflect well on them, for if they have the perfect child, spouse and so forth, that tells them that they, in turn, are perfect.

Angry/vindictive people love to be with each other. They play off each other, and fan the flames of anger, hatred and destruction. They really hate themselves, and project this hate onto others. They feel wronged, victimized and have to seek vengeance. This justifies their vindication, criticism and judgment. They cannot forgive because that, somehow, excuses the person who has hurt them. They must always remember the hurtful incident. They are martyred, filled with self-pity and want you to feel sorry for them.

It's not enough for the angry/vindictive game player to be angry, he wants you to be angry, also. If he can't get you angry, this makes him angrier, and he'll keep on trying until he does. Some angry/vindictive game players are out front with their temper while others hide it. You always know that the "out front" player is going to explode about something, and that it's just a matter of time before he does. Some angry/vindictive players are in such denial that they can fool themselves and not even know they are angry.

Angry/vindictive players have had choice taken from them by their possessive, controlling parent or family member. Until they make up their minds to take responsibility for their minds, accept they have choice and choose, they will be forever doomed to a life of anger and destruction.

As long as the angry/vindictive player continues to hate himself, he will continue to destroy himself, and will project his hate onto others, justifying his destruction of them. The only way to end this is to love himself, for if he loves himself, he can then love others.

When the angry/vindictive player sees and faces how destructive he has been in this strategy, he experiences grief. If he chooses to end this strategy forever, he then automoatically moves into the defensive/paranoid strategy.

The Defensive/Paranoid Strategy

When the game player is in the third level of the game he is using the defensive/paranoid strategy. Those game players in this strategy are always compensating for the "not-good-enough" message they received as children by forever striving to defend themselves from this message. They live their lives in terror of making a mistake and being told that they are not good enough and, at the same time, expect it. In an effort to avert the inevitable, they constantly defend themselves from anticipated rejection, and mentally rehearse conversations in preparation for this rejection. They are terrified that the ax is going to fall, know it is going to happen, and feel relieved when it does. At least then they have some relief, if only temporary, from the constant tension and pressure of their terror. Their lives are about defending themselves for not getting the job done, protecting themselves from being told they're not good enough and pulling away without really leaving. If the defensive/paranoid player turns his terror inward, he becomes depressed.

Defensive/paranoid players have incredible opposite desires which cause inconsistency, and contribute to the failure of their relationships. These opposite desires make communication difficult with this game player. It is this inconsistency that can make you think you're crazy. The defensive/paranoid player feels not good enough, and wants his spouse to confirm it. If his spouse tries to convince him that he is good, he begins to feel like "somebody," and becomes proud. However, this pride is short-lived and quickly followed by a fall.

The life of the defensive/paranoid game player is spent living on the edge of a deep chasm into which the slightest "not good enough" message sends him plummeting. Trying to get good enough is an addiction in which he has no choice, no rights and no control. Almost all his thoughts are consumed by his imaginary defenses against anticipated not good enough messages. He lives in total denial because he can't stand the pain of being not good enough.

> *Staying in the defensive/paranoid strategy destroyed one man's life. He was part of the allied invasion of Normandy, France during World War II. When the troops hit the Normandy beach, they had no cover or protection. They were out in the open, totally exposed to enemy fire, and thousands lost their lives. In order to protect himself, this soldier covered himself with the bodies of two dead soldiers and pretended to be dead while his best friend moved on with the rest of their company. The soldier has lived a tortured life of regrets, remorse, guilt, sorrow and anguish every day for fifty years. After the war he lost track of his best friend. Fifty years later they found each other. Tearfully he begged his friend's forgiveness for having "played dead" to avoid being shot. His friend told him that there was nothing for him to forgive, that his life was filled with happiness because once the war was over he was able to leave it behind, but that the soldier needed to forgive himself. Living in the defensive/paranoid game has been what has tortured him and destroyed his happiness.*

The defensive/paranoid player has to always be right. When confronted on a mistake, he makes excuses, justifies, presents facts, and defends himself rather than simply solving the problem.

> *When Judy, on retreat with her team, failed to let her spiritual coach know what time it was, she was afraid her coach would get angry at her. Instead of taking responsibility for not doing her job, she began to mentally build her case and defend herself by thinking that her coach was ganging up on her and her co-producer. Her coach was not ganging up on her, but simply telling her what she wanted, which was to know the time.*

The defensive/paranoid player is afraid you will see him as less than perfect and reject him. This fear of rejection prevents him from saying, "I want" and "I don't want." He does allow others to say, "I want," but not, "I don't want." He feels defensive when someone says, "I want" and paranoid when they say, "I don't want."

Nancy and her teacher were writing a paper together. Her teacher dictated the words "bad and not good enough," which Nancy did not hear. When her teacher called her on this, Nancy swore she had not mentioned them. Her teacher then asked Nancy, "Are you playing the game with me?" Nancy realized she was playing the defensive/paranoid game. She truly believed, and would have been willing to swear to and defend her belief that her teacher had never said "bad and not good enough." However, the one thing she did know was that she was playing the defensive/paranoid game and, therefore, knew her teacher was right. Had she not known she was playing the game, she would never have believed her teacher was telling the truth. At this point she moved out of the defensive/paranoid strategy and automatically moved in the cooperative strategy. Seeing her change of strategy, as a learning tool, her teacher asked, "How does it feel to be using the cooperative game strategy now?" Nancy replied, "It feels like I am doing everything I can to be good, and don't know what else I can possibly do. I feel like a hamster on a treadmill going 'round and 'round with no thought of getting off. I know that this game will not end until I face me."

Once the defensive/paranoid player becomes aware of this strategy and the emotional and physical pain it causes, he experiences sorrow and anguish. He can then choose to let go of it forever. If he does he automatically moves into the cooperative strategy.

The Cooperative Strategy

When the game player is in the fourth level of the game he is using the cooperative strategy. This strategy is the one in which "nice" boys and "good" girls live. This strategy is about hiding out by looking good; about pleasing instead of giving pleasure. These players stay in their heads and figure out what it will take to make them look good. The cooperative game player wants to give you what HE wants to give you and expects you to be grateful for it. He wants to fool you into believing that his motive is sincere and that he is not trying to destroy you.

Self-deception and denial play a large part in the cooperative strategy. The cooperative game player creates chaos and confusion. He feels he is being his highest and best, and deceives himself into believing that he is giving you what you want, but in truth, he is doing what it takes to look good and is giving you what HE thinks you want so you won't leave. He <u>wants</u> to give you what you want, but because he can only think of himself and what <u>he</u> wants, he thinks that what <u>he</u> wants is what <u>you</u> want. He gives you what <u>he</u> wants <u>you</u> to give <u>him</u> or what he thinks you want, expects gratitude and acknowledgement for it, and doesn't give you the space to say that you don't want what he is giving you. If you say, "I don't want," he feels confused, takes it personally and feels you're telling him he's not doing it good enough, when all you're saying is, "This is not what I want." He feels he can never please you, that nothing he ever does is good enough and wonders why you don't get someone else who <u>can</u> please you. He doesn't blame you---he just doesn't take his responsibility.

> *Ever since she was small, Jane's mother gave her gifts she didn't want. Jane complained to her friend, "My mother gives me what I don't want and expects me to be grateful for it."*

The cooperative strategy is an act designed to convince you that he <u>is</u> good by <u>looking</u> good; that he <u>is</u> innocent by <u>looking</u> innocent. This strategy is designed to fool you, to convince you that he is giving you what you want, and to divert your attention from the fact that he is out to destroy his relationship with you for his possessive, controlling parent or family member. He is NOT nice, good or cooperative, but is ACTING nice, good and cooperative. He is deceptive and is still destructive. He is in denial and cannot tell himself the truth: that he is still giving his possessive, controlling parent or family member what he wants by destroying his relationship with you. If you confront him on this, he responds with terror. To his mind, you have exposed him. To the game player, everyone with whom his possessive, controlling parent or family member won't let him have a relationship is his enemy. This includes his teacher, who he has asked to tell him the Truth. The teacher (the Truth) is a threat to his possessive, controlling parent's or family member's control. The cooperative strategy is the diversion he uses to keep his teacher and himself from seeing that he is out to destroy their relationship for this parent or family member.

The cooperative game player is eager to please, feels numb, has a nervous energy about him and looks confused, therefore what he says is confusing and difficult, if not impossible, to understand. This game player has a constant need for praise, acknowledgement and approval for doing his job, instead of doing the job because it is his responsibility to do so. He gives in order to get acknowledgment, rather than doing what he does because he wants to. If the cooperative game player doesn't get the constant recognition and reassurance he needs, he will ask for it. There is no flow in his relationships. It always feels as if he is doing you a favor. His attitude is, "I'm doing a good deed because I'm doing something for you." He gives what appears to be so much, yet it is not what you want. You must act as if it is, though, so as not to hurt his feelings. The cooperative game player feels that he is his highest, best and most altruistic when in the cooperative strategy.

> *One day in class, Lisa used the cooperative strategy with her teacher by asking a question designed to get her praise and acknowledgement. Her teacher listened to the question and gave Lisa a clear, simple, truthful answer. Because Lisa was in the cooperative strategy and, therefore, could not hear or listen, she ignored the answer and did not hear it. Instead, she gave an answer of her own, one designed to be more flattering to her. Lisa did not want the truth; she wanted to be publicly praised and acknowledged. When her teacher's answer did not do this, she overruled her answer and gave one of her own, which let the teacher know what Lisa expected. Her message was, "Don't give me what I verbally ask for; give me what you should already know I want." If her teacher had not been aware of what was going on, it would have been incredibly confusing.*

The cooperative game player cannot say, "I don't want," nor can he allow others to say, "I don't want." If someone says, "I don't want," it implies to him that he is not good enough because he has not already given the other person what he is asking for. He cannot be held accountable and works diligently to impress upon others his purity of motive.

The difference between the cooperative strategy and true cooperation is that in the cooperative strategy the game player gives to get, whereas in true cooperation we do what we do because we want to and, in so doing, when something doesn't work, we simply face the mistake, solve the problem and do whatever it takes to get the job done without playing games. There is enormous inconsistency in the cooperative strategy, and total consistency in true cooperation. It is the inconsistency of the game that drives people crazy. The cooperative game strategy is designed to destroy relationships while, at the same time, hiding this from the victims and expecting praise and acknowledgement. It is all about betrayal: acting like a friend and betraying the friend, acting like a spouse and betraying the spouse, acting like a student and betraying the teacher for the possessive, controlling parent or family member. In true cooperation if something isn't working, the problem is solved by finding someone who wants to cooperate, be on the team and be willing to solve the problem.

There is no winning with game players because, unknowingly, the game is designed to destroy all their relationships for their possessive, controlling parent or family member. However, if you choose to interact with one, the easiest time to deal with him is when he is in the cooperative strategy. Here he thinks he is giving you what you want though, in truth, he is giving you what _he_ wants to give you.

When the cooperative player sees and faces his destruction, he experiences sorrow and anguish. He can then choose to let go of the cooperative strategy forever.

Game players can change strategies instantly when the situation calls for it. However, each game player has a predominant strategy which he uses the most.

The game is triggered when someone says, "I want" or "I don't want" or forces the game player to say it. These words are heard differently in each strategy. The game player in the pompous strategy doesn't even hear the request because his thinking is, "I am royalty, so don't ask anything of me." Underneath this pompous attitude he is terrified of having to say, "I want" and "I don't want," and of your saying, "I want" or "I don't want." Instead he blames you for asking him to help you solve _your_ problem. The game player in the angry/vindictive strategy becomes angry when he hears, "I want," and enraged when he hears, "I don't want." He feels that you are putting demands and expectations on him, and blames you when he does not live up to your perceived expectations. He cannot say, "I want" or "I don't want," and blames you for putting him in the position of having to ask. Because <u>he</u> doesn't have the freedom to say, "I want" and "I don't want," he does not give you that freedom, either. The defensive/paranoid game player is filled with self-doubt. He, too, is not free to say, "I want" and "I don't want," nor can he give you that freedom, either. He believes he is not able to do anything "good enough" for you, so he cowers in terror when you say, "I want." He thinks that you think that he has messed up when he doesn't succeed at doing it "good enough" in his mind, and blames himself. The cooperative player <u>wants</u> to give you what <u>he</u> wants to give you because he can only think of himself and what <u>he</u> wants. When you don't want what he is giving you, he takes it personally. He hears you telling him that he is not good enough when all you're saying is, "This is not what I want." He doesn't blame you or himself, but he does not take his responsibility.

Pompous players lie to themselves and others. Angry/vindictive players lie to themselves and others. When they see the destruction they have created, they experience grief. Defensive/paranoid players do not lie to themselves, but <u>do</u> lie to others. When they see the destruction they have created, they experience sadness. Cooperative players do not tell themselves or others the truth, but do not lie to themselves. When they see the destruction they have created, they experience sorrow and anguish.

> *Sue, a game player, was married to Bob, a better game player. They both used the angry/vindictive game strategy. He won with her so often and caused her so much pain with his torturing that she saw that her game playing wasn't working. Because she wanted a warm and loving relationship with him she decided to stop playing the game. She chose love over the game; a warm and loving relationship over winning. She knew it was risky, but she had to take the risk. As soon as she ended the game and began loving and cooperating with him, she ceased being a challenge. Though he loved her, he still had to play the game and destroy his marriage for his possessive, controlling parent. When the marriage ended, Sue became romantically involved with John, who she later married and who, until his death, was the love of her life. Bob, on the other hand, also married and was divorced two years later. Many years later Sue saw that by ending the game she found true love and everything she had ever wanted.*

A group of Betty's friends confronted her on her destruction as she was about to leave to visit Claire, a close friend. While she realized that her friends had served her by telling her the truth, and told this to Claire, she was in the defensive/ paranoid game strategy and wanted Claire's support. Claire informed her that she was not about taking care of anyone and refused to comment. The next day, when Claire was elated after a spiritual lesson with their teacher, it became apparent to Betty that she could not hold Claire down. Betty was terrified of being left behind and alone. She instantly moved into the cooperative strategy where she stayed. In the meantime, Claire's husband arrived home in the angry/ vindictive strategy, and tried get her to cancel her out-of-town trip with Betty. When Claire refused to change her plans, her husband moved into the defensive/paranoid strategy. Both Claire and Betty were in the cooperative strategy and "enjoyed" their trip.

COMPARISON OF THE FOUR GAME STRATEGIES

The Pompous Game Player

- Bossy. Tells others what to do, and knows they will do it without being asked.
- Goes through life totally unaware of his destruction.
- Believes he is "royalty," and buys his own sale.
- Treats others as underlings, servants and sometimes, slaves.
- Believes that everyone is responsible for him and his well-being.
- Totally self-centered, and unaware of anyone as a person.

The Angry/Vindictive Game Player

- Can't say, "I want" and "I don't want."
- Doesn't allow others to say, "I want" and "I don't want."
- Feels anger when someone says, "I want," and rage when someone says, "I don't want." Rage triggers his vindication.

- Pretends he is perfect, and is terrified of being told he is bad.
- Has to be right. When confronted on being bad says, "See, I'm right. I told you I was bad and not good enough." Then feels that it's hopeless and he's helpless.
- Always trying to prove himself to be good and good enough.
- Experiences grief when he's caught being "bad" and sees his destruction.
- Blames you.

The Defensive/Paranoid Game Player

- Can't say, "I want" and "I don't want."
- Allows others to say, "I want," but not, "I don't want."
- Feels defenseless when someone says, "I want," and paranoid when they say, "I don't want."
- Lives his life terrified of losing the game. Lives in terror of being told he is wrong, not good enough and less than perfect, and is always defending himself from that message.
- Avoids telling others the truth.
- Experiences sorrow and anguish when he sees his destruction.
- Blames himself.

The Cooperative Game Player

- Can say, "I want," but cannot say, "I don't want."
- Allows others to say, "I want," but doesn't allow them to say, "I don't want."
- Feels confused when someone says, "I want" or "I don't want."
- Impatient and always scrambling and hurrying to get the job done.
- Creates chaos and confusion.
- Feelers out all the time.
- Driven to look good.
- Doesn't tell the Truth to himself or others.
- Experiences sorrow and anguish when he sees his destruction.
- Doesn't blame himself or others, but doesn't take his responsibility.
- Fakes cooperation instead of truly cooperating.

You can't play the game and be committed to anyone or anything. The only thing you value are accolades and glory, and glory becomes an addiction. You play the game to get what you want without having to ask, and to destroy your relationships for your possessive, controlling parent or family member. Winning the war is a shallow victory. In the end, you realize that you have lived your life trying to get perfect by being good enough for your possessive, controlling parent or family member. When you finally see how you have been used, duped and betrayed by your possessive, controlling parent or family member, you rebel against him and, because the game is all you know, and glory is all you have sought, you then use this lifetime of training to go for your OWN glory. Once you taste the glory you previously sought for your possessive, controlling parent or family member, glory becomes the master of your life and, unconsciously, you become your own hero, and victim of your own game. Once you see the hollowness of this glory and how addictive it is, then you can cease being a warrior in a useless war, and become a peacemaker. Only then can you grow up and begin to create your life YOUR way. Only then can you appreciate and value warm and loving relationships. And only then can you be yourself, be refreshing, and express your talents and abilities.

Let go of your old programming, turn your back on it, and take responsibility to create a new program that works for you.

SYNOPSIS

When we left God in the Garden of Eden we, unknowingly, gave up our identity as God's children, stopped relying on Him to protect and take care of us, and began relying on our parents. At this time we gave them control of our lives and took on an ego for our identity. We began playing the game to destroy the relationships that our possessive, controlling parent or family member did not want us to have, to avoid cooperating with others and to get what we wanted without having to ask. The minute we began playing the game, everyone our possessive, controlling parent or family member did not want us to have a relationship with became the enemy. He told us that they were the "outsiders" and were out to destroy us. The game became a very complex, manipulative, conniving tool, which we sharpened and honed with age and experience.

Playing the game is life to the game player. It is what he does. In truth, it is all-out war, and it is this war that destroys homes, marriages, people, organizations and relationships. It breeds hate, deception and the destruction of either the relationships or the people you love the most. In the end the game destroys you and your dream. It causes heartache, cold hearts, hardened hearts and, worst of all, loss of heart. It destroys caring, giving, receiving, loving and, most important of all, being---being you, being all you can be, being your highest and best. Its faith is in facts rather than Truth. Its method is destruction by not giving others what they want, withholding, resistance and denial. Forget having a warm and loving relationship with game players. It's impossible. You have to start over every time you see them. Nothing that's gone before builds on itself. It's a new game with every meeting, a new beginning with every encounter, no matter how old the relationship. The game is based on fear, insecurity and hatred.

It takes enormous courage to <u>face</u> the game, to <u>face</u> yourself and to <u>face</u> your possessive, controlling parent or family member. It also takes enormous courage to tell yourself the truth about the relationships you've destroyed. If you face the game, you can end it forever and not look back. If you don't choose to face the game, the destruction of your relationships and loved ones will continue throughout your life. The game and the possessive, controlling parent or family member have to be faced and each has to be released on all four levels (see chapter: The Power of Releasing Four Times). The choice is yours. The problem is that your possessive, controlling parent or family member took choice from you. You are like an elephant with a thin string tied around his leg, powerless and chained by the string. Choice is yours for the taking, but, unconsciously, it means betrayal of that parent or family member. It means ceasing to give him what he wants and beginning to give yourself what you want. So it comes down to <u>your</u> life or his, betraying him or yourself. The only one who can save you from this betrayal is you. If you choose to end this self-betrayal you can then and only then end the game and begin to live a life of true cooperation, not the fake cooperation that game players use.

The opposite of game playing is true cooperation. Game players resist true cooperation, and, instead, use the cooperative strategy, believing that they are truly cooperating. If the game player cooperated, he would give you what <u>you</u> wanted and not what he wanted to give you.

When the game player lets go of the game, he is in a transitional place between the cooperative strategy and true cooperation. He feels neither happy nor unhappy, neither secure nor insecure. He feels unanchored and in limbo. He knows he is not going back to the game, but he doesn't know where to go. This is the time to move into true cooperation. In limbo he relies on himself to take care of himself; in true cooperation he relies on God to protect and take care of him. He feels anxiety in the limbo state and peace in true cooperation. By moving into true cooperation he feels happy, secure and comfortable for the first time. He can stop destroying his relationships and start creating warm and loving relationships. The walls he built while in the game are now down and he can start giving and receiving. For the first time he can be real. He can start taking <u>his</u> responsibility instead of others' responsibilities. He can stop pleasing and learn to give pleasure. In the limbo state he could begin to cooperate with others and still not cooperate with himself. In true cooperation he can cooperate with others, himself and God and, in so doing, love himself, love God and love others. Negative thinking is not cooperating with himself. As he begins to cooperate with himself he begins to see the Truth, to eliminate untrue thoughts from his mind and to tell both himself and others the Truth. It is important that he let go of his negative mind and accept that he has a positive mind. It is important that he take full responsibility for his mind and his thinking. Due to old habits, a negative thought can enter his mind, but because it is his mind and he is in charge of it, he can now see the negative thought, release it and replace it with a positive one. It is important that he make up his mind he has choice, that it is <u>his</u> life, that he <u>does</u> have choice and that he chooses to live it <u>his</u> way. It is important that he choose to have warm and loving relationships. It is important that he take full responsibility for his happiness, for what he does and does not do, and for all his relationships, especially his relationship with God. It is also important that he make up his mind that he is free to say "I want" and "I don't want." Once he declares what he wants, asks God for it and believes he will receive it, God will show him his first step. As soon as he takes the first step, he will be shown the next step, and the next, until he gets what he has asked for.

When you reach this point, don't think about it, just do it. Accept you have only one thing to do. After you do that one thing, you will be shown the next. It will come to you as a thought. It's a new life, a new beginning. You are both the clay and the potter. Make up your mind to have fun every second of your new life. Make up your mind to enjoy creating your dream and warm and loving relationships.

End making your possessive, controlling parent or family member your god, and make God your God. Know without question that God is always there for you to love and to guide you. Make up your mind to go to God to protect, love and take care of you forever. Let go of sorrow and anguish, and choose to be happy all the time. It's your mind and you can be as happy as you choose to be. Let go of self-hate and forgive yourself. There's nothing for which to ask God to forgive you. He's never seen anything in you but a precious, adorable angel. Accept yourself as you are, accept that you love yourself, and accept that you are a precious, adorable angel. Let go forever of punishing yourself, and make up your mind that you reward yourself forever. Let go of all hatred toward your possessive, controlling parent or family member, and forgive him. Accept him as he is, and accept that you love the angel within him. Make up your mind to express all of your talents and abilities. Place your hand in God's hand. By placing your hand in God's hand you are then free to have a warm and loving relationship with anyone you want, and you are free to place your hand in anyone's you choose. Open up your heart and invite God in. He will fill any void. He will protect you where all else fails. He will take care of you. Come as a little child into His loving arms. What you want most and have been fighting is loving and being loved. Your possessive, controlling parent or family member did not allow you to love or be loved, so you have resisted love in every way possible in every area of your life. Now it's time to love and be loved. Return home to God, love and be loved, and be free at last, free at last, free at last.

12 Mind Sets

THERE ARE FOUR PATTERNS OF THINKING which determine our actions. We call these patterns of thinking "mindsets." By learning the thought processes of each mindset, you can better understand yourself and others. These mindsets were beautifully illustrated in the classic, "The Wizard of Oz," by L. Frank Baum. For clarity and understanding we have chosen to call them by the names which were made famous by this work.

LION MIND SET

Lions will only take responsibility in front of an audience---of one or a million. They come alive in front of a crowd. As soon as the audience moves away, however, they lose energy, and let go of all responsibility for themselves.

Everything the Lion does is designed to avoid getting the job done. He volunteers to do something in order to look good, be accepted, and receive praise and recognition. However, once he receives this praise and recognition, he begins to procrastinate, and doesn't do what he said he would. He creates problems, chaos, and confusion as a result of his resistance to getting the job done. He denies to himself that he made the offer, and feigns innocence as a cover to not getting the job done. He has carefully thought-out excuses to justify his position, and will, if necessary, become ill to prove to himself and others that he is right and blameless. If you confront him on this, he will become angry. Asking him why he did not follow through terrifies him because the very word, "why?" implies that there is something he didn't do or should have done. The reasons he does not get the job done are: 1) he is terrified of making a mistake because, 2) he is terrified of being less than perfect, and 3) he cares what people think. His ultimate fear is being rejected (being left or being asked to leave). So he does only enough to look good and get by, hoping you won't call him on what he hasn't done. His life is about performing and resting, promising and procrastinating---all because of his terror of being rejected. This terror manifests as extreme resistance. This is why it requires such an enormous amount of effort for him to do anything.

Because his life is a sham, he is vulnerable to the shams of others. He attracts people who lie, con and deceive him, as he does them. They join hands in an unspoken agreement and form a closed "club" in which the members feel a kinship, and protect each other by buying and selling their own sale (that they are right and blameless) to one another. Only those who live this lie qualify for membership; those who tell the truth are excluded. Some are more adept at the lie, and are instantly recognizable by the other club members. They form their own club within the larger club. Other clubs-within-the-club are formed based on the members' ability to lie. All this because the Lion is so terrified of being rejected.

Denial is characteristic of a Lion. He doesn't know what the truth is, so he can't tell the truth to himself or others. Another Lion characteristic is undependability---you can't count on him because he doesn't do what he says he will do. He goes through the motions of life to avoid taking his responsibility---especially his responsibility for what he doesn't do.

Lions are masters at riding the coattails of successful people. They have an enormous fear of being seen as weak in any area---they feel that they will die if found out. Because they can't tell the truth about any weak areas which need strengthening, they never learn to be successful. They look like leaders, and are frequently thrust into positions of authority without any experience, but don't want to take the time to learn. Instead, they look for shortcuts to success.

Lions will torture you, stalking you the way a cat stalks its prey, toying with you, losing interest when you give up the fight, and deriving pleasure from pouncing on you the minute you try to get away. Lions hold themselves out as the prize, promising, then withholding, staying just out of reach. They remember past hurts and withhold forgiveness, "rubbing your nose" in your transgression, in an attempt to continually make you feel guilty for what you did to them.

Synopsis

- Lions don't take their own responsibility. They appear to take other people's responsibility, but usually end up backing out of it. They are quick to say they will do something in order to get credit and recognition, and then they drop the ball. Soon the original offer is dropped from their consciousness. This failure to accomplish what they offer causes them to experience a gnawing feeling of guilt, so they are never free to express their talents and abilities to the highest.

- Lions appear confident, powerful, enthusiastic and sincere. They will offer to do something for you to support you in making your life easier and happier, and then resist doing it. Quite often, after a few days, their enthusiasm begins to fade. Nothing happens. Even though they accepted the job, they may begin avoiding you, and deny to themselves that they ever offered to help. Their resistance to doing the job, and desire to take back the offer comes from the fear that they won't do it perfectly and would, therefore, feel bad because others would see them as less than perfect. They cannot stand to face the music. Their resistance manifests as procrastination. Their greatest fear is that the world will find out they are less than perfect and, therefore, failures. In some rare cases, they will keep the agreement and proceed, but with great resistance and irritation. If you dare mention instances in which they have dropped the ball, they become angry, blame you, and make you bad and wrong for wanting them to follow through as agreed upon.

- Lions hate to be held accountable, and feel pressured when checked on to see if they've done the job. The truth is that they really don't want to do it. When they offer, they are not thinking about following through. They want your appreciation, thanks, love, a chance to be in the limelight, and praise and recognition of their graciousness. They feel that just offering assistance will win them a place in your heart. Once the offer is made and it's time to begin doing what they said they'd do, they resist to the point of totally forgetting the agreement. That is why, in some cases, you may get the response, "What are you talking about?" when you ask how the task is coming along.

- Lions lack the courage to admit to themselves or others that they have not followed through on their offer. They create havoc by not doing what they say they'll do, and will lie, if necessary, rather than face what they haven't done. They're great talkers and salesmen, and can con you into thinking they're the best at getting the job done---and they may be the best, but they just can't do it.

- Lions act confident, self-assured and fearless. In reality they are scared, vulnerable and insecure. They despise weakness in others because it mirrors their own.

- Lions are very vindictive, and if you refuse to give them what they want, no matter what it is, whether your spouse, your car or your mind, they will "get" you by cutting you off in traffic, publicly humiliating you, dropping your favorite vase, etc. They have a knee-jerk reaction to any perceived attack, and are unaware of this. Often, they see enemies where there are none, and are super sensitive to enemies where they exist. However, they are their own worst enemy because they do not take responsibility for what they do and don't do, and deny it to themselves.

- Lions build walls so that others won't get close enough to see their vulnerabilities, weaknesses and imperfections. They are not there for you (though they would have you believe that they are), but want you to be their friend and be there for THEM when they need you. The relationships that they do have are superficial ones, although they deny this, and believe they are a true friend. They will tell you to your face that you are their best friend, while stabbing you in the back and denying that they are doing t.

- Lions want to feel <u>needed</u> and <u>indispensible</u>. It hurts them deeply if they feel you don't want them. They want you to see them as your hero and savior, because this is ego-building, but don't want you to put any expectations on them. The reason they offer to do things for you is so that they will be valuable to you. This is designed to make you desire them, because if you desire them, you won't reject them. That puts them in control. They dangle the carrot and say they will deliver. At the time of the offer they really believe that they want to deliver, and fully intend to do so. That doesn't mean that they will. The truth is that they never wanted to do it, but choose not to see this. They don't take the responsibility to be truthful to themselves and, therefore, to others. If confronted on this, they become angry, vindictive and vengeful. You have exposed their clay feet. It's almost impossible to discuss this with them. They don't want to hear what you are saying, and will respond to you as if you are crazy. Often, they will blame it on someone else. Their ears are closed to anything other than your praise and recognition of them. They shut down and lose touch with their feelings, which leaves them confused. The more they are confronted, the more deeply they go into either inferiority or superiority. If they go into inferiority, feelings of being bad and guilty surface immediately. If they go into superiority, they become angry and vindictive toward you. They want admiration and recognition more than anything. In extreme cases, they brag about themselves, and want you to brag about them, too.

- Lions love the limelight. It empowers them. The majority in this mindset feel comfortable in front of an audience, even while experiencing nervousness. They don't like too many questions asked of them while up front, though, because often they do not know all the facts and, if questioned too closely, would be exposed. They like being the authority, but don't want leadership positions requiring ongoing follow through. They have a tendency to exaggerate and overdramatize. People are usually entertained by them. They so cleverly <u>evade</u> the issue by <u>changing</u> the subject, that it is difficult for a responsible person to deal with them, because they won't be <u>accountable</u>. They give the impression of being in great demand, and loved by lots of people.

- Lions can never appear needy in public. Only in private, with someone they totally trust, will they reveal their true feelings of inferiority. Most Lions love the limelight because stars are loved and desired. On those rare occasions when they offer to share the limelight with anyone, they will end up backing out because they are afraid that the audience may be more impressed with the other person than with them.

- Lions cannot be depended on. To do so is to set yourself up for disappointment, disillusionment and/or anger. However, they are dependent on you and hide this with a fake independence. The only way to have a successful relationship with a Lion is to not want anything from him. If you don't want or expect anything from him, but just enjoy him, you can have fun with him. Lions are players, so most of their recreation is for fun, which doesn't necessarily have to be constructive, productive or educational.

• Lions are extremely sensitive, and the most difficult mind set to confront on not taking their responsibility. When confronting them or assisting them to see something in themselves, it takes gentle loving care to keep them from running away.

• Lions appear courageous and powerful, but know subconsciously, if not consciously, that they lack courage. They want real <u>courage</u> more than anything, so that they can drop the <u>act</u> and be <u>free</u> to be their true selves.

• Lions see themselves as special, like a king or queen.

TIN MAN MINDSET

Tin Men want everything smooth, easy and comfortable. They want everyone to like them and take care of them, and they enjoy taking care of others. This works until they destroy the person they are taking care of through pity and sympathy, or until the person decides to leave. They walk a fine line between keeping the other person down (so he won't leave) and needing to be taken care of, and keeping the other person up enough so that they will be desirable and taken care of. When it comes to taking action, to taking a risk, terror arises. The choice between taking responsibility for their own lives or going back into their Tin Man mindset causes great inner tension because taking responsibility is a risk. Tin Men interfere in others' business, checking up on them to make sure the job is done.

Tin Men have opposite desires---they want to go out in the world and go for it, and they want to stay home and play it safe. And they want others to do the same. Tin Men substitute being busy for being responsible. They avoid looking at a problem so that they won't have to do anything about it. One of the hardest things for Tin Men to face is that they blame others for not taking care of them. This blame is always just below the surface. Their actions assist them to hide out from the truth. Tin Men can lie in order to get a "good" message, but they feel horrible and guilty for doing it.

Synopsis

- While Tin Men can take care of themselves and enjoy helping others to do the same, they do not take their own responsibility---or anyone else's.

- Tin Men are behind-the-scenes people. They "lay low" and don't make waves. They are afraid to take a stand because they are afraid that someone might get angry with them, or they might be blamed for hurting someone. They won't take charge of or responsibility for anything, but will help the ones in charge to do so. They almost always resist when anything is asked of them. They don't want the limelight because they are afraid someone might see that they are bad, less than perfect and not good enough. They often won't even take responsibility as a guest, by socializing or mingling with people they don't know.

- Tin Men take care of themselves by being impeccable in their personal grooming, and their homes. You would never see a Tin Man with a tear in his clothing, even in his own backyard.

- Tin Men give to get. They seek out and find strong, powerful, successful, outgoing people to take responsibility for them, the kind who love to be told they are wonderful, because Tin Men will tell them they are. Tin Men are always extremely loyal to the ones who are taking responsibility for them, and will come to their defense as long as they don't run the risk of being told they are bad.

- The Tin Man's idea of being good is being agreeable, compliant, sweet, helpful and sympathetic. This is how they are with people who will take responsibility for them. This type of person likes to be sympathized with, taken care of emotionally, and have their egos built up. This is what Tin Men do so well, but, again, only with the ones who will take responsibility for them.

- Tin Men associate with Lions, Scarecrows and Dorothys because those mind sets look strong and powerful, and like having Tin Men support them so blindly. They do not associate with other Tin Men because Tin Men lack the power and strength that appeal to them. This is not a very angry or vindictive mind set, but Tin Men can become extremely angry when someone who they believe had promised to take responsibility for them "drops the ball." They will support the one who is taking responsibility for them by seeing him as the victim of another's mistreatment, if that is what he asks. Tin Men will truly believe there has been mistreatment, will feel sorry for him and will join his team. They will put him on a pedestal and make him their hero and savior. If by chance, they get a peek at a "chink in his armor" they will pretend not to see it, because they need so desperately to see the other as strong, powerful and capable of taking responsibility for them.

• Without realizing it, Tin Men's sympathy can be extremely destructive to their partners. Sympathy is crippling and holds a person down. Example: One woman had a good job, earning enough money to live in the style of her choice. Then she married a Tin Man who took care of her emotionally. After awhile, she quit her job and began traveling with her husband in his job. She felt that she couldn't be away from him for very long, and soon was almost unable to go out and work again because she had lost her confidence.

• Tin Men are great listeners. They listen to and are entertained by stories of what goes on in others' lives. This is valuable to others, but Tin Men aren't aware of their value, and feel lucky to have the other person around. They feel flattered and gratified that others want to receive their attentiveness, strokes and sympathy.

• Tin Men use the strong people they connect with as their shield to cower behind in the world. They are "coattail-riders."

• Tin Men don't associate closely with each other or anyone else who isn't going to take, or at least promise to take, responsibility for them. When two Tin Men get together, nothing happens because neither one will take any responsibility. Most Tin Men do not go out into the world and get involved. They rely on their friends to fill them in on what's happening out there.

• Tin Men have great resistance when someone wants them to take responsibility in a relationship. The resistance comes from their great fear of not living up to the real or imagined expectations of the other person. They won't look to see what their responsibilities are. They put their heads in the sand. If they looked at their own responsibility, they might have to do something and, if they did, they would run the risk they are so afraid of: being told that they are bad, less than perfect and, therefore, not good enough.

• Tin Men want everything peaceful, harmonious and loving. They avoid a scene and act as peacemakers. It's scary to have people warring around them. They live in the fantasy that they have no problems with others, that nothing is bothering them.

• Tin Men don't want leadership positions because of the responsibility, even though they can be great leaders. To them leadership means setting themselves up for a fall---being told that they did it badly or not good enough, both of which are less than perfect. Some Tin Men desire to be perfect while others desire to be good enough.

• Tin Men spend a lot of time on their personal appearance, pampering, re-doing, and fixing up their homes and themselves. This is one of the ways in which they attempt to be perfect, and therefore, good enough.

• If someone tells a Tin Man that he did something wrong, he will believe it, even if he did nothing inappropriate. Tin Men often let people abuse them (mentally and/or physically), rather than take responsibility to see what is happening, for fear of having to take a stand.

• Tin Men give the impression that they are givers, but resist and get angry when something is asked of them. They are afraid that their gift won't be good enough, and are terrified of being rejected. Tin Men appear to be kind and loving, but they know, subconsciously, if not consciously, that their kind and loving gestures are an act, and they want to be real. What they want more than anything is a good heart and courage.

• Tin Men have an ability to communicate clearly and tactfully. They enjoy teaching, and are generally excellent at it. They are great at helping others. They are good listeners and add to an occasion rather than detracting from it. They support others in having the spotlight. They support the star, and are very loyal to their leaders. They are efficient, and some are organized as well. They are very structured, and if they say they are going to do a job, they will do it. They have a sixth sense about what makes relationships work. They do well in service professions, and make excellent right-hand men. They are kind, gentle, creative souls who love their homes, and make wonderful homemakers and providers.

SCARECROW MIND SET

Scarecrows obligate you in their minds by taking your responsibility and then, without saying anything, expecting you to take theirs. Because you are unaware of this non-verbal expectation you can become confused, since it is all going on beneath the surface. This is referred to as the "make-you-crazy game." If you don't fulfill their expectations by taking their responsibility, they get angry to the point of rage, and make you think they will leave. Sometimes they do. Scarecrows have the gift of making themselves indispensible to you. They do this to manipulate you into taking responsibility for them because, in their minds, you owe them something. They think they know what's best for everyone, and if you dare step out of their pre-conceived plan for you, they will force you to leave so that you will look like the bad guy to the world, and they will be seen as right and blameless. If you won't leave, even after all their attempts to get you to do so, then they will, leaving the words, "after all I've done for you..." streaming behind them. They are blind to what they do, and can't stop it. They maintain a precarious balance between pushing you to see how far they can go, while feigning innocence to themselves and others. Ultimately they go too far, destroying the balance and finding out it's too late. They've chosen this mindset in order to remain right and blameless. Unknowingly, they are on a treadmill of self-destruction. The only way off it is to let go of having to be right and blameless, and to choose God and follow Him every moment.

Insanity is doing the same thing over and over again, and expecting different results. The Scarecrow does the same thing over and over again, then blames you for not giving him different results---and convinces himself that he is doing something different.

Scarecrows keep score, and use it to "get" you. They want to kick you in the teeth---and want you to be grateful to them for doing it. If you don't allow them to, they will hate you and then "get" you for not allowing them to.

Another Scarecrow characteristic is that they are masterful liars---to themselves and others. They live in denial, which is how they are able to lie to themselves. Deep down they know the truth, but won't face it. The terror of being blamed for being bad or not good enough, coupled with the desire to be right and blameless runs, controls and directs their lives.

Synopsis

• Scarecrows take on other people's responsibility in order to control them.

• Scarecrows want to be taken care of, loved, and seen as perfect. They expect obligation from you. As long as you make yourself available for them whenever they want you, everything will run smoothly. But if you're not there for a Scarecrow, even ONE time, watch out! It can, and most often will, bring out irritation in them to the point of rage, even if you've been there for them a hundred times before. They don't remember all the other times you were available and supportive. They will lie to themselves and others in order to convince themselves of their lie. In so doing, they blame you instead of taking their own responsibility for what they have done or not done. Scarecrows need you there for them because they are so insecure. They feel that they can't survive without someone taking care of them and being responsible for them.

• Scarecrows are out-front people, visible and willing to take risks. It might scare them, but they will do it anyway.

• Scarecrows are constantly looking at your problems and responsibilities, and figuring out ways to solve them. They do this whether they are asked to or not. They want to be your savior and/or hero so that you will feel obligated and unable to live without them. They believe that this will ensure your being there for them. However, Scarecrows are extremely resistant to anyone telling them about their own responsibilities. They won't look at their own problems or responsibilities, or even find out what they are, because the thought of taking responsibility for them is terrifying. The underlying reasons for their not taking their responsibilities are the fear of not doing it good enough, the fear of failure and the fear of being less than perfect.

- Failure is a Scarecrow's greatest fear. Anything less than perfection is failure in their eyes, which makes them feel bad and, therefore, not good enough. And feeling bad, less than perfect and not good enough must be avoided at all costs. No mistakes are allowed in this mind set, and since mistakes are "stepping stones" to success, it's extremely difficult to achieve the success they so greatly desire. In Scarecrows' minds, their success in business, relationships, etc., is put off to the future. For example, "when I get married," "when I have my first child," "when we move to another city," "when I turn 30," "after I totally know myself," etc. These are excuses for not facing their own fear of failure.

- Scarecrows seek out and thrive on credit, recognition, praise and acknowledgement, and get quite a lot of it by taking others' responsibilities, but it is never enough. It makes them feel good for the moment, but they need a constant dose of it. They don't really want to do all the jobs they volunteer to do, but they're afraid of being told that they are bad, less than perfect and not good enough if they don't, and terrified of being asked to leave and being replaced. Scarecrows feel resistance to getting the job done, but will ride over the top of the resistance, and, in most cases, complete the task at hand. Sometimes they do "drop the ball," but it's usually because they've taken on so many jobs, that they either forgot or "couldn't find the time" to do it. Scarecrows become fatigued from riding over the resistance, and get to the point where they can't push themselves, and have to rest. A lot of time is spent resting or playing because it takes enormous amounts of energy to fight resistance.

- Scarecrows want leadership positions because they want power and important-sounding titles. They are not interested in doing the work that leadership requires, and usually don't look to see how much responsibility is involved before they take it on. Even after they take a leadership position, Scarecrows have difficulty understanding that enormous responsibility goes with it. They deny that they are the ones responsible for getting the job done, since they didn't want the responsibility in the first place. They just want the power that comes with the title. They want a job at the top without having to work their way up, and a position of power gives them some security. However, they live in constant fear that a more powerful person will come along and take it away. It's extremely important to a Scarecrow to be the one with all the answers. He feels that if he knows the most, he will be indispensible, and will never be left. Scarecrows have an extreme fear of being left, but if they become indispensible to another person by taking on HIS responsibilities, there's a good chance he will stay, and the Scarecrow will be in control. The catch is that they eventually get fed up with doing the other person's work, and start blaming HIM for not taking his responsibility. They resent him for giving them the responsibility, when the truth is, he didn't give it to them---they just volunteered to take it. The Scarecrow just didn't take his own responsibility to begin with.

• Scarecrows want to delegate jobs, but they have great difficulty praising and acknowledging others for their support in making the Scarecrow look good. As a result, they have a hard time keeping friends, employees and supporters. They feel that it takes something away from them to give acknowledgement, credit or recognition to others.

• Scarecrows don't like working for others, because they feel that others place expectations on them. They don't like this even though that's what they do to others. They fear not being able to measure up to those expectations, and this fear creates failure for them. Scarecrows have a tendency to get fired, or at least quit before they are fired, due to the resistance to taking responsibility for what they do and don't do. They are game players who resist anyone saying "I want" or "I don't want" to them. For example, a Scarecrow mother will instantly become angry while making dinner if her child asks her when it is going to be ready. To her, the child is saying, "You are not perfect because it's not already on the table, therefore you are bad and not good enough." The child might simply want the information so that he knows how long he has left to play. A Scarecrow husband might become angry if his wife asks when he plans to mow the lawn. He feels that she is putting pressure on him and saying, "You are bad because it is not already done." She may simply be asking because she has not yet bought gas for the mower, which is her responsibility. Scarecrows are very systematic, rigid and analytical in their efficiency to get the job done. Some of this efficiency is due to their desire to avoid problems, which they are not allowed to have.

- It is extremely important to Scarecrows to know everything and be right. To them, knowledge is power, and power is security. (Money is important to them for the same reason.) They feel very insecure if they find themselves in a situation where the topic of conversation is something they know nothing, or very little, about. They are usually very smart, although upon closer examination, they often appear to know more than they really do. They don't like being questioned about details, unless it's a subject they've studied thoroughly, because they can't acknowledge that they don't know everything, and are terrified of others finding out.

- Scarecrows are not usually sympathetic, empathetic or compassionate. Sometimes they will appear to be, but it is an act. When they take on a project which could bring them lots of credit and recognition, they hold on to it even though they don't really want it. The thought of letting someone else take over, maybe do it successfully and get the acknowledgement, is unbearable to Scarecrows, because they believe it will make them look bad by comparison. It's either perfection or failure---there is no middle ground. Risks are difficult. There is always a built-in excuse for failure. This is their compensating mechanism because they constantly compare themselves when others are praised and acknowledged. They take it as a personal affront. It says something about them: what they've done is not good enough. They are the captains who would rather go down with the ship and die a martyr than turn it over to a second mate who could keep it afloat. Scarecrows don't like having assistants---it's too risky. The assistant might get some credit and recognition. The Scarecrow might, however, accept assistance from someone he can control and dominate.
-
- Scarecrows connect well with Tin Men because the Tin Man builds their egos, tells them they are great, and cheers them on. They provide background support which the Scarecrow needs.

- Scarecrows are scary to others because they have so much anger in them. They use scare tactics to keep others from getting too close because they feel vulnerable, afraid and insecure. They don't like others getting close enough to see that they are made of straw and can be blown away very easily. When the time comes to be held accountable for not taking their own responsibilities, Scarecrows will blame those whose responsibility they've taken for not reciprocating and handling the Scarecrows'. When caught not getting their jobs done, they say it's someone else's fault.

• When Scarecrows get the praise and recognition they seek, they become cocky, arrogant and superior. They want all attention on them, and are extremely uncomfortable when it is given to another. They watch very closely to try to catch the other person not taking their own responsibilities. They try to get you to commit to doing something, and then watch to see if you keep your commitment. It makes them feel superior when others make mistakes or fail, and it is this feeling of superiority which makes them arrogant and cocky. However, they have contempt for anyone they can control and dominate, and hatred for anyone they can't. All Scarecrows speak with such authority that when they accuse someone of controlling them, it puts the Scarecrow back in control. The other person is so shocked and scared, that it gives the Scarecrow the upper hand.

• The Scarecrow is looking for someone who is brave, strong and courageous who will inspire them to be brave, strong and courageous, too.

• Scarecrows love telling others what to do, and directing their lives. If they are responsible enough, and this is possible because they can force themselves to ride over their resistance, they make great critics and directors.

• Scarecrows usually take care of themselves the least of all the mind sets. For example, they might go past the time for a needed haircut. Most scarecrows are sloppy in their looks and clothes. Their homes and cars often reflect the same. However, once they get their homes neat and in place, you dare not move a thing.

• As long as Scarecrows work for themselves and create relationships in which others believe they are indispensible, they will stay in a position of power. They never allow others to know that they need them because, if they do, the balance of power shifts and the other person gets the upper hand. The truth is, they are the neediest of all. Scarecrows can't stay long in a position where someone else is directing, out of fear of falling short of their own personal expectations of perfection. They cannot see anyone but themselves as the authority, while, at the same time, they are looking for someone they can trust enough to be their authority. This creates great inner conflict.

- Scarecrows are very detail-oriented and very critical of others who are not. They are organized, great at running meetings, managing others, and trouble-shooting. They are structured, logical, and always anayzing YOU. Every piece of the puzzle must build upon the previous one, in order to make sense to a Scarecrow. They are good at systematizing others' ideas. They are creative, but not innovative---musicians, rather than composers. They would do very well writing directions and manuals. They make excellent judges and lawyers. Scarecrows would do well in the military where they have some authority, since they love giving orders!

- Scarecrows are direct, and communicate logically and precisely. They are able to confront when necessary. They are good teachers on an impersonal level. Scarecrows are constantly checking to make sure they are getting their fair share. They are able to see immediately what is, what isn't, and what needs to be done. Once they give their word, they usually keep it and get the job done.

DOROTHY MIND SET

Dorothys take on others' responsibilities as well as their own. They take their responsibilities so seriously that they can neither enjoy, nor have fun. Wonderful things happen to Dorothys in spite of themselves. They are natural leaders. They are popular, and successful at what they do, yet never feel successful or desired. Relationships mean more to them than anything. As a result, they might hold themselves back from being their highest and best because their success creates jealousy in others, and they are terrified of others leaving them out of jealousy. A relationship would have to get to the point of betrayal before they would end it. They will not, however, allow themselves to be used or taken advantage of, under any circumstances. They are principled. They have authority. Their self-respect means more to them than anything. Dorothys appear to be disciplined but, the truth is, they are committed and dedicated. They are always empathetic and feel others' hurt and pain. Dorothys are problem solvers. They are creative, organized, departmentalized and prioritized, but are often not neat. They love neatness, though, and will take responsibility to get the job done. Dorothys are excellent delegators. They will take a stand for what they feel is right, even if they are terrified. Rather than make another person jealous, Dorothys will keep their own accomplishments quiet, and will sabotage themselves if their shining casts a shadow on someone else. They love people, and are interested in and fascinated by them. Their greatest desire is that people receive their love so that they may create peace and harmony in their environment. The most characteristic feature of a Dorothy is that they will NEVER "get" you or be vindictive in any way, for any reason.

Synopsis

- Dorothys take their own responsibilities and everyone else's.

- Dorothys are the peacemakers. They go to any and all lengths to have peace and harmony. They do and overdo in their families and with their friends. They can work long hours with little sleep, and usually do. They are busy "doers," with all their own responsibilities and everyone else's. They get the job done no matter what, regardless of the circumstances.

- Dorothys take up the slack for others, whether their spouse, children, friends, etc. They feel totally responsible for everyone's happiness, and will do anything to make others happy. If it makes others happy for Dorothys to be sad, be depressed or get out of the way, they will be sad, be depressed or get out of the way. Dorothys cannot be happy when the ones for whom they are responsible are unhappy. Because they can never achieve their goal of happiness for others, they feel that they have failed and are, therefore, bad.

- One Dorothy said, "I worked, worked, worked to make them happy, and then I'd say, 'How's that?' and they would say, 'Well, if you would just do this one thing more...'" It's like a carrot always being held out in front of them. They keep going for it, but the carrot keeps moving just out of reach, keeping them from the success they so desperately want. They feel that if they could just achieve success, then they could rest.

- Dorothys are trusting of others and believe in them. They always look for and see the best qualities in people, and never look for flaws or faults. They are taken advantage of and betrayed many times because of their openness, trust, and sincerity.

- Dorothys are natural people. They will take a stand for their own truth, saying how they see it, even in the face of total opposition. They must say what is true for them.

- Dorothys' recreational activities are productive learning experiences. When they see a movie, they always find a deep meaning in it regardless of the subject matter. They may go camping and hiking for recreation, but it is also for fitness, to learn about nature, wilderness survival, etc. They glean everything they can from every experience.

- If Dorothys have children, they train them to go out into the world and be responsible human beings. One Dorothy read all the books she could, including the Bible, in order to teach her children about what works in business, relationships and life. They all became highly successful adults. Training children takes much time and energy, but Dorothys never think of how much time anything takes---they just get the job done.

- Dorothys are always neat and clean in their personal appearance. If they don't have time to clean their homes, because of all their other responsibilities, they hire someone to clean for them.

- Dorothys assume leadership roles and get the job done. They never resist, and almost never "drop the ball" or forget. They are natural and creative, and if others' rules and ways don't work for them, they find what does. This doesn't mean that they are rebellious. They are not. They simply break away from the crowd to live their lives their way.

- Dorothys are truly generous, loving and giving. They will avoid causing others hurt or pain at all costs.

- If you push Dorothys too far and step over their line they can go into revolt. Revolt says, "Don't you mess with me." It takes a lot to get them to this point, but when they reach it, you'd better duck. They are not vengeful, they just won't take it. Dorothys mean what they say. They are not bluffing. They are totally honest, and never covert. Revolting will get the other person "off their back", but revolt is hell for a Dorothy. When in revolt, they cannot feel love for others. Instead, they judge. Both are painful, and totally against a Dorothy's nature.

• Dorothys have incredible perseverance, tolerance, and patience, and are accepting of others to a fault. They are optimistic, and always see ways to make it work, no matter what "it" is.

• Dorothys adore their friends, and will do ANYTHING for them, as long as it is not destructive to anyone. If a Dorothy has a sick friend, she will take dinner to them, clean their house, and see that their children are fed, bathed and bedded.

• Dorothys do not know what they want because they do not think about what they want. Instead, they think about what others want.

• Dorothys aren't after a heart like Tin Men, courage like Lions, or a brain like Scarecrows. They just want to go Home to God.

• A Dorothy can make you feel like you are the most important person in the world. They can create a cozy atmosphere and make everyone in the room feel comfortable, important and valued. They are sincere and trustworthy. They tell the truth, and can get to the bottom line. They make commitments and follow through with them.

• Dorothys are in their element when inspiring others to be the best they can be. They think of others, and love to be with them. They love people, life, animals and flowers.

• Dorothys are innovative and creative. They can see the big picture and are also good at details. They know what needs to be done and can delegate and direct people. They are leaders, and are usually found in positions where there are opportunities for creativity and involvement with others.

The Tin Man hides out; Dorothy is out in the open without defense; the Lion is harmless until cornered, and the Scarecrow is a predator who feels that the best defense is a good offense.

You can have one or more mindsets. For example, if your mother was a Dorothy/Scarecrow combination and your father was a Lion/Tin Man combination, you can be all four mindsets due to your programming. However, most people are a combination of two.

Those with opposite desires play a role in a role, which is a combination of mindsets. They can flip from one role to the other in mid-stream. This can be confusing to those with whom they interact.

The way to fully express yourself is to let go of the fear of making a mistake, the need to prove yourself, the need to be right, blameless, and perfect, and the terror of being rejected. Accept that you are accepted in every area of your life, and accept that you are good enough just as you are. Most important of all, accept that you are the spirit that is, was and ever will be. Accept that you are life itself, love itself. Accept that you are free to be all you can be. Accept that you are free to be YOU.

13 Impatience

MOST OF US HAVE BEEN BROUGHT UP to view impatience as one of those minor, annoying habits some people have, like nail-biting or gossiping. Actually, impatience is a strongly negative way of life, one which is cruel and overly demanding of perfection of self and/or others. It is "hurrying up to die." Impatience is caused by our mother's, father's or family's impatience with us, perfection, living in the future, and living someone else's dream. Living someone else's dream causes the "JITS," which is an anacronym for judgment, impatience, trapped and superior. The "JITS" create impatience with whatever you're doing, making you want to hurry up and end, even if it's the thing you love to do the most.

We become impatient when we are stuck in traffic. We feel trapped, and our minds move into the future, where our bodies cannot follow. This creates inner tension and stress, which compound the problem. When we are in the future, we feel very nervous and want to leave, even if we are with loved ones and even if we are doing something we enjoy. This causes those we are with to feel we don't care about them or want to be with them. Our impatient energy destroys both their peace and the atmosphere. We are not there with them because we are in the future, and they can feel it. And if we stay, we hold back. Once we get where we wanted to be, we don't want to be there, either. Being in the future destroys enjoyment and fun, and prevents us from focusing on the task at hand. We feel there is SO much to do, and we have to hurry up and get it done. Others don't feel they have the space to talk around us when we are in the future. And when someone else speaks, we can't hear or listen. Being in the future creates enormous nervous tension, keeps us on the outside, and prevents us from having peace.

We see impatience around us every day. A boss becomes impatient with an employee who takes too long to understand his instructions. A mother becomes impatient with her child for not getting dressed fast enough for school.

Impatience generates enormous anxiety, pressure and restlessness in order to hurry up, complete the immediate task and rest. The present can never be enjoyed because the impatient person lives for something in the future: a drink at 5:00 p.m., dinner at 6:00 p.m., television at 7:00 p.m., a weekend party, summer vacation, children's college graduation or retirement. The truth is that the anxiety does not end until he lays down to sleep or lays down to die. Therefore, enjoyment of the moment, even for those things eagerly anticipated, is destroyed by impatience. Impatience can cause frustration and anxiety when our desires and ambitions do not arrive in the allotted time. Some impatient people become discouraged, disillusioned and, at some point, may abandon the chosen project in order to be relieved from the inner pressure, while others make up their minds to accept the pressure as something with which they have to live, and go all the way with the project.

Impatient people feel contemptuous of others. They blame, criticize and make others bad and wrong.

Impatience destroys peace within and without. Do you want inner peace? Do you want warm and loving relationships? Do you want to create destruction or love? Impatience is a technique which the right and blameless destroyer uses to destroy his relationships (see chapter: The Roles). He denies to himself that he is doing this, and is totally unaware that his spouse or friends don't want to be around him. Because impatience is so destructive to relationships and such an undesirable human trait, some people put on a complex, intricate act to cover it up. The most patient-appearing people can be the most impatient of all.

Impatience can be so very subtle in its expression and so all-consuming in its victims' lives that, knowingly or unknowingly, people who are controlled by impatience may seek one of three paths to relieve their pain and suffering:

- Procrastination, laziness and avoidance of responsibility,
- Compulsive doing, and
- Impatient fantasizing.

The person who chooses procrastination, laziness and avoidance of responsibility feels that he will never live up to his parent's expectations of perfection and, therefore, his own. This manifests as feelings of extreme inferiority and defeat. To deal with the overwhelming feelings of anxiety and internal pressure, he escapes into procrastination or laziness. This is a way of saying, "I can't work it all out, so I won't even try. What I will do is just enough to get by. Don't ask or expect anything of me because I am not capable enough, smart enough, talented enough or good enough to get the job done." This person gets attention by acting helpless. Often, he is gentle, kind and easy-going.

Even though procrastination offers some relief from the anxiety of living in the future, it creates countless problems in the present. It is probably the most expensive habit that anyone can have because of monetary fines, interest on unpaid bills, and all the anger generated from other people who expect the person to live up to his obligations, responsibilities and claims.

The second manifestation of impatience is compulsive doing. The compulsive doer never finds fulfillment in a task. There is never a feeling of having done it "good enough," only a need to do better and better. To the impatient person someone else is always creating problems in the project on which he is working, causing it to fail or destroying its momentum. The impatient one then loses his patience and fails to persevere. He abandons the project, breaks the contract or leaves his job, marriage or children, blaming those left behind for the failure.

Impatient doers stay very busy. They believe that if they hurry up and get everyone and everything fixed and perfect, then they will be acceptable to themselves and others, and then they can rest. The truth is that they just keep hurrying from one thing to the next, always busy and always anxious.

Impatient doers are often domineering and quick-tempered, constantly finding fault with others. They feel it is their right and their duty to criticize everyone else's imperfections.

The last manifestation of impatience is the impatient fantasizer, who has accepted in his mind that he is already perfect. He doesn't have to do anything to improve his state of perfection. He is forever finding fault, criticizing and judging others.

Impatient fantasizers are difficult to live with because no one ever measures up to their expectations. They have an inflated opinion of themselves and are overdemanding, domineering and, at times, tyrannical. Their anger can be fierce or dangerously threatening in a covert way. They resist being successful and, therefore, don't want you to be successful because they feel they would pale in comparison. They want you to be good enough, but don't want you to be as good as they are, out of fear you will surpass them. They hold you back by withholding their permission for or approval of your success, and by creating doubt in your mind about your abilities. They have opposite desires (see chapter: Programming). It is impossible to please them.

The impatient fantasizer holds incredible power over his loved ones, allowing them to love only those he has chosen for them. To love anyone else is seen as disloyalty to the fantasizer, which triggers his impatience and anger. His commitment to his fantasy of perfection is so great that nothing anyone can say penetrates the brick wall of his belief. He does not see that his impatience and anger are destroying his relationships. His greatest fear is being left and, therefore, alone. To prevent this, he manipulates and controls people to keep them from leaving and to give him what he wants without having to ask. He must always remain blameless in his own mind, and never do anything for which he could be openly accused. At the same time, he has a strong desire to be taken care of but, because of his pride, is unable to ask for it.

The impatient fantasizer's manipulative skills are formidable. His impatience won't let him go through the traditional pecking order. He has to go straight to the top without paying the price to get there. He is patient with himself and impatient with others.

It is our parents' responsibility to give us their dream for us while we are growing up. Once we become adults and begin to live our own lives, it then becomes our responsibility to cease living our parents' dream for us and begin living our own. If we were not permitted to have choice as children, choosing our own dream is impossible. At this point it is important that we make up our minds we are adults and have choice. In order to deal with the impatience caused by living our parents' dream for us, we must decide what WE want for our lives, and what OUR dream is.

Impatience keeps us in a jail to which only we have the key. To unlock the door, all we have to do is surrender our need to live our parents' dream, choose our own, let go of the "JITS", begin living our dream and accept that we are patient on all four levels.

John was an impatient fantasizer and believed he was already perfect. He was married to Sue, a patient, loving wife and mother who was living her own dream of being a home-maker. John was living his father's dream which was to work for and travel with him in his business. He was impatient with Sue and always looking for an excuse to leave because she was not living his father's dream. John married her because he knew she would be a wonderful wife and mother, which she was, but his father felt she wasn't good enough for him. After ten years of marriage he left her for another woman who, he thought, would be good enough.

Some people are impatient with themselves, while others are impatient with others, and a few are impatient with both themselves and others. It's important to see where your impatience lies.

This is your life. You have both the right and the responsibility to get clarity on what your dream is and go for it. You are no longer a child. It's time to grow up and assme your adult responsibility to choose and live your dream. Impatience is a crippling disease that has a solution. The solution is to face impatience, let it go and accept that you are patient.

The truth is that NOW is the only moment we have. We exist only in the now, not in the past or the future. Since this is the only moment we have, why destroy it with impatience? We will never get good enough or be perfect, so why not live each moment to its highest and best by choosing to live it now and enjoy it now? <u>Do it now</u>.

14 Destructive Powers

DESTRUCTIVE POWERS ARE THE MOST POWERFUL TACTIC that one person can use to control, hold down or hold back another. The purpose of putting these powers on someone is to get him to destroy all those relationships, both personal and professional, that the one controlling his life doesn't want him to have. These powers are so debilitating that they prevent the one inflicted from doing what he wants to do, being who he is, and having what he wants to have. They destroy him by taking choice from him, leaving him imprisoned, and preventing him from being free to say, "I want" and "I don't want." Unknowingly, the one who places these powers of control on him becomes his god, his life and his jailer. He has no choice but to protect and take care of his controller at all costs, which means giving him everything he wants. He makes an unspoken pact with his controller without being aware of it, and it is this pact that determines the rules by which he lives.

Destructive powers originate in childhood when a parent or family member puts them on the child. Because this happens at a very early age, it is soon lost from memory. The memory can only be recalled if, as an adult, his desire to be free and have everything he wants becomes great enough for him to face himself, his life, and his controlling parent or family member. These powers are so much a part of him that he, unknowingly, becomes susceptible to seduction by others with these same powers. Consequently, more than one person can have destructive powers on him at the same time.

When someone has destructive powers on you they play games with you, mentally and sexually seduce you, and can get IN you, which result in your living in a fantasy. Destructive powers cause you to destroy your relationships and your ability to even think about what you want. They cause you to destroy yourself or others, your happiness and, sometimes, your life. These powers prevent you from being involved with family members or friends because the only one with whom you can be involved is the one who has placed these powers on you. Destructive powers can also be placed on inanimate objects, such as a car, a house, a piece of furniture or a business.

Barbara was one of the few successful women in her field. When Susan, who was equally successful, arrived and threatened her position, Barbara put destructive powers on her in order to hold her down.

Some of the destructive powers that can be put on you by those who have the power to do so are the power of aging, the power of low energy, the power of nervousness and the power of negativity. Let each of them go with a made up mind, and accept that you are ageless, that you have high energy, that you are calm, and that you have a positive mental attitude.

One of the most debilitating destructive powers is the power to hypnotize you. When you are hypnotized, the hypnotist takes your heart, mind and soul, leaving only a shell. Unknowingly, the hypnotist becomes your god, and you become the hypnotist's slave. You are unable to think, feel or care about anyone but the hypnotist or those he allows you to have. You are owned by the hypnotist and, unknowingly, do only what he tells you to do. You shut down, become "the living dead", and move like a zombie. You are hollow and without life. Some hypnotists instruct their victims to cover the hypnosis with personality. This act makes them appear alive. The hypnotist keeps you striving and never arriving by making you feel you are not good enough, and by mentally seducing you into believing that no one is good enough for you, even those you love and care about.

If, at some point in time, you let go of being hypnotized by your original hypnotist, you have to make up your mind to be free from allowing yourself to ever by hypnotized again. This is necessary because your mind is vulnerable to being hypnotized by someone else. You have to let go of the hypnotic spell the hypnotist has over you, and take back your mind, your heart and your soul.

After someone puts destructive powers on you, four sequential steps always follow. The first step is game playing. He uses your weaknesses to hook you into playing his game, in which he makes all the rules and always wins (see chapter: Game Playing). This makes you feel less than and not good enough, and opens you up to the next step, mental seduction. He, then, mentally seduces you and, in so doing, causes you to think like him. If he hates women or men, you will hate them also. If he is an obsessive eater, you will eat obsessively. If he is obsessed with physical fitness, you, too, will be obsessed with physical fitness. However, the one exception to this is rebellion. If you rebel against this obsessive behavior you will do the opposite, but, at the same time, you will still not be able to do what you want to do (see chapter: Rebellion). He weakens you by getting you to doubt yourself and believe you are bad. He further enslaves you by getting you to believe that you are not good enough. When you doubt yourself, you are unable to believe in yourself. Without belief in yourself you can't even think about what you want, much less, have a purpose, a dream or a reason to live. He expects you to fail, which causes you to have a fear of failure, and anything you fear you draw to you. By withholding his permission and approval, he keeps you coming to him, and sets you up to be sexually seduced, the next step. Sexual seduction is an unspoken mind game in which the message is "I desire you sexually," but is not acted on. Sexual molestation can follow in some cases. Sexual energy is a powerful tool which he uses to arouse your desire for him. Sexual seduction promises, but doesn't deliver. You unconsciously believe that the sexual desire you feel from him is what love is, and believe that others who desire you sexually love you. This belief opens you up to hurt and disappointment. Once he has gotten you to this point, he is then able to take the final step and get IN you. Being in you is the ultimate control. Unknowingly, when he moves in, you move out. You become a physical shell through which he lives. By this time, you are thinking, acting and being like him. You cease being you and become him. Unconsciously, you think he IS you, so to expose him and face him feels like you are destroying him and, in turn, yourself. This is why facing someone who has put destructive powers on you is as terrifying as putting your hand in a hole in the ground, not knowing what's inside. The terror of exposing him, and his subsequent rage, is what keeps you from facing his power over you. It is important that you face him and his destructive powers, let them go and then let go of the four steps in sequence in order to be free to have warm and loving relationships and success in every area of your life. Make up your mind that you are free from anyone putting destructive powers on you ever again. When you release these destructive powers you can feel scattered, confused and in limbo because you're no longer going to that controlling person to tell you what to do. It is imperative, at this point, to go directly to God. Unknowingly, the one who put destructive powers on you became your god and told you, either verbally or non-verbally, that you didn't need anyone but him, and that he would take care of you in every way. In so doing, he kept you from growing up, from taking your adult responsibilities, from taking care of yourself and from relying on your True Source. Therefore, it is important at this time to rely on God to take care of you. This makes you feel secure, safe and protected. Make up your mind to focus center on God and stay there. Drop down to the bottom of your stomach and focus center. By staying there everything you've ever looked for in another you find in yourself: inner peace, love, joy, happiness, ecstasy, power and caring. In focusing center you will move through four levels. As you move into each level, your body will relax and you will feel calmer and more peaceful. It now becomes necessary to begin the process of forming the habit of focusing center. As you develop your new habit, old thoughts and programs will naturally surface and scream for their lost position. Therefore, it is important to ignore the mind and continue to focus center. By staying focused center, these thoughts will find no space and, after awhile, will cease to exist. Focusing center gives you a direction, a place to go to put your attention and a reason for living.

Once you are relying on God to protect and take care of you and are focused center, you can face your pacts (see chapter: Programming). When someone is in you, they get you to agree to an unspoken pact with them. A pact is an agreement which tells you what they allow you or don't allow you to do, be and have. They may allow you to have a pet, but not a spouse, in which case you will destroy your marriage. They may allow you to have a job, but not a career, in which case you will destroy your business. If, for example, you make a pact with them to be liked by everyone, you will wear a thousand faces. Because you have a different pact with each person who has placed destructive powers on you, it is important to face and let go of each pact individually.

Once you have let go of someone's destructive powers over you, game playing, mental seduction, sexual seduction, gotten them out of you and released your pact(s), it is important to forgive them and yourself, and let go of any hatred you might have toward them or yourself. Then accept them just as they are, accept yourself just as you are, and accept that you love them and yourself. If you find it difficult to love them, accept that you love the angel in them. Should you feel sorrow and/or anguish, let each go and accept that you are happy. Let go of your negative mind and accept that you have a positive mind. Should you experience anger, make up your mind that you are free to say, "I want," and should you experience rage, make up your mind that you are free to say, "I don't want." Allowing anyone to put destructive powers on you can make you feel stupid for having done so. The truth is that you were unaware of what was happening. Let go of any feelings of stupidity that you might have, and accept that you have wisdom. Once you have done this, turn your back, walk away from your past and your old programming, move into your new life, and make up your mind that you are free from ever looking back. The slate has been wiped clean and you are now free to express yourself and to acknowledge your talents and abilities. Some have been hidden from view due to these destructive powers. Discover yourself and learn to enjoy every moment of your life.

The final steps in going beyond the mind are to move into the zone and ecstasy, and then to move into bliss. The zone is that glorious space that is right in front of your center. Being in the zone is much like being in a capsule where you are protected and always feel peaceful, powerful and quiet inside (see chapter: The Acceptances). By moving into the zone you avoid pain, and can always feel inner peace, regardless of what is going on in your life. In the zone you experience ecstasy and "the peace that passes all understanding."

The ultimate experience is bliss. Bliss can be experienced by moving from the zone to the top of your head. Make up your mind you are blissful, your natural state of being.

With Destructive Powers On You, You:

- Cannot be involved.
- Don't care.
- Cannot love or be loved.
- Are a loner.
- Can't say "I want" and "I don't want."
- Can't do, be or have what you want.
- Can't express your talents and abilities.
- Can't appreciate or value anything or anyone.
- Can't have warm, loving relationships.
- Can't have a dream or a purpose.
- Have to destroy all relationships.
- Can't see others as they are.
- Are imprisoned.
- Have someone else in you, and think and act the way they do.
- Have opposite desires.
- Are mean.
- Are afraid of the person who put the powers on you.
- Can't be yourself.
- Can't see yourself as you are.
- Have a negative mental attitude.
- Don't do what you say you'll do.

When You Are Free of Destructive Powers, You:

- Are free to be you.
- Are free to be real.
- Are free to be your highest and best.
- Are free to express your talents and abilities.
- Are free to see what's blocking you from having it all.
- Are free to have it all.
- Are free to get clear answers.
- Are confident.
- Have inner power.
- Believe in yourself and others.

- Appreciate yourself and others.
- Love, care and acknowledge.
- Are free to know what you want and what you don't want.
- Are free to be happy regardless of the circumstances.
- Are free to have joy, ecstasy and bliss.
- Are free to have a positive mental attitude.
- Are God-centered versus self-centered.
- Are free to know your labor of love.
- Are free to have a labor of love.
- Are free to be successful.
- Are free to let go of fears and self-doubts.
- Are free to have self-worth and self-esteem.
- Are free to do what you want because you want to.
- Are free from proving, making excuses and explaining.
- Are free to know, accept and be what you're good at.
- Are free to do what works.
- Are free from the fear of failure.
- Are free to be successful in every area of life.
- Are free to enjoy others' successes.
- Are free to be creative.
- Are free to see beauty everywhere.
- Are free from thinking you're not wanted.
- Are free from thinking you're bad and not good enough.
- Are free to feel.
- Are free to be focused center.
- Are free to move into the zone.
- Are free to make up your mind to stay in the zone forever.
- Are free to live your life YOUR way.
- Are free to be free.

15 Rebellion

ONE OF THE MOST DIFFICULT things to understand in life is why a loved one, friend, or co-worker cannot or will not give you what you want. He understands what you're asking for and often agrees to give it to you, but fails to deliver.

Why would someone be in a job, and resist doing what he is paid to do? And why would someone in a relationship which means a lot to him not give the other person what he wants or asks for?

Rebellion is often the cause of this lack of cooperation or support. This rebellion began as retaliation toward an authority figure from the past who made unfair or unrealistic demands. When a child is forced to obey authority figures, be they parents, teachers, doctors or ministers, against his will or sense of justice, he thinks that he has no means of defense but rebellion. When the child chooses rebellion as a means of protection against unfair treatment, he doesn't give the authority figure what he wants, and, unknowingly, doesn't give anyone else (including himself) what they want.

Adult hypocrisy is often the cause of rebellion. Inconsistency in discipline, having different rules for different children, and telling a child to "do as I say, not as I do" is perceived as unfair treatment, and it is this unfair treatment which causes the child to rebel.

Rebellion manifests itself in several ways: "If there's anything you want, I'll do the opposite," or "I'll prove you right (or wrong)," or "If you expect anything of me, I refuse to live up to that expectation."

Rebellion can be expressed either openly or silently.

OPEN REBELLION

An open rebel does the opposite of what family, friends or society asks of him. He enjoys the response he gets from others as a result of what he believes is his courageous stand. Quite often, open rebels call themselves nonconformists or free spirits. They do what they want to do, whether or not it is socially acceptable.

An example is Robert, who married into a very wealthy family. On one occasion, he was required to wear a tuxedo to an exclusive club. He wore white tennis shoes with his tuxedo so that he could express his rebellion and still attend the party.

Open rebels think their behavior is due to honesty, courage and being true to themselves. The truth is that their actions are motivated by rebellion against authority figures. At one traumatic moment, their anger became so great that they committed themselves to rebellion.

The commitment to open rebellion takes a positive or negative direction, based on what the rebel perceives as the desire of the authority figure. Joe's father held him back in every way he could, because his father felt threatened by Joe's success. He was afraid that his son would surpass him. Joe rebelled against his father's negative control in a positive way by making all A's.

Patti rebelled in a negative way against the high expectations for perfection her mother placed upon her. She did this by using drugs, alcohol and, often, sex.

With any request, the rebel experiences a stabbing contraction in the stomach. His immediate response to the request is, "Don't ask anything of me."

Open rebels openly express anger. They can have a confrontation with someone close to them one day and, by the next day, have forgotten it completely. This open attack leaves the one attacked feeling angry and hurt, while the rebel feels relief from the inner pressure to rebel. The relationship is often destroyed because the one attacked won't allow it again. In the case of a close family member, it leaves the one attacked feeling humiliated and abused. The open rebel has the capacity to deny, and so, goes through life dropping little bombs everywhere and feeling no remorse.

The rebel is terrified of any commitment. He originally rebelled to gain freedom from overbearing domination and control, and to him, commitment looks very much like submitting to control once again. The truth is, he is already committed to rebellion.

Open rebels choose work where they can be independent of others. Having a boss tell them what to do causes conflict, anxiety and frustration for all involved. Many open rebels turn to "creative" pursuits, which involve working with objects, rather than people.

Open rebels enjoy being with other rebels because they are of like minds. Even though the open rebel may pursue a spiritual path in his search for freedom, he is resistant to the truths he is learning. He finds fault with them and tries to prove them wrong. Even if he hears the truth, he may delight in discussing his doubts and looking for flaws.

An open rebel, unknowingly, applies resentment or hate of unjust treatment from the past to the present. As an example, for years a mother described the type of man she thought her daughter should marry. The daughter always dated the opposite type of man. She was unaware of this because her rebellion was unconscious. She was 35 years old before she finally saw that she had chosen the men out of rebellion against her mother. In truth, she really did want the same type of man her mother wanted for her, but because of her rebellion, she was not free to be involved with him.

> *As a child, Maddy was told she had to practice the piano every day. Now, as an adult, she hates being told that she HAS to do anything.*

> *Unknowingly, Susan rebelled against men because her first husband was unfaithful to her. As a result, she was always suspicious of her second husband, Bob. One day Bob asked Susan, "How long am I going to have to live with the memory of your ex-husband's betrayal?" This opened her eyes to her rebellion, and she made up her mind to end it.*

Open rebels are generally domineering, and overcome injustice by force and control. They are very strong-willed and possess a singleness of purpose. They feel that they have the right to own others and tell them what to do. They can be brutally honest, and can be reformers, saviors or shrews depending on how they express their rebellion.

The open rebel thinks that if he were to arrive at success in his work or relationships he would have nothing to do and life would be over. Consequently, he has to constantly sabotage his successes, which gives him something to do, and keeps him striving and never arriving.

Until the rebel sees his behavior in clear vision, he is unaware of what he is doing. If confronted, he becomes defensive because he is exposed. Until he is ready to face his rebellion honestly, it is very difficult, if not impossible, to remove himself from the grasp that it has on his life. Not only does he not give others what they want, but he is unable to give himself what he wants, as well.

Open Rebellion and You

If everything you are trying to do in your life feels as though it is stuck in mud, this a good indication that you are in rebellion. There is a war going on inside of you---you want something, yet you resist going for it. You do this unconsciously, but nevertheless, it manifests itself in your circumstances. Its many symptoms are visible, though, such as clumsiness, accidents, breaking things, forgetting things and/or losing things. Another symptom is the knife-like stab in your stomach when anyone tells you what to do or even asks anything of you. Everything seems to take so much effort. You feel as if you are swimming upstream. You have little energy or motivation, and compensate for this by willing yourself to get the job done.

Physical symptoms include a constricted feeling in the jaws, neck, shoulders and back. Often there is a tight, band-like constriction around the chest in the area of the heart. Other symptoms are a "tight" stomach, indigestion, shallow breathing, shortness of breath, lethargy, over-sleeping and extreme stress. Most experiences generate impatience and anger, and cause you to blame others instead of taking responsibility for your rebellion.

> *Mary Ann's husband said to her, "Every time I compliment you on a certain dish you make for dinner, that's the last time I get it." Although she denied it to him, deep down inside she knew that he was telling the truth. She thought that his compliment meant that he wanted the meal again, but because of her rebellion she could not give him what he wanted.*

The biggest block to releasing open rebellion is the fear of losing control. You may also have a strong fear of becoming like the person you've rebelled against. Your rebellion only solidifies this. One reason this person's qualities are especially offensive to you is that you, subconsciously, recognize them in yourself.

Releasing rebellion is difficult if you don't have the truth with which to replace it, which is that you have choice, that this is your life and that you have the right to live it your way. Releasing rebellion can be threatening because it appears to the mind that you are going to do away with its protective shield. Your mind is afraid that you will be swallowed up by unjust, overly demanding domination and control.

Rebellion is a powerful commitment to a way of life. To release rebellion is to give up this way of life. The truth is that constructive creativity replaces rebellion. Instead of denying what you want, you can create what you want. You stop destroying relationships, and begin to create them the way you want them to be. That stab in your stomach, which appeared whenever anyone asked you to do something, will be gone. You will be free to act naturally or spontaneously, rather than reacting out of rebellion.

By releasing rebellion you are free to cooperate. You are then able to take charge of your life. You can't take charge of your life if you are in rebellion. Taking charge is another step toward freeing yourself from resistance, domination and control forever. Once you take responsibility and take charge of your life, there is no need for rebellion. It was a childhood defense mechanism, and, as an adult, you no longer need it.

SILENT REBELLION

Silent rebels are completely unaware of their rebellious behavior. When confronted with their actions, they deny them, or say that they did not know what they were doing. They are sincere, but the target of silent rebellion sees the situation entirely differently. Silent rebellion can provoke extreme emotions, especially in a spouse who is treated with contempt for no apparent reason.

As an example, Roy resented his mother bitterly for insisting upon bathing him until he was nine years old. This

> *bathing experience humiliated and embarrassed him to such a degree that he chose to rebel silently. He hated his mother, and later projected this hatred onto other women. His feelings were "I'll show you! I will always have power and control over women. They will never control me again!" Years later, during his marriage, he unconsciously treated his wife with hate, contempt and disrespect. When she pointed it out, he denied it. Communication was impossible. The frustration of not being able to discuss things upset his wife enormously. In Roy's mind, his wife was the cause of the problem.*

As difficult as it is to comprehend, the silent rebel is totally unaware that he is making trouble. He looks at the person who loses his patience or temper with utter disbelief and blame. What begins as a power struggle between parent and child over who is going to have his way, ends in silent rebellion. From that moment on, the child withholds what others want.

The silent rebel sabotages his own happiness by withholding from himself as well. Roy, in the previous story, actually wanted a warm and loving relationship with his wife. However, his commitment to his rebellion, to retaliation and to making women, in general, unhappy, was stronger than his desire to have what he wanted: a loving relationship with one woman, his wife.

Silent rebellion causes other problems. In business, for example, a silent rebel may want to give his boss what he wants, and knows that if he does not, he will lose his job. But it takes so much energy to rebel and, at the same time, give the boss what he wants that, by the end of the day, the rebel is exhausted.

A person will act out his rebellion, silently or openly, to the extent that he feels powerless. The more powerless he feels, the more silent is his rebellion. If he should see that he has power over someone, by virtue of being needed or desired, the silent rebel then becomes more overt in expressing his rebellion.

The stronger his rebellion, the more difficult it is for him to work for someone else. The silent rebel also experiences that knife-like stab in the stomach with all requests from others. His tension, anxiety and anger are in direct proportion to his degree of rebellion. Because the silent rebel does not want to make a scene or cause an open war, he usually retaliates covertly, by performing badly, not getting the job done, forgetting, not cooperating, breaking things or doing other destructive acts for which he feels blameless.

Constant tension and anxiety cause the silent rebel to always be ready for the "attack" of another request. He feels he must be on guard in order to know how to size up and handle any request. As a result, his energy is drained.

The silent rebel is so wrapped up in his own feelings, and so involved in protecting himself, that he is unaware of others' feelings. This creates self-centeredness. He is afraid of being exposed. He is vulnerable because, on a subconscious level, he knows that he can be destroyed by being hurt or rejected. He avoids serious conversation about his behavior in order to prevent revealing his weaknesses. To survive, he thinks that he has to "get" others before they "get" him. By silently observing others' weaknesses, he can be prepared for any attempt by them to expose him and, thereby, "get" him. Finding others' weaknesses also lets him feel right, blameless and self-righteous by comparison. Life becomes an endless power struggle. It is him against them and, unknowingly, him against himself.

Rebellion is futile. It's a dead-end street with no way out. Face the truth that there has always been and always will be injustice in the world, but there is total justice with God. He will always be there for you, will always support you, will always love you, and will lead you, one step at a time, to anything you want, as long as it's not destructive to you or anyone else.

Let go of rebellion, let go of the world and get yourself off your hands. Then turn to your Heavenly Father for guidance, for support and for love. Accept Him as your God and Creator, and rely on Him to protect and take care of you. Assume the sale that He is there for you and will always be there for you. Tell Him your dream, and He will lead you to it one step at a time. Follow Him. Don't think about it, just do it.

CORE OF REBELLION

If you go to cause and find the problem, you can solve it and eliminate all of its effects. Since rebellion is generally established in childhood, it disappears from your conscious memory and creates problems in your life without your being aware of it.

Once you release rebellion, a large portion of your rebellious behavior is gone. What is left is the core: impatience with everyone and resistance to everything. You will, unknowingly, almost immediately resist any request made of you out of a subconscious desire to rebel, and will feel that the one making the request is imposing on you. You become annoyed when those close to you want to be with you, and have to get away from them. You blame them for making you feel like leaving and, in turn, exclude, ignore and reject them, thereby making warm and loving relationships impossible.

Anyone coming from the core of rebellion doesn't want to do anything. To him, any request is an imposition. He instantly hears the most innocent request as a demand or expectation, and interprets it as an attempt to control him. His resulting resistance keeps him from cooperating, supporting or working with those with whom he is closely involved and cares about the most, and stands in the way of his success, happiness and the creation of relationships that work.

Rebellion begins when a child feels he has been treated unjustly by his possessive, controlling parent or family member. Opposite desires are created by the conflict between making his possessive, controlling parent or family member his one and only and only one and, at the same time, rebelling against their unfair treatment (see chapter: Programming).

If you make a possessive, controlling parent or family member your one and only and only one you, unknowingly, give them control over your life and choices. This control, once given, prevents you from having a committed relationship with anyone else. In order to have a warm, loving, committed relationship with someone other than your one and only and only one, rebellion against that controlling parent or family member becomes the only option. Once you choose to rebel and develop a relationship with someone else, the feeling of guilt for having betrayed your one and only and only one kicks in. You can't understand the guilt because you know that you haven't done anything wrong. The need for relief from the guilt and the desire to leave become so unbearable that you automatically rebel and turn against the spouse you wanted so much to begin with and, in so doing, destroy the relationship.

> *Tommy's friends played kickball in the summer outside his house till 9:30 p.m. His mother's curfew for him was 9:00 p.m., which she refused to change. Because he felt that his curfew was unfair, he silently rebelled against his mother, who*

he had made his one and only and only one. His opposite desires created a tug of war within him which affected his future relationships with women.

The core of rebellion, making a possessive, controlling parent or family member your one and only and only one, and the resulting opposite desires are three of the most debilitating controls over your life.

Susie, who was her father's one and only and only one, rebelled against her husband, Johnny. At a recent party, Susie both resisted him and was impatient with him when he tried to be with her. She kept moving away while he kept running after her. Unknowingly, because she was rebelling against Johnny, she was laying the foundation for the demise of their relationship.

Everyone wants romance in their relationships. If one of the two people involved in a romantic relationship is coming from the core of rebellion, the relationship is doomed from the start.

Tammy truly wanted a warm and loving marriage. Because she had rebelled against her possessive, controlling father who would not allow her to have a husband, she made up her mind she would find one, which she did seven years after his death. Once married, her one and only and only one message kicked in. She stopped rebelling against her father and began rebelling against her husband, which caused her marriage to fail.

The mind can cause you to rebel or revolt against external circumstances. Revolt is making a choice to go no further under the existing circumstances with an attitude of "Don't mess with me!" Some people rebel, some revolt and some do both.

The resistance at the core of rebellion causes such exhaustion, tension and destruction to relationships that some form of escape is the only relief from it, but because escape is a compensation, not a solution, it becomes a greater trap. A few of the many escapes chosen are: sleep, drugs, work, play, travel, alcohol, fantasy, reading, television, movies, hobbies, forgetting, sickness and disease, sex, eating, injuries and accidents, denying reality, insanity, apathy, non-involvement and the void.

THE VOID

The void is the least obvious, and least understood escape. Yet, it is quite common. People enter it without any awareness, and for many, living in the void becomes a way of life. Those who live with a parent who is in the void are vulnerable, susceptible and subconsciously programmed to do the same. The void produces a negative energy which some turn inward and others turn outward. The person in the void feels as though he is in a fog. When this fog is directed inward, it forms a safe haven from perceived external threats. No one can get to him or touch him emotionally and cause him pain. In effect, the void creates a protective shell and produces a zombie-like state in which the individual can neither feel nor think clearly. His mind goes blank and everything said is instantly erased. Life becomes gray, with no emotional highs or lows. Love is neither given nor received. This absence of any kind of emotion provides safety and nothingness. It creates a void of emotion designed to avoid feeling pain, fear or love. Those in the void fear loving and being loved. They don't want to be touched or loved, and pride themselves on being unemotional. Because emotions are so unbearable, the void is a safe place in which to live without them. Being in the void enables people to function without feeling. The one in the void recognizes external stimuli, such as conversations and events, but sees them happening at a distance. Some people in the void are "spacey" and out of touch, while others develop a personality to appear alive.

Some live their lives in the void, while others go in and out of it. If, as children, they were taught that they were perfect or had to be perfect, they'll escape into the void at any threat of criticism, and any problem is perceived as criticism. Those who, as children, were not allowed to love or be loved escape into the void at the threat of love. And those who were given both messages are threatened by both criticism _and_ love. Those in the void unconsciously have to retaliate for these threats by punishing anyone who either criticizes or loves them.

When the negative energy produced by the void is directed outward, it creates an intangible but powerful atmosphere that incapacitates those present, and protects the sender. This negative energy occurs when either love or criticism threatens an individual to the point of intense fear. Feeling as though he is sinking into this fear, he directs negative energy outward like a life-line which consumes other people's energy. This is all done on an unconscious level. This outwardly directed negativity manifests as a sort of vacuum, sucking energy out of the room, and leaving those present exhausted to the point of sleepiness. The pull is so strong that the urge to sleep is almost irresistible.

Those who turn this negative energy inward do so in order to be alone. Turning it inward depletes their energy, forcing them to rest.

Neither the victims nor the perpetrators of the void are aware of what's going on. Awareness and choosing to come out of the void are the only ways to end being its victim or its perpetrator.

Mary and her husband, John, were driving along with an aunt who was in the void. The vacuum she created was so powerful that both of them felt sleepy and drained of energy. As soon as the aunt left the car they felt awake and energized.

Things can be going well in a business meeting, for example, when suddenly the atmosphere in the room becomes heavy, and people begin to yawn and want to end the meeting. What has happened is that the threat of either criticism or love has caused someone to move into the void.

Bob was selling a life insurance policy, but when it came time to sign the contract, the prospective buyer became so fearful of making a wrong decision that he retreated into the void. Bob instantly felt its effects and became very drowsy. His pen became almost too heavy to hold, and speaking became difficult for him. The experience left him so exhausted that he had to go home and go to bed.

A person who lives with someone in the void lives his life alone, because the one in the void is there physically but not emotionally or mentally. Those living in the void protect themselves from any outside threat, while at the same time, they threaten their every relationship with their indifference and non-caring attitude.

You can come out of the void by facing it and making up your mind to come out of it. Then you will be able to see how it has stifled your life and destroyed all your relationships, especially your relationship with yourself. Make up your mind to stop escaping and start facing and solving your problems. Once you see how the void has deprived you of warm and loving relationships, you will never want to escape into it again. Let go of the core of rebellion and begin a life of cooperation. Accept that you cooperate in every area and accept that you are in the flow of life.

At some point everyone chooses one of three directions in which to live life: your self, the devil or God. When you come from your self, your whole focus is on obtaining and gathering facts and information, which gives temporary relief from mental conflicts and proof that you are right and blameless. When you come from your self you stay in your mind, which permits you to live by your own rules. The only people you allow into your world are those who will live by and obey your rules, which are defined in minute detail and conveyed through powerful mental techniques. The second choice is the devil, who wants you to make him your one and only and only one, destroy all other relationships and doubt yourself and others. He enters through greed, hatred and fear, and disguises himself as one who will give you everything you want, whereas in truth, he gives you DOUBT, DOUBT, DOUBT. The third choice is God, Who gives you peace, belief and love. Love breaks down all barriers, fills the heart with joy and thanksgiving and restores life. Unconditional love cannot be stopped, interfered with or destroyed. Any love that is withdrawn or withheld is not love, but a fake technique posing as love, designed to control. God is Love and Love never ceases.

16 Escaping Responsibility

Many people go through life escaping their responsibilities in one form or another without realizing how self-destructive it is. Unknowingly, they are so afraid of failure, humiliation, making a mistake, criticism and being blamed that they turn to escape to keep from feeling guilty, bad or not good enough. The greater the fear of failure, the greater the need for escape. Those who were raised to be careful, perfect and safe are the ones who avoid risks at all costs, escape into a comfortable lifestyle and become satisfied with mediocrity. Problems are either avoided, denied or blamed on others. Many deceive themselves into believing that they could be successful if they wanted to, and think this is their choice, but in reality, they can't be successful because of their prior commitment to fail for their possessive, controlling parent or family member. This parent or family member does not want them to express their talents and abilities for fear of their becoming so successful that they would leave and he would lose them. His message to his children when they were young was, "Be careful. You might fail." This suggestion causes them to doubt themselves and be held down and back. The moment they begin to succeed, they feel as if they are doing something bad or wrong. One word from the possessive, controlling parent or family member sends them plummeting.

Others, who have been taught that they can do what they want, will take risks in spite of their fears. Both are afraid, but the one who was allowed to take a risk and say, "I want" and "I don't want" will do it and grow from it.

The possessive, controlling parent or family member is unaware that he doesn't want his child to express his talents and abilities, and would be highly offended if this were suggested to him.

Most people deal with the effects of their problems rather than their causes because they don't want to acknowledge that they have any, for to do so would mean, to many, that they were less than perfect. The truth is that the mountain of success is crowded at the bottom and sparsely populated at the top, so it serves us to look at the causes of our problems.

The difference between taking responsibility and avoiding it is like day and night. The child who is given responsibility performs his tasks without complaint, resistance or escape, and without having to be watched. If he has to be watched, he hasn't been given the responsibility. The child who has not been trained to be responsible resists, complains, tries to escape when asked to do anything, and, in many cases, becomes angry and vengeful for having been asked. He feels put upon, burdened and controlled. The child who is given responsibility is prepared for success as an adult, while the child who is not given responsibility remains an emotional child and is prepared for failure. He may be successful in one area, but success in all areas of life eludes him.

> *Judy's job involved cleaning a small roomful of furniture. This was a simple task, easily handled in a short period of time, but because Judy resisted taking her responsibility, she complained when asked to do it, felt obligated, and blamed the one asking for causing her anger.*

> *Bobby, Johnny and David were brothers. Growing up, they knew that each one of them had a responsibility to clean their rooms and to practice the piano for 30 minutes before school. Because their mother believed in them and knew that they would take their responsibility, she never checked on them. This training has been invaluable to them as adults. It has enabled them to get the job done without resistance and to become successful in life.*

Some parents avoid giving their child responsibility in order to protect him from failure. One of the major reasons they avoid teaching him responsibility is it's difficult to teach something they know nothing about. It's easier to do the job themselves than take the humiliating risk of their child's possible failure. Because these parents are more concerned with what others might think of them as parents than about their child's training, the child then grows up without knowing what responsibility is. When he becomes an adult, he resists it. His fear of being exposed keeps him on the alert for any attack and always prepared for a fight while, at the same time, hating to fight. His feelers are constantly out for this threat at all times. This is his life. Because he believes that he has to defend himself at all costs, his life is, unknowingly, motivated by not taking responsibility, and remaining right and blameless. If he took responsibility in all areas of his life there would be no need for defending, protecting, flipping from inferior to superior, denying and blaming.

Many people take inappropriate responsibility--responsibility for others--and deceive themselves into believing that they are taking their own. They take others' responsibilities because it's easier, they don't have to be responsible for the outcome, it helps them avoid their own fear of being blamed or criticized or of failing, and it gives them credit, recognition, praise and acknowledgment without risk. Taking inappropriate responsibility interferes with others and prevents them from learning their necessary lessons.

The person who takes responsibility welcomes suggestions and requests, for he knows that he has choice. The person who doesn't take responsibility is offended by suggestions and requests, and doesn't know that he has choice.

Escapes from responsibility vary from being socially acceptable and seemingly harmless, to being self-destructive and illegal. It is the degree to which they are practiced that determines whether or not the activities are an escape. Sleep, play, fantasy, movies, going blank, eating, drugs, travel, reading, hobbies, sickness/disease, work, alcohol, television, forgetting, sex, injuries/accidents, apathy, denying reality, non-involvement and going into the void are some of the ways used to escape responsibility.

FANTASY

One of the most common escapes is fantasy. Some people live their lives in a fantasy, while others move in and out of it. To the one in a fantasy it is reality. Those who live in a fantasy eat, breathe and live their fantasy. Their fantasy is their life. People have as few as four or as many as thirty fantasies, and it is possible to have more. Unconsciously, the fantasizer lives each fantasy sequentially and, when he chooses to face and eliminate them, comes out of them sequentially. The fantasizer watches to see how the fantasy he is in is working and, if it's not and he feels threatened, he automatically slips into the next one. Fantasies prevent the fantasizer from loving and being loved, and having warm and loving relationships, including the relationship with himself and God. Fantasy creates a life of not telling the truth to himself or others, while at the same time, expecting others to believe his fantasy, and becoming angry or enraged when they don't. Fantasy gives the fantasizer the excuse to leave in order to find someone who WILL believe his fantasy. Fantasizers base their fantasies on movie or cartoon characters, television characters, fairy tale characters and characters in books. They can even make real life people who they respect and admire the characters of their fantasies. Most people step into the role and become the part.

> *One of Susie's many cartoon character fantasies was Jerry, from the cartoon series "Tom and Jerry." Susie wanted to be remembered forever, to always win, to play games with people, and to trip them up and never get caught---while having fun doing this. Cartoons are fun, ageless, and the characters get away with everything. Jerry, who never got caught by Tom, the cat, always won and was never found out. He fulfilled all Susie's fantasies.*

Fantasies are hidden from the fantasizer as well as those who are involved with him, making love, truth, intimacy and involvement on the part of the fantasizer impossible. Because the fantasizer is one person acting like another there are two different agendas going on.

> *Rachel had many fantasies in which she lived, and could flip into several different ones in the course of one conversation. This made communication impossible because no one knew which fantasy was going to emerge, and she would become enraged if you saw her as she was, rather than as the fantasy character she was presenting. Her inconsistency made it impossible to create a warm and loving relationship with her.*

> *Maddy had lived in fantasies her whole life. To her, they were her reality. Her first fantasy was Glinda, the good witch from "The Wizard of Oz," who was a sweet, kind, loving fairy godmother. In this fantasy, Maddy could---and did---solve everyone's problems. Her career as a counselor enabled her to get paid while doing this. She also made herself available to her friends to call whenever they were in need. When she was in this fantasy, it made her feel good to help them. In the beginning of her marriage, her husband sought her advice, only to later reject and ignore her. This rejection propelled her into her second fantasy, which was Scarlett O'Hara in the movie "Gone With the Wind." Her husband became Rhett Butler, rejecting her with a "Frankly, my dear, I don't give a damn" attitude. However, she continued to feel like the belle of the ball. When, at some point, she realized that the Scarlett O'Hara fantasy wasn't working, she moved into her next one, which was that of a space alien disguised as a beautiful earthling, who had come to earth to destroy it. When her husband left her, she turned to her next fantasy, that of Salieri in the movie "Amadeus" and pursued, full force, the destruction of her friend, Judy, of whom she had always been jealous and envious. She was shown this fantasy when Judy was confronted by their teacher in front of Maddy. Maddy was thrilled that Judy was being confronted, and gloated over this. Their teacher then confronted Maddy on what she was doing, and exposed her fantasy. Maddy knew that this was the truth because of the terror she had been feeling. Maddy had asked God why she was feeling this terror, but because she was in fantasy when she asked, she was unable to tell herself the truth. To do so would have ended the fantasy, and this was terrifying to her. So instead of ending terror, the fantasy compounded it. When she saw this fantasy, she felt disgusted and foolish. She was amazed by the stubborn persistence of her fantasies.*

When two people are living together and one is in a fantasy and the other is in reality, they are living in two different worlds. This can be hell for both. It is unbearable for the one in reality to live with someone in fantasy, and then it becomes unbearable for the one in the fantasy because the one in reality isn't believing the fantasy he is presenting. Ultimately, the one in reality will leave, divorce or turn to God and totally rely on Him.

> *Tom came out of the fantasies in which he had lived for thirty years and into reality. Reality was so painful that he could see why he had moved into fantasy. He knew he couldn't go back into fantasy because it no longer worked for him, so here he was, in reality, which was unbearable. Unknowingly, he was in the greatest place he could be, for this place forced him to take a leap of faith to rely on God to be there for him, to protect him, to take care of him, guide him and love him for the rest of his life. He felt an incredible sense of relief, peace and joy beyond anything he had ever experienced. He left hell on earth and entered heaven on earth.*

Fantasizers rely on their fantasies to protect and take care of them, instead of relying on God. As a result, when the fantasy they are in is not working, they become terrified because they feel vulnerable and without protection. Reality, which is where they go when they come out of fantasy, is so painful because seeing life as it is is not easy. Neither fantasy nor reality works because, while in them, the fantasizer has to destroy his relationships for his possessive, controlling parent or family member. He can be in a fantasy and think he is relying on God because, while he is in fantasy, he can't tell himself or others the truth. The fantasizer thinks he can only be in either fantasy or reality, but the truth is that he can live in heaven on earth if he is willing to face his fantasies, let them go and totally rely on God to protect and take care of him.

If, as a child, you were not taught to believe in yourself, nor allowed to be who you were, fantasy can become a way of coping and of making life bearable.

RESPONSIBILITY

We may experience a need to escape when life forces us to take a risk, when circumstances become so grave that failure appears to be the only option, or when having to face the truth. To ask for help at this time would be to take responsibility for the solution of our problems.

Not asking for help becomes part of the escape. The need to be perfect or to know everything makes asking for help impossible. Fear of failure prompts the retreat from responsibility, and once the wall of our escape mechanism has gone up, sadness, sorrow, anguish and unhappiness become the jailers which rob us of our energy and happiness. Then denial sets in and we escape, either mentally or physically, into this self-imposed jail of fantasy while our minds delude us into believing that we are escaping into freedom from worldly pressures. This denial of reality can manifest as believing we are perfect, justified, and right and/or blameless. We often believe that our problems will go away if we don't look at them, so we choose to sweep them under the rug, rather than deal with them.

Responsibility is one of the most feared, resented and misunderstood words in our language. Yet, the truth is that once a decision is made to take full responsibility for our lives, for our relationships, for what we do and don't do, for our happiness, for our bodies and for our work, we find it to be an incredibly freeing experience. To not take our responsibility is to feel trapped, fearful and burdened. We learn that responsibility is totally the opposite of how it appears to be. To take responsibility is to take charge of our life and to freely create warm, loving and caring relationships. To take responsibility is to create everything we want, and not to take it is to destroy everyone and everything we love. By not taking our responsibility we listen to our possessive, controlling parent or family member; by taking our responsibility, we can listen to God and to our heart. Discovering and taking all of our responsibilities is the key to total enjoyment.

The way out of being trapped, destroying your relationships with yourself and others, and flipping between superior and inferior is to make up your mind to take charge of your life and take full responsibility for what you do and don't do, for your happiness, for your body, for your work and for your freedom. To do so will free you to get clarity on your dream and do what is necessary to have it. This step is important to take before moving into the Light of God's love, wisdom and joy. It frees you to complete the circle of freedom---freedom to soar, freedom to love and, most importantly, freedom to be who you are.

Escaping responsibility doesn't work, which is why we let it go. Doing what works is easy, and doing what doesn't work (escaping responsibility) is hard. The reason we avoid responsibility is the fear of being blamed if something goes wrong. Escaping responsibility assures you of not being able to have your dream. So, it's important to look at the consequences of not taking responsibility, and make a conscious decision to do what works for you. The other cause of escaping responsibility is not believing in yourself and doubting you can get the job done. Make up your mind that you have confidence. With self-confidence, your way of thinking about everything changes. Make up your mind you rely on God to protect you, take care of you and guide you one step at a time.

Your purpose for being on this planet is to love and be loved. Accept that you are love itself, and accept that you both give and receive love.

It is important to know that this is your life, so make up your mind that you are in charge of it. Let go of your old programming and take responsibility to create a new program that works for you. Take charge of your mind, take charge of your life and take charge of your happiness. Make up your mind you have choice, choose your dream and accept that you have it now because it's a done deal. When you are directed to take a step toward the achievement of your dream, don't think about it, just do it. Face any blocks that come up and let them go. Accept that you have the power of a made-up mind. This power frees you to make up your mind to do whatever that next step is to achieving your dream. Take responsibility for your life, your mind and your happiness---and live.

17 Programming

ONE MUST COME TO A CLEAR UNDERSTANDING that he or she has been programmed from an early age. By this I mean that some dominant relative or group influenced each of us so that we adopted their beliefs, their solutions, their fears, their outlook on life, their everything. And we have spent our lives in the same manner as a marionette, having as little control over our movements and thought processes as does a marionette. We believe what we were programmed to believe, and the patterns of our lives are the summation of these beliefs. Our decision-making ability, moment by moment, down through the years, has been totally influenced by our programming. And the position we find ourselves in at any given moment is the result of these decisions. It's a crying shame that these decisions were made as a result of someone else's thinking, and not our own. The biggest misfortune is that we do not have the slightest idea that it is happening, and for anyone to suggest it is offensive. However, most people's lives follow the same pattern, different names and different places, but always the same results. Successive marriages to alcoholics, limited success in business, relationships which fall apart at the same point each time, and so on. If we are to ever change the pattern of our life, it can only be done if we recognize that we are programmed, and then do what it takes to get rid of the old program and replace it with something more to our liking. There is no other way. People spend a lot of time and money going to positive thinking seminars, and I think they're grand. But the success rate over a period of time has been less than five percent, and the reason is that their prior programming takes precedence, and until it has been removed a new program can't just fall into place. The place is already full. If a glass of water is full, one can't put in another glass. Obviously, the glass must be emptied. Then options are available. One can put in water or tea or milk or whatever. At least it will be an individual selection, not something selected by someone else.

All this to say that TROB is a process by which one becomes aware of his programming and, by seeing it in clear vision, is able to come to grips with it and release it. Then reprogramming according to his own individual yearnings can take place.

Kent Hovis

FAMILY COMMITMENT

Unknowingly, each of us is committed to thinking like our mother, acting like our father and being like our family. The commitment that we made to our family is as controlling as our commitment to our mother and father. Family is defined as all close relatives, such as aunts, uncles, cousins, grandparents and, especially, brothers and sisters. The strongest family commitments are made to those who lived with us when we were growing up, like brothers and sisters, because we saw them on a daily basis, but they are not necessarily the only commitments we made. Often commitments were made to grandparents, cousins, aunts and uncles to whom we were close. This unconscious family commitment controls our lives, allows us to be only the way our family wants us to be and prevents us from being ourselves and being how *we* want to be.

> *Maddy, who was vivacious and effervescent by nature, remained silent in the presence of her sister because her sister always demanded the limelight.*

A child's commitments to being the way he is vary according to each family member. If two family members give opposite messages, as in the case of a grandmother wanting the child to be outgoing and a brother wanting him to be quiet, they create opposite desires in the child, and these opposite desires lead to failure. The person caught in this double bind feels incapable of moving, out of fear of making a mistake and experiencing subsequent pain, suffering and guilt. Unknowingly, the cause of this fear is his commitment to his family. As long as he is committed to being how his family wants him to be, he is not free to be how *he* wants to be, which results in conflict, frustration, moving into the void and, in many cases, fantasy (see chapters: Rebellion and Escaping Responsibility).

Our commitment to thinking the way our mother wants us to think, acting the way our father wants us to act, and being the way our family wants us to be prevents us from wanting to be where we are, makes us want to leave, and causes us to escape.

Because we are unaware of our family commitment, we are also unaware that we are to others how our family members were to us. In truth, our family members are being the way their family members were to them, and until we face this in ourselves, we will continue to treat others the way our family members treat us. To avoid facing this, we often project onto those we love the most that they are treating us the way, in fact, we are treating them.

The strongest family commitment is to brothers and sisters. Unknowingly, many children want to destroy their siblings so that they might be their parents' only child.

> *From the beginning, Tom did not want his younger sister, Joan, to have a relationship with their mother because he wanted to be her only child. Their mother wanted successful children to show off to the world. Tom wanted to be his mother's only successful child. Therefore, he did not want Joan to be successful in anything she did, and wanted to destroy her. When they were children, Tom criticized and tattled on Joan at every opportunity. Unknowingly, Joan's commitment to Tom, then, was to give him what he wanted by being unsuccessful at everything she did and to be destroyed. As a result, she attracted people who tried to destroy her in every area of life. She held herself back for many years until she saw how her commitment to him ran her and controlled her life. With this new awareness, Joan saw her talents and abilities for the first time. She acknowledged these talents and abilities, began to express them and believe in herself and turned her life around. Years later, she realized that her desire to fly airplanes was motivated by her brother, who had been a pilot. Once she saw this, she released all desire to fly a plane and was able to spend her time developing her own talents and abilities.*

When we are close to aunts, uncles, cousins or grandparents, we often commit to being how they want us to be.

> *Barry spent his summers with his invalid grandmother. She had specific ideas about how she wanted him to be and, because she cared intensely about what others thought, she controlled him by keeping him at her beck and call. Barry's commitment to her was to be the perfect grandson, which meant giving her everything she wanted, keeping her alive and making her happy. He was so burdened by her demands and by his commitment to fulfill them, that he sought help at an early age. Once he saw and released his family commitment, he was free from his inner turmoil and was able, for the first time, to think about how he wanted his life to be.*

Serious marital problems can be created when our primary commitment is to put our original family first.

> *Barbara's grandfather did not want Barbara to be married. This resulted in great inner conflict when she did. After marriage, she tried to put her husband first, but was unable to do so because of her prior unconscious commitment to her grandfather. By the end of her first year of marriage, torn by the need to be how her grandfather wanted her to be and the desire to have a happy marriage, she sought help. Once she became aware of this commitment, she was able to release it and, in so doing, free herself to be happily married.*

When seeing in clear vision how your family wants you to be, you may feel anger or resentment toward them. Should this occur, just remember that your family members are living out their family commitments, and are no more aware of this than you were of your commitments to them. Neither their family, your family or you are to blame. So, forgive them and accept them just as they are. Take your responsibility to get clear how you want to be, and be it. You don't have to leave your family to take this responsibility. By taking your responsibility, both your family and your life can be the way you want them to be. It is important for you to prioritize your life, choosing who is number one, number two, and so forth, in order of importance to you. And it is also important to grow up emotionally so that you can become an emotional adult. Growing up emotionally allows you to accept your responsibility, and frees you to be of one mind by being congruent in your heart and mind. Accept that your emotional age is the same as your chronological age. Give thanks for the knowledge and understanding that you are gaining about yourself, and give thanks for your family. Knowing the truth will set you free to be your highest and best, to be all you want to be, to be you.

After you release your commitment to being how your family wants you to be, you sense a freedom, and yet it feels as though something is still holding you back. You feel a reluctance to move on. You no longer identify with your previous commitment, but you have not yet decided on a new one. You are in a state of limbo. It is important to find your niche by discovering what and how you want to be. Once you decide, take your responsibility and make a new commitment to being that.

Arriving at this new awareness is fun and exciting. Spend time alone and ask yourself what you want to be, how you want to be and who you are. Sometimes it helps to begin by looking at what you <u>don't</u> want in order to arrive at what you <u>do</u> want. Make a list of everything you want and a picture will emerge. Ask those whose opinions you value and trust what they perceive your talents and abilities to be. This will assist you greatly in finding your niche. It is important to know that blocks will come up at this point. Face them, let them go and move on.

Once you have your list, prioritize it. Prioritizing eliminates anxiety and frustration, and helps your life to flow.

We strive to be how our family wants us to be so that they will approve of us, accept us and love us. We want to please them so that they will be happy with us. We will even imitate them in order to achieve this. We hope they will, in turn, accept us so that we can accept ourselves. Instead of giving them power over our lives, it is important that we accept ourselves, whether they, or anyone else, does.

> *Don's brother was always jealous of him and wanted him out of the way. In order to give his brother what he wanted, Don contracted diabetes, bone cancer and heart problems. Once Don saw how he was destroying his body for his brother, he let go of his family commitment and began to heal.*

It takes a great deal of time, effort and examination to see clearly how each family member wants us to be. However, the time spent examining and releasing this commitment is the turning point in our life. Releasing this commitment frees us to decide and commit to being how we want to be. We are now adults and we CAN make that choice based on what is right and best for us. By letting go of our family commitment, we free ourselves to begin to live our life the way that works for us, to be how we want to be, to be who we are. It's time for us to accept that we have choice, and to choose.

FAMILY CODE

Within each family there is a code. This family code is both implicit and explicit. Implicit, in that it is largely felt, rather than spoken; explicit, in that the lines are very clearly drawn. There's no doubt about the agenda and there's no stepping over the lines because, to do so, would create terror and evoke wrath.

This unspoken code is passed down from family member to family member. Within this code there is a leader who demands power, allegiance and control. This leader is more important than the God within and/or the god of society. To look at, let alone face, this code would cause tremendous family turmoil, for to do so would necessitate exposing someone with whom the family has been in collusion to defend and protect from the truth of his destructive control. Due to this protection, the one causing the problem remains the hidden power behind the throne. He makes it look as though someone else is running the family. He's setting it up so that he has his way in every situation, and he is the one deferred to. He has absolute power, and is protected from exposure by the whole family, no matter what he does. He is the one who gives the orders and controls the family. The fear of arousing his anger is what keeps him in control. This fear paralyzes some and motivates others to leave. Facing this arouses the same fear that was there when, as a child, you were yelled at, screamed at and, in extreme cases, physically abused. Why put yourself through this fear? Why experience this pain? Why take the risk of exposing your family code? You do this in order to be free to have your dream and to live the life that works for you and your own family.

Unbeknownst to you, this family code has total power and control over your life. It can keep you unmotivated, unproductive and destructive. It is important to see that you are not supposed to look at this code. Take advantage of and use each emotion that surfaces. Face each one and release it, and in so doing, free yourself to have your dream and live your life the way you choose---the way that works for you.

THE CODE BEARER

Everyone has a code of rules by which he lives. This code is determined by the family member who has the greatest influence, power and control over the family: the code bearer. Quite often, there is more than one code bearer. In most cases, the code bearer is obvious, but in others, he is cleverly hiding behind another family member. Accept your code bearer as he is, and face the power that his unknown control has had over your life, so that you may be free from this control forever. The code bearer's influence persists even after his death, and is often responsible for those emotional responses which are difficult to explain. For example, a husband can hardly wait to come home and be with his wife, yet he finds himself walling off, shutting down and feeling trapped as he approaches the driveway. Another example is the girl who looks forward to playing with her friend, yet who becomes inexplicably fearful and physically ill on her way to her friend's house. Or the daughter-in-law who, at a dinner with the in-laws she loves and her code bearer, becomes so ill that she has to go to bed.

The code bearer determines what we are to do, how we are to be, and what we can have in every area of life. His influence permeates each cell in our bodies. Because our subconscious minds have accepted his code, he pulls our strings like a puppeteer, and yet, we are totally unaware of it. His code influences our relationships with those who mean the most to us because it prevents us from being honest with ourselves and with them. Under the guise of love and friendship, our code bearer causes us to use our friends and loved ones, take advantage of them and destroy them, all because the code determines the rules by which we live. It is important to make up our mind to create our own rules. Once we do this, it is helpful to make three lists: what we were allowed to do, what we were allowed to be, and what we were allowed to have, according to our code bearer. It's like working an exciting puzzle. It often takes several days or weeks before we are able to unravel it totally and become fully aware of these codes of living. For example, we might begin to unravel a thread that leads us to see that we were the family scapegoat, and have lived this role in every area of life (see chapter: The Roles). Or we might see that we were the destroyer for our code bearer, destroying our relationships, our businesses and/or our bodies for him. Once we see the enormity of the power this code has for running our life, we will be inspired and motivated to let it go on a level we never dreamed possible. Once our lists of what we want to do, be and have are complete, it is important to accept that we have them now.

The tyrannical code bearer overtly controls every encounter. He suppresses the creative expression and uniqueness of everyone in his life by his overbearing personality. The covert code bearer uses the manipulative technique of scapegoating in order to remain innocent and deferred to. Scapegoating is a technique he uses to blame others for being bad and wrong, while he remains innocent, right and blameless. The scapegoating code bearer is both judge and jury. He has the right to punish his scapegoat for not living up to his expectations. Some code bearers, after scapegoating others, then scapegoat themselves. In this way they, unknowingly, punish themselves for having scapegoated the ones they love. Other code bearers simply get stronger as they scapegoat others.

More often than not, we are in denial and block our feelings, making it difficult, if not impossible, for us to see or believe that anyone else has had control over our life. In fact, the code bearer can get us to destroy for him, while we remain totally unaware that we are doing it. He can do this in one of several ways: by seducing us, by projecting onto us what is in him, by scapegoating, or by transferring another person onto us and treating us as if we were that person. For example, he might, subconsciously, make us his mother, and react to us the way he reacts to her.

Our code bearer doesn't want us to believe in ourselves or have self-confidence, because if we did, he would lose control. Self-doubt originates with the code bearer.

A child's programming is determined by how his mother thinks, how his father acts, how his family is, and what his code bearer allows him to have. It is the code bearer who has the power to determine whether we are for someone or against them, because he tells us who we can or cannot have. If he tells us that we cannot have friends, we won't have them. If he tells us that we cannot have a spouse, and we rebel and marry anyway, we won't be on our spouse's team.

Your code for living life is so powerfully strong that the only way you can begin permanent change is by being born again of the Spirit. Invite God into your heart. To get you off your hands and to be born again is to know joy without bounds, to experience incredible peace, and to have unconditional love. Unconditional love crosses all color and race lines. It sees beauty everywhere, and is friendly and loving to all, even those who betray or turn their back on it.

You have to die to the old program in order to create anew. Your code bearer directs, patterns and controls your life. So, let go of the code bearer who you have, unknowingly, worshipped as your god. Hard as we try to make the God within our God, our code bearer keeps pulling us back. Even the death of the code bearer makes no difference. The die has been cast. The good news is that we are told to know the Truth, and the Truth will set us free. So in knowing the Truth, we are free to let go of the code bearer as our god, and make the God within our God. By prioritizing our life, we can begin to create it the way that will work for us: making God #1, walking with Him, relying, trusting, being the Light, listening and following Him. Then, by making ourselves #2 after God, our spouse #3, and so forth, we are able to create the life that each of us wants. A life of love: love of God, love of self, love of family, love of teams, love of friends, love of work, love of play, love of grandchildren, love of animals, love of all races, all colors, all people. A life of having fun while loving and being loved. This is what life is about.

PACTS

Unbeknownst to us, our lives have been systematically designed by a master architect or architects who had the greatest influence over us as children. We have made either our mother, father, brother, sister, grandparents and/or godparents our authority, and have given them the power to design, direct and control our lives. A pact is made in childhood between us and this authority figure (figures) and, once made, becomes our belief system. The authority figure with whom we formed this lifelong pact can also be someone influential outside the family, such as a teacher, minister, doctor, etc.

A pact is a binding agreement between you and an authority figure to be what they want you to be.

> *As a child, Barbara made a pact with Patty, her younger sister, to give Patty whatever she wanted, in exchange for which Patty would not throw temper tantrums. Because of*

this pact, even as adults, Patty was able to control Barbara with the threat of a raised voice. And, as a result, Barbara gave Patty control over their joint inheritance, and was unable to ask her any questions about where all the money had gone.

Along with a pact, you can have an addendum with an authority figure. An addendum is an addition to the pact, but involves a third party. The addendum is made with someone who has influence over the person with whom you have made a pact (the one who has influence over YOU.) This is a double bind because of the power the third party has over the person with whom you've made a pact. It is harder to see this addendum because it is deeply hidden behind two people instead of one.

Barbara's mother threatened (nonverbally) to banish her from the family if she were not obedient. Barbara made a pact with her mother to protect her image as the perfect mother by not letting the world know that she did not have the perfect family, in return for which her mother would allow Barbara to stay.

Her mother gave Barbara to her (the mother's) older sister to be her authority, so in addition to the pact with her mother, Barbara had an addendum with her aunt. She agreed to make her aunt the matriarch of their family, if the aunt would include and accept her. The matriarch had the power to control all family relationships by determining who was included and who was excluded.

Unknowingly, most people make at least one pact (and some make two, three, or many), and some have an addendum. Every decision and choice you make in your life is based upon these pacts and addenda. These decisions and choices make up your belief system, which determines your future. The persons with whom you made these pacts could have passed away years before, but their power over you through these pacts continues to control your life.

When a child is unjustly accused and unfairly punished, he feels hurt, abandoned and betrayed by God and/or his family, and, in a moment of despair, can choose to rebel and defiantly make a pact with the himself to never be treated this way again. Many people make a pact with the devil to be taken care of and protected. For example, there have been cases in which passengers on hijacked airplanes have joined forces with the hijackers because they feared for their lives, and in so doing, formed a pact with the devil. At some traumatic time in your life, out of fear of losing your life, a parent or a friend, your desperate need for help can open you up to being available to or hypnotized by the devil. On a subconscious level, it feels like the devil will protect you from harm, pain, hurt, death or any other fear the mind can conjure up. But in reality, the devil not only does not protect you, but makes you more vulnerable, by opening you up to doubt and fear. The devil hides behind smoke screens designed to keep up his cover. The deception by those who have made pacts with the devil is impeccably hidden. They are awesome actors and actresses who are masters at covering up their destruction. They work beneath the surface, behind the scenes in the dark, while looking innocent. They get others to do their dirty work for them. They have a hidden agenda. When someone has made a pact with the devil, what you see is not what you get.

An addendum to the devil can be the result of having been given to the devil by an authority figure with whom you've made a pact. Or it can be the result of some traumatic emotional experience which, out of terror, caused you to make an addendum with the devil for help and protection. If you have been given to the dark side, you become its slave, and have no voice. It feels like there is a leash around your neck by which the architect of your pact can jerk you back if you try to step outside of his pre-arranged boundaries. This is so powerful in its control over your life that it is important to see if you have a pact and an addendum, and especially important to make up your mind to face them and end them. It will take a strong desire, time and continued focus to unravel these pacts and addenda. Remember, an addendum is an addition to a pact which you have with a parent or another authority figure. It could even be with a childhood friend. The addendum is more hidden than the pact and, therefore, more powerful. The addendum can be the most destructive of all because of its capacity to hide out. All your attention is on the big issues which keep occurring in your life, but the addendum, since it is an addition, is buried under tons of weight from the pact, holding you down and keeping you from having your dream and living your life. Once you see that you have an addendum, it is necessary to face the fears which caused you to make it, in order to let it go. Because these pacts and addenda are so painful, most people move into a fantasy to protect themselves from the pain. They live out their lives in this fantasy, which keeps them from seeing how things really are (see chapter: Escaping Responsibility).

Many of these pacts and addenda require that you be the perfect human being (see chapter: Perfection). Many pact architects define perfection as having no problems. Perfect people don't have problems. To have a problem, therefore, would reflect on the pact architects, and would make them look less than perfect. If you can't look at a problem, or face a problem, there's no way to solve a problem. This keeps you doing what is necessary to avoid making a mistake or having a problem and, in turn, keeps you from ever having a dream. If you were taught, as a child, that problems mean you have made a mistake, then you believe that problems say something about you---that you are less than perfect. As a result, you are so terrified of making a mistake that you can't even begin to look at having a problem. You have to deal with the mistake before you can deal with the problem. As a result, problems get swept under the rug because you can't get past the mistake in order to arrive at the problem. Being called on a mistake can trigger vengeance, violence, terror, anger, fear, hurt---the gamut of emotions. Once you make a pact, you will do anything to be perfect and avoid making a mistake. Because a mistake says that you are less than perfect to the pact architect, and is a reflection on him, the terror of his abandoning you or kicking you out is so great that you either totally submit or totally rebel. And so, your life is run by the terror of making a mistake.

Anyone who becomes successful in life does so by making many mistakes and learning from them. If you're not free to make a mistake, you can't achieve your goals or reach your dreams. Instead, you sit back and criticize others for doing something, not knowing something or offering you something. You become superior, snobby or vindictive, all because you are not free to make a mistake or to fail. If you're free to fail, you're free to succeed.

The only way out of this jail is to cease putting your faith in facts, and put your trust and belief in Truth. The difference between facts and Truth is that facts will let you down because they are fickle and changeable, but Truth is consistent and unchanging. Truth will lift you up and guide you, step by step, to your dream. The fact is that you made a pact with a family member as a child. The Truth is that you are an adult, and responsible for everything you do or don't do. As long as you come from facts, you will turn Truth into facts, in order to comply with your pact. As long as you come from facts you are stuck in doing, proving and justifying, which keeps you from being. By being loyal to Truth, you find inner security, inner power and inner direction.

Being free to make a mistake and solve problems is freedom. Being free to make a mistake and solve problems makes life exciting. Being free to make a mistake and solve problems is having a life.

Facing these pacts, telling yourself the truth about them, and releasing them frees you to begin to live, and frees you to see what you have done to be true to or rebel against the architect of your life.

It is necessary for you to take responsibility for what you did prior to your awareness of these pacts, instead of blaming the architect(s) of your life. Blaming keeps you locked into the pact. Making up your mind to end it is the only way out of it. This will free you to begin to express your talents and abilities, and to be free to be you. It is an adventure to know yourself, for you are the most important person in your life.

In order to live life joyfully, happily and successfully, there comes a time when you have to take full responsibility for the choices you made as a child, and full responsibility for the choices you make now and for the rest of your life. It means ending blame, ending proving and ending having to be perfect or good enough for some unknown source with unconscious rules and selfish intent. The choice is between freedom and jail, heaven and hell, life and death.

Within each of us is a source of limitless love. Within each of us is a source of abounding energy. This source, which we call God, is a master coach, a master producer and a master director. To find this combination in one source is unheard of in the world. This source is available the moment we choose to invite Him to direct our path. When we choose to totally rely on Him for everything, when we choose to make Him our belief system, when we choose to go Home and live with Him, when we choose to put our hand in His hand, when we choose to be crushed by Him, when we choose to be willing to die for Truth, when we choose to make Him our number one priority in life, then we will find everything we have ever looked for, asked for and dreamed of. Until then we will not be free to do what we want to do, be what we want to be, and have what we want to have. Until then we will not be free to express all of our talents and abilities, and enjoy every moment of our life. And, until then we will not be free to know that every man is equal, that every man is the same, and that every man has unique talents and abilities. This frees us from judgment, and allows us to love, enjoy and have fun with everyone, every second of our life.

It's time to be good to yourself. It's time to love you and be kind to you. This is your greatest gift to yourself. Take the time to become aware of those choices that have blocked you from doing all you can do, from being all you can be, and from having all you can have. Be to yourself the way you have so desired that others be to you. It begins with you. Express, enjoy, love and be you.

OPPOSITE DESIRES

The Life Pattern

Each of us has a life pattern that determines our actions. We are born into a family that creates, supports and reinforces this pattern. Each of our family members has his own life pattern which, though different, fits hand in glove with ours. Our life pattern is set in cement and becomes the blueprint by which we live. Because this blueprint is comfortable and familiar to us, it makes change, goals and resolutions very difficult and, at times, impossible.

> *When Stan's father saw his daughter-in-law drive up to his house he remarked, "Here comes the outsider," thus reinforcing what his son already felt to be true: that his wife <u>was</u> the outsider. In a few years Stan and his wife were divorced. This fulfilled his life pattern, which was to destroy his relationships.*

Why does the pattern of our life make change so difficult? What is it about our life pattern that feels like it holds us back and causes us to resist change, even when we want to change? THE BIGGEST PROBLEM IS BEING UNAWARE OF ITS EXISTENCE AND THE CONTROL IT HAS OVER US. But once we learn of its existence, we can then acknowledge it, take responsibility for it and let it go. Without facing and letting go of the pattern of our life, lasting change is very difficult.

There are different messages that combine to make up the pattern of our life, which is dictated by our possessive, controlling parent or family member. If two of these messages are opposites, such as good girl/playgirl or nice boy/playboy, opposite desires are set up and, because opposite desires are the cause of failure, failure is inevitable.

Opposite Desires

Unknowingly, many parents don't want their children to grow up. They tell their child non-verbally, and sometimes verbally, to remain their "little girl" or "little boy" forever and, simultaneously, they tell him to grow up and take responsibility for what he is doing. Most parents want their child to marry and have children while, at the same time, remain their child. Rather than teaching the child responsibility, they teach him how to act responsibly, by being a "nice boy" or "good girl." At the same time, they want the child to go out and play so that they won't have to be responsible to teach and train him at home. Finally, the message from the possessive, controlling parent or family member becomes abbreviated and carried into adult life as "be a nice girl/playgirl" or "be a nice boy/playboy." This message causes the child to resist growing up and to resist responsibility. When adult responsibilities are required of him, he becomes angry, and can subsequently escape into various addictions, such as food, alcohol, drugs, reading, movies or sleeping. Unknowingly, the life pattern creates enormous sorrow, anguish and frustration.

Opposite desires are created by our possessive, controlling parent or family member's two contradictory desires for us, such as wanting us to relocate in order to be president of the company while, at the same time, wanting us to stay home to take care of him.

Opposite desires force us to sit on the fence where it feels safe and comfortable. They also promote laziness because the fear of failure or feeling bad which occurs when moving in either direction, and the ensuing guilt, are too unbearable. The desire for comfort is one of the most debilitating, crippling, failure-oriented desires we can have. Comfort squeezes all of our ambition, dreams and aspirations from the very core of our being, and leaves laziness in its wake. We become angry and fearful if anyone asks us about anything we have not done, because we can't stand to be held accountable, and we become angry and fearful if anyone asks us to do anything because we don't want to do anything. We resist the request and may retaliate for being placed in this uncomfortable position. We HAVE to retaliate instantly in order to maintain our own "rightness." As a result, we fire the first shot. This knee-jerk reaction reveals that we would rather be right and blameless than happy, successful or have what we want. We would rather prove that we are right and blameless than be ourselves and create our lives successfully. This attack instantly poisons the atmosphere around us, destroys our relationships and prevents us from solving the problem and getting the job done. Because we are not free to say, "I want" or "I don't want," we can't give anyone else the freedom to do so.

Opposite desires are the secret of failure. They are what force us to sabotage our plans, and keep us from achieving our goals and dreams. They create enormous resistance in us and cause us, unknowingly, to destroy what we want, destroy our success and prevent us from focusing our attention on one task for any length of time. Opposite desires can range from mild---wanting to be in two places at once---to extreme---being married and, at the same time, wanting to be divorced. An example of the mild expression of opposite desires occurred when Mary Jane was invited to a shower for her best friend's daughter. She wanted to attend and made plans to do so, but, at the same time, wanted to go out of town with her husband. Even though her husband was fine with either choice, Mary Jane felt tense, indecisive and pulled from within when faced with this decision. However, once she made up her mind to attend the shower, the tension, indecisiveness and inner pull immediately left.

> *An example of the extreme expression of opposite desires happened to Don, who wanted to marry Joan and who, while walking her down the aisle, changed his mind and wanted to live alone. After ten years of marriage and two children, they divorced. Not long after the divorce, Don wanted Joan back. In the meantime, Joan had met, fallen in love with and married Jim. By the time Don realized he had made a mistake, it was too late---Joan was already happily married. Because they had children together and because Don was willing to face himself and his opposite desires, they were able to remain friends.*

Opposite desires prevent us from including our loved ones in our life, and are a major cause of the demise of our relationships.

The energy emitted by a person experiencing opposite desires is unbearable to sensitive people, making them feel that the one with opposite desires is always leaving. The truth is, he is. He just doesn't say so.

With opposite desires, we can be going in one direction and suddenly change directions in mid-stream without being aware of it. When we become exhausted from trying to live up to our own or others' expectations of how we should be, our mind flips to the opposite direction. The flip occurs when the pressure to be who we said we were becomes too great, when we feel bad and guilty for doing what we want to do, when we give our plans, dreams or desires to someone who influences us in a destructive way by causing us to doubt our ability, or when we want relief from the fear of being found out. This flip then becomes an escape from telling ourselves and others the truth and taking responsibility for what we have done or not done, or from how we are being or not being. The flip is used to take the attention off our possible destruction and to avoid being blamed or told we are bad or not good enough. We become angry at those who want us to do what we said we'd do, and project onto them that they expect us to live up to what we said we'd do. In truth, we want to do it, but we know we're not going to, so in order to get it done we have to deny to ourselves that we're not going to do it, and then will ourselves to get the job done. However, willing ourselves can last only from three days to two weeks.

In the absence of someone to blame for our not keeping our promises or expressing our talents and abilities, we seek various mental and emotional escapes: denial, deceiving ourselves and others, moving into the void, fantasy, not telling the truth to ourselves or others and creating mental blocks (see chapter: Escaping Responsibility). Often we become angry with those who have spontaneity and the courage to "go for it," and out of envy or jealousy, challenge them to hold them down. On some level we know that we're not going to do what we said we'd do because we can't, but we don't know why.

> *Mary was married and had four children. She had opposite desires. She both wanted to be a wife and mother, and didn't want to be. Because she resisted her responsibilities as a wife and mother, she was continuously exhausted. To replenish her low energy, she would mentally and emotionally drain her husband of his energy and, in so doing, created a low energy household. She felt alone, unloved and unwanted. She believed that her husband was able to have more fun and enjoyment than she could. She wanted to leave, and blamed her husband for her unhappiness. As soon as he apologized, accepted the blame for her unhappiness and felt guilty, she flipped from feeling unhappy, powerless and inferior to him to feeling happy, right, blameless and superior to him. She would go from fear to anger, from self-pity (martyrdom) to meanness, and in so doing, expressed her opposite desires.*

Paul, a master salesman, was loved by everyone. Though sales were the perfect vehicle for him, he was never able to meet his financial needs. The pressure of having to live up to his self-imposed expectations to be family provider became so great that he both resisted and resented selling, and decided to become a professional golfer. He felt he could play golf and meet his financial obligations without pressure. He practiced and worked hard to get on the professional tour, while remaining in sales in order to pay his bills. He wanted to both make money and play golf; to work and play. For him, these were opposites. When he became a professional golfer and money was involved, golf ceased being fun. He was also pulled by his wife's opposite desires. She wanted him to be there for her all the time, emotionally and physically, and, at the same time, wanted him to go out and earn money. As a result of flipping from one to the other, opposite desires prevented him from focusing his attention in one direction and being a success at either career.

There are several symptoms of opposite desires: having energy, then suddenly, inexplicably, becoming exhausted; loving what you're doing, then suddenly hating it; love/hate relationships; excitement/depression; happiness/sadness; lack/abundance; winning/losing; passivity/aggression; superiority/inferiority; self-assurance/doubt; giving to others/taking back; feeling good enough/feeling bad; confusion/clarity; frustration/freedom to say, "I want;" impatience/patience; taking things personally/going to cause and being torn between being where you are and wanting to be elsewhere. Inconsistency reflects opposite desires.

Maddy loved food and, at the same time, wanted to lose weight. As a result, every time she prepared to eat something she loved, she would ask herself if she really wanted it. If she ate it, she felt guilty; if she didn't eat it, she craved it. Her inability to make a decision was caused by opposite desires.

Those with opposite desires create disharmony in their environment and destroy the atmosphere because of their desire not to be where they are. They are always leaving mentally, emotionally and/or physically for fear of being found out for not being who they claim to be, and for fear you will ask them to do something. They don't want to do anything, and truly believe you are lucky to have them. They develop different techniques which provide valid excuses to stay away from you. Some people travel, some are always sick, and some stay away by going in and out of the hospital.

Love/Hate

If you ask someone with opposite desires to do something, he can both love and hate to do it, and both love and hate you for asking him to do it. Opposite desires make him blame and criticize you for "making" him do it. He will procrastinate and finally will himself to get the job done. Upon completion of the task, he must immediately escape to the safety of his car, home or office and reward himself by doing nothing.

The opposite emotions of love and hate can co-exist in the same person. In the love/hate cycle, each emotion has an equal duration. The swings are visible and predictable. Because of its inconsistency, the up and down roller coaster of these cycles destroys relationships and inner peace.

By staying uninvolved and remaining an observer, the lover/hater keeps all relationships at a distance, including those closest to him. He reacts to life instead of living life. He acts the part rather than being it. Life becomes a play, a fantasy, rather than reality.

Love/hate is a commitment that stems from opposite desires and is created to destroy your relationships for your possessive, controlling parent or family member. Opposite desires can result in the tendency to see both sides of every situation and to feel noble for doing so. In truth, opposite desires produce an inability to take a stand for one side or the other for fear of taking a risk, taking the wrong stand and, thereby, making a mistake. The excuse for not taking a stand is that the one with opposite desires is able to see both sides; the truth is, he does not have choice. Love/hate is a clue to realizing that he has opposite desires and that choice has been taken from him by his possessive, controlling parent or family member.

The lover/hater can never be happy for any length of time. His life is about ups and downs. For everything he does on the positive side of the ledger, he offsets it by doing something on the negative side. If he makes money, he expects to lose it; if his relationships are going well, he expects them to fall apart. Nothing lasts. When he's in the hate cycle, he has to have a scapegoat on whom to vent his hate and blame (see chapter: The

Roles). He thinks, "After all I've done for you," and feels that the scapegoat should allow him to hate and blame him---and becomes angry if the scapegoat won't let him. When he's in the love cycle, the lover/hater builds the relationship, and sees the other person through the eyes of love. Then, suddenly, he sees the other person through the eyes of hate. The lover/hater has to punish his lover for being the object of his love.

If we are lover/haters, love/hate is our way of life. It is how we live our life. We can tell the truth as long as we keep our relationships superficial. We all want to love and be loved, but when we find love, our programming from our possessive, controlling parent or family member causes us to pull back and hate the object of our love. Surface truths create surface relationships. Telling the truth about how we feel creates intimate relationships. In a marriage, there is an intimacy which involves sexuality and deep feelings. In the mind of the lover/hater, these feelings are not allowed to be expressed. The lover/hater feels threatened because he's afraid he'll be asked to do something he can't do or doesn't want to do, which is everything, and that expectations will be placed on him which will expose him. He's not free to say, "I want" or "I don't want," nor does he give others the freedom to do so. He feels trapped and held down. He can't say, "no" to an "I want" request because it makes him feel bad. When he's in the hate cycle, he hates the one who requests anything of him because that person is exposing him as being less than perfect for not having already thought of it. When he's in the love cycle, he hurries to fulfill the request while he has energy. The lover/hater does just enough to get by, and always has an excuse in order to remain right and blameless. He feels that everyone puts expectations on him, but in truth, he is projecting _his_ expectations onto others. He believes that expectations lie behind every request, and he's afraid of not measuring up to them. He blames his scapegoat for holding him down while, in truth, he is holding himself down by his opposite desires.

As awareness grows, the love/hate cycle shortens, with love and hate following each other in rapid succession.

> *A lover/hater and her teacher were in the teacher's office. The teacher asked her to close the air conditioning vent, which she did lovingly because she was in the love cycle. The teacher immediately requested that she place a large object over the vent. Instantly and unknowingly, the lover/hater felt hatred for her teacher, and punished her by not giving her*

what she wanted. She heard the request, but chose to ignore it.

The lover/hater has to do everything his way. To give others what they want is to take away the lover/hater's right to do it his way, which makes him feel held down or held back. When he's in the love cycle, the lover/hater wants to give others what they want. In the hate cycle, the slightest request feels like an imposition, as if he's being put upon. In this cycle he doesn't want to give anyone what they want, and their request angers him. He punishes them by being vindictive.

The way out is to make a choice between love and hate, between the world and God, between the dark side and the Light. Let go of opposite desires, let go of hate and accept that you love.

The truth is that everyone with opposite desires wants to be free from their inner conflict. We avoid facing our opposite desires by compensating for them: doing simple, insignificant and/or fun things, making it look like we're getting the job done. In truth, we are doing just enough to get by. We become trapped by comfort and laziness. We go through the motions of doing what we've been told will work, and believe it will. This is the story of opposite desires: stick our head in the sand and "hope for the best while expecting the worst." When we have opposite desires, even if we get comfortable, we can never fully enjoy our comfort because of the guilt which comes, on some level, from knowing that we haven't done our job. We know that we feel guilty, but we don't know why. We know we haven't done anything wrong---we just haven't taken our responsibility for doing what we said we'd do.

The person with opposite desires both wants to do what he said he'd do and doesn't want to do what he said he'd do.

> *Tammy loved to help her busy friend, Maddy, put together large parties. On one occasion, Tammy bought the groceries, cooked the main dish and brought it to Maddy's house. Later, Maddy thanked her and said she could not have had the successful party without her. Because Tammy had opposite desires, she both wanted to help Maddy and didn't want to. She knew that the only way she'd gotten the job done was through effort and will, and so, felt both happy and guilty accepting Maddy's gratitude. This describes Tammy's life.*

When we have opposite desires, it is difficult, if not impossible, to receive a gift of gratitude, whether verbal or material.

The only time we do not have the low energy which accompanies opposite desires is when we're playing. Some people who have opposite desires can get things done, but it takes great effort and will to overcome their resistance. They live in the future. The whole time they're working, all they can think about is getting through with what they're doing so that they can rest. They have a low-grade anger as a result of their resistance to being asked to do anything.

To end this living death that has run our life we must:
- Face opposite desires,
- Choose to end opposite desires forever,
- Decide what we want,
- Make up our mind that we deserve to have what we want, and get a program and do it.

It is important to let go of opposite desires on all four levels. When we are on the first level, we don't see what we are doing, and are unable to hear or listen. On the second level, we feel confused. On the third level we see what we are doing, but can't stop doing it. And on the fourth level we face our opposite desires, tell ourselves the truth about them and make up our mind to let them go forever. Once we let go of opposite desires and make up our mind to follow our program, it will be easy and effortless. Letting go of opposite desires ends the inner tug of war: once we let go of one side of the rope, the pull is over.

Opposite desires are indigenous to the life pattern of many people. Seeing our life pattern clearly is necessary in order to understand what our life has been about.

> *Sara's possessive father wanted her to destroy all men in her life in order to remain his one and only. The pattern of her life was right and blameless/know-it-all/good girl/ playgirl. Unconsciously, she established a pattern of flipping between the four. Unknowingly, she was destroying her relationships with men for her possessive father. After two divorces and many destroyed relationships, she chose to unravel the pattern of her life. Once it was unraveled and faced, she took responsibility for her destructiveness. She let*

go of each of the four parts of her pattern. Old friends immediately recognized and acknowledged the spectacular changes in her. After releasing her life pattern she no longer had to be right and blameless, but instead, could be real. She was then able to take responsibility for her life and for all of her relationships. She accepted that she loved and was loved on all four levels. Then she accepted that she cared and was cared about on all four levels. As a result, her relationships moved to a profound new level in which she was able to love, care and support everyone. Now, looking through the eyes of love and caring, she sees everyone and everything in her life differently.

SYNOPSIS

The pattern of our life is either positive or negative, constructive or destructive, resistant or cooperative. With opposite desires it is a combination of these. The person with a negative belief system has to be right and blameless. To the one with a positive belief system, IT JUST DOESN'T MATTER if he is right or wrong. The one with a negative belief system sees everything as life or death---being right is life; being wrong is death. The one with a positive belief system only cares about getting the job done; being right and blameless just doesn't matter. The one with a negative belief system destroys his relationships with himself and others by HAVING to always be right and blameless, while the one with a positive belief system is able to create warm and loving relationships because he is willing to be wrong and can solve problems. Because the one with a positive belief system doesn't have to be right and blameless, he can do what it takes to get the job done. Because the one with a negative belief system has to be right and blameless, he does just enough to get by in order to look good. The person with a positive belief system is a problem solver; the person with a negative belief system is a problem creator who denies it. His attitude is, "I don't have a problem. You have a problem." Many people are driven by the need to be perfect. The negative person believes he's already perfect so he doesn't have to do anything about it. The positive person knows he's not perfect and works hard in his pursuit of perfection. The negative one has enormous resistance to anyone saying, "I want" or "I don't want" because that tells him he is less than perfect and, therefore, not good enough. He perceives others' wanting something from him as their saying he should have already known and/or done what they wanted without their having to ask, and that, because he has not already done it, he is wrong and to blame. In his mind they are saying he's not good enough. In truth, what he is, unknowingly, doing is projecting onto them his belief that he is not good enough, which triggers his anger. The negative one has two different agendas going on: perfect and not good enough, and it's these two different agendas that keep him terrified that others will see that he is not who he says he is. To the negative one, when someone says, "I want," in his mind they are saying, "I want you to get it for me," or "I want you to do it for me." He hears them telling him what to do, and this arouses his anger, when all they are doing is verbally sharing their wants with him. He cannot hear what they are saying because he is so busy living the pattern of his life and scrambling to be right and blameless. Because the negative one feels that the positive one is making him wrong and blamed, threatening his belief that he is perfect, the positive one becomes the enemy, and the negative one must either resist him, destroy him or leave. Conversely, he gets angry when he has to ask for something because he believes others should already know what he wants without his having to ask. He projects onto them, believing to his core that they are saying or doing what, in fact, he has said or done, and that he is right and blameless and they are wrong and to blame. In his mind, the projection justifies his anger and subsequent destruction. In the end, his destruction backfires and he begins destroying the things that mean the most to him: his relationships, his career and, in the end, his body. At this point he has the opportunity to face his destruction, the cause of it and end it.

Because our life pattern was established in childhood and does not work for us in adulthood, it is important to face and let go of each of its four parts on four different levels. Because nature can't stand a vacuum, and a vacuum is created when we release the four parts of our life pattern, it is necessary to replace the four old ones with four new ones of our choosing. It is exciting to know that we can let go of our old life pattern and select a new one. In order to do so, it is necessary to accept that we have choice. Choice is freedom, freedom to create and choose how we want our life to be. Do we want our life to be free, creative, happy, loving, caring, enjoyable, truthful and fun? In order to be free to live our new life pattern it is necessary to forgive anyone from our past who has hurt, betrayed or disappointed us. To do so, first, we forgive him. If there is any hate toward him, we let the hatred go. (Sometimes, there is no hatred.) Then, we accept him as he is and accept that we love the angel within him. Sometimes it is necessary to forgive the same person as many as 100 times. We do this until we get assurance from God that we have completely forgiven him.

Before letting go of our old life pattern, we were not taking responsibility for our mind. Now, it is important that we take full responsibility for our mind, for our happiness and for all our relationships. To do so frees us from anyone else running our life, frees us to accept others as they are without blame, and frees us to give others the freedom to be themselves. This freedom allows for open communication, freedom to express our talents and abilities, freedom to love and be loved, freedom to tell the truth, and freedom to see beauty everywhere. And most important of all, freedom to care, have joy and have fun every second of our life.

18 From Role to Reality to Your Dream

From the beginning of time, man's biggest problem has been ignorance: ignorance of knowing who he is, ignorance of knowing what he wants and doesn't want, and ignorance of knowing that he can have it all. If he knew that by telling himself the truth, taking a stand for it, and taking responsibility for it, he could have everything he wants, telling himself the truth would then become easy. What was before, complex, would then become simple. The beginning of the solution to this problem of ignorance is to truthfully answer a few simple questions. What do you want? What is holding you back from having it? Do you block your feelings? Why? Can you say, "I want" without becoming angry or depressed? Can others say, "I want" to you without your becoming angry at them or depressed? Can you say, "I don't want" without becoming enraged or depressed? Can others say, "I don't want" to you without your becoming enraged at them or depressed? Do you have a dream? Can you set up a step-by-step plan to achieve your dream? Are you willing to face any blocks to doing this? Do you escape into a role, a fantasy or the void rather than making up your mind to express your talents and abilities, making up your mind to have your dream, and going for it? Do you care what other people think? Are you willing to withstand the possible attacks, humiliation or rejection that can come from friends, family and loved ones when you have a dream and go for it? Are you willing to end cowardice by taking a stand for Truth, if it means your death, even if it is just your truth? Do you exclude certain people? Do you feel that you're being excluded? Have you avoided problems at all costs, to the point of denying that you have a problem? Has your mind gone blank while reading this? Are you in denial? Are you willing to face the truth that a life without problems is a life of boredom, blame and mediocrity, resulting in escape into roles, wars, rebellion, the void or fantasy? Have you been critical of those who have gone for and achieved their dream, while you resisted yours? IT IS IMPORTANT TO SEE THAT YOU ARE DOING TO OTHERS WHAT YOU ARE AFRAID WOULD BE DONE TO YOU IF YOU EXPRESSED YOUR TALENTS AND ABILITIES. It is also important to see that without a dream in which you can express your talents and abilities and without a made up mind to go for it, you will become destructive to yourself or to those who are going for theirs, without being aware of it.

Most people let external circumstances and others determine how they feel or how they SHOULD feel, instead of going to the cause of their problem and finding its solution. Those who have had to be perfect for their parents or other authority figures, more often than not, were not free to have problems, for having problems would mean that they were less than perfect. Being free to have problems, facing them, and finding their cause and solution is a necessary step toward having your dream. This is one of the most freeing things you can do for yourself. Many people live their lives doing everything they do to avoid problems, so that they can remain right and blameless. They react with anger, rage or depression to any request prefaced by the words, "I want" or "I don't want," out of fear of being asked to do something they don't want to do and/or out of fear of making a mistake and, thereby, being told they're not good enough and seen as less than perfect. These fears keep them on the defensive at all times and prevent them from being themselves, having a dream and expressing their talents and abilities. The fears keep them from going forward in life. Until they see this in clear vision, they will be unable to see that they are living a role.

THE ROLE

There are four roles: right and blameless destroyer, wrong and blamed scapegoat, controller and controllee. The role is what people take on to escape from their responsibility to be who they are. They choose a role in order to have an identity and be "somebody." Deep within them is a strong need to be both approved of and taken care of. The roles are created out of this need. These roles prevent them from having a dream and expressing their talents and abilities (see chapter: The Roles).

The right and blameless destroyer has to destroy his relationships. He creates a scapegoat who he makes wrong and blames for everything---and the scapegoat accepts the blame. He deceives the scapegoat into believing that he will take care of him, but in truth, the destroyer dominates him, stifles him and gets the scapegoat to take care of <u>him</u>. In order to be approved of and taken care of, the wrong and blamed scapegoat both invites and allows the destroyer to dominate him. The controller needs to maintain control in order to feel secure and comfortable. Unless he is in control, he is confused and doesn't feel at home anywhere. At the same time, the controllee is dependent on the controller for his self-worth, self-esteem and value. Like the wrong and blamed scapegoat, the controllee wants to be taken care of, but in order to maintain his control, the controller attempts to hold the controllee down and back by withholding what the controllee wants, and what he (the controller) said he would give him. The controller and controllee roles are subtler than those of the right and blameless destroyer and the wrong and blamed scapegoat. The controller gives the controllee more freedom than the destroyer gives the scapegoat in that the controllee is controlled, but not dominated and stifled.

> *Susan, a right and blameless destroyer, was married for 50 years to Robert, a wrong and blamed scapegoat. She was overly demanding, while he asked for nothing. She became angry at him when he retired and stayed at home with her because she didn't want him around while she sat and watched TV all day. Susan spent the last year of Robert's life not speaking to him. After this year of silence, Robert died, from no apparent cause. Susan finally got what she wanted.*

> *When Darlene, a scapegoat, fell in love with Don, a destroyer, they seemed made for each other. He was fun, he made her laugh, and he acted warm, caring and attentive. Unbeknownst to Darlene, Don began stealing small items and cash from her. This became clear in retrospect because she was always short of cash, but couldn't figure out why. Although she had very little money, she let him move in with her. Because he had even less money, she paid all the bills. After he moved in with her, she realized that he contributed nothing*

to the relationship, but did not say anything to him about it. He stopped acting like he cared and became verbally abusive. She accepted his criticism because she thought she deserved it. Her eyes were opened when she gave him money to pay a utility bill and he never did, but instead, lied to her. He told her he had given the money to his friend, who was going to pay the bill. Still, she did nothing about it because she wanted to believe him. When she finally saw how much he enjoyed his sadistic cruelty, she ended the relationship.

If the right and blameless destroyer sees that his role isn't working, he changes his tactics and moves into the role of controller, where he begins the process of controlling instead of destroying and stifling. If the wrong and blamed scapegoat revolts, he moves into the controllee role.

Tom, a former destroyer who moved into the role of controller, volunteered to handle the financial records for a school he attended. When he took on the project and saw the mismanagement that had taken place, he did not want anyone else to handle it. He felt that he was the person to straighten things out, and wanted control over the finances. While he wanted control over the project, he felt that he was being controlled. He resented anyone questioning him about what he was doing because their questions made him feel that he was being watched and that he was not good enough. When he saw that he could not control the people in his life and could not hold them down and back, he began pulling away to be by himself. Although he took responsibility for the school's finances, he did not take responsibility for the sizable debts he had accrued in his own business. When he let go of his controller role, he no longer felt defensive, paranoid, or that he had to be in total control of the school's finances. He could now take responsibility for his own finances as well.

Nancy, a scapegoat, dated Stan, a destroyer, for three years, at which time she got so fed up with being a scapegoat that she moved into the controllee role. While they dated, Nancy adored Stan, and would do anything he asked. As a scapegoat, her honesty left her open to blame. She was so

> *terrified of making a mistake that she took the blame for everything that went wrong in the relationship. She even accepted blame for what <u>he</u> did wrong. Stan treated Nancy like a servant, and constantly caused her to doubt herself by criticizing her, asking questions she could not answer, mentally entrapping her, and telling her that she needed psychiatric help. It was only when Nancy learned that Stan had treated his former girlfriend like a queen (because she didn't want him, which made her more desirable) that she was able to see his destruction to her and end the relationship.*

The reason we take on a role, rather than being who we are, being real and taking our responsibility, is to have an identity, to be approved of and to be taken care of. We live our lives protecting and defending our ego and whoever we have chosen to take care of us. To be taken care of is to give up our freedom to do what we want to do and to be real---without being aware we are doing it.

Needing the approval of a possessive parent or family member keeps you on his team and prevents you from being on anyone else's team unless he approves of it. To have a successful marriage, the Bible tells women to submit to their husbands, and men to love their wives (Ephesians 5:22, 24, 25, 28, 33). This is often misinterpreted by husbands or wives as allowing the husband to control or dominate the wife. For a wife to submit to her husband is to make him the ultimate authority and spiritual leader of the family. For a husband to love his wife is to take charge and take responsibility for his wife and family, to be openly affectionate with his wife, and to take responsibility to be the spiritual leader of the family.

To accept that you have the power of a made-up mind means you have the power to make up your mind to do anything you want to create your life the way you want it to be. This is life transforming. Without a made-up mind, it's so difficult to even get started, and to accomplish anything requires a strong will, which soon becomes exhausting, whereas making up your mind and taking responsibility makes whatever you choose to do easy.

REALITY

Reality involves taking your responsibility and taking charge of your life. Reality involves telling yourself and others the truth, and taking a stand for your truth. Reality is being yourself, being real, having congruency between your emotional and chronological ages, being all you can be, and being your highest and best. Reality means not allowing anyone to control or dominate you. Reality means wanting, but not needing anything from anyone. Reality means forgiving yourself, accepting yourself as you are, and loving yourself. Reality means that the buck stops here---that you are responsible for your life and happiness, that you are responsible for what you do and don't do, that you are responsible for each of your relationships. Reality is letting go of all resistance, and accepting that you are in the flow. Reality means making up your mind to do anything it takes to create your dream.

YOUR DREAM

Going for your dream gives purpose, direction and excitement to your life. You have to have a made up mind to stay focused and look neither to the left or the right, but straight ahead to your dream. Accept that you have your dream now and get the feeling that you have your dream now. While there will often be attacks from those who want to hold you down and back from going for your dream, once you make up your mind to go for it, the attacks stop. A made-up mind is essential to eliminate attack. A dream presents you with the opportunity to focus. Focus is absolutely necessary to keep you from being pulled down and back by those who feel threatened by your dream and your determination to go for it. Focusing, maintaining singleness of purpose, and not thinking about it---just doing it are the stepping stones to the achievement of your dream. Make up your mind that you will not allow ANYONE to stop you or your dream. You can't care what people think, you can't need to be taken care of, and you can't need anything from anyone. You can want it, but not need it. Need, the inability to focus, being a taker, and the feeling of lack are all obstacles to your dream.

The Taker

In order to have your dream, you have to be a giver and receiver instead of a taker. Lack is caused by being a taker. For example, a taker will take all the apples off a tree and horde them. Because he has taken more than he can eat, many of the apples spoil. The giver and receiver takes only what he wants from those that fall to the ground and are naturally ripe. He leaves the rest for others. He knows that there will always be an abundant supply of apples, whereas the taker is fearful that there won't be enough for him. The taker believes in lack.

Being a taker destroys having your dream. Because takers doubt that they can have a dream, they try to take other people's dreams. If you are a taker, you've got to grow up and cease wanting to be taken care of by anyone, in order to have your dream. If you don't go for your dream, you will become critical and judgmental of others. A taker always has a low-grade anger which keeps those close to him walking on eggshells for fear that his anger will erupt. Rather than take responsibility for his anger, the taker projects his feelings onto others, and believes it's the other person who is angry. The taker always feels anxiety and tension. There's never enough, he is never good enough, and others are never good enough. This feeling of not being good enough keeps him on the treadmill of lack, always feeling that there's not enough, and always afraid that someone will take what he has from him. He clings tenaciously to what he has, which prevents him from taking a risk to achieve his dream. He can't look at what he wants, but looks at what others have, and determines what he wants from that---and he's never grateful for what he has. He is always comparing, and what he has is never good enough. Not being able to have happiness, abundance and peace causes him to wall off and makes him angry and mean. His fear of losing what he has makes him guard what is his, and this makes him mean---he has to scare you and keep you away so you won't steal what he's got. The main reason for his meanness is his inability to say, "I want" and "I don't want." He can't let people know what he wants because if he does, he will be denied it. So he has to charm you into giving it to him without having to ask for it. He develops a strong personality and charm to manipulate you. He has a facade, and acts pitiful to control you. He is narcissistic, and no one else matters.

Being willing to go for a dream, and being willing to do whatever it takes to achieve it are necessary in order to change this unconscious pattern of taking instead of giving and receiving. Sometimes it takes a tragedy or losing something or someone who means a lot to you to get you to see this pattern and make up your mind to change it.

The Code

Most every child has one or more authority figures in his life who become his code bearers and determine the code by which he lives (see chapter: Programming). These code bearers can be teachers or coaches, as well as family members. They write and devise a plan for the child's life. Unknowingly, the child makes a pact with these code bearers in order to please them, and these code bearers then become the architects of his life (see chapter: Programming). Each pact has an accompanying code which the child, unknowingly, lives out. The code or codes are the way in which the pacts are expressed. Until you see these codes and face them, you are not free to express your unique talents and abilities, nor are you free to be you. You are, unconsciously, acting out the code that you and your code bearer mutually agreed upon for you. The code is the way in which you express what your code bearer wants you to do, be and have. If your code bearer tells you you're not good enough, this belief will create physical, as well as emotional, pain. When you let go of being not good enough, and accept that you are good enough four times, the pain will dramatically disappear. If there are two or more code bearers giving conflicting messages, living out these codes produces such suffering that most children create a fantasy in which they escape to safety. Living in this fantasy shields them from the pressure of the conflicting codes. Reality for them is the codes their code bearers have given them, by which they live, and the fantasy is what they created in order to cope with this reality.

Jane had four code bearers: her mother, her father, her grandmother and her brother. In an effort to please her code bearers and receive their approval, she flipped between the two roles of Right and Blameless Destroyer and Wrong and Blamed Scapegoat. The code she had to live out for her mother was the perfect woman who worshipped the god of society and, consequently, was controlled by what people thought. Her father's code for her was to be an aggressive bully and tyrant, as well as a victim. Her grandmother's code was to revere her grandmother for having religious and intellectual superiority, see her as a perfect, god-like woman, make her the matriarch of the family, and follow in her religious footsteps. Lastly, her code for her brother was to hold her opponent down and back, and be a snake in the grass, appearing innocent, while striking her victims from behind. She expressed whatever code would work to get her taken care of.

In looking at these four codes given to her by her code bearers, we can see how diametrically opposed they are. How is she to be? Which code is she to carry out? She found that the only way for her to survive this inner tug-of-war was to move into a fantasy where she sat still so that she would be safe. She learned that she could paint while sitting still, but, after having her self-expression criticized by her brother, turned to reading novels and living her life vicariously through the characters in the novels she read.

Polly was a playgirl/seductress as a result of her pact with one code bearer, and a good girl who didn't like sex for her other code bearer. These two different codes created such opposite desires in her that they caused her to destroy all of her relationships.

Some children are so sensitive and so eager to please that they take on many code bearers and are, consequently, pulled in many directions by the need to please them.

Bob, who came from a large family, had fifteen code bearers: aunts, uncles, his father, his sister, a cousin and two athletic coaches. After letting go of all these code bearers and his attachment to them, he felt joyful and blissful. Before the releasing he felt dead; afterwards he came alive.

The number of codes that we have and live by are determined by the number of code bearers we invite and allow to direct our life. We take on different personalities to both express their codes and receive their approval. We can change personalities so rapidly that we confuse others. This sudden change in personalities often causes the destruction of our relationships.

We are given a code by each of our code bearers by which to express who they want us to be. This is often determined by their unfulfilled needs. They can want to live vicariously through us, and either want us to do, be and have everything they couldn't, or want to hold us back to keep us from leaving them. Jane, in the first example, was unable to openly express the aggressive/bully code she got from her father because it was in conflict with her mother's code of being the perfect lady. She appeared to the world to be lazy because she moved as little as possible. The truth was, she didn't move because of the inner tug-of-war resulting from these conflicting codes, and from her terror of making a mistake. Most people are controlled by the terror of their code bearers' leaving them and, in the end, being left alone and lonely. This terror keeps them constantly seeking their code bearers' approval. Often we can express the aggressive, bullying code with a spouse or a child because we can get away with it with them. We learn that there are certain circumstances in which we can express our code without loss of family or friends.

There are those rare souls who are allowed and encouraged to be themselves by a parent or family member who is not playing a role, and for whom code bearers don't exist. These people are given positive principles by which to live, rather than restrictive, controlling codes. These people are unique in that they are always refreshing to be with.

One of the requirements of growing up is to let go of these code bearers' control, take charge of your life, and establish your own code. That's not to say that many of the codes you were given were not positive, but being pulled by all these code bearers, and wanting to please them, is what creates such pressure, and can often lead to rebellion or escape into destructive habits.

Once you start stepping outside your code, you'll hear, "Don't get too big for your britches," "Who do you think you are?" "Money doesn't grow on trees," "You're too smart for your own good," "Watch out. Don't let success go to your head," or "Watch out. You might fail," in order to snatch you back into your role so you can be controlled. It seems as though those who have the greatest talents and abilities are held down the most for daring to outshine their code bearers.

If you decide to end these codes and be yourself, it is important to know that all the forces within you are going to scream, "Watch out!" or "Don't do it!" or "Danger ahead." That is the time to pull out all the stops and make up your mind to go for it, no matter what. That is the time to "cut the rope to the mainland," and to do the thing that scares you the most. It serves you to face and remove your blocks to this, and then to release each new block one at a time as it appears. Don't think about it, just do it. In order to eliminate the codes from your life, get a mental image of them, one at a time. Find a character in a movie, television series, book or fairy tale with whom you can identify, one that represents your codes and your code bearer. Walk into a steel-lined room with a steel door. Close the door behind you. Pull a key out of your back pocket with a picture of this code on it. Walk to the steel door, unlock it with the key, push the door open, and walk out onto a veranda that overlooks the ocean. With your left hand, reach into your head and pull out the code with which you identify. With your right hand, throw the key with the picture of your code on it out into the ocean. Repeat this process with each code which originated with your code bearer. Let go of each code bearer individually, and let go of your attachment to each of them. Some may have long since passed away, but they still maintain control over you through this code. Forgive yourself, accept yourself as you are, and accept that you love yourself.

Releasing these codes will free you to create your own code for your life.

Responsibility

Everyone wants to be happy and feel good about themselves. In order to do so, it is necessary to take full responsibility for your life and your happiness. When you take this responsibility, you take the time to find out what works for you and what doesn't. Taking full responsibility frees you to do what you do because you want to, and frees you to let go of the escapes you have provided for yourself to avoid taking it, such as denial, blame, destruction, roles, fantasy and the void. Two of the major escapes are not being free to say, "I want" and "I don't want" and resistance. Unknowingly, resistance creates a wall between you and all your relationships, and the unspoken message the wall sends out is, "Don't ask me to do anything, because I don't want to." Some of the things which people resist are: change, having to do anything they don't want to do, losing control, acknowledging, valuing, loving and being loved, giving and receiving, problems, fun, responsibility and life. And some people resist everything. When you are resisting, you feel intruded upon, irritated, bothered by any request, and unable to feel grateful for anything, whereas, when you take responsibility, you see beauty everywhere, you're free to say, "I want" and "I don't want," to express your talents and abilities, have a dream, love and be loved, give and receive, and you are grateful for everything. To go from resistance to responsibility is to go from hell to heaven, and move into a whole new world. What does resistance do to a marriage? It destroys marriage, even if the resistant spouse is very much in love with the non-resistant spouse. The worst thing about this situation is that the resistant spouse doesn't know he's doing it. How do you deal with someone who doesn't know he's destroying the relationship that means the most to him? You don't. All you can do is gently tell him how it feels on the other side. The problem with this is that when a spouse is in resistance, he resists hearing he's in resistance and, therefore, can't do anything about it. And because he is not taking responsibility, he won't do anything about it. Many say, when a marriage is over, "I don't know what happened." When someone is resistant, he is inconsistent, walled off, and non-verbally saying, "I don't want to be with you." Unknowingly, he is continually pushing away those who care about him.

The resistant person resists everything, including those things he loves to do the most. For example, when he goes to play, he becomes impatient to finish his playing. His resistance overpowers everything he does. He can't stand happiness in any form because he has to resist his own happiness. He has opposite desires---he both wants to be happy and resists being happy, he both wants to be successful and resists being successful, he both wants to make money and resists making money, he both wants to have warm and loving relationships and resists having warm and loving relationships, and he both wants to be creative and resists being creative (see chapter: Programming). Resistance is so hard on the resistant one's body that it can cause physical problems, and the ensuing denial prevents him from being aware of what is going on. The worst part about resistance is that the resistant one doesn't know he's doing it. He's trapped in his own resistance. And if he's fortunate enough to know he's in resistance, he can't stop it until he sees it on the fourth level of awareness and lets it go. To the observer, his resistance is obvious, whereas the resistant one is totally unaware of what he is doing---and would be humiliated if he knew that everyone knew.

> *After enjoying a delightful dinner party with friends, Tim verbally attacked Bob for something he innocently said. The attack was so unexpected and so uncalled for that it destroyed the atmosphere, broke the flow of the evening, and was obvious to everyone but Tim.*

After letting go of resistance, and taking full responsibility for your life and your happiness, you can start being all YOU can be, doing what YOU want to do, and having what YOU want to have. Now you can create your life the way YOU want it. To go from resistance to responsibility is to create miracles every day. It's exciting, freeing, fun, creative, rewarding and, most importantly, it feels good.

When you realize that your resistance came from your possessive, controlling parent or family member, there is a natural tendency to become angry at that parent or family member for having denied you your freedom to create warm and loving relationships. Taking responsibility for being the creator of your life instantly ends any anger, resentment or vengeance. "Vengeance is mine; I will repay, saith the Lord" (Romans 12:19). Leave all vengeance to God. Forgive those who have wronged you. Forgive all who have harmed or betrayed you. Forgive yourself so that you might be free to be, free to love, free to create, free from caring what others think---free to take full responsibility for your life, your mind, your happiness and your relationships.

The biggest problem in learning responsibility is facing not only what it truly means, but also what yours is. Your training just begins when you take responsibility. You learn what is your responsibility versus what is others', how to take your responsibility instead of theirs, and to be so focused on getting your job done that you cease looking at what others do or don't do. As a famous actor once told his actress daughter when she complained about negative publicity, "I raised you to be a race horse. Race horses look neither to the left nor the right, but straight ahead." Not caring what people think about you is absolutely necessary in order to stay focused on your dream. It is necessary to face your relationships with your parents and family members, even if they are deceased, in order to take full responsibility for your life, mind, happiness and relationships. Because your relationships with your mother and father were established in childhood, they have the strongest and most powerful emotional control over you, and can either give you the greatest pain and conflict or the greatest peace and joy.

When Sandy, who was having difficulty with her husband, was told to look at her father, she said, "It's not my father who is the problem, but my husband." What she did not know was that she was still attached to her father, and that this emotional attachment and his possessiveness of her was, unknowingly, what caused her to destroy her relationship with her husband.

To take full responsibility for your life and happiness is to live your life moment by moment, free of regrets, free from feeling it's too late, and free from the chains of fear, anger or hatred. It is your responsibility (responding to your abilities) to live every moment in peace and happiness, your natural state of being. You will draw to you each person necessary to assist you to see what is blocking you from having peace and happiness. Give thanks for them. They will stay long enough for you to complete whatever it is you need to complete. You will draw to you those thoughts and ideas necessary to assist you. If a thought comes to mind, it is there for you to deal with it. How do you deal with a parent or sibling who is not relating to you in a positive way, or who has betrayed and hated you your whole life? You deal with him by taking each emotion that surfaces, facing it, letting it go, and accepting its opposite. For example, if you're terrified of a parent or sibling leaving, let go of the terror of their leaving four times, and accept that they are free to go four times. It won't work to deal directly with them, firstly, because they will think you're crazy and, secondly, because they don't have the problem, you do.

Any time you are bothered by the way someone is being, that is an indication that YOU have a problem. What will work is to deal with any emotion that surfaces within yourself. Emerson wrote an entire thesis on this entitled, "As a Man Thinketh, So He Is." It's time to end being a victim of your repeated circumstances with only a change of people and places. Ask yourself, "What is it about me that responds to them the way I do? Why do I feel fear or anger with them? Why do I feel guilt or hurt?" Does it make you angry or hurt that your friends or relatives don't trust you? Ask yourself if you trust yourself. Are you angry with yourself for not trusting yourself? If you feel these emotions with those closest to you, you will feel them with everyone, including yourself, until you deal with them within you.

Do you trust God? Are you angry with God because you can't trust Him? Are you finding it difficult to create what you want in your life? If this is so, and you can't trust yourself or God, you can see how difficult it would be to create abundance and have it all. Do you tell those closest to you what you want without anger or rage? Ask yourself if you're free to say, "I want" and "I don't want." If you're not, you won't be free to say either without anger or rage.

Begin by facing your relationship with your parents and siblings. Use them to mirror those blockages within you which are preventing you from creating what you want. If you cannot, ask yourself if your mother, father, siblings or teams want you to have what you want. Let go of the resistance to having what you want because of your mother, the fear of having what you want because of your mother, the hate of having what you want because of your mother, and the desire not to have what you want because of your mother. Accept that you have what you want now and you always will. Do this release with your father, family, teams, spouse, self, children and people if this is your programming. Ask yourself if your mother wants you to remain her little boy or your father wants you to remain his little girl and, thus, remain a child emotionally. This possessiveness is one of the most crippling things a parent can do to a child because it assures the destruction of all the child's relationships when he becomes an adult.

> *Sally's father wanted her to remain his sweet, little girl. She talked "baby talk" after she was married and had children, and eventually developed Alzheimer's out of her need to be taken care of and remain her father's sweet, little girl.*

It's time to grow up and take full responsibility for your life. Accept that your emotional and chronological ages are the same. Make up your mind to take full responsibility for what you do and don't do, and let your code bearer, who is still controlling your relationships, go. This is how you begin to take responsibility for the relationships that mean the most to you. If you don't like the way your life is going, change your invitation. Decide the way you want your life to go, and create it that way. As long as you look outside yourself at what others are doing or not doing, you can be assured that your life will stay the same. If you want change, rely on God to show you how to do so, one step at a time. Don't think about it, just do it.

It is time for you to have it all by removing those blocks that have stood in your way. Until you take responsibility for your happiness and success in every area of your life, nothing will change. The good, exciting, freeing news is that you, and you alone, have the power to do this. Knowing this gives you total power over your life and circumstances. Isn't it wonderful to know that no one can take it from you? You can give it away if you choose, and, should you choose, you can take it back at any moment.

The next question is, do you have choice? Yes. However, if you have this freedom of choice and don't know it, or if you take it and don't use it, you might as well not have it. What good does it do you if you have a million dollars in the bank and live in poverty and squalor? So, see that you accepted that you had no choice, and let go of not having choice. Tell yourself the truth: accept that you have choice and always will. Were you taught that you were bad if you did what you wanted? Were you taught that you were bad if you asked for what you wanted? Were you taught that all rich people are thieves, that only poor people are honest and, therefore, you can only be honest if you're poor? These are some of the myths which control your life. Family programming has been passed down from generation to generation and followed, unconsciously. It's time to think about your programming and see if it is working for you. If it's not working for you, it's time to change it. Albert Schweitzer said that man doesn't think. The truth is he <u>can't</u> think because of his programming, which he blindly follows. Use your relationship with your family and friends to show you what is blocking you from having a warm and loving relationship with them, with yourself and with God, that source of energy within you, that can and will provide you with all things. The way to tap into that energy is to first accept that you're centered. Focus your attention on your center, which is located at the bottom of your stomach. It's important to focus your attention there in order to pull your energy in, rather than allowing it to be dissipated.

Often we look out there to a man, a woman, a job or a move to save us from our present circumstances. Upon close examination, we begin to see that we have to save ourselves. We do this by letting go and allowing our Heavenly Father to save us. It is like the story of the man who sat on his porch, refusing help, while his house flooded. The first offer of help came from a man in a boat. He refused, saying, "God is going to save me." As the flood waters rose and he climbed closer to his roof, another boat arrived, offering help. Still he refused, saying, "God is going to save me." When he had climbed up to the roof, a helicopter arrived. Once again he refused help, saying, "God is going to save me." Finally, the waters rose so high that he drowned. When he got to heaven, he asked God why He hadn't saved him. God's reply was, "I <u>sent</u> you two boats and a helicopter!"

Our next step is always right there before us, and we always have the choice to take it or not. It is important to know that this step never leaves. Should you choose not to take it, and then later decide to do so, the same step will be there. Your next step is always waiting for you.

Taking your responsibility means going for it at all times, and using all of your talents and abilities in that direction, just as the archer sends his arrow directly to its target. Your mind will ask, "When can I rest?" Resting is a state of mind. Resting supports comfort, and comfort invites boredom, negativity, resistance and immobility.

There are times while you are climbing that mountain to high places, your legs burning and your lungs screaming for air, when a little rest gives your body time to refill with energy, and when a little drink of water rejuvenates, fulfills and energizes. It is a good rest when you know that you have pushed beyond what you thought yourself capable of doing. But, as soon as the filling of the vessel has been completed, it is time to get up and keep going up the mountain. As the mountain comes closer to your face, you know by your body's response that it is steep. You know from your life's experiences that you can take one step, and then one more, and you know that by living in this moment and taking one step at a time, there is nothing you cannot do. Clarity of direction, willingness to train, a made-up mind and a commitment to rely within on God will take you, one step at a time, up any mountain in life, regardless of height.

The more dedicated and committed you are to realizing your dream, the more quickly you will discover your next step. It is like being on a scavenger hunt. The treasure is hidden there, and you alone can find it. It is so exciting to know that your next step is always there waiting for you. And it is freeing to know that there are leveling off moments, like a path with no hills, where you are given time to discover, face, and let go of the blocks that are keeping you from continuing on the road to your dream. Make up your mind that you are free from anyone ever taking your dream from you. Guard your dream and keep it close to your heart. SHARE IT ONLY WITH THOSE WHO WILL SUPPORT YOU. Always ask for the wisdom to know the ones who will and those who won't. This is your responsibility. This is your life.

Who do you want to take care of? Face the truth that if you don't want to take care of anybody, nobody wants to take care of you, either. In telling yourself this truth, you can immediately end the games you have devised to be taken care of.

There are a few major reasons you resist taking responsibility for your life, mind and happiness:

- Reluctance to grow up and wanting to be taken care of because a possessive parent or family member wants you to remain his little boy or little girl. In order to grow up, it is important to make up your mind that your emotional and chronological ages are the same. For example, if you are 54 years old, and are emotionally a 14-year-old, accept that you are 54 years old emotionally. How do you tell if you are emotionally a child? The best way to tell is that you resist taking your responsibility, that you're still blaming someone in your life for your lack of success, whether it is emotional, mental or physical, and that being right and making others wrong is more important to you than having warm and loving relationships.
- Caring what others think.
- Not being free to say, "I want" and "I don't want."
- Not being free to express your talents and abilities.
- Not being free to have a dream.
- Being dominated or controlled.

Examine, face and move through the above taking full responsibility for your life, mind and happiness.

To get that you have choice, and that you have a right to lead your life YOUR way is the beginning of total freedom and the beginning of taking full responsibility for your life, your happiness and your mind. How you're thinking now, what you're doing now and how you're being now determines your tomorrow. It is important to take responsibility and decide how you want your tomorrow to be, for, in so doing, you will take charge of your today.

If you want to end living a role, if you want to be yourself and know and be the Truth, get your dream and make up your mind to go for it. The secret to living life successfully is to have a dream that will motivate you to move from your role into reality into your dream, and finally, into love, where you ARE love, give love and receive love, not just words, gifts or flowers, but rather, where you ARE love in the face of fire, give it unconditionally in the face of attacks and conflicts, and receive it regardless of anyone who wants to keep you from doing so. Make up your mind and accept that you are true to yourself, and that you are being your highest and best. And make up your mind and accept that you are the Source and Creator of your life. Make up your mind to rely on God to take care of you, protect you and guide you, one step at a time. Make up your mind to learn and express your talents and abilities, and make up your mind to enjoy every moment of your life.

Loving, being loved, feeling good and being happy all the time is what we're here to learn. Ecstasy and bliss are the results. Discovering your niche is necessary in order to express your dream. Make up your mind to know and express your niche. Nothing can stop a made-up mind. Make up your mind to move from role to reality to your dream. Make up your mind to be centered down deep within and to listen to God within for your directions. He will guide you, one step at a time, to your dream. Just listen and follow.

19 The Destruction Caused By Your Belief System
Building Your Life On Rock Versus Sand

UNKNOWINGLY, WHAT YOU HAVE BELIEVED all of your life to be true is 180 degrees off course. Facing your belief system and unraveling its truth for you will free you to see the real truth about you and your life. It will also free you to be the Truth and to have the Truth. The Bible says, "And ye shall know the truth and the truth will make you free," John 8:32. To be, have and live the Truth is to be free.

Unraveling Your Old Belief System

In order to begin unraveling your belief system, you must first face your need to be perfect. When you have a need to be perfect, any praise or acknowledgement says that: 1) expectations are being placed on you and you feel put upon (you must live up to the standard you have just set), or 2) you are being told that you have not lived up to that standard until now and are, therefore <u>not good enough</u> or less than perfect, or 3) the person praising and acknowledging you is criticizing and judging you. You can never live up to any expectations you feel are being placed on you. Facing this will free you from the terror of being wrong and the absolute necessity of having to be right, a vicious cycle in which you have felt trapped for most of your life. Facing this will also destroy everything you've ever believed to be true and, consequently, will make you "wrong." It will destroy the very foundation upon which you've built your life. To be free, it is important to face that you have built your life on sand, rather than on rock, and that the sand is shifting beneath you. You will have to face that you have built your life on a lie, which you have chosen to believe was the truth.

Facing this will take more courage than anything you will ever do and yet, to be free, it is absolutely necessary to do so.

> *Peggy related, "Yesterday I saw that I was like a life-sized, cardboard cut-out of myself which I held up in front of me and presented to the world. It was not me---it was my presentation of me. I was a fake. I was not real. I saw that the only way anyone can be with God and move into heaven was to first see that they have been and are WRONG---wrong about everything. If you have bought your own sale, as I did, you have to see that that's all it is---a sale. When you reach the point where you see that you are simply a cut-out of a perfect human being, and that nothing about you is real---and that you are wrong---it can be devastating. I was at my desk at work when I got a flash of this and started crying. I can see why people become suicidal at this point because, without God, there is no place to go. You believe that you and your ego are one and the same, so when the ego finds out it is wrong, that it is not real, that it is simply a cardboard cut-out being presented to the world, it knows it has been found out and it must die. This is the time for it to be crushed. I saw that my world revolved around my ego and was based solely on self-protection and, therefore, the destruction of anyone who threatened it. A former employee returned to the office yesterday to show me my ego. She left our office to produce a play---and is pretty impressed with that. When she asked what I was telling people who called asking for her, I told her that I told them she no longer worked here. She instantly said, 'They should be given my home phone number immediately if they ask for me.' I was shocked---she no longer works here, yet was giving me orders in an imperious tone. It was too close to home to ignore. She showed me how I had always been."*

Your desire for freedom must be so great that you are willing to face and tell yourself the truth about what, before, had been you and your life: the belief system by which you chose to live. You will no longer be able to go to your grave saying, "The one thing I could always say and know to be true is that I was always right."

THE DESTRUCTION CAUSED BY YOUR BELIEF SYSTEM

The secret (that you are wrong) is the secret which you have kept from yourself, and which you have lived in terror of finding out and of others finding out. Anyone who approaches or comes close to exposing this secret becomes the enemy and has to be destroyed, left or made to leave. While the secret is that you are wrong, but don't know it, you do know that something isn't right, since you feel guilty with some people and terrified with others, and you have to, of necessity, blame them for your discomfort. The fear of finding out, or of being found out, that you are wrong is worse than death itself. Herein lies one of your greatest FEARS, which must be protected at all times and at all costs. In order to maintain your secret, you have to always be right in your own mind. If you have a possessive, controlling parent or family member, a pact is often made with him early in childhood to not do anything other family members want you to do, and on some level, you know you don't have to. You know that you are always protected and have someone on your side. Life within the family becomes a war of divide and conquer. You are given the pact and the rules by your possessive, controlling parent or family member, and are sent into battle. This pact and these rules become your belief system. And it is this belief system which forms the foundation of your life, and dictates what you do and who you are. Being right is an integral part of most belief systems. Having to be right prevents you from being free to have problems. Not being free to have problems, the terror of making a mistake, and the necessity to be perfect are all part of having to be right. Being right protects your secret and keeps you in denial. "I'm right. You're wrong." "It's not my problem; it's yours. I don't have a problem; you have the problem." You protect yourself by not having a problem and, when confronted with a problem that can no longer be ignored, you respond by doing just enough to get by, by overdoing or by flipping between the two. Part of the secret is that if you think I'm telling you you're wrong, no matter how close we are or how much you might love me, you'll have to destroy me and/or our relationship. If I praise or acknowledge you, you think I am expecting you to continue to do the same or more, which you don't want to do. You don't want to do anything I want you to do, because your possessive, controlling parent or family member doesn't want you to do anything for anyone but him. If I say, "I loved your bringing me a glass of water," you interpret that as my saying that I want you to bring me water all the time. If you give me something that I praise you for, you think you'll have to do it over and over. So, you never want to get anything for me or give anything to me again. Instead, you make excuses to keep from giving me what I want, like, "I forgot this morning." "I was too busy." "The phone was ringing." "The baby was crying," etc. The insanity of this is that you <u>do</u> want me to praise you and tell you you're great, but if I <u>do</u>, you'll have to retaliate ("get" me) and destroy our relationship. This is called opposite desires (see chapter: Programming). Opposite desires are caused by a possessive, controlling parent or family member who gives you opposite messages. For example, he might want you to stay home and take care of him, while, at the same time, want you to go out into the world and be a success. Or he might want you to get married so he can have grandchildren, while, at the same time, want you to remain single. Anyone who is in a relationship with someone who has opposite desires is in a no-win situation. The relationship is doomed to failure.

> *Mary, who had opposite desires, said that being loved by her teacher was driving her crazy and, at the same time, she wanted her teacher to love her. Her pact with her possessive, controlling parent and her opposite desires were what were driving her crazy. Yet, she blamed her teacher for her own resistance to being loved.*

In order to maintain your belief system, you have to destroy any relationship which threatens it, which is a relationship with anyone your possessive, controlling parent or family member won't allow you to have. Anyone who threatens your belief system becomes the enemy and has to be destroyed, left or made to leave.

> *One woman's belief system required her to be successful and popular and, at the same time, to sit on the sofa, not moving, for fear of making a mistake or doing something wrong. Her belief system was also one of opposite desires.*

Many belief systems are based on opposite desires. For example, you want to have warm and loving relationships, yet you have to destroy them if your pact with your possessive, controlling parent or family member prevents you from having them (see chapter: Programming). Accepting and believing praise and acknowledgement means you have to go against your belief system, while, at the same time, you crave praise and acknowledgement.

THE DESTRUCTION CAUSED BY YOUR BELIEF SYSTEM

Having a pact with your possessive, controlling parent or family member makes creating warm and loving relationships in your life impossible.

Jane destroyed her marriage because of opposite desires. Her father wanted her to go out into the world and be famous <u>and</u>, at the same time, be with him. She wanted more than anything to stay home to create a warm and loving family with her husband and children. Because of her belief system and the pact with her father, she divorced her husband and continued to pursue fame. One day she woke up and asked herself, "Where is my husband?---What have I done?" She instantly became filled with remorse. She realized, for the first time, what she had done to her marriage. What she didn't know was why, and it was that desire to know why that sent her in pursuit of her answer. Her opposite desires kicked in when she began to experience the pain resulting from what she had done and, because she thought the truth would kill her, she escaped into denial, which ended her search for the truth.

The inability to be praised and acknowledged, and the necessity to remain true to your programming, keeps you trapped in a lie that runs your life. The terror of facing and knowing yourself keeps you blaming others instead of taking responsibility for your life. And until you do so, you won't be able to create your dream. This is the greatest gift you can give to yourself. DO IT FOR YOU. What are your options?: a life of denial in which you don't see anyone as they are or anything as it is, in which you stubbornly cling to a belief system that doesn't work, and don't tell yourself or others the truth. Unknowingly, many try to get out of this trap by rebelling against the program their possessive, controlling parent or family member has set up for them, but the rebellion throws them onto a track that traps them even more.

The world, as we have known it, is over. It has come to an end. All the circuits within our belief systems have been jammed and blown. The insanity is that praise and acknowledgement put expectations on us and, in our minds, become criticism and judgment. Seeing this truth will help us to end the pact with our possessive, controlling parent or family member and free us to praise and acknowledge others, and to be praised and acknowledged. Seeing this truth will help us to end our old belief system and form a new one, one that works for us as adults. We are clearing away the old belief system to make way for the new. Not only have we found out that we are not right and blameless, but we have seen things totally backward, totally opposite from the truth. It's time to face that the loyalty to the pact with our possessive, controlling parent or family member has been more important to us than life itself. It's time to face the truth and be free.

CREATING YOUR NEW BELIEF SYSTEM

Now you can begin to build your life on rock. After facing and letting go of your old belief system, you can begin to create your new one. Facing the old belief system can cause you to feel disoriented, shell-shocked, distraught and sorrowful. Your legs may feel wobbly, making it difficult to do physical exercise. Your body is going through a detoxification, so it is important to drink eight to ten glasses of purified water a day, eat raw foods, take extra vitamin C, and allow your body to rest. Give yourself time to see everything as you've never seen it before. Be with people who support you and your dream. Refrain from sharing your dream with those who don't support you. "Give not that which is holy unto the dogs, neither cast ye your pearls before swine, lest they trample them under their feet, and turn again and rend you," (Matthew 7:6). Share all your dreams and your new belief system only with those who support you. The world will do everything it can to hold you down. That's just the way it is.

All of the above is a result of making your possessive, controlling parent or family member your god. It's time to let go of making him your god, and honor, value and rely upon the true God within. He wants you to have everything you want and everyone you want. By going to Him first, you will find peace, the freedom to have the whole world and the freedom to have it all.

Go to God. Invite Him into your heart to walk with you and to guide your path. This is the secret to being real and to feeling ecstasy, bliss and joy every moment of your life. It is the secret to being child-like instead of childish. And that's the Truth.

20 Ending Destruction & Moving Into Love

Destroying yourself or allowing others to be destructive to you, is caused by the desire to punish yourself for having made a mistake and, consequently, being wrong. When the mind accepts that it has to be right, it has to, of necessity, make others wrong. The mind believes that you have to punish yourself and pay for what you have done, before you can start anew. Self-destruction manifests in many ways, but its most destructive form is scapegoating. Scapegoating is both self-blame, and inviting and allowing others to blame you. Scapegoating clouds the mind and prevents you and others from seeing your fine, positive qualities, and from seeing you as you really are. Self-punishment, by way of scapegoating, is very destructive because you won't allow yourself to be praised or acknowledged, nor will those who are scapegoating you praise or acknowledge you, unless it serves their own ends. This self-inflicted sentence of self-punishment, for having accepted you were wrong, ends when, and only when, you make up your mind to end it and cease trying to prove yourself.

Viewed in the light of reality, self-punishment is paralyzing, self-destructive and doesn't solve the problem. Self-punishment keeps you mentally and physically imprisoned. If a man is punished and put in jail for having committed a crime, he can neither work nor provide a living for his family. However, his sentence ultimately ends and he is free to begin anew. Whereas, self-punishment keeps you in a mental and physical jail, and prevents you from ever enjoying life, loving yourself and others, and being at peace. Life is about feeling good, being happy and creating success in your work and all your relationships. Make up your mind to end doing what doesn't work, and begin doing what does. Self-punishment keeps you from doing what you want to do, being yourself and having what you want to have. Facing self-punishment and how you do it is necessary for you to end it. Self-punishment eliminates everything from your life which makes you feel good. It destroys the quality of your life. It stifles your freedom to live your life your way. Self-punishment is caused by living out someone else's concept of how you should live your life. Self-punishment makes you feel that you don't deserve to have your own life. It's time to accept that God loves you, and it's time for you to love you, also. It's time for you to listen to God and to yourself, and cease listening to your possessive, controlling parent or family member. When you listen to your possessive, controlling parent or family member you have to destroy your relationships with others. You do this by always being right and then blaming them for being wrong, or by withholding, walling off, not listening to them, resistance, indifference and projection. You project in order to remain right. When projecting, you unconsciously project onto the other person what *you* are feeling, and believe that it is what *he* is feeling. In order to have a relationship with someone your possessive, controlling parent or family member won't let you have, you unconsciously transfer that parent onto the other person and mentally make him that parent. Projection is a way to destroy without guilt; transference is a way to have a relationship without destroying it.

> *Jane, who was sexually abused in childhood by her possessive, controlling father, punished herself by overeating. She made a pact with herself to be undesirable to men by going from 125 pounds to 220 pounds. This subconscious desire to stay overweight became apparent to her when she almost passed out upon entering a weight loss clinic. Her mind clouded and she felt as if she were under water. Her self-punishment was designed to prevent her from expressing her sexuality and keep her loyal to her possessive, controlling father. Finally, her own needs and desires for a mate were so strong that she faced her allegiance to her father, ceased listening to him, and began listening to God, which freed her to begin to create the body of her dreams.*

Punishing yourself or others is the automatic reaction to the acceptance that you are wrong. Some people punish themselves, some people punish others, and some people do both. The way out is to cease all punishment and allow God to handle the retribution. The Bible says, "Vengeance is mine, I will repay, saith the Lord" (Romans: 12:19). Face your destruction to yourself or others, tell yourself the truth about it and end it. Take responsibility for your destruction, become consciously creatively constructive, and take charge of your life, your happiness and the expression of your talents and abilities.

Can you imagine a loving God wanting His children to punish themselves? You must face that you don't deserve to be punished. Facing this, letting it go and facing that you deserve to have it all is one of the hardest, and yet, one of the greatest things you can do for yourself. To get through this, make up your mind to face what you are doing to yourself, and make up your mind to be good to you. Face that God loves you and face that punishment is not yours to administer. Let down your wall to love, accept that you are love itself and accept that you both give and receive love. Invite God into your heart to walk with you, to sup with you, to be with you and to guide and direct your path.

Your mind is a finely-tuned instrument which reacts to vibrations according to its programming. Your programming is designed by a master architect, and comes with a detailed blueprint. Both punishment to others and self-punishment are products of this architectural plan. If there were a way to get a printout of this plan, so that you might look at and revise, as an adult, what you accepted as a child, it would make your life so much easier. The truth is you can. Being unaware of this architectural plan keeps you making the same mistakes over and over again. Once you become aware of this plan, you can begin to bring it up, one step at a time. It's like playing a game or putting a puzzle together, looking for each piece until you have the complete architectural drawing. Some have one architectural plan while others have many, because they have many architects who direct their lives. With time and attention, all are revealed. These plans were drawn up, accepted by you in your childhood, and determine your life. Your life is not your own, as you thought, nor can you have a dream until you face these plans and let them go. How can you begin with something which feels so complex? You begin by taking charge of your life, full responsibility for your mind, and full responsibility to face these architectural plans, and end them. A pact is a powerful agreement you made with someone else which determines and controls your life (see chapter: Programming). Exposing the pact puts light on the plan. This plan keeps you from seeing people as they are, and from living your life the way you want to. If the architect of your life did not give you freedom to express yourself, your natural talents and abilities are squelched. The architect was expressing what he wanted for your life, often <u>without you in mind</u>. It is by taking charge of your life, instead of blaming, that you can pull up this detailed architectural plan, face it, tell yourself the truth about it, and let it go. It is in dealing, as an adult, with what you accepted as a child that you can change your life and design your own plan, based on choices that work for you now. When you begin to see this architectural plan, you may experience anger, remorse, or both, but in order to be your own architect, it is necessary to take full responsibility for every bit of your destructiveness to yourself and others, which includes forgiving yourself and them. Once this is done, you can then begin to draw up a plan that works for you as an adult, and become your own architect. Taking charge of your life frees you to live and to decide how you want your life to be. It's time to end the old and begin the new. If the architect of your life wanted you to stay his baby or little child, you will remain emotionally crippled and unable to take your adult responsibilities, while blaming others for your inability to do so. You will continue to live in an adult body with adult responsibilities, living out the architectural plan you chose as a child. You can see the number of problems that are created once you take on various adult responsibilities, when the architect of your childhood demands obedience. If you take responsibility for your architectural plan, even though you accepted it as a child, often under traumatic circumstances, you are then able to cease destroying your life, and can turn it around and create it your way.

You cannot create your dream as an adult while your architectural plan from childhood is still directing your life. You can whine and cry and blame others, or you can grow up and assume your adult responsibilities. It's so exciting to know that you can create your life the way <u>you</u> want to. Once you take responsibility for being the architect of your life, you can create your plan to be loving, creative and successful. This is the first step to moving from your destructive mind into your heart and into love. Invite God into your heart to walk with you, to guide you and to direct your life. Refuse to allow feeling you're not good enough to keep you from this joy, this inner peace and this love, for you <u>are</u> good enough just as you are. You're God's child. Go Home and be with your Heavenly Father.

On Being Right

The terror of making a mistake keeps you bound to your programming and driven to <u>always</u> be right. The drive is so great that, in the face of a mistake, you deny it to yourself. You make the same mistakes over and over again, expecting different results. Having to be right causes you to be contemptuous, judgmental, and impatient with others. Because you are so terrified of being wrong and disapproved of, you, unknowingly, project onto others what is going on in you. Most importantly, it prevents you from telling yourself and others the truth. Driven by the need to protect your possessive, controlling parent or family member and give him what he wants, you destroy all the relationships that mean the most to you. Why is having to be right so important? Why would you allow yourself to be restricted by something so consuming and so confining as having to be right?

Having to be right traps you and prevents you from expressing your talents and abilities. It makes you critical of others and keeps you on a treadmill going nowhere. The addiction to having to be right is so all-consuming that it becomes your life. It is caused by the terror of making a mistake and the need to protect and defend your ego, as well as your possessive, controlling parent or family member. You are always on the alert for the slightest threat of blame or criticism. If you are confronted on making a mistake, you become angry. You can either turn your anger outward and retaliate by becoming vindictive; or you can turn it inward and punish yourself by becoming depressed---or you can make up your mind that you are free to say, "I want," and live a life of peace.

Because you are in constant terror of being told that you're wrong, you have to judge others before they judge you, blame them and make them wrong. Because you have to be right, you can't have a problem. Any time a problem arises, your attitude is, "They have a problem; I don't have a problem." Projection is one of the ways you use to remain right. Projection is attributing your feelings to others.

> *Jane said to Terry, her employee, "I want you and I to develop a new fitness program." Terry said, defensively, "You know I have already developed a lot of different fitness programs." Jane said, "I'm not criticizing what you've done or haven't done or criticizing you, Terry. I'm just saying that I want a fitness program now." Because Terry wasn't free to say "I want," she couldn't give her boss what <u>she</u> wanted.*

> *Terry projected onto Jane that Jane was judging her, but in truth, Terry was judging Jane for not acknowledging what she had done in the past. In order to remain right in her own mind, she projected onto Jane that Jane was judging her. In truth, Jane was not judging Terry; Terry was judging Jane. Terry then faced what her mind was doing and knew the truth: that she was projecting, and Jane was not finding fault with her. At that moment she made up her mind to end projection and judgment forever and to take her responsibility.*

With projection, the belief is so real to the one projecting that he would willingly go to court and swear on the Bible that he is telling the truth. At the first level of facing having to be right/projection, it feels like the one you are projecting onto is crazy. Your mind asks, "Can't he see he's wrong? I'm not doing what he says I'm doing." If confronted by someone you care about and trust, you may begin to open the door to the possibility that you might be wrong. Then you can begin to face the truth. At the second level, you feel, "I'm doing this but I can't stop it. Don't let me do it to you." At the third level, you recognize it as you are doing it and can stop on many occasions. You are still in denial at this point. At the fourth level of facing having to be right, something has to mean enough to you that you are willing to face the ugliest ways in which you destroy your relationships.

> *Lisa said she was at the brink of insanity while she was facing having to be right. She knew she would go insane if she ever again went down that road of having to be right. She couldn't stand to be cold and indifferent to her loved ones ever again. Her dream in life is to be sweet, loving and caring to her loved ones and to everyone. And yet, until she ended having to be right, she couldn't have her dream.*

Your ego has a belief system upon which it bases its life. If you have a belief system that has to be right and your ego believes that everyone is out to "get" it, it must either "get" them first or leave before it is "gotten". If the ego is "gotten", it is proven wrong and must prove itself right by retaliation. Being proven wrong is its greatest fear because it is driven by its belief system to always be right. Because you, unconsciously, believe that you and your ego are the same, this belief system entraps you in its web and keeps you from ever learning from your mistakes. It prevents you from telling yourself and others the truth. With this belief system, the only way to accomplish anything is through effort and will. Some people can effort and will themselves forever, while others can do it for only short periods of time, creating inconsistency in and destruction to their relationships. The worst thing about having to be right is that you've always got to blame everyone else when you've made a mistake---and you can't tell yourself the truth, for to do so feels like it would be death.

Your belief system requires you to be perfect, and demands that others see you as perfect, also (see chapter: Perfection). In order to remain perfect, you are unable to hear or listen to anyone. Being right makes you cocky, arrogant, and superior, which destroys humility and creates contempt. By constantly judging, you see everyone as less than you: less attractive, less intelligent, etc. This is how you destroy your relationships.

Having to be right demands that you live in a fantasy, and keeps you from having a dream. This fantasy takes over and becomes your life. Having to be right keeps you in either the past or the future, and prevents you from staying in the present. When you are right and someone gives you a suggestion, you think they are making you wrong by implying that you should have already thought of what they are suggesting.

People use gossip and mental or sexual seduction to get you on their side against others. Once they've gotten you on their side, they often withhold what they promised. This game of destructions makes warm and loving relationships impossible (see chapter: Game Playing). Some game players wants to beat you, while others only want to win over you. With both types of game players, if you say, "I want," they will do one of several things: 1) become angry and make you wrong and blamed for asking, 2) "forget" to bring you what you asked for, even through they agreed to, 3) deny hearing your request, or 4) take back gifts they gave you and not do what they said they'd do, which gives them sadistic pleasure. They'll borrow money and not pay it back, which causes them to destroy many of their relationships.

You can choose to live your life one of three ways: either consciously destructively (evil), or coming from the mind (analyzing), or coming from Love (in the flow). The first way, destruction, either to yourself or others, is taking from life; the second way, mentally analyzing and/or manipulating, is getting from life, and the third way, coming from Love, is both giving to and receiving from life. Many choose to live their lives coming from destruction. While they may deceive themselves through the mental techniques of denial, fantasy, projection or living in the void, they consciously know what they are doing when they are destructive to another human being. The next level is the level of the mind. To the mind, love appears out of control, weak, scattered and, at times, threatening. This mind level manipulates, analyzes and controls in order to have its way. It is selfish, self-centered and egotistical. It relies on the ego. The size of the ego determines the mind's degree of selfishness. It is exclusive, cannot ask for help and demands perfection from itself and others. The choice is between a creatively destructive life in which you are either the victim or the victimizer, or a consciously, creatively constructive life of giving and receiving love and expressing your talents and abilities.

Decide how you want your life to be. Until you make up your mind to be consciously creatively constructive each new day, and to begin your day coming from the deepest level of love, the mind, out of old habits, will pull you back under its control.

Life is about doing what you do because you want to, life is about doing what works, life is about being free to say, "I want" and "I don't want," life is about enjoyment, life is about living in the moment, life is about being centered, life is about being focused, life is about being grateful, life is about having fun in everything you do, and most of all, life is about love---loving and being loved, giving and receiving love. So make up your mind that you are love itself and accept that you both give and receive love.

Once you see how you've been destructive to yourself and others---how you've done it and why you've done it---you'll feel repentant and remorseful. And if you don't, that's a good sign you're in denial, and not taking responsibility for what you've done or haven't done. Make up your mind to let go of denial and make up your mind to take responsibility for your mind, your happiness, for what you've done or haven't done, and for what you're doing or not doing. It's been said that man can't change; however, by letting go of your old programming on all four levels, and creating your own new program, you can change. The cause of your inability to change is that you have been denied choice by your possessive, controlling parent or family member. In reality, choice is your for the taking. Realizing this allows you to choose. Seeing that you have been denied choice is enough to motivate you to make up your mind to choose. Because your possessive, controlling parent or family member rarely allows you to have a relationship with anyone but him, everyone else becomes your enemy, even those you care about the most. Once you let go of your old programming, those who, before, were your enemies, become your friends. What, before, was war, now, becomes peace. This simple choice is life-transforming. Your old programming forces you to live in the past or the future. Once you let go of your old program, you can let go of the future and live in the present. Then you can create warm and loving relationships which, before, were impossible.

Everyone has a subconscious way of expressing life, whether creatively or destructively, positively or negatively, and it is necessary to face this modus operandi in detail and let it go in order to be free to establish your own new program. The modus operandi is your belief system, how you act on it, and how you react to it. It's important to see <u>how</u> you destroy your relationships for your possessive, controlling parent or family member, and what technique you use to do so. For example, do you fail to do what you say you'll do? Do you interfere with the flow? Do you become indifferent or, in extreme cases, do you feel like you want to kill when asked to do something or when you can't have your way? Must you maintain a perfect facade while withholding from peole what you know they want?

In her desire for attention, Judy, unknowingly, destroyed her relationships by interfering with the flow. She did this by talking too much and repeating herself, which caused people not to listen to her or believe her, and made them want to get away from her.

Until you face how you destroy your relationships and let it go, you will not only continue to destroy them, but you'll become angry or enraged at anyone who confronts you on your destruction. Anyone who tells the truth is the enemy according to your possessive, controlling parent or family member and must, therefore, be destroyed in order for you and that parent or family member to remain right and blameless at all times. Make up your mind to let go of your resistance to not protecting and defending your possessive, controlling parent or family member. And make up your mind to let go of your resistance to not destroying your relationships for him.

Sue and Stan were destroying their marriage and each other. Because they loved one another and wanted the marriage to work, they sought the advice of Rick, an honest, *wise, loving counselor. When Rick told them the truth about what they were doing, they instantly stopped destroying each other and united in destruction against their common enemy: Rick. They <u>had</u> to in order to protect and defend their respective possessive, controlling parents. Even though they had asked Rick to tell them the truth (and had paid for it), when he gave them what they asked for, they turned on him.*

As long as you listen to your possessive, controlling parent or family member, you will continue to give him power and control over your life. Listening to him keeps you living in the future in order to make him right, and being perfect for him so you will get his approval. Consequently, life is, and has been, about getting your possessive, controlling parent or family member's approval. Anything you HAVE can be taken from you; anything you ARE is yours to keep. So, it's important to accept that you have his approval in order to be free. A beautiful message on a greeting card says, "Yesterday is history, tomorrow is a mystery, today is a gift, that's why we call it 'the present.'" Accept that you ARE, and move into being---being you, being your highest and best, being all you can be, and accept that you are the Creator of your life. In order to create your life in a way that works for you, it's very important to have a higher power on which you can rely at all times to protect and guide your every step. It's not until then that you are able to recognize and express all of your talents and abilities, and see and remove any blocks to their expression. Once you see clearly that your life has been about making that possessive, controlling parent or family member proud for having created a perfect human being, you can stop. But until you face and end both your old program and your modus operandi, and tell yourself the truth about them, they will continue to run your life until the end.

Forgive your possessive, controlling parent or family member whose program you have loyally followed, for he knew not what he did. If you hate him, let that hatred go and accept him as he is. Accept that you love the angel in him. No matter how destructive they have been, everyone has an angel in them. Love that angel. Forgive yourself and accept yourself just as you are, for you knew not what you did, either. Accept that you love yourself, and that you're ready to begin anew, that you're ready to learn and express all of your talents and abilities, that you're ready to enjoy yourself and have fun every moment of your life. Life is about having fun and feeling good. It's time for you to have fun and feel good every second of your life.

Face that your old program hasn't worked, and begin anew by designing a new one that does, one that creates warm and loving relationships. Make up your mind to take a public stand for truth so you'll have courage. Courage will prevent you from becoming trapped again in another destructive relationship. Make up your mind that you create warm and loving relationships, that you both give and receive love, and that you do what you do because you want to, rather than out of duty or obligation.

Surrender your life to God and let the Light of His Love flow through you and from you. Until you make the choice to move into love, you will automatically punish yourself and feel guilty for your destruction. It's important to face that self-punishment through guilt is neither noble nor beneficial to you. It just keeps you walled off from those you care about the most, and prevents you from having warm and loving relationships with them. If not stopped in its early stages, it can maintain its control over you for life. At some point, you may become aware that you feel guilty all the time without knowing why. It is important to end this guilt and self-punishment and become aware of who you are listening to. Are you listening to your possessive, controlling parent or family member or to God? You might say, "My possessive, controlling parent (or family member) is no longer living." However, death does not end the control. You end the control from your possessive, controlling parent or family member by letting go of your old program and modus operandi, establishing a new program and modus operandi that work for you, ceasing to listen to him, and making up your mind to listen to God.

By making up your mind to take full responsibility for your mind, your life, and your relationships, you can end the power your possessive, controlling parent or family member has over you. Getting and accepting that you are responsible for your mind, life and relationships frees you, rather than entrapping you. It makes what was, before, difficult, easy. How can you understand this without making up your mind that you tell yourself the truth and tell others the truth? You can't. So make up your mind to tell yourself the truth and make up your mind to tell others the truth. Know that nothing can stop a made-up mind to free you from your self-inflicted prison. Make up your mind to end proving that you and your possessive, controlling parent or family member are right and blameless, and that others are wrong and to blame. Cease protecting and defending your possessive, controlling parent or family member, cease destroying for him and move into being.

Make up your mind that you are the spirit that is, the spirit that was, and the spirit that always will be. Make up your mind that you are the Light, and that your Light shines so brightly that others can see their path by it. Unless you make up your mind, you will move back into being a right and blameless destroyer when you come face to face with what has kept you from having warm and loving relationships, with what has kept you from being your highest and best, and from being the Source and the Creator of your life. Unless you make up your mind to let go of your old program and modus operandi, tell yourself and others the truth, and rely on and listen to God, you will continue to listen to and obey your possessive, controlling parent or family member, who wants you to destroy all your relationships. There's no greater power over your mind than the power you give him. IF YOU'RE NOT FREE IN YOUR MIND, YOU'RE NOT FREE IN YOUR LIFE. Only a made-up mind to be free mentally, spiritually and creatively, only a made-up mind to take responsibility for your mind and your relationships, and only a made-up mind to turn your life over to God will allow you to end the power your possessive, controlling parent or family member has over you. You're not supposed to look at this power, for to look feels like you're betraying him. So, the choice is between looking or not looking, between being controlled or being free, between listening to your possessive, controlling parent or family member or to God. Something or someone has to mean enough to you to look at and face his control, otherwise you'll sink back into your destruction and not know it. You have to end the comfortable control which your possessive, controlling parent or family member has had over you or you will unite with him against your common enemies which, more often than not, are the ones you care about the most. The choice is yours.

The decision to end destruction is necessary, followed by the decision to replace it with love. Love is what works, and doing what works makes you feel good. And you can feel good all the time by accepting that you are good enough, living in the present, and walking hand in hand with God. Make up your mind that you are love itself. Make up your mind to give love and make up your mind to receive love.

> *Nancy had to get clear what her belief system was. She saw that she lived a life of fantasy and projection. She was always in the future and, therefore, got nothing done in the*

present. Because she handled everything in her mind, her fantasy was that there was nothing to do. If she did happen to notice a problem, she would think it was your problem. She projected onto you whatever was going on with her, saying, "You have a problem, I don't." For example, she frequently offered to do things for others, then would forget and make excuses when reminded. Projection is knowing, beyond question, that someone else did something or said something when, in fact, it was you. Your mind will go to the ultimate, to the death, to remain right and blameless, never taking responsibility for your actions. To project and not see it is one thing (sticking your head in the sand), but when you do it and see yourself doing it, the need for self-punishment is so great that you can go to the extreme of feeling like committing suicide. To end projection, take responsibility for your mind, for your life and for your happiness. Make up your mind that you are free to say, "I want" and "I don't want," and, most importantly, make up your mind to let go of your old program and your old modus operandi, and create a new one. Creating a new program will take some time. Give yourself a couple of hours, write down everything you want, and accept that you have your new program and modus operandi now.

The choice is yours to move into love and take responsibility to stay there. Begin your day there. If you move out, just move back in without punishing yourself or making yourself bad or wrong.

Your possessive, controlling parent or family member tells you which relationships you can have and which relationships you can't have. Rarely will he allow you to have a relationship with anyone but him. In order to have a forbidden relationship with someone you want, you will, of necessity, transfer your possessive, controlling parent or family member onto him, mentally making him that parent or family member. If he won't allow you to transfer onto him, you have to destroy the relationship. If you can't destroy the relationship by doing everything it takes to get him to leave, you either have to destroy him or turn your destruction inward on yourself, or leave. In other words, you can't have the relationship because you are listening to your possessive, controlling parent or family member, and he won't allow you to have it. This problem can be solved 1) by letting your possessive, controlling parent or family member go, ceasing to listen to him, and making up your mind to listen to God, 2) by making up your mind to cease destroying your relationships for him, 3) by letting go of your programming, 4) by making up your mind that you have the power of a made-up mind, 5) by making up your mind that you are free to say, "I want" and "I don't want," 6) by making up your mind that you have choice, 7) by making up your mind to tell yourself the truth, and making up your mind to tell others the truth, and 8) by making up your mind that you want, and can have, that person. Nothing can stop a made-up mind, but you have to do it. No one can do it for you.

If you don't or can't tell yourself the truth, or don't or can't tell others the truth because your possessive, controlling parent or family member won't allow you to, you are trapped by not being able to think, by not being free to make a decision, and by not being free to have choice.

It is important that parents and grandparents assist their children and grandchildren in the great adventure of discovering themselves, being themselves, loving themselves, expressing their talents and abilities and creating happy memories. It is also important that they teach their children and grandchildren that they are good enough. What the children are doing or not doing may not be working, but their actions do not imply that they are not good enough. There is no greater lasting gift than this.

PERFECTION

The reason you destroy your relationships is to be perfect for your possessive, controlling parent or family member, so that he will approve of you (see chapter: Perfection). He demands perfection from you at all times and requires that you protect him at all costs. This is how your programming entraps you. Face your programming, and it will reveal to you the way in which you have to be perfect for your possessive, controlling parent or family member. Your concept of perfection is different from anyone else's. Facing it will unlock the doors to your programming and how you have to live your life for your possessive, controlling parent or family member.

Some of the ways in which you have to be perfect for your possessive, controlling parent or family member are:

- Resistance to everything and everyone

- Indifference to everything and everyone
- Always leaving
- Killing yourself
- Killing others
- Rebellion
- Being pitiful
- Projection
- Not listening
- Having to be right
- Criticism
- Judgment
- Trying to make others perfect so that they will be good enough for you
- Having to know it all
- Comparing
- Not needing anything or anyone
- Not saying, "I want" and "I don't want"
- Exaggerating
- Living in the past or the future
- Not expressing your talents and abilities
- Proving yourself
- Doing just enough to get by
- Feeling guilty all the time
- Not telling the truth to yourself or others because it would expose you and, therefore, your possessive, controlling parent for having raised a less-than-perfect child
- Being popular
- Speaking only when you are spoken to
- Being exclusive
- Making your possessive, controlling parent or family member your god
- Never telling anybody what goes on at home
- Protecting and defending your possessive, controlling parent or family member
- Seeing everyone else as less than perfect, bad or not good enough

- Seeing your possessive, controlling parent or family member as perfect

One of the benefits of not having to be perfect is the freedom to make mistakes---and to learn and grow from them. This way, your life is about getting better and better instead of sweeping problems under the rug.

INDIFFERENCE

One of the greatest controls your possessive, controlling parent or family member has over you is to get you to be indifferent. Indifference is a cruel, controlling technique that excludes and doesn't include. The superiority, aloofness, disgust and disdain of the indifferent person tells you, nonverbally, that you are not good enough for him. Because his message is often unspoken, he can't (and won't) be held accountable. Indifference says you don't count, that you and your feelings are of no worth or value, and that whether you live or die doesn't matter. It's as if the indifferent person belongs to an exclusive club to which only he and his possessive, controlling parent or family member belong. He surrounds himself with a wall which distances him from everyone. Because indifference destroys feeling and the expression of emotions, the indifferent one can't feel, and so he resists loving and being loved, and has contempt and disdain for those who do. He puts a mental lead blanket on you to hold you down, back and at a distance. He can't be happy or free. He can't be involved with anyone his possessive, controlling parent or family member won't allow him to, which can include another family member, his spouse or even his child. More often than not, the only one with whom he can be involved is his possessive, controlling parent or family member. This is his reality, and he is unaware of its existence. However, those closely involved with him are totally aware of it. He becomes fearful of success in any area his possessive, controlling parent or family member doesn't allow, and can only do what that parent or family member tells him to do. Many people rebel as children against this unfair restriction and, in so doing, free themselves to do what they want to do. At the same time, their programming kicks in, causing their relationships to be destroyed.

So, let go of rebellion, and accept that you are free to have warm and loving relationships. Only a made-up mind to let go of your programming and modus operandi on four levels will free you from a life of limitation and control. Because your possessive, controlling parent or family member is afraid of losing you, of your leaving and of your being revealed as less than perfect to the world (thus exposing him as a less than perfect parent), he holds you down and back. Unknowingly, this creates a fear of success in you, for your success could take you from him. This is not about making your possessive, controlling parent or family member bad or wrong, but about your being free to have warm and loving relationships with anyone you want, including God and yourself, to express your talents and abilities, to have financial success, and success in your labor of love.

> *Bob and Joan, two indifferent game players, were married to each other. Because their respective possessive, controlling parents would not allow them to have a relationship with each other, they kept everything separate: their food, their money, their time and, in the end, their friends. They loved each other yet, because they were not allowed to have each other, kept themselves separated by indifference. For years, Bob did everything he could to get Joan to leave, but she refused because she so wanted the marriage to work. In the end, when Joan would not leave, Bob divorced her.*

With indifference comes judgment and projection in order to protect and defend your possessive, controlling parent or family member by always making him right.

It comes down to making up your mind that you have choice, then choosing to make the true God Who resides within you your God, rather than your possessive, controlling parent or family member. Make up your mind to choose to listen to God, rather than your possessive, controlling parent or family member.

The only way out of the prison of indifference is to let go of your programming and your modus operandi, and make up your mind that you are there for your loved ones. Make up your mind to love yourself, and make up your mind to both give and receive love. Let go of resistance four times, and accept that you are responsible for your mind, for your life, for your happiness, and for each of your relationships four times. Accept that you are in full charge of your life. Accept that you ARE the Light, that you are surrounded by Light, and that the Light of God's love illuminates your path. Accept that you are free to say, "I want" and "I don't want." Accept that you are happy and always will be four times. Forgive yourself, accept yourself as you are, and accept that you love yourself. Forgive your possessive, controlling parent or family member. Accept him as he is, and accept that you love the angel in him. Observe how wonderful forgiveness feels. Accept that you are the spirit that was, that is and that ever will be. Accept that you are the Source and the Creator of your life, and that because you are, you can create it any way you want. Make up your mind that you rely on God to protect you, take care of you, guide you, and direct your every step, and make up your mind that you listen to God always. Accept that four times. Make up your mind that you have warm and loving relationships with God, with yourself and with everyone in your life. Make up your mind that you express all of your talents and abilities, that you know what they are and what your niche is. And make up your mind that you enjoy every moment of your life. Accept that four times. Make up your mind that you have fun every second of your life. Accept that four times. Let go of your old programming. Let go of the feeling that you are bad, not good enough or both four times, and accept that you are good enough just as you are four times. This is the secret of being happy. Let go of all need to punish yourself for expressing your talents and abilities, and accept that you reward yourself four times. Accept that you're free at last to be all you can be, to be your highest and best, to just be---YOU.

BEING THERE

Love can be expressed in many different ways: by giving gifts, through communication (by saying, "I love you," or calling to ask, "How are you?"), through correspondence (by sending cards, letters), by praise and acknowledgement, by wanting to be with your loved one, and by doing things for him. But the greatest expression of love is being there for a loved one. Being there means you are there for him in his times of need and his times of success. It means being trustworthy and consistent. Being there means that you don't wall off when your loved one has problems or wants something from you. When you are there for a loved one, you're there because you want to be, because you care, and you show that you care by giving him what he wants. Being there means that if your loved one needs space, you give him space; if he needs company, you give him company. If he's going through something difficult, you let him know that you care, and you don't withdraw or withhold from him. If he wants to be alone, you don't take it personally and don't exclude him, but continue to "keep your hand in his hand." This doesn't mean that you're "on call" all the time or that you give up your life for your loved one, but that you do what you do because you want to. Being there is an expression of love--not necessarily romantic love, but true love.

We all want our loved ones to be there for us. Being there can be active or passive. To be there for someone, you have to be free of control or manipulation, and have to have the courage to take a public stand for him. Most people don't have the courage to take a stand for a loved one. They care too much about what others think and about being disapproved of, and they're controlled by the terror of their possessive parent's anger. To be there for a loved one is to let others know publicly that this is the person you love, in spite of the fact that others can hate you for it because it makes them feel less by comparison. Were they to take a public stand for a loved one, they would not be approved of by their possessive, controlling parent or family member. Taking a public stand for anyone other than this parent or family member is not allowed. Children of possessive, controlling parents or family members are so driven by the need for their parents' or family members' approval, and the terror of their disapproval and subsequent anger, that they have to be perfect and always right in order to get this approval. If not faced and ended, this terror remains for life. Until you make up your mind to let it go forever, it will recur. Their need to be right keeps them totally self-centered. If they do give to another, they automatically pull back, wishing they had not given the gift or made the offer. They feel guilty and fearful because they know, on a subconscious level, that what they're doing is not allowed. They learn early on that it is not acceptable to give to or receive from anyone other than those their possessive, controlling parent or family member allows them to---which, in most cases, is only that parent or family member.

> *Joan had been in a potentially life-threatening situation which she shared with two of her closest friends, Bob and Mary. After telling them what had happened, rather than being concerned about her and what she was going through, they both walled off and instantly felt fear for themselves. Their inability to be there for her prevented them from caring. Joan felt so hurt by their lack of caring that she cried.*

The choice is between being right and being there. There's no way to have true love or to be there for a loved one until you face and let go of your programming and modus operandi.

Being in a relationship with someone who is not there for you causes you to feel uncared about and hurt all the time. Because he's not allowed to be there for you, he automatically turns cold and walls off when you want something from him or if, in a rare moment of caring, he should offer to do something for you.

The minute someone they know becomes controversial, most people drop them for fear of being criticized. Later, if that former friend becomes successful and well-known, they return, claiming to have been friends forever.

> *Tom, a controversial leader, warned Betty, at a banquet, not to talk to him because people would hate her. Betty, a loving friend who did not care what others thought, disregarded what Tom said and, instead, sat down beside him and put her arms around him and his wife. Because Betty had been there for him, twenty years later, when Tom became highly successful, Betty, Tom and his wife were still friends.*

Many people rebel against the control of their possessive, controlling parent or family member so that they can have the caring relationships they want.

To create a successful, happy, warm and loving marriage, it is important for both parties to be there for each other. And to create secure, confident children, it is necessary for both parents to be there for <u>them</u>. Many parents believe they are there for their children until the children create a problem and then, instead of being there for them, the parents become angry at them. They act as if they are there for their children by doing things for them and giving them things, instead of being there for their children when they children made a mistake. They can't be there because of their possessive programming. Being there for their children doesn't mean that the parents agree, support or condone what they've done, if what they've done has been destructive. What it does mean is that the parents separate what the children have done from who they are.

> *John, a very self-confident, successful young professional was told by his mother to <u>always</u> leave any place he wasn't*

wanted and, if he ever found himself without transportation, to call her and she would come get him regardless of the time or place. Just knowing that she would always be there for him contributed to his self-confidence and success in life.

In "Julius Caesar," Shakespeare said, "Cowards die many times before their deaths; the valiant never taste of death but once." If you don't allow or encourage your child to take a public stand for truth, he will feel fear daily. He'll wall off, destroy the relationships that mean the most to him and learn to put on an act instead of being himself.

When Steve was being sued, he asked his friend Sue if she would testify on his behalf. Sue, a true, loving friend said, "I would be honored to do so." Sue was there for him in his time of need.

Being there for someone, whether a family member, friend or stranger, makes them, as well as you, feel good, and this feeling lasts, in memory, forever. Not being there for someone you love makes that person feel unloved, unwanted and causes you lifelong regret, whether you are aware of it or not.

Forty-six years ago, Susie, an American traveling through France, was on a train that had stopped to take on new passengers. Susie reached down to assist a small child onto the platform. The child's mother, who was grateful to Susie for being there for her child, said, "Merci beaucoup, mademoiselle." Although Susie did not speak a word of French, she remembers this incident now as if it were yesterday. Remembering this scene still makes her feel good.

Taking a Public Stand for Truth

Many mothers teach their children to avoid risks, play it safe, and choose cowardice rather than going for it and becoming courageous by taking a public stand for truth, whether it is a popular or unpopular stand. We're developing a world in which people play it safe, a world that cares more about what others think, more about being right, and more about sitting in the middle of the road doing nothing than about daring to take a risk and going for it.

THE FREEDOM TO SAY, "I WANT" & "I DON'T WANT"

Having the freedom to say, "I want" and "I don't want," and giving your loved ones the same freedom, eliminates most of the anger and rage from your relationships. If you are not free to say, "I want" or "I don't want," it makes you angry or enraged to have to say it, or when it is said to you while, at the same time, you deny your anger and rage to yourself and others, so you don't know you're doing it. The only way to deal with others' calling you on your anger is to deny it and blame them by accusing them of being wrong. And if you say, "I want" or "I don't want," others become angry or enraged at you, which causes you to retaliate or not want to be with them.

Don adored his Uncle Mike and Aunt Ann. When he found out that his uncle Mike was having an affair with a friend of his, he was very upset. When Ann found out about the affair and about how upset Don was, she told Mike that she did not want him hurting her family. When she said, "I don't want," Mike went into a rage and threw her across the room.

The heart of our programming is not being allowed to say, "I want" and "I don't want," and, subsequently not allowing others to say it. Parents teach their children not to say, "I want" and "I don't want" in many ways.

When Tom was five years old, he asked his mother for a sip of the soda she was drinking. She refused, saying, "My doctor prescribed this soda for me, so I can't give it to you." Tom's request said, "I want." Because she was not free to say, "I want," she was unable to give her son the same freedom. She taught Tom, by example, not to give others what they want and to lie about it. Her refusal to give Tom a sip of her soda gave him an "I don't want" message. This enraged him, although he did not express it outwardly. Instead, he made up his mind that he would never ask her, or anyone else, for anything again. And he didn't. Her refusal to give him what he wanted created a fear of rejection in him and established a pattern for his life.

Some of the interactions which destroy relationships and prevent you from being there for your friends and loved ones are: indifference, resistance, possessiveness, choosing sides, denial, not being willing to take a public stand, caring about what others think, listening to others instead of your friends and loved ones, and competition.

COMPETITION

The competitor and the non-competitor have two different agendas, and what appears to be poor timing to a non-competitor is impeccable timing to a competitor. Competition is the opposite of warm and loving relationships (see chapter: Competition). Competition, by its very nature, destroys relationships.

There are four levels of competition: it begins with the level of thought, and is followed by the second level of feeling, the third level of habit and the fourth level of mood. Unless you are willing to face each and let it go, competition becomes your way of life. It is the tool many use, unconsciously, to destroy all of their relationships. Competition in relationships turns you into a warrior, makes you mean, and prevents the creation of warm and loving relationships. On the fourth level, you have a sense that competition is going on, but are afraid to look at it out of your need to be right. Until you face competition and why you do it, you will continue to destroy your relationships, because you believe you can't stop. Competition is like a runaway horse that won't allow you to stop until you make up your mind that this is YOUR life. Make up your mind to take full responsibility for what you do and don't do, make up your mind that you are free to say, "I want" and "I don't want." Let go of your old programming and let go of your old modus operandi that perpetuates your programming. You are unaware that your possessive, controlling parent or family member doesn't want you to do anything, and you, unknowingly, destroy your relationships for him by not doing what you say you'll do. Make up your mind to face this, and let go of the pact that you made with your possessive, controlling parent or family member. A pact is an unspoken agreement you made in childhood with that parent or family member. You are either driven to fulfill the pact or to rebel against it. If you've chosen to rebel against the pact, make up your mind to let go of rebellion, and then let go of the pact. Make up your mind to take charge of your life and to live it <u>your</u> way. Nothing can stop a made-up mind. It's time to stop destroying your relationships with the ones who mean the most to you in order to get the approval of your possessive, controlling parent or family member---who may not even be alive. It's time to end cowardice and become courageous. It's time to end the fear, the terror and the guilt that has resulted from being controlled. It's necessary to end competition on all four levels. Be aware that there is a strong pull to hold back on the fourth level.

> *Tammy made up her mind to end competition and to do her best in every area of her life. She was able, for the first time, to become a fully-functioning member of the team---and loved it. Nevertheless, when this fourth level of competition surfaced, she felt resistance, which caused her to hold back and depleted her energy, making it difficult to do her job on the team, even though she loved what she was doing.*

Until you let competition go on the fourth level, you cannot see it for what it truly is. It is a weapon designed to kill all the relationships your possessive, controlling parent or family member will not allow you to have. Competition is always laying in wait for that perfect moment in time to get its victim at his most vulnerable point. Its timing is impeccable. Competition is as vicious as a rattlesnake waiting in the grass for that perfect second to strike.

Mothers and fathers, unknowingly, compete with their children, destroying their self-confidence and making them feel unwanted, unloved, insecure, angry, enraged, and often, depressed. Parents who compete with their children don't want to be with them because they feel that their children are a bother or a burden. These parents feel this way toward anyone with whom they compete. Asking yourself how you want your children to turn out is very important in facing competition. Do you want your children to feel secure, self-confident, responsible and mature? Competition is so painful to look at that, without a strong enough motivation, it is impossible.

> *Mary was hurt by her mother every day of her life growing up and did not know that the hurt was caused by her mother*

competing with her. The final coup occurred on the day of Mary's wedding. Mary produced the entire wedding herself without any help from her mother, who had previously produced a friend's daughter's wedding. The only request Mary made of her mother was that she move two buttons on her trousseau robe. The day of the wedding, when Mary asked her mother if she had moved the buttons, her mother said she hadn't, at which point, because of hurt, disappointment and total exhaustion, Mary burst into tears and cried the whole day. This was the most important day of her life and she allowed her mother to destroy it for her.

Larry, a boating enthusiast, married Sue, who didn't like boats. Soon after marriage, Sue asked him to sell his boat to help her financially in her new business. He resisted, but finally, resentfully gave in to support her. However, she used most of the money to buy him an expensive car, which he didn't want. He blamed her for making him give up his boat and, unknowingly, waited years for the perfect time to punish her. Just before she left her old business and began a new one, he bought a brand new boat. This caused her to become enraged with him. He had waited 14 years for the opportunity to retaliate.

Both men and women want warm, loving, intimate relationships, but competition destroys them. The competitor will "cut off his nose to spite his face."

Bobby refused to make love to Maddy after four and a half years of marriage, denying her what she wanted. His relationship with his family was very important to him. To punish him in their competitive war, she constantly belittled him for working in his father's business. The marriage ended after nine years of competition.

Competition destroys friendships as well as marriages and families.

> *Sally and Betty were close friends. Sally made disparaging remarks about Betty's career to a potential client in front of Betty. Sally was attempting to take the client away from Betty by making the client her friend. Betty wanted to talk about this so that it would not destroy their friendship, but was unable to do so because Sally denied it had happened. This created war between the two until, eleven years later, they put it to rest because they decided that their friendship was more important than winning in the game of competition.*

Unknowingly, husbands and wives compete with each other to destroy their marriage for the approval of their possessive, controlling parent or family member and to give that parent or family member what he wants, which is to make him their one and only and only one. When you make your possessive, controlling parent or family member your one and only and only one, you can neither hear nor listen to those you care about the most and will, unconsciously, twist what they say into what you want to hear. Consequently, you think the other is going crazy. Unconsciously, you deny your projection and, in some cases, your transference to yourself. You can't have loving friendships; you have to have surface relationships. You end up at the end of your life with regrets and sorrow because you've lived your life based on what your possessive, controlling parent or family member wanted you to do, be and have. The thought will become consuming that divorce or leaving is the only way out and, in so doing, you destroy the relationships that mean the most to you. And this will never end until you make up your mind to end being controlled by your possessive, controlling parent or family member. This is *your* life, and you alone are in charge of it. It's time to take responsibility for it and cease blaming, criticizing, and judging those who mean the most to you. You have to be willing to take a public stand for Truth and be willing to tell yourself and others the truth. It's time to take a public stand for what you want. In order to do so, you've got to be willing to tell yourself and others, in minute detail, what you want, and be willing to take the disapproval of that possessive, controlling parent or family member. You've got to be willing to die for what you want so that you can begin to live. The only way to establish a new program for your life that works for you is to first let go of your old program. The Bible says "And no man putteth new wine into old bottles: else the new wine doth burst the bottles, and the wine is spilled, and the bottles will be marred: but new wine must be put into new bottles" (Mark

2:22). No one is going to take care of you. And no one wants to, any more than you want to take care of someone else. The only ones we take care of are the children, the old people and the infirm in our lives. As citizens we are responsible to assist those who are incapable of helping themselves, if we are able. We're responsible for all of our relationships, but responsibility does not involve taking care of others. We're to enjoy them, have fun with them, appreciate and value them, and give to and receive from them.

In order to change your old programming, you have to face it, tell yourself the truth about it and let it go. This takes time, but it is, without question, the greatest thing you can do for you. If you were handed tickets to a world trip or given one million dollars, they're not even close to what this will do for you by comparison. Facing your programming and making up your mind to let it go is the only way out, and until you've had enough, you won't do so. This is how powerful it is. Facing and letting go of your programming is about being free to be you, to be all you can be, to express your talents and abilities every moment of your life, and to have fun.

Be there for your friends and loved ones now, because this may be the only chance you'll ever have to do so. Love means being there for them. Form the habit of creating happy memories.

LOVE

The choice is heavenly and divine. The choice is Love. Love is given unconditionally, effortlessly, tirelessly, limitlessly, continuously and without expectations.

Love allows you to express your real self, and your talents and abilities. Love gives space and is kind. Love is caring. If you're hurting, love wants to know, because it wants to help ease the pain. If you are coming from the mind and can't receive help, love backs off and gives the hurt a chance to heal in the way it is asking to be healed. To the mind, it might appear that love is walling off, but in truth, love is giving what is asked for. The mind and love can't understand each other, for they see everything totally differently. Evil hates love, for evil sees love as a weakness, something to be disdained, something of which to be contemptuous, something to be used. Evil uses hate and anger to motivate, to get itself to move into action. When love is present, evil sits back, does nothing and blames love for holding it back, or it flees---and love just keeps on loving, which offends evil even more. True love can't be destroyed; it just keeps right on loving. One day, it sees the destruction that evil has created, and its heart breaks. In this way, love learns that evil HAS to do evil things and that the mind can only be what it is: the mind. Evil and love are like oil and water. They can't mix. So evil has to leave love because it can't stand being unable to destroy love. Sometimes love's heart is broken, but it can be mended by letting the broken heart go. Not being free to give or receive love causes the mind to wall off to love, making those walled off uncomfortable, scared, nervous, anxious and vulnerable in love's presence. After awhile love learns that it is only by being with love that it can create, cocreate, play and have fun, give and receive love and share. And it learns that it is only with love that it can just BE without demands, controls, hidden agendas, walls or anger.

Love never has to prove or defend, for love IS. True love neither expects nor requires anything in return. It wants love, but doesn't withdraw when love is not returned. Love is not angry, for love is free, and freedom knows no anger. Love doesn't compare. It doesn't have to, for it is secure within itself. Love doesn't have opposite desires because it is of one mind. With love everything works. Love is not terrified of making a mistake or having problems. Love knows that problems are stepping stones, and that the solving of problems increases confidence and carries its possessor to a higher level. Love does not know doubt or fear; Love is confident. Love doesn't play roles. It doesn't have to. It is. Love doesn't have to be protected and taken care of to feel safe, for it is secure in itself. Love doesn't have to be a hero, for it needs no glory. Love doesn't have to play games because it doesn't compete. Love doesn't have to punish, for Love forgives. Love doesn't have to resist or be defiant. It wants to give you what you want. Love is not vengeful. It always supports. Love doesn't have to create destruction because it is creatively constructive. Love does not hate; it is too busy loving. Love does not have to withdraw; it is always there for you. Love does not have to face destruction because it is always creating. Love is not afraid of not being wanted because it has no awareness of being unwanted. Love is not afraid of being excluded because it is so inclusive. Love has no fear of being scapegoated, for it is unaware of blame. Love is not afraid of projecting, for it takes responsibility for its actions. Love is not afraid of being transferred onto, for it is. Love is not afraid of being a fool, for it is not self-conscious. Love is not afraid to say what it wants, for it is free to express itself. Love is not afraid to enjoy itself, for Love is fun. Love is patient, kind and persevering. Love cares.

And above all, love is free to give others what they want joyfully, happily and lovingly, without strings.

Putting your hand in God's hand and allowing Him to guide your every step, being the Light, believing in Him and listening to Him is the way to Love. God is Love, Truth and Light. You are Love, Truth and Light.

REACH

RESPONSIBILITY
SUCCESS IN BUSINESS
WARM & LOVING RELATIONSHIPS
YOUR NEW PROGRAM

CONSCIOUSLY CREATIVELY CONSTRUCTIVE

LIVE YOUR DREAM

THE GAME

TAKE CHARGE AND LIVE!!!

SITTING ON THE FENCE

RIGHT AND BLAMELESS DESTROYER

WRONG AND BLAMED SCAPEGOAT

YOUR OLD PROGRAM

21 You Are a Precious, Adorable Angel

BY ACCEPTING AND BELIEVING that you are a precious, adorable angel, you cease working to get good enough. With this acceptance you feel grounded, peaceful, calm, and secure in your relationships. You instantly become creative, see your opportunities, and know you can get the job done.

It is important to get the one or two words that clearly and succinctly describe the programming which became the belief system you accepted about yourself in childhood. This word(s), unknowingly, has become the mood from which you live your life.

For example, if your brother or sister was jealous of you from birth, and, consequently, didn't want you, the word that describes your belief system about yourself would be "unwanted."

> Tom's mother wanted him to be perfect and, because he never measured up to her concept of perfection, he felt incompetent. His belief system about himself was that he was "incompetent." After letting his false belief system go, and accepting that he was competent, he was able to tell his friends about the top performance awards he had received at work.

Once you find the word that describes your belief system about yourself, let it go four times, and accept its opposite four times.

While growing up, Mary Ann's entire family constantly called her an "asshole," which, to them, meant she was a total jerk. When her teacher told her the truth, that she was a precious, adorable angel, it so disagreed with her belief system that, in her mind, the truth was a lie and the lie was the truth. But, by letting go of the lie and accepting the truth, she was instantly transformed.

It is possible that, after letting go of the lie and accepting the truth, you may find yourself punishing yourself. Just let go of punishing yourself four times, and accept that you reward yourself four times.

Put your hand in God's hand by inviting him into your heart to walk with you and guide you. This will give you a Light that will illuminate your path, one step at a time. It will eliminate the past and give you a new life, a new beginning. The biggest block of all will be eliminated, and what is naturally there---and has been all along---is the truth that you are a precious, adorable angel, that you are real, that you already ARE important, that you ARE somebody, that you have value and self-worth, and that you are free---free to be you, free to be all you can be, free to be your highest and best, and free to know and express your talents and abilities. So, turn your back on the past, make up your mind that you are free from EVER looking back, and walk into the Light.

22 How to Live a Life of Ecstasy and Bliss

1: Let go of your 7 emotional attachments: mother, father, family, teams, spouse, self and children, and any individual attachments you have.

2: Accept the 7 basic acceptances: taking charge, child of God, being, the source, relying within, expressing talents and abilities, enjoyment, and fun.

3: Accept the 7 basic I Ams: I am centered, I am in the zone, I am the Light, I am joy, I am love, I am listening within to God, I am relying within on God, I am enjoyment.

4: Let go of the role you have chosen to live: right and blameless destroyer, wrong and blamed scapegoat, controller or controllee.

5: Let go of the need to be right, the terror of being bad, the terror of making a mistake, the terror of not being good enough, and the terror of being wrong.

6: Accept that you are good enough just as you are, and accept that you are free to make mistakes.

7: Let go of opposite desires: success/failure, love/hate, patience/impatience, construction/destruction, good/bad, take charge/escape, the desire to be praised and acknowledged/the expectation of being criticized, past/future, and fantasy/reality.

8: Accept that you are of one mind.

9: Let go of doubt, and accept that you believe in God, in yourself and in others.

10: Accept that you have the power of a made-up mind.

11: Make up your mind to tell yourself and others the truth.

12: Make up your mind to take a stand for the truth.

13: Let go of your old programming---establish a new program that works for you.

14: Let go of rebellion, revolt and/or resistance, whichever applies to you.

15: Accept that you cooperate.

16: Accept that you have choice.

17: Accept that you are free to say, "I want" and "I don't want."

18: Cease being held down and back, and cease holding others down and back.

19: Let go of the terror of being wrong or less than perfect.

20: Let go of the need to be perfect.

21: Face how your family solved problems. Accept that you are free to have and solve problems, personal or otherwise.

22: Let go of the resistance to being praised and acknowledged, and/or praising and acknowledging others.

23: Let go of the false belief that praise and acknowledgement = expectations and criticism.

24: Accept that you have self-respect.

25: Let go of the need to be vindictive toward those who praise and acknowledge you.

26: Cease being a know-it-all.

27: Let go of having to listen to and hear only your possessive, controlling parent or family member.

28: Let go of having to make your possessive, controlling parent or family member your one and only and only one.

29: Cease making your possessive, controlling parent or family member your god, and giving him control over your life.

30: Let go of rebelling against your possessive, controlling parent or family member.

31: Make the true God your God, and invite Him into your heart to guide and direct you.

32: Let go of resistance, and enter into the kingdom of heaven within.

33: Let go of all controlling techniques, such as withholding love, walling off, pity, anger/rage, charm, the threat of leaving, mental seduction, sexual seduction, dividing and conquering, negative suggestion, non-stop talking, excluding, not including, and choosing sides.

34: Accept that you are free to be you.

35: Ask for, listen to and follow God's directions.

36: Know your niche.

37: Find your labor of love.

38: Find your dream.

39: Accept that it's a done deal.

40: Accept that you value yourself and others.

41: Recognize the five steps of training:
- You recognize you did it after it's over.
- You recognize you're doing it while you are doing it but can't stop.
- You recognize you're doing it while you're doing it and stop in midstream.
- You recognize you're about to do it and stop.
- You make up your mind it's over.

42: Accept that you have understanding and wisdom.

43: Let go of guilt, remorse, regrets, sadness and unhappiness, and accept that you are happy, joyful, in ecstasy and blissful.

44: Let go of caring what others think.

45: Be consistent.

46: Take responsibility for what doesn't work, and do what does work.

47: Give pleasure rather than pleasing.

48: Be involved.

49: Fear neither success nor failure.

50: Get the job done. Don't think about it, just do it.

51: Accept that you care and are considerate.

52: Accept that you are love itself, and accept that you both give and receive love. Accept that you cherish your loved ones and yourself, and accept that you allow your loved ones to cherish you.

53: Accept that you have warm and loving relationships with everyone.

54: Be there for your loved ones.

55: Accept that you are grateful, and give thanks for everything.

56: Accept that we are ALL the same, that we are ALL equal and that we are ALL God's children.

57: Accept that you are a precious, adorable angel.

58: Accept that you are in the flow.

59: Praise:
    Let go down to your toes and let God run your life.
    Move into the deepest level of love.
    Move into the deepest level of joy.
    Accept that you are centered.
    Focus center on the fourth level.
    Move into the fourth level of the zone.
    Move into the fourth level of listening to God within you.
    Move into the fourth level of the I AM vibration.
    Move into the fourth level of the light.
    Praise God.

AFTERWORD

Because we accepted that we are bad and not good enough in childhood, we unconsciously allow others to influence, direct and/or control our belief systems, and we blame them for our life not working. It is not until we take full responsibility for our life, for what we want or don't want and for what we do or don't do that we can be free to do what we want to do, free to be ourselves, and free to have what we want to have.

A FINAL WORD

Desire is the key that opens the door to your Source, to God within. When this desire is followed by a made-up mind to live life lovingly, joyfully and blissfully, nothing on the planet can stop you. Learning to take full responsibility for each creation in your life keeps you from veering off course, and assists you to move quickly through blocks.

Time spent alone in meditation (stilling the mind) in the early hours of the morning is necessary to experience union with God. This union is achieved by using concentration to go beyond the mind to your Source deep within. Stay in this state of union until the mind is completely still. There you find the peace that passes all understanding, the Kingdom of God within.

How do you carry this incredible experience out into your daily life? You do so by concentrating, by keeping your attention on your Source, God within all day long. Anything you keep your attention on grows stronger and more powerful.

May you walk hand in hand with your Heavenly Father forever and ever.

JOYCE HOVIS

Joyce Hovis exudes unconditional love for all. Her confidence, inner security and power are the result of a lifelong search for Truth, Beauty and Happiness. She is a living example of her message: you CAN realize your dreams.

At age 68, instead of retiring to the serenity of her beautiful Atlanta home, she arises before dawn to spend fourteen hours a day directing the activities of TROB, Inc., a school of self-knowledge, which she founded. Her love of people and desire to serve were so great that for ten years, as a young mother, she went into the most dangerous parts of Atlanta to teach the illiterate to read and write. Her work was a forerunner of Atlanta's Literacy Action Program.

Her belief in the balance of Mind, Body and Spirit motivates her to constantly stretch and go forward. She learned to play tennis in her 50's, and began taking flying lessons in her 60's. She has climbed mountains and tackled the challenges of the Ropes Course. She works out with weights on a regular basis, and still has time for weekly outings with her ten grandchildren.

In 1989, she became the first Ms. Senior Georgia, and has traveled the state inspiring Seniors to reach for their dreams. She was chosen one of the "Outstanding Women of the '80's" by the TBS program, "Good News." She is an inspiring radio and TV personality.

Her book, TAKE CHARGE AND LIVE!, has transformed the lives of those who have read it. This book is the culmination of 18 years' work, and the result of her own struggle for happiness. In it, Joyce explains the cause of man's failure and unhappiness, in business and relationships, and shares the remarkable solution which has worked for thousands of people.

She has been successful in creating her dream, which was to have a warm and loving nuclear and extended family. This dream motivated her to originate the TROB work.

TROB

TROB is a global school of self-knowledge that was created for people to discover and express their talents and abilities. TROB was founded in 1982 by Joyce Hovis, an Atlanta homemaker who searched for years to find the Truth of how to live life successfully. TROB students are encouraged in their uniquenesses, and loved for their differences. TROB is a team that supports, loves and cares about each team member. Students are encouraged to both stand on their own, and to embrace and receive the support of the whole. TROB empowers everyone to discover their own courage, self-reliance and integrity and, in so doing, fosters their self-confidence. Students are taught to solve problems by going to cause versus dealing with effects.

TROB is a school that assists people to eliminate what doesn't work, and supports them in finding and doing what does work; to eliminate the old program they were given as children, and create a new program that is suited to their present lifestyle. TROB is a school which assists its students to create warm and loving relationships with everyone in their lives, to live successfully, to find and create their dream, and to be happy, peaceful and joyful.

TROB'S MISSION

To provide you with the opportunity to:
- Walk hand-in-hand with God,
- Be yourself,
- Have your dream,
- Express love, success, and peace ALL the time.

HOW WILL TROB ASSIST YOU?

- By teaching you to see beauty everywhere.
- By leading you to live a life filled with love, inside and out.
- By providing a haven from the world where it is safe to learn and grow and love.
- By helping you to see the value and importance of warm, loving relationships, and enabling you to create them.
- By assisting you to see that your problems were created by the choices you made, and that you can make new choices which work for you.

Index

A

Abraham Lincoln 56
abundance 145
acceptance
  by family 96
acceptances
  technique for 48
addendum 296
addiction 209, 220
addictions 301
adult relationship 47
affair 197
aggressive 216
agreement 73
anger
  11, 98, 122, 125, 204, 268
  turned inward 70
angry/vindictive 214, 216
anguish 221
anxiety 72, 112, 230, 254
approval 13, 96, 111, 190, 203
architectural plan 341
arrogance 170
arrogant 210
asking for what you want 208
atoning 99
attachments 1
  individual 43
  releasing technique for 48
authority figure 160, 295, 320
authority without responsibility 136
avoidance of responsibility 255

B

bad 95, 98
bad message
  releasing 100
balance 41, 54
be-er 116
beater 186
beaters 140
beauty 93
Being 54, 65
being careful 72
being there 356
belief system 309, 333
  negative 309
  positive 309
  unraveling 333
belief systems
  false 53
  letting go 53
bipolar illness 113
birthright 145
blame 9, 13, 145, 202
  eliminating 54
  in marriage 9
bliss 263, 331
blocks 81, 92, 327
  mental and emotional 81
  releasing 47
blueprint 300, 341
  family 71
boundaries 25
bushel basket 78, 203

C

caring what others think 109
caring what people think 318
centered 87, 112
chameleon 25
chaos 222
charm 12, 122, 206
Child of God 54, 61
childhood programming 45, 85

children
　emotional attachment to 40
　responsibility for 40
choice 59, 114, 125, 328
choosing sides 12, 122, 206, 211
code bearer 112, 293, 320
　tyrannical 294
codes
　eliminating 323
comfort 301, 307
coming from Love 345
coming from the mind 345
commitment 81
comparing 105
compensation 61, 96
competition 19, 75, 82, 183
　four levels of 361
　in marriage 184, 193
　in relationships 183
　recognizing 197
compulsive doing 255
condescension 178
confidence 75, 77
conformity 22, 24, 26, 67
confrontation 154
consciously destructively 345
contempt
　　108, 131, 137, 177, 201, 254
control
　by fear 72
control tactics 11, 203
controllee 97, 99, 121, 127, 315
controller 75, 97, 98, 121, 315
cooperate 159
cooperation 224, 230
cooperative 214, 221
corral 156, 188
courage 231, 349
coward 137, 212
creating your dream 230
criticism 106
cynic 184

D

dark side 307
deception 131
defensive attitude 152
defensive/paranoid 214, 219
dementia praecox 113
denial 98, 156, 209, 222
dependency 34
depression
　　67, 70, 100, 107, 125
desire for freedom 334
desire for recognition 155
destruction 339
destructive powers 259
　sequential steps 261
　symptoms 264
detoxification 338
devil 278, 297
divide and conquer 12, 122, 205
doer 116
doing what works 346
doing what you do because you
　　want to 346
domination 27
Dorothy 248
doubly special 179
doubt 72
dream 256, 318, 342

E

ecstasy 145, 263, 331
ego 62
　as identity 230
　belief system 344
ego self 35
　and self expression 36
　attachment to 35
　emotional attachment to 37
egomania 113
emotional adult 291
emotional age 167, 327

emotional dependencies 61
empower 54
enjoy 80
Enjoyment 54, 79
escape 109
escapes 2, 26, 113, 275
Escaping Responsibility 279
escaping responsibility 285
evil 345, 365
excluding 12, 122, 202, 206
exclusive star 149
expectations 97, 105, 216
expressing life 347
Expressing My Talents and Abilities 54, 78
expression of love 356

F

facts vs. truth 298
faith 64, 65, 67
false concept 95
false concepts 33, 53, 97
false identity 62, 65
false image 125
family 17
  and self worth 18
  emotional attachment to 17
  influence 18
family code 292
family commitment 288
  and marriage 290
family programming 328
family scapegoat 293
fantasy
  60, 72, 125, 167, 281, 345
father
  emotional attachment to 13
  role 41
fear 16, 65
fear of being blamed 58
fear of being different 63
fear of being humiliated 79

fear of being left out 26
fear of failure 4, 66, 279
fear of humiliation 137
fear of loss 66
fear of making a mistake 70
fear of public speaking 67
fear of rejection 26, 58, 181, 221
fear of success 66, 355
fear of the unknown 66
fears 124
fence 301
flip-flopper 96, 116, 130, 188
focus center 262
forgive 310, 348
Franklin Roosevelt 66
freedom 310
  to be yourself 21
freedom to be yourself 124
freedom to make a mistake 152
freedom to say, "I want" and "I don't want," 360
Fun 54, 85
future 68, 112, 253, 348

G

game
  core of 208
game playing 131, 160, 199
game strategies 214
Garden of Eden 62, 230
give 196
giver and receiver 319
giving and receiving 196
glory 228
God 62, 63, 65, 67, 69, 91, 119, 230, 278, 331, 338, 341, 352, 370
  trusting 326
good 101
gossip 345
grandparents 352
grief 70, 219
grow up 327

grudge 217
guilt 6, 8, 24, 95, 99, 103, 349

H

happiness 56
happiness within 56
hatred 262
   and competition 195
having a problem 134
having to be right 343
heaven 112
hidden agenda 132, 156
hiding out 221
holding back 132
hypnosis 260
hypnotic spell 260
hypocrisy 267

I

I am 88
I Am Centered 87
I Am Enjoyment 93
I Am in th Zone 88
I Am Joy 89
I Am Listening 91
I Am Love 90
I Am Relying 92
I Am the Light 89
I don't want 25, 59, 117, 207
I want 25, 117, 123, 207
   and anger 123
identifying
   with children 42
identity 71, 314
ignorance 313
impatience 107, 253, 274
impatient fantasizer 255
inability to be on a team 160
inadequacy 133
inappropriate responsibility 281
incongruency 167
inconsistency
   96, 174, 189, 213, 224, 267
indecision 70
indifference 354
indispensible 242
inferior 65, 137
inner conflict 307
insanity 242
insecurity 95, 106
interference 109
interrupting 82
intimacy 196, 210, 282
irritated 59

J

JITS 253
joy 145
judging 14
judgment 355

K

knowing what you want 28

L

lack 319
law of cause and effect 202
leadership 149
   squelching 149
learning responsibility 325
leaving 200, 302
   threat of 11
less than perfect 98
letting go and letting God 62
liar 243
life pattern 300, 308
limited supply 207
Lion 233
living vicariously 72
loners 24, 134
love 90, 350, 365
love-making 196
love/hate cycle 305

loving 331
low energy 70, 260, 308

M

made-up mind 318
making up your mind 73
manipulation 122
marriage 31
  destruction of 166
  warm and loving 358
master mind 212
masters of destruction 186
mate
  desire for 75
mental illness 113
Message to Garcia 56
mind 68, 92, 346
  subconscious 73
mindsets 233
mixed messages 32
modus operandi 355
mother
  emotional attachment to 4
  good 40
  surrogate 5
mother/child relationship 47

N

narcissistic 319
natural person 124
natural star 149, 158
need 10, 32, 184, 189
need for power and control 155
need to be right 139, 335
need to be taken care of
  121, 127, 318
negative attention 184
negative attitude 14, 25
negative energy 276
negative mental attitude 180
negative special 180
negative star 149
and scapegoat 152
negative suggestion 12, 122, 205
negative thinking 191, 230
nervous 210
non-caring attitude 176
non-game player 200
not giving you what you want 208
not good enough 4, 25, 68, 106
not included 24
not including 12, 122, 206
not-good-enough 219
nurturing
  need for 8

O

obligation 131
one and only 83, 155, 166
only one 83, 155, 166
opposite desires
  72, 105, 116, 132, 151, 189, 197, 219, 301
  and belief systems 336
  letting go 308
  symptoms of 304

P

pact 295, 320
pain and suffering 61, 74
paralyzed non-doer 115
paranoia 113
parental fears 41
parents
  good 42
past 68
pathological lying 113
peace 69
perfect 4, 298
  need to be 333
perfection 68, 105, 253, 352
  cause of 107
  concept of 105
  concepts of 68

permission
    6, 8, 47, 57, 59, 73, 96, 111
pitiful 11, 204
pity 122
pleaser 96, 127
pleasing others 60
pompous 214
possession 82
possessive, controlling parent 190
power of a made-up mind 317
praise and acknowledgement 336
precious, adorable angel 369
preparing for failure 56
prioritizing 161
problem solver 248
problems
    inability to have 26
procrastination 233, 255
programming
    53, 93, 287, 341, 369
projection
    82, 131, 340, 343, 355
protect and defend 199
protecting and defending 125
protective mechanism 40
protective shell 276
proving 95, 102, 134
psychotic master mind 213
public humiliation 150
punishment 99, 144, 155
purpose 286

R

rage 11, 122, 204
real 230
reality 283, 318
rebellion 5, 14, 73, 96, 167, 267
    core of 273
    one and only, only one 274
    open 14, 268
    physical symptoms 270
    releasing 271

silent 14, 271
recognition 203
reformer 109
rejection 156
releasing four times 51
releasing technique 45
relying 92
    on God 91
    on self 91
relying on God 262
Relying Within On God 54, 74
resentment 60
resistance
    14, 61, 191, 274, 302, 323
responsibility
    13, 54, 74, 80, 284, 323
    for one's life 13
    for parents happiness 96
    lack of 116
revolt 275
right and blameless
    26, 125, 199, 301
right and blameless destroyer
    75, 97, 98, 121, 131, 315
    and impatience 254
    and negative star 149
    origin of role 133
role 97, 100, 108, 121
role concepts 32
role model 13, 71
roles: 314
royalty complex 155
running from problems 26

S

sadness 70
savior 110
scapegoat 315
scapegoating 339
Scarecrow 242
schizophrenia 113
secret of failure 302

security 66, 77
seduction 155, 261, 345
    mental 11, 204
    sexual 12, 122, 204
self concept 6
self expression 36
self-blame 339
self-centered 37, 68, 150, 189
self-conscious 38
self-deception 101, 134, 222
self-destruction 339
self-esteem
    low 95, 106
self-hatred 71
self-punishment 339, 349
self-reliance 75
self-worth 215
selfishness 205
separation from God 62
sequential levels of learning 215
serenity 69
sexual molestation 205
sibling rivalry 19, 20
single people 34
sociopathy 113
sorrow 221
special 149, 150, 166, 214
spirit 350
spontaneity 135
spouse
    and relying 31
    emotional attachment to 30
stars 149
Stonewall Jackson 66
stress 123, 253
subconscious mind 293
subconscious resistance 72
superior 137, 210
symbiotic relationship 143

T

take a public stand
for truth 349, 359
Take Charge 54
take charge 54
taker 318
taking a stand 144
taking risks 29
talkativeness 39, 206
team players 149, 159
teams 22
    and having 22
    and inner security 27
    and relationships 23
    effect of 24
    emotional attachment to 22
    parental attitude toward 23
teenagers 7
tension 46
terror of being rejected 234
terror of making a mistake
    114, 298, 343
the peace that passes all understanding 263
The Source 54, 71
Tin Man 238
transference 82, 131, 171, 340
trigger 208
TROB 288
turning point 91, 151

U

unconditional love 65, 69, 278
unfair treatment 274
unhappiness 59

V

verbal repartee 210
victim 200
void 113, 276

W

walling off 12, 26, 122, 206, 340
war 210
winner 187
winners 140
withdrawal of love 11
withholding
    106, 202, 256, 272, 340
withholding love 122
withholding of love 203
Wizard of Oz 233
wrong and blamed scapegoat
    97, 99, 121, 143, 315

Z

zone 88, 263